FACTS AND RESEARCH IN GERONTOLOGY

1992

FACTS AND RESEARCH IN GERONTOLOGY

1992

Editors

B. VELLAS, J.L. ALBARÈDE (Toulouse)

Corresponding Editors

– A.J. CAMPBELL (Dunedin, N.Z.)
– J. Grimley EVANS (Oxford)
– D. GUEZ (Paris)
– F. JIMENEZ HERRERO (Madrid)
– L. RUBENSTEIN (Los Angeles)
– L.G. SERRO-AZUL (Sao Paolo)
– H. WERNER (Frankfurt)
– H. SHIBATA (Tokyo)
– B.P. YU (San Antonio)

Distributed in U.S.A. by
Springer Publishing Company
536 Broadway
New York, NY 10012-3955

Distributed in Europe and other countries by
Serdi Publisher
29, rue de Saint-Pétersbourg - 75008 PARIS

Serdi Publisher, 29, rue de Saint-Pétersbourg ; 75008 Paris, France
Springer Publishing Company, 536 Broadway, New York, NY 10012-3955

CONTENTS : FACTS AND RESEARCH IN GERONTOLOGY 1992

IV - FACTS AND RESEARCH IN PHARMACOLOGY, AGING AND THERAPEUTICS

V - FACTS AND RESEARCH IN CLINICAL GERONTOLOGY

VI - FACTS AND RESEARCH IN SOCIAL GERONTOLOGY

VII - FACTS AND RESEARCH IN INTERNATIONAL GERONTOLOGY

CONTRIBUTORS

J.-L. ALBAREDE, Département de Médecine Interne et Gérontologie Clinique, CHU Purpan-Casselardit, 170, chemin de Casselardit, 31000 Toulouse, Fr. EUROPE.

C.M. ALDWIN, Human Development & Family Studies, University of California, Davis, CA, USA.

E. ALIX, Département de Gériatrie, Hôpital du Mans, Fr. EUROPE.

A. ALPEROVITCH, INSERM U 169, 16 bis avenue P. Vaillant-Couturier, 94807 Villejuif Cedex, Fr. EUROPE.

P.H. ANDREWS, Iowa Geriatric Education Center, Department of Internal Medicine, The University of Iowa Hospitals and Clinics, Iowa, USA.

J.-M. AZORIN, Clinique de Psychiatrie, CHU Timone, rue Saint-Pierre, 13385 Marseille Cedex 5, Fr. EUROPE.

L. BALDUCCI, Oncology section, James A. Haley Veterans Hospital, Tampa, Florida, USA.

P. BARBERGER-GATEAU, INSERM U 330, Université de Bordeaux II, 146, rue L. Saignat, 33076 Bordeaux Cedex, Fr. EUROPE.

M. BARKATS, URA CNRS 1294, UFR Biomédicale, 45, rue des Saints-Pères, 75006 Paris, Fr. EUROPE.

R.N. BAUMGARTNER, Clinical Nutrition Laboratory, University of New-Mexico. School of Medicine, Albuquerque, NM 87131, USA.

C. BERR, INSERM U 169, 16 bis av. P. Vaillant-Couturier, 94807 Villejuif Cedex, Fr. EUROPE.

F. BEZIAT, Département de médecine interne et gériatrie, CHU Purpan-Casselardit, Toulouse, Fr. EUROPE.

A. BIANCHETTI, Geriatric Research Group, Via Romanino 1, 25122 Brescia, Italy, EUROPE.

N. BONS, Lab. de neuromorphologie fonctionnelle, EPHE, Université de Montpellier II, place E.-Bataillon, 34095 Montpellier Cedex 5, Fr. EUROPE.

R. BOSSE, Normative Aging Study, Department of Veterans Affairs Medical Center, 200 Springs Road, Building 70, Bedford, MA 01730, USA.

A. BOULIER, Hôpital Charles Foix, 94200 Ivry-sur-Seine, Fr. EUROPE.

K.C. BUCKWALTER, College of Nursing, The University of Iowa, Iowa, USA.

J. BUREMA, Department of Human Nutrition, Wageningen Agricultural University, PO Box 8129, 6700 EV Wageningen, The Netherlands, EUROPE.

P. BUSTANY, Lab. Pharmacologie, CHU, 14033 Caen Cedex, Fr. EUROPE.

C. CANET, Lab. de Santé Publique Dentaire, Université de Bordeaux II, 146, rue L.-Saignat, 33076 Bordeaux Cedex, Fr. EUROPE.

G. CHAPOUTIER, UFR Biomédicale, 45, rue des Saints-Pères, 75006 Paris, Fr. EUROPE.

N. CHAU, Unité INSERM 115, Faculté de Médecine, allée de la Forêt de Haye, 54500 Vandœuvre-lès-Nancy, Fr. EUROPE.

W.C. CHUMLEA, Department of Community Health, Wright State University, Yellow-Spring, Ohio, USA.

T.A. CLEARY, Educational Measurement and Statistics, The University of Iowa, Iowa, USA.

C. COHEN-SALMON, URA CNRS 1294, UFR Biomédicale, 45, rue des Saints-Pères, 75006 Paris, Fr. EUROPE.

J. CONCEICAO, Département de Médecine interne et Gérontologie clinique, CHU Purpan-Casselardit, Toulouse, Fr. EUROPE.

D. COMMENGES, INSERM U 330, Université de Bordeaux II, 146, rue L.-Saignat, 33076 Bordeaux Cedex, Fr. EUROPE.

Y. COURTOIS, INSERM U 118, 29, rue Wilhem, 75016 Paris, Fr. EUROPE.

G. CUNY, Service de Médecine B, CHRU de Nancy, rue du Morvan, 54500 Vandœuvre-lès-Nancy, Fr. EUROPE.

J.F. DARTIGUES, INSERM U 330, Université de Bordeaux II, 146, rue L.-Saignat, 33076 Bordeaux Cedex, Fr. EUROPE.

M.J. DEALBERTO, INSERM U 169, 16 bis, avenue P.-Vaillant-Couturier, 94807 Villejuif Cedex, Fr. EUROPE.

G. DEBRY, Centre de Nutrition Humaine, Université de Nancy I, 40, rue Lionnois, 54000 Nancy, Fr. EUROPE.

A. DECAMPS, Centre de Gériatrie, CHR Bordeaux, 33210 Lormont, Fr. EUROPE.

L.P.G.M. DE GROOT, Department of Human Nutrition, Wageningen Agricultural University, PO Box 8129, 6700 EV Wageningen, The Netherlands, EUROPE.

F. DENIS, Département de Bactériologie-Virologie, CHU Dupuytren, 87042 Limoges, Fr. EUROPE.

A. DONNET, Clinique de Neurologie, CHU Timone, rue Saint-Pierre, 13385 Marseille Cedex 5, Fr. EUROPE.

R. DUFETELLE, Université du Troisième âge, Université des sciences sociales, Toulouse-I, 31000 Toulouse, Fr. EUROPE.

M. FERRY, Centre Hospitalier, 26008 Valence, Fr. EUROPE.

N.A. FOX, Center for Economic Studies in Medicine, Reston, Virginia, USA.

S. FRANZONI, Geriatric Research Group, Via Romanino 1, 25122 Brescia, Italy, EUROPE.

M. GAGNON, INSERM U 330, Université de Bordeaux II, 146, rue L.-Saignat, 33076 Bordeaux Cedex, Fr. EUROPE.

S.R. GAMBERT, New York Medical College, Munger Pavilion, Room 170, Valhalla, New York 10595, USA.

A. GHISOLFI-MARQUE, Département de Médecine interne et Gérontologie clinique, CHU Purpan-Casselardit, 31000 Toulouse, Fr. EUROPE.

J.S. GILMER, Office of Consultation and Research in Medical Education, The University of Iowa, Iowa, USA.

Y. GUIGOZ, Nestlé Ltd Research Center, Vers-Chez-Les-Blanc, CH-1000, Lausanne 26, Switzerland.

S. GUO, Department of mathematics and statistics, Wright State University, Dayton, Ohio (USA).

X. HÉBUTERNE, Service de Gastro-entérologie, Hôpital de l'Archet, route de St-Antoine de Ginestière, BP 689, 06012 Nice Cedex, Fr. EUROPE.

E. HEIKKINEN, Department of Health Sciences and Gerontology Research Centre, University of Jyväskylä, Finland, EUROPE.

P.F. HIGGS, Division of Geriatric Medicine, Department of Medicine, St George's Hospital Medical School, Cranmer Terrace, Tooting, London SW 17 ORE, United Kingdom, EUROPE.

J. JACOBS, Center for Economic Studies in Medicine, Reston, Virginia, USA.

C. JEANDEL, Service de Médecine B. CHRU de Nancy, rue du Morvan, 54500 Vandœuvre-lès-Nancy, Fr. EUROPE.

Y. JUILLET, Roussel-Uclaf, Paris, Fr. EUROPE.

B. KARK, Frankfurt/Main, Germany, EUROPE.

K.V. KOWDLEY, Gastroenterology Division, University Hospitals of Cleveland, 2074 Abington Road, Cleveland, Ohio 44106, USA.

J. LABAT-ROBERT, URA CNRS 1174, Faculté de Médecine, 8, rue du Général-Sarrail, 94010 Créteil, Fr. EUROPE.

B. LESOURD, Hôpital Bichat, 75 Paris, Fr. EUROPE.

L. LETENNEUR, INSERM U 330, Université de Bordeaux II, 146, rue L.-Saignat, 33076 Bordeaux Cedex, Fr. EUROPE.

M.R. LEVENSON, Human Development & Family Studies, University of California, Davis, California, USA.

J. LITVAK, Research Program on Aging, W. H. O., National Institute on Aging, Bethesda, Maryland 20892, USA.

F. LOEW, Institutions Universitaires de Gériatrie, CH-1226 Thonex-Genève, Suisse.

S. MAGGI, Research Program on Aging, W.H.O. National Institute on Aging, Bethesda, Maryland 20892, USA.

A.P.N. MAJUMBAR, VA Medical Center and Wayne State University School of Medicine, Allen Park, Michigan 48101, USA.

S.A. MAYER-OAKES, Department of Medicine, Division of Geriatrics, A-671 Factor Building, Los Angeles, CA 90024-1687, USA.

S. MAYENCE, Inter-University EUROPEan Institute on Social Welfare, 179, rue du Débarcadère, B-6001 Marcinelle, Belgium, EUROPE.

N. MESTRE, Lab. de neuromorphologie fonctionnelle, EPHE, Université de Montpellier II, place E.-Bataillon, 34095 Montpellier Cedex 5, Fr. EUROPE.

P.H. MILLARD, Division of Geriatric Medicine, Department of Medicine, St George's Hospital Medical School, Cranmer Terrace, Tooting, London SW17 ORE, United Kingdom, Fr. EUROPE.

J.P. MICHEL, Institutions Universitaires de Gériatrie, CH-1226 Thonex-Genève, Suisse.

J.L. MIQUEL, Lab. de Santé Publique Dentaire, Université de Bordeaux II, 146, rue L.-Saignat, 33076 Bordeaux Cedex, Fr. EUROPE.

J. MOREAU, Service de Gastro-entérologie et de Nutrition, CHU Rangueil, 31054 Toulouse Cedex, Fr. EUROPE.

J.E. MORLEY, Geriatric Research Education and Clinical Center, St Louis VA Medical Center, St Louis, Missouri, USA.

W.W. MORRIS, College of medicine, The University of Iowa, Iowa, USA.

M. MOUNIER, Département de Bactériologie-Virologie, CHU Dupuytren, 87042 Limoges, Fr. EUROPE.

D.K. MROCZEK, Psychology department, Boston University, Boston, MA, USA.

B.D. NALIBOFF, Department of Anesthesiology, UCLA School of Medicine, Los Angeles, California, USA.

C. NEJJARI, INSERM U 330, Université de Bordeaux II, 146 rue L.-Saignat, 33076 Bordeaux Cedex, Fr. EUROPE.

A. NIEOULLON, Unité de Neurochimie, 31, chemin J.-Aiguier, 13402 Marseille Cedex 9, Fr. EUROPE.

J. ORGIAZZI, Service de Médecine Interne, CH Lyon Sud, 69310 Pierre-Bénite, Fr. EUROPE.

H. ORIMO, Department of Geriatrics, Faculty of Medicine, University of Tokyo, Tokyo, Japan.

J.G. OUSLANDER, Jewish Home for the Aging of Greater Los Angeles, 18855 Victory Bld, Reseda, CA 91335, USA.

A. PETTER, Musée d'Histoire Naturelle, 55, rue Buffon, 75005 Paris, Fr. EUROPE.

J.M. POW-SANG, Department of Urology, H. Lee Moffitt Cancer Center and Research Institute, Tampa, Florida, USA.

P. RAMPAL, Service de Gastro-entérologie, Hôpital de l'Archet, route de Saint-Antoine de Ginestière, BP 689, 06012 Nice Cedex, Fr. EUROPE.

S. RANGER, Departement de Bactériologie-Virologie, CHU Dupuytren, 87042 Limoges, Fr. EUROPE.

F. RAUL, INSERM U 61, 3, avenue Molière, 67200 Strasbourg, Fr. EUROPE.

D.B. REUBEN, Multicampus Division of Geriatric Medicine and Gerontology, UCLA School of Medicine 32-144 CHS, 10833 Le Conte Av., Los Angeles, CA 90024-1687, USA.

M. REVILLE, INSERM U 61, 3, avenue Molière, 67200 Strasbourg, Fr. EUROPE.

A. RIBET, Unite INSERM 151, CHU Rangueil, 31000 Toulouse, Fr. EUROPE.

L. ROBERT, URA CNRS 1174, Faculté de Médecine, 8, rue du Général-Sarrail, 94010 Créteil, Fr. EUROPE.

M.J. ROSENTHAL, GRECC 11E, Sepulveda VA Medical Center, 16111 Plummer Str., Sepulveda, CA 91343, USA.

R. ROZZINI, Geriatric Research Group, Via Romanino 1, 25122 Brescia, Italy, EUROPE.

L.Z. RUBENSTEIN, GRECC, Sepulveda VA Medical Center, Los Angeles, CA, USA.

R.M. RUSSELL, USDA, Human Nutrition Research Center on Aging at Tufts University, 711 Washington Street, Boston, Massachussets 02111, USA.

R. SALAMON, INSERM U 330, Université de Bordeaux II, 146, rue L.-Saignat, 33076 Bordeaux Cedex, Fr. EUROPE.

P. SCHWED, Département Universitaire de Psychiatrie, Service de Psychogériatrie, Hôpital de Prilly, CH-1008 Prilly-Lausanne, Switzerland.

M. SEDEUILH, Gerontology Research Department, University of Toulouse I, Fr. EUROPE.

W.O. SEILER, Medizinisch-Geriatricsche Klinik, Kantonsspital, CH-4031 Bale, Switzerland.

C. SHOVLIN, Islington Health Authority, Royal Northern Hospital, Holloway Rd, London N7 GLD, Great Britain, Fr. EUROPE.

A.L. SIU, Multicampus Division of Geriatric Medicine, UCLA School of Medicine 32-144 CHS, 10833 Le Conte Av., Los Angeles, CA 90024-1687, USA.

A. SPIRO, School of public health, Boston University, Boston, USA.

H.B. STÄHELIN, Medizinisch-Geriatricsche Klinik, Kantonsspital, CH-4031 Bale, Switzerland.

L. STERU, President, Institute for the technical evaluation of Medicine, Paris-France, EUROPE.

A.E. STUCK, GRECC, Sepulveda VA Medical Center, School of Medicine, Los Angeles, CA, USA.

A. STUCKELBERGER, Institutions Universitaires de Gériatrie, CH-1226, Thonex-Genève, Switzerland.

A. TEBI, Centre de Nutrition Humaine, Université de Nancy I, 40, rue Lionnois, 54000 Nancy, Fr. EUROPE.

J.F. TESSIER, INSERM U 330, Université de Bordeaux II, 146, rue L.-Saignat, 33076 Bordeaux Cedex, Fr. EUROPE.

A.L. THOMASSET, Université Claude-Bernard, 69000 Lyon, Fr. EUROPE.

M. TRABUCCHI, Dept. Experimental Medicine, 2nd University of Roma, Roma, Italy, EUROPE.

J. TRETON, INSERM U 118, 29, rue Wilhem, 75016 Paris, Fr. EUROPE.

A. TROTTI, Radiation Oncology, H. Lee Moffitt Cancer Center and Research Institute, Tampa, Florida, USA.

W.A. van STAVEREN, Department of Human Nutrition, Wageningen Agricultural University, PO Box 8129, 6700 EV Wageningen, The Netherlands, EUROPE.

B. VELLAS (coordonnateur de la rédaction), Département de Médecine Interne et Gérontologie Clinique, CHU Purpan-Casselardit, 170, chemin de Casselardit, 31000 Toulouse, Fr. EUROPE.

P.M. VELLAS, Groupe de Recherche Architecture, Urbanisme et Vieillissement, Université de Toulouse I, Fr. EUROPE.

J.M. VETEL, chef du service de gériatrie, Hôpital du Mans, Fr. EUROPE.

H. WERNER, Frankfurt, Germany, EUROPE.

L.E. WOORRIPS, Department of Human Nutrition, Wageningen Agricultural University, PO Box 8129, 6700 EV Wageningen, Ther Netherlands, EUROPE.

TT YOSHIKAWA, Office of Geriatrics and Extended Care (114), Department of Veterans Affairs, 810 Vermont av. NW, Washington D.C. 20420, USA.

I

FACTS AND RESEARCH IN BIOLOGICAL GERONTOLOGY

NEUROBEHAVIORAL AGING : GENETICALLY DEFINED RODENTS AS PROMISING MODELS

Charles COHEN-SALMON, Martine BARKATS, Georges CHAPOUTHIER (*)

Summary. – Animal studies have led to promising models for the study of cerebral aging. In the normal aging process, the use of inbred strains of mice allows the analysis of genetic and non genetic determinants of brain aging. Several recent models (senescence accelerate mice, transgenic mice...) have provided possibilities for studying accelerate aging phenotypes. Among the transgenic strains, transgenic mice for the gene of human superoxide dismutase, an enzyme whose excess seems to be linked with accelerated aging in Down's syndrome and Alzheimer's disease, seems especially promising. Pharmacological approaches offer models for the modification of cerebral neurotransmitters in aging. Cholinergic, catecholaminergic and GABAergic models have been the most useful until now. (Facts and Research in Gerontology 1992)

Key-words : Aging, animal models, brain, genetics, mouse, inbred strains, transgenic mice, hippocampus, learning, memory.

The development of experimental medicine has entailed extensive use of animal models and the present emphasis on studies concerning aging is no exception to this rule. The question of the ethics of such an approach, which has been the theme of bitter controversy between scientists and animal lovers, extensively discussed elsewhere (1), will not be reanalysed here. We will only discuss, from a strictly scientific point of view, and by giving some examples, the validity of the increased use of ani-

(*) Laboratoire Génétique, Neurogénétique et Comportement, URA CNRS 1294, UFR Biomédicale, 45, rue des Saints-Pères, 75006 Paris (France).

Adresser toute correspondance concernant le manuscrit à : G. Chapouthier, Laboratoire Génétique, Neurogénétique et Comportement, UFR Biomédicale, 45, rue des Saints-Pères, 75006 Paris (France). Téléphone (1) 42.86.22.05 - Fax : (1) 42.86.22.50.

This work was supported by CNRS (URA 1294), Université Paris V (UFR Biomédicale) and the Fondation pour la recherche médicale.

mal models for the improvement of our knowledge of brain aging in general, and of human brain aging in particular. We will also limit our discussion to *models involving rodents,* since models using primates or insects constitute a clearly different problem which would require an extensive separate discussion. Without the ambition of being exhaustive, this topic involves three main areas of investigation : animal models of normal brain agig ; animal models of accelerated brain aging and models of brain biochemical mechinisms, which are greatly modified during aging. We will analyse the most exciting of these models.

NORMAL BRAIN AGING

One of the first approaches to aging using animal models was the study of the genetic determinants of aging. Although aging certainly involves strong environmental determinants, its genetic bases also seem to play a very important role both in humans (2) and in animals (3, 4). Furthermore, the use of animal models enables some of the genetic and epigenetic mechanisms implicated in aging to be identified. For such studies, the laboratory mouse offers an excellent model. This is justified by several facts :

– genetic studies of normal aging on humans are rare. The study of Jarvick et al. (5) on senescent twins is an exception and its results are biased by effects of both selection and hospital environment ;

– an animal model enables the simultaneous collection of transversal and longitudinal data (6) ;

– an animal model allows selection biases to be avoided (7) ;

– the individual history of subjects, an important factor of variation, can be controlled in animals by a rigid standardization of the environment as early as embryonic life. For this purpose, techniques of ovary and embryonic transplantation (8, 9) in addition to adoption procedures (10) allow an excellent control of the respective effects of cytoplasm, prenatal environment and post-natal maternal factors (nutritional and care-linked) ;

– the use of the mouse is justified by the existence of nearly 400 inbred strains of mice, obtained by several brother x sister crosses, offer, within each strain, individuals homozygote for all loci and thus identical for their genotypes ;

– for these inbred strains, a great deal of data is known on the physiological (life span, for example), biochemical, hormonal as well as anatomical aspects ;

– sophisticated and well-defined techniques can be used for analysing the mouse nervous system and behavior.

For example, our work in this field has attempted to compare susceptibility to aging in virgin females of 3 inbred strains of mice (BALB/c, C57BL/6 and DBA/2) as well as their reciprocal F1s. Thus, 27 independent groups were tested : 3 parental strains and 6 reciprocal F1 at 3 ages : 150, 400 and 750 days. Systematic studies were performed on 15 different behavioral and neurological traits ranging from actual survival percentage (11), body weight, sensory or motor ability and circadian rhythms to morphology of the hippocampus. The first results concerning senescence of motor behavior show that this can only be described by a group-by-age interaction, since certain groups for certain parameters show no link between activity and age, and since deterioration rate and the deteriorated abilities at a given age vary from one group to the next within the same group and the behavioral variations are not identical for all variables (12). These data have led us to abandon any attempt to establish a general index of aging, just as Roubertoux et al. (8) rejected the hypothesis of a general early development factor.

ACCELERATED BRAIN AGING

Since the study of normal aging is, by definition, very long, even in animals such as mice whose lifespan does not exceed 2-3 years, scientists have tried to devise models of accelerated aging.

a) The « Senescence Accelerated Mice »

One recent animal model of accelerated aging is the « Senescence Accelerated Mouse » (SAM) characterised by Takeda's group at Kyoto University. It includes, on the one hand, six strains showing characteristics of accelerated aging and a marked short lifespan, the « SAM-Prone » lines designed by SAM-P/1, SAM-P/2, SAM-P/3, SAM-P/4, SAM-P/6 and SAM-P/8, and, on the other hand, three strains whose aging does not present any pathological aspect, the « SAM-Resistant » lines called SAM-R/1, SAM-R/2 and SAM-R/3 (13, 14).

According to Sprott and Combs, these lines could be recombinant inbred strains derived from AKR breeding pairs and one unknown genotype (15). Concerning the implication of the AKR genotype, one question emerges : do some of these strains maintain certain pathologies specific to AKR line, particularly leukemia ? In this case, some consequences of aging in these lines would be nothing but a trivial phenomenon, i.e. a pathology having no link with aging *stricto sensu.* Moreover, the uncertain origin of these lines makes the localization of eventual genes implicated in their precocious aging, rather difficult.

The method in this kind of study, consisting of comparisons of genotypes or generations, uses the « scending » strategy, i.e. from phenotype to gene, and is therefore time-consuming for the discovery of the genes responsible.

b) Transgenic animals

An alternative method lies in the use of transgenic animals which pave the way for an investigation of physiological pathways from genes to pathological aging phenotypes.

A very interesting model has been offered by the indirect use of Down's syndrome : it has been shown in humans that a trisomy 21 is characterized by early aging and is accompanied by the appearance of histopathological cerebral abnormalities, similar to those observed in Alzheimer's disease (AD) : these abnormalities range from neuronal death, neurofibrillary degenerescence to amyloid plaques (16, 17, 18). It could, thus, be assumed that the overexpression of one or several genes mapped on the chromosome 21 could be responsible for certain aspects of AD (19, 20). Several of these candidate genes have been transfected on to the mouse genome.

– *The Amyloid Precursor Protein*

One of the transgenic strains used in pathological aging research carries the human gene encoding for the Amyloid Precursor Protein (APP) which leads to the formation of A4 amyloid peptide, which accumulates in senile plaques under certain conditions.

These transgenic mice may provide a useful model for resolving the link existing between the A4 amyloid peptide and neuronal cell death (21).

– *Cooper-Zinc Superoxide dismutase*

A second interesting candidate is the gene coding for Copper-Zinc Superoxide dismutase (SOD-1) (22). At physiological doses, SOD-1 is assumed to be an enzyme protecting the cell against the free radical superoxide anion, produced during oxidative metabolism. SOD-1 catalyses the dismutation of these free radicals into H_2O_2, thus limiting their damaging effects ; but, at higher doses, instead of protecting the cell, SOD-1 tends to increase the oxidative shock by generating the hydroxyl radical °OH, known to be highly toxic for membrane lipids, proteins, sugars and nucleic acids (23). This extreme reactivity of the hydroxyl radicals could induce, for example, the appearance of abnormal constituants of the cytoskeleton, such as hydroxyproline, found in neurofibrillary degenerescence (24).

The hypothesis of an overexpression of the gene coding for SOD-1 in Alzheimer's disease can be tested in an animal model : transgenic mice for the gene of the human SOD-1 (hSOD-1 mice) have been obtained (25). They are obtained by introducing fragments of human DNA into the pronuclei of the mouse eggs. Later it is verified, by DNA hybridation techniques, whether some of these fragments have been integrated into the mouse genome. Some of these mice carry the hSOD-1 coding gene. Measured by several biochemical markers, the level of expression of this gene is very high in the brain of hSOD-1 mice, whereas the global SOD-1 is increased twofold, a situation approaching that of the human trisomy 21. This gene expression is particularly increased in the hippocampus and especially in the pyramidal cells and in the granula cells of the dentate gyrus (26).

This data is compatible with that known in human : in subjects suffering from Alzheimer's disease, a specific localization of SOD-1 has been found in hippocampal pyramidal cells showing neurofibrillary degeneration (27). Similarly, at the human behavioral level, both normal and accelerated aging are known to affect the treatment of temporo-spatial information and memory ability, which are related to hippocampal function (28, 29, 30).

Thus the analysis of hippocampal modifications in the transgenic hSOD-1 mice seems to be a very promising animal model of accelerated aging, which could give new clues to the mechanisms underlying Alzheimer's disease.

Discovery of homologic fragments between the human chromosome 21 and the murine chromosome 16 (31) has stimulated new work using trisomic mice for the chromosome 16 (32, 33, 34). The main limitation of this model is the very precocious death (in utero) of these trisomic mice. A novel promising application of this model consists in transplants of mouse trisomy 16 hippocampus into the brain of recipient mice (35). This recent application of neural graft has permitted this difficulty to be avoided by extending the survival period, at least to an early stage of development.

This new model represents a valid tool for the investigation of the pathology of Alzheimer's disease.

BIOCHEMICAL AND PHARMACOLOGICAL APPROACHES

The brain is a biochemical factory. Among the other chemicals, transmitters allowing the transfer of impulsions at the synaptic level are among the most important agents for its function. Thus, a great deal of work has attempted to analyse the modification of the transmitters in aging, both by biochemical studies and by the pharmacological study of the action of compounds which affect transmitter metabolism or secretion. Though most of the work in this field is not based on genetically controlled animals, it is clear that the models proposed would benefit from the use of some of the genetically controlled animals mentioned earlier, whether inbred strains of mice or transgenic subjects. In inbred strains of mice, it is already well-known that several important differences exist in the metabolism of brain transmitters. These differences could be useful for the analysis of the pharmacological effects we will now describe.

In humans, Alzheimer's disease is linked with cholinergic deficits in the nucleus basalis of Meynert, one of the two main systems of cholinergic projection in the cerebral cortex (36). It is obvious that Alzheimer's disease does not limit itself to these cholinergic deficits. It is, however, possible to find animal models of such deficits, either by lesion of the nucleus basalis magnocellularis in rodents (the nucleus basalis magnocellularis is the equivalent in rodents of the nucleus basalis of Meynert), or by administration in this area of pharmacological agents (37, 38, 39). The subsequent decrease in cortical cholinergic activity is linked, in rats, with memory deficits. These hypotheses are, however, limited by a clear obstacle : it is not possible up to now, to alleviate the effects of Alzheimer's disease in human subjects by an action on the cholinergic system, just as Parkinson patients can be treated by an action on the dopaminergic system (40).

Thus, the research on animal models has involved other transmitters. Several authors have emphasized the importance of the decrease with aging of catecholaminergic activity in rodents (41), in non human primates (42) and in humans (43). These last authors suggested a possible improvement in Alzheimer's disease patients by a selective action on catecholamines. Animal models will be of great use for confirming this assumption.

Some authors have proposed more sophisticated models where a combination of cholinergic and catecholaminergic mechanisms is involved. Thus S. Sara (44) provided evidence in the rat for the role of the septo-hippocampal cholinergic pathway and of the interaction between acetylcholine and norepinephrine, in the hippocampal formation, for determining memory dysfunction. The author performed a series of experiments in rats in which hippocampal cholinergic activity had been reduced. The hypothesis was that a lesion of the cholinergic pathway leads to an enhancement of norepinephrin activity which inhibits the spare cholinergic neurons. By pharmacologically *decreasing* norepinephrin release, Sara improved memory ability in rats with cholinergic impairment. Another interaction between cholinergic and catecholaminergic mechanisms has been found by Jaffard et al. (45). These authors showed, in mice, that progressive attenuation with aging of memory abilities is linked to an attenuation of central cholinergic activation. Contrary to Sara, they found that septal administration of noradrenergic antagonists produced similar impairments to those observed with aging. Thus, in this model, catecholamines *improve* rather than impair age-related deficit. Though these two studies are not in total agreement for reasons (animal used, site of injection...) which still remained to be elucidated, they clearly support the idea of an interaction between catecholaminergic and cholinergic hippocampal mechanisms in age-related behavior deficits. However, they still leave open the question of the non-hipocampal cholinergic mechanisms, such as those involving the nucleus basalis-frontal cortex system.

Finally another approach to the effects of transmitters in cerebral aging could be found in the GABAergic mechanisms. Benzodiazepines, well-known ligands of the GABA receptor complex, impair memory processing (46). Conversely, we have recently provided evidence that inverse agonists of the benzodiazepine site, called B-carbolines, are able to improve learning in adult mice (47). The possibility that some of these compounds could also be used in aged human patients to alleviate the effects of senile dementia has been suggested (48). However, since at higher doses most B-carbolines are potent anxiogenic (49) and convulsive (50) agents, only less powerful B-carbolines, such as ZK 93426, could be proposed for this role (48).

CONCLUSION

The few, but promising models described here, give an idea of how the use of animal studies can provide new areas of investigation for the study of aging. Many of these models emphasize the genetic bases of aging, and mice seem to be among the most useful animals for this type of research. It is clear, however, as we mentioned earlier, that no species can offer a general model of aging but rather that several animal models must be used for the study of separate « symptoms » of.aging. This is also true for age-related diseases such as Alzheimer's disease ; it is not possible to obtain animal models of the disease itself, but animal models of the biological or behavioral effects of the disease will be of great use. They could eventually lead to discoveries in both the empirical treatment of aging (51) and the theoretical basis of this essential phenomenon.

REFERENCES

1. CHAPOUTHIER G. : *Au bon vouloir de l'homme, l'animal.* Denoël, Paris, 1990.
2. CONNEALLY : Aging genes and diseases of the aging nervous system. *Advances in Neurology,* 1991, *56*, 233-236.
3. SLAGBOOM P.E., VUG J. : Genetic instability and aging : theories, facts and future perspectives. *Genome,* 1989, 31.
4. YONEMURA I., MOTOYAMA T., HASEKURA H., BOETTCHER B. : Relationship between genotypes of longevity genes and developmental speed in drosophila melanogaster. *Heredity,* 1991, *86*, 143-149.
5. JARVICK L.F., BLUM J.E., VARMA A.O. : Genetic components and intellectual functioning during senescence : A 20 year-study of aging twins. *Behav. Genet.,* 1972, *2*, 159-166.
6. ELIAS P.K., ELIAS M.F. : Motivation and activity. In J.E. Birren & W.K. Schale Eds., *Handbook of the psychology of aging,* New York : Van Nostrand Rheinhold, 1977, 357-383.
7. SIEGLER I.C. : The terminal drop hypothesis : fact or artifact ? *Exp. Aging Res.,* 1975, *1*, 169-195.
8. ROUBERTOUX P.L., CARLIER M. : Differences between CBA/H and NZB on intermale aggression : II. Maternal effects. *Behav. Genet.,* 1988, *18*, 175-184.
9. ROUBERTOUX P.L., NOSTEN-BERTRAND M., CARLIER M. : Additive and interactive effects between genotype and maternal environments, concepts and facts. *Adv. Stud. Behav.,* 1990, *19*, 205-247.
10. CARLIER M., ROUBERTOUX P.L., COHEN-SALMON C. : Early development in mice : I. Genotype and post-natal maternal effects. *Physiol. Behav.,* 1983, *30*, 837-844.
11. COHEN-SALMON C., PEREZ-DIAZ P., LHOTELLIER L. : Lifespan in virgin female mice of three inbred strains and their reciprocal F1s. *Mouse Genome,* in press.
12. LHOTELLIER L., COHEN-SALMON C. : Senescence of motor behavior in mice : contribution of genetic methods. *Eur. Bull. Cognit. Psychol.,* 1991, *11*, 27-53.
13. TAKEDA T., HOSOKAWA M., TAKESHITA S., IRINO M., HIGUGHI K., MATSUSHITA T., TOMITA Y., YASUSHIRA K., HAMAMOTO H., SHIMIZU K., ISHII M., YAMAMURO T. : A new murine model of accelerated senescence. *Mech. Ageing Dev.,* 1981, *17*, 183-194.
14. KUNISADA T., HIGUCHI K., AOTA S., TAKEDA T., YAMAGISHI H. : Molecular cloning and nucleotide sequence of cDNA for murine senile amyloid protein : nucleotide substitutions found in apolipoprotein A-11 cDNA of senescence accelerated mouse (SAM). *Nucleic Acids Res.,* 1986, *14*, 5729-5740.
15. SPROTT R.L., COMBS C.A. : Genetic aspect of aging in Mus Musculus. *Review of Biological Research in Aging,* 1990, *4*, 73-80.
16. EPSTEIN C.J. : Down's Syndrome and Alzheimer's Disease, implications and approaches. In : *Biological aspect of Alzheimer's Disease,* Ed. Katzman R., Cold Spring Harbor Laboratory, 1983, 169-182.
17. EPSTEIN C.J. : Down's Syndrome and Alzheimer's disease. What is the relationship ? In : *Advancing frontiers in Alzheimer's disease research.* Eds. Glenner G.G., Wurtman R.J., University of Texas Press, Austin, 1987, 155-173.
18. MANN D.M.A., YATES P.O., MARCYNIUK B. : Alzheimer's presenile dementia of Alzheimer type and Down's Syndrome in middle age form : an age related continuum of pathological changes. *Neuropathol. Appl. Neurobiol.,* 1984, *10*, 185-207.
19. SCHWEBER M. : A possible unitary genetic hypothesis for Down's Syndrome and Alzheimer's Disease. *Ann. N.Y. Acad. Sci.,* 1985, *450*, 223-239.

20. SCHWEBER M. : Unitary genetic hypothesis for Down's Syndrome and Alzheimer's Disease. *Am. J. Hum. Genet.*, 1986, *39*, A 100.
21. UNTERBECK A., BAYNEY R.M., SCANGOS G., WIRAK D.O. : Transgenic mouse models of amyloidosis in Alzheimer's Disease. *Review of Biological Research in Aging*, 1990, *4*, 139-162.
22. SINET P.M., ALLARD, LEJEUNE J., JEROME H. : Trisomie 21 et Superoxyde dismutase. *Exp. Cell. Res.*, 1976, *97*, 47-55.
23. SINET P.M. : Metabolism of oxygen derivatives in Down's Syndrome. *Ann. N.Y. Acad. Sci.*, 1982, *396*, 83-94.
24. VOGELSAND G.D., ZEMLAN F.P., DEAN G.E. : Purification and solubilization of paired helicoidal filaments from Alzheimer's brains. *J. Neurochem.*, 1990, *54*, 148-155.
25. CEBALLOS-PICOT I., NICOLE A., BRIAND P., GRIMBER G., DELACOURTE A., DEFOSSEZ A., JAVOY-AGID F., LAFON M., BLOUIN J.L., SINET P.M. : Neuronal specific expression of human copper-zinc superoxide dismutase gene in transgenic mice : animal model of gene dosage effects in Down's Syndrome. *Brain Research*, 1991, *552*, 198-214.
26. CEBALLOS I., JAVOY-AGID F., HIRSCH E.C., DUMAS S., KAMOUN P.P., SINET P.M., AGID Y. : Localization of copper-zinc superoxide dismutase in the human hippocampus by *in situ* hybridization. *Neurosci., Lett.*, 1989, *105*, 41-46.
27. DELACOURTE A., DEFOSSEZ A., CEBALLOS I., NICOLE A., SINET P.M. : Preferential localisation of copper-zinc superoxide dismutase in the vulnerable cortical neurons in Alzheimer's Disease. *Neurosci. Lett.*, 1988, 247-253.
28. BARNES C.A. : Memory deficits associated with senescence : a behavioral and neurophysiological study in the rat. *J. Comp. Physiol. Psychol.*, 1979, *93*, 74-104.
29. WALLACE J.E., KRAUTER E.E., CAMPBELL B.A. : Animal models of declining memory in the aged : short-term and spatial memory in the aged rat. *J. Gerontol.*, 1980, *35*, 355-363.
30. LISTON E.H. : Clinical findings of presenile dementia. *J. Nerv. Ment. Dis.*, 1979, *167*, 337-342.
31. COX D.R., EPSTEIN L.B., EPSTEIN C.J. : Genes coding for sensitivity to interferon (IfRec) and soluble superoxide dismutase (SOD-1) are linked in mouse and man and map to chromosome 16. *Proc. Nat. Acad. Sci., U.S.A.*, 1980, *77*, 2168-2172.
32. COX D.R., SMITH S.A., EPSTEIN L.B., EPSTEIN C.J. : Mouse trisomy 16 as an animal model of human trisomy 21 (Down's Syndrome) : formation of viable trisomy 16 — diploid mouse chimeras. *Dev. Biol.*, 1984, *101*, 416-424.
33. COYLE J.T., GEARHART J.D., OSTER-GRANITE M.L., SINGER H.S., MORAN T.H. : Brain neurotransmitters : implications for Down's Syndrome from studies of mouse trisomy 16. In : *The neurobiology of Down's Syndrome.* Ed. Epstein C.J., Raven Press, N.Y., 1986, 153-169.
34. OSTER-GRANITE M.L., GEARHART J.D., REEVES R.H. : Neurobiological consequences of trisomy 16 in mice. In : *The neurobiology of Down's Syndrome.* Ed. Epstein C.J., Raven Press, N.Y., 1986, 137-151.
35. RICHARDS S.J., WATERS J.J., BEYREUTHER K., MASTERS C.L., WISCHIK C.M., SPARKMAN D.R., WHITE C.L., ABRAHAM C.R., DUNNETT S.B. : Transplants of mouse trisomy 16 hippocampus provide a model of Alzheimer's Disease neuropathology. *The EMBO Journal*, 1991, *10*, 297-303.
36. BARTUS R.T., DEAN R.I. III, BEER S., LIPPA A.S. : The cholinergic hypothesis of geriatric memory dysfunction. *Science*, 1982, *217*, 408-417.
37. MAYO W., DUBOIS B., PLOSKA A., JAVOY-AGID Y., LE MOAL M., SIMON H. : Cortical cholinergic projections from the basal forebrain of the rat, with special reference to the prefrontal cortex innervation. *Neurosci., Lett.*, 1984, *47*, 149-154.
38. MAYO W., KHAROUBY M., LE MOAL M., SIMON H. : Memory disturbances following ibotenic acid injections in the nucleus basalis magnocellularis of the rat. *Brain Res.*, 1988, *455*, 213-222.
39. DUBOIS B., MAYO W., AGID Y., LE MOAL M., SIMON : Profound disturbances of spontaneous and learned behaviors following lesions of the nucleus basalis magnocellularis in the rat. *Brain Res.*, 1985, *288*, 213-218.
40. CHAPOUTHIER G. : The search for a biochemistry of memory. *Arch. Gerontol. Geriat.*, 1989, *suppl. 1*, 7-19.
41. HOCK F.J. : Drug influences on learning and memory in aged animals and humans. *Neuropsychobiol.*, 1987, *17*, 145-160.
42. ARNSTEN A.F.T., GOLDMAN-RAKIC P.S. : Catecholamines and cognitive decline in aged nonhuman primates. *Ann. N.Y. Acad. Sci.*, 1985, *444*, 218-244.
43. McENTEE W.J., CROOK T.H. : Age associated memory impairment : a role for catecholamines. *Neurology*, 1990, *40*, 526-530.
44. SARA S.J. : Noradrenergic-cholinergic interaction : its possible role in memory dysfunction associated with senile dementia. *Arch. Gerontol. Geriat.*, 1989, *suppl. 1*, 99-108.
45. JAFFARD R., DURKIN T., TOUMANE A., MARIGHETTO A., LEBRUN C. : Experimental dissociation of memory systems in mice : behavioral and neurochemical aspects. *Arch. Gerontol. Geriat.*, 1989, *suppl. 1*, 55-70.
46. LISTER R.G. : The amnesic action of benzodiazepines in man. *Neurosci., Biobehav. Res.*, 1985, *9*, 87-94.

47. CHAPOUTHIER G., RAFFALLI-SEBILLE M.J., VENAULT P., SIMIAND J., DODD R.H. : Comparison between the effects of the benzodiazepine receptor ligands methyl beta-caroline-3-carboxylate and diazepam in two learning situations in mice. *Psychobiol.*, 1991, *19 (1),* 58-63.
48. SARTER M., SCHNEIDER H.H., STEPHENS D.N. : Treatment strategies for senile dementia : antagonists B-carbolines. *Trends Neurosci.*, 1988, *11,,* 13-17.
49. PRADO DE CARVALHO L., GRECKSCH G., CHAPOUTHIER G., ROSSIER J. : Anxiogenic and non-anxiogenic benzodiazepine antagonists. *Nature,* 1983, *301,* 64-66.
50. PRADO DE CARVALHO L., GRECKSCH G., CAVALHEIRO E.A., DODD R.H., CHAPOUTHIER G., ROSSIER J. : Characterisations of convulsions induced by methyl B-carboline-3-carboxylate in mice. *Eur. J. Pharmacol.*, 1984, *103,* 287-293.
51. RAFFALLI-SEBILLE M.J., CHAPOUTHIER G., CLOSTRE F., CHRISTEN Y. : Learning improvement in adult and aged mice induced by a Ginkgo biloba extract. In : *Ginkgo biloba extracts (EGB 761) and brain,* edited by M. Lacour and Y. Christen, Elsevier, in press.

NEWS IN BIOLOGICAL GERONTOLOGY

We present here the abstracts of articles published in the international editions of Facts and Research in Gerontology 1992. Reprint are available to the authors (see contributors directory) or to Serdi : 29, rue de Saint-Pétersbourg, 75008 Paris.

1 - AGING AND SKIN : L. Robert, J. Labat-Robert

Summary. – We present a short review of the mechanisms of connective tissue aging. Such tissues are composed of cells and extracellular matrix (ECM). Mesenchymal cells are mostly mitotic and their aging was studied by the Hayflick model in conventional culture conditions. The decrease of proliferative capacity can be preceeded or not by the decrease of the biosynthetic capacity of matrix macromolecules. Some of these biosynthetic processes increase with passage number, this is the case for fibronectin. It appears that proliferation capacity and matrix biosynthesis are independently regulated. The aging of matrix macromolécules can be divided in two independent processes : the age-dependent modifications of their biosynthesis and the post-synthetic modifications of the macromolecules. The age dependent increase of collagen III/I ratio and of fibronectin biosynthesis are exemples of the Ist class of events. Post-synthetic modifications comprise increasing crosslinking of collagen fibers (by the Maillard reaction) increasing interactions with lipids and calcium salt (elastin) and proteolytic degradations (fibronectin, elastin). Degradation products of matrix macromolecules do exhibit biological properties possibly involved in age related modifications. Elastin peptides are recognized by the elastin receptor which might well be involved in the age dependent calcium deposition. Uncoupling of receptors may also represent an important mechanism of aging as shown by the loss of interaction between G-protein and the elastin receptor in aging cells.
(Facts and Research in Gerontology 1992)

Key-words : *connective tissues, extracellular matrix, mesenchymal cells, collagen, elastin, proteoglycan, fibronectin, receptor, aging.*

2 - MITOCHONDRIA AND AGING : J. Tréton, Y. Courtois

Summary. – The mitochondria is an intracellular organel which is found in all living cells. It participates in the production of free radicals. This process is involved in the aging mechanism. Thus, any change in the morphology and structure of the mitochondria will be the first sign of a modification or alteration in the mitochondria. It is therefore very important to examine and to analyze the factors which act on the mitochondria. There are three cases in which nutrition affects the mitochondria morphology : 1) nutritional change (weaning) ; 2) overfeeding ; 3) underfeeding. These data are analyzed and discussed in this paper. They underline that mitochondrial homeostasy plays a crucial role in the nutritional changes occuring in relation with pathology or aging. (Facts and Research in Gerontology 1992)

Key Words : *Mitochondria, Aging, Nutrition.*

3 - NEURITIC PLAQUES, AMYLOID DEPOSITS AND NEUROFIBRILLAR CHANGES FOUND IN THE BRAIN CORTEX OF A LEMURIAN PRIMATE : POSSIBLE ANIMAL MODEL FOR ALZHEIMER'S DISEASE : N. Bons, N. Mestre, A. Petter

Summary. – Microcebus murinus *(body weight 100 g), originating from Madagascar, has in nature a life span about 4-5 years but in captivity this primate dies about after 8 to 12 years. A population of 27 microcebes (15 young and 12 old animals) has been studied. The old animals showed physical and behavioral changes compared to the young individuals. In different aged microcebes these changes were accompanied by deep anatomo-histological brain changes. In particular, various brain areas displayed dramatic atrophy associated with a conspicuous increase in the size of the cerebral ventricles. These modifications seemed not to be correlated to the brain weight. But these morphophological brain changes were accompanied by certain histological profiles indicative of pathology. In the cortex, these histological changes consisted of : 1) numerous neuritic debris ; 2) dense bundles of argyrophilic filaments in many pyramidal neurons ; 3) amyloid deposits in and around the vascular walls, and 4) in two animals, a large number of neuritic plaques. So far, all these histological lesions recalled some of those observed in human senile dementia ; they may indicate that* Microcebus murinus *may well be a good model for studies on cerebral aging. (Facts and Research in Gerontology 1992)*

Key-words : *cerebral aging, neuritic plaques, filamentous changes, amyloid, Alzheimer's disease, primate, lemurian.*

SELECTION OF LITERATURE

1 - AGING AND SKIN : L. Robert, J. Labat-Robert

1. VERZAR F. : Aging of collagen fibers in D.A. Hall Ed. *Int. Rev. Conn. Tis. Res.* (Acad. Press, NY), 1964, *2,* 244-300.
2. HAYFLICK L. : Aging under glass. *Exper. Gerontol.,* 1970, *5,* 291-303.
3. Pour plus de détails voir L. ROBERT : « Les Horloges biologiques », *Flammarion,* Paris, 1989 et « Mécanismes cellulaires et moléculaires du vieillissement », *Masson,* Paris, 1983.
4. EL NABOUT R., MARTIN M., REMY J., KERN P., ROBERT L. LAFUMA C. : Collagen synthesis and deposition in cultured fibroblasts from subcutaneous radiation-induced fibrosis. Modification as function of ageing. *Matrix,* 1989, *9,* 411-420.
5. MOCZAR M., OUZILLOU J., COURTOIS Y., ROBERT L. :Age dependence of the biosynthesis of intercellular matrix macromolecules of rabbit aorta in organ culture and cell culture. *Gerontol.,* 1976, *22,* 461-472.
6. Development and maturation of the crosslinks in the collagen fibers of skin. In : « Frontiers of Matrix Biology ». L. Robert, B. Robert, Eds, 1973, *1,* 130-156 (Karger, Basel).
7. BROWNLEE M., VLASSARA H., CERAMI A. : Nonenzymatic glycosylation and the pathogenesis of diabetic complications. *Ann. Intern. Med.,* 1984, *101,* 527-537.
8. TARSIO J.F., WIGNESS B., RHODE T.D., RUPP W.M., BUCHWALD H., FURCHT L.T. : Nonenzymatic glycation of fibronectin and alterations in the molecular association of cell matrix and basement membrane components in diabetes mellitus. *Diabetes,* 1985, *24,* 477-484.
9. KERN P., SEBERT B., ROBERT L. : Increased type III/type I collagen ratios in diabetic human conjonctival biopsies. *Clin. Physiol. Biochem.,* 1986, *4,* 113-119.
10. KERN P., MOCZAR M., ROBERT L. : Biosynthesis of skin collagens in normal and diabetic mice. *Biochem J.,* 1979, *182,* 337-345.
11. BOYER B., KERN P., FOURTANIER A., LABAT-ROBERT J. : Age-dependent variations of the biosyntheses of fibronectin and fibrous collagens in mouse skin. *Exper. Gerontol.,* 1991, *26,* 375-383.

12. « Frontiers of Matrix Biology » Biology and pathology of elastic tissues. A.M. Robert, L. Robert Eds, 1980, *8* (Karger, Basel).
13. Elastine and Elastases. ROBERT L., HOTNEBECK W., eds *CRC Press*, Boca Raton, 1989, vol. I, II.
14. FULOP T., WEI S.M., ROBERT L., JACOB M.P. : Determination of elastin peptides in normal and arteriosclerotic human sera by ELISA. *Clin. Physiol. Biochem.*, 1991, *8*, 273-282.
15. ROBERT L., JACOB M.P., FULOP T., TIMAR J., HORNEBECK W. : Elastonectin and the elastin receptor. *Pathol. Biol.*, 1989, *37*, 736-741.
16. FULOP T., JACOB M.P., FORIS G., VARGA Zs. : Effects of elastin peptides on ion fluxes. In : « Cell calcium metabolism ». Gary Fiskum Ed., pp. 617-622 *(Plenum Publishing Corporation)*, 1989.
17. VARGA Z., JACOB M.P., CSONGOR J., ROBERT L., LEOVEY A., FULOP T. : Altered phosphatidylinositol breakdown after K-elastin stimulation in PMBIs of elderly. Mechanisms of ageing and development.. *Elsevier Scient. Publish. Ireland Ltd*, 1990, *52*, 61-70.
18. ROBERT L., MOCZAR M. : Age-related changes of proteoglycans and glycosaminoglycans. In : « Glycosaminoglycans and proteoglycans in physiological and pathological processes of body systems ». Varma R.S., Varma R. Eds, 440-460 (Karger).
19. VOGEL H.G. : Influence of maturation and aging on mechanical and biomedical properties of connective tissue in the rat, Me. *Aging Develop.*, 1980, *14*, 283-292.
20. REDINI F., LAFUMA C., FULOP T., ROBERT L., HORNEBECK W. : Effect of cytokines and growth factors on the expression of elastase activity by human synoviocytes, dermal fibroblasts and rabbit articular chondrocytes. *Biochem. Biophys. Res. Commun.*, 1988, *155*, 786-793.
21. Frontiers of Matrix Biology, Structural glycoprotein in cell matrix interactions. J. Labat-Robert, R. Timpl. L. Robert Eds, 1986, *11* (Karger, Basel).
22. HYNES R.O. : Molecular biology of fibronectin. *Ann. Rev. Cell. Biol.*, 1985, *1*, 67-90.
23. PLANCHENAULT S., LAMBERT VIDMARK S., IMHOFF J.M., BLONDEAU X., EMOD I., LOTTSPEICH F., KEIL-DLOUHA V. : Potential proteolytic activity of human plasma fibronectin. FN gelatinase. *Biol. Chem. Hoppe Seyler*, 1990, *371*, 117-128.
24. ROBERT L., LABAT-ROBERT J. : Aging of extracellular matrix, its role in the development of age-associated diseases. In : « *Sandoz lectures : Crossroads in aging* », 1988, 105-127.
25. LABAT-ROBERT J., ROBERT L. : Aging of the extracellular matrix and its pathology. *Exper. Gerontol.*, 1988, *23*, 5-18.

2 - MITOCHONDRIA AND AGING : J. Tréton et Y. Courtois

1. MENSZIES (R.A.) and GOLD (P.H.) : *Popular Science Monthly*, 71, 1971, 481.
2. MIQUEL (J.) and FLEMING (J.E.) : *Exp. Geront.*, 19, 1984, 31-36.
3. HAMMER (C.T.), WILLS (E.D.) : The role of lipid components of the diet in the regulation of the fatty acid composition of the rat liver endoplasmic reticulum and lipid peroxydation, *Biochem. J.*, 174, 1978, 585-593.
4. SONAWANE (B.R.), COATES (P.M.), YAFFE (S.J.) and KOLDOVSKY (O.) : Influence of prenatal nutrition on hepatic drug metabolism in adult rat : *Dev. Pharmacol. Them. 6*, 1983, 323-332.
5. POLLAK (J.K.) : The maturation of the inner membrane of fœtal rat liver mitochondria, *Biochem. J.*, 150, 1975, 477-488.
6. POLLAK (J.K.) : Mitochondrial heterogeneity in fœtal and suckling rat liver, differential leucine incorporation into the proteins of two mitochondrial populations : *Biochem. Biophy. Res. Comm.*, 69, 1976, 823-829.
7. SUBRAMANIAN (H.) and KATYARE (S.S.) : Oxydative phosphorylation in mouse liver mitochondria during weaning. *Mech. Age. Develop.*, 54, 1990, 121-129.
8. RAJAN (R.) : Studies on hormonal regulation of brain development and drug interaction. Ph'D. thesis, *University of Bombay*, 1989.
9. REGIUS (O.), BÖRZSÖNYI (L.), GERGEGELY (I.) and LENGYEL (E.) : The effect of family background on body weight and on the number and morphological changes in lymphocytes in old age. *Z. Gerontol.*, 22, 1989, 96-100.
10. MICOZZI (M.S.), ALBANES (D.), JONES (Y.) and CHUMLA (W.C.) : Correlation of body mass indeces with weight, stature, and body composition in men and women in NHANES I and II, 1-3. *Americ. J. Clin. Nutr.*, 44, 1986, 725-731.
11. BEREGI (E.) and REGIUS (O.) : Lipofuscin in lymphocytes and plasma. *Geront. Geriatr.*, 2, 1983, 229-235.
12. LAGANIÈRE (S.) and YU (B.P.) : Anti-lipoperoxydation action of food restriction. *Biochem. Biophy. Res. Comm.*, 145, 1987, 1185-1187.
13. LAGANIÈRE (S.) and YU (B.P.) : Effect of chronic food restriction in aging rat liver subcellular membranes. *Mech. Age and Devpt.*, 48, 1989, 207-219.
14. SOHAL (R.S.), SVENSSON (I.) and BRUNK (U.T.) : Hydrogen peroxyde production by liver mitochondria in different species. *Mech. Age Devpt.*, 53, 1990, 209-215.

15. SMITH (R.E.) : Quantitative relation between liver mitochondria metabolism and total body weight in Mammal. *Ann. N.Y. Acad. Sci.*, 1956, *62*, 405-422.

16. OUDEA (M.C.), COLETTE (Z.M.) and OUDEA (P.) : Morphometric study of ultrastructural changes induced in rat liver by chronic alcohol intake. *Digest. Dis.*, 1973, *18*, 398-402.

17. OUDEA (M.C.), COLETTE (Z.M.), DEDIEU (P.M.) and OUDEA : Morphometric study of ultrastructure of human alcoholic fatty liver. *Biomedicine*, 1973, *18*, 455-459.

3 - NEURITIC PLAQUES, AMYLOID DEPOSITS AND ALZHEIMER DISEASE : N. Bons, N. Mestre, A. Petter

1. WISNIEWSKI H.M., BERNADINO GHETTI M.D., TERRY R.D. : Neuritic (senile) plaques and filamentous changes in aged rhesus monkeys. *J. Neuropathol. Exp. Neurol.*, 1973, *32*, 566-584.

2. EARNEST M.P., HEATON R.K., WILKINSON W.E., MANKE W.F. : Cortical atrophy, ventricular enlargment and intellectual impairment in the aged. *Neurology*, 1979, *29*, 1138-1143.

3. PRICE D.L., WHITEHOUSE P.J., STRUBLE R.G., PRICE D.L. Jr., CORK L.C., HEDREEN J.C., KITT C.A. : Basal forebrain cholinergic neurons and neuritic plaques in primate brain. *Bandbury Report*, 1983, *15*, 65-77.

4. PETERS A. : in : Cerebral cortex : 9 : Normal and altered states of function. A. Peters and G. Jones ed., *Plenum*, New York, Londres, 1991, 485-510.

5. WISNIEWSKI H.M., JOHNSON A.B., RAINE C.S., KAY W.J., TERRY R.D. : Senile plaques and cerebral amyloidosis in aged dogs : a histochemical and ultrastructural study. *Lab. Invest.*, 1970, *23*, 287-296.

6. FUENTES C., ROCH G., KÖNIG N. : Etude morphologique de l'écorce cérébrale temporale de l'hippocampe et du noyau basal de Meynert en microscopie optique et électronique après injection de cholinotoxine chez le rat. *Z. mikrosk. Anat. Forsch.*, Leipzig, 1987, *101*, 439-450.

7. FUENTES C., KÖNIG N., ROCH G. : Regional and laminar distribution of nodules in rat cerebral cortex after injection of the cholinergic neurotoxin : AF64A. *Z. mikrosk. - Anat. Forsch.*, Leipzig, 1987, *101*, 1035-1039.

8. QUON D., WANG Y., CATALANO R., MARIAN SCARDINA J., MURAKAMI K., CORDELL B. : Formation of ß-amyloid protein deposits in brains of transgenic mice. *Nature*, 1991, *352*, 239-241.

9. WIRAK D.O., BAYNEY R., RAMABHADRAN T.V., FRACASSO R.P., HART J.T., HAUER P.E., HSIAU P., PEKAR S.K., SCANGOS G.A., TRAPP B.D., UNTERBECK A.J. : Deposits of amyloid Protein in the central nervous system of transgenic mice. *Science*, 1991, *253*, 323-325.

10. SELKOE D.J., BELL D.S., PODLISNY M.B., PRICE D.L., CORK L.C. : Conservation of brain amyloid proteins in aged animals and humans with Alzheimer's disease. *Science*, 1987, *235*, 873-876.

11. FELDMAN M.L., DOWD C. : Loss of dendritic spines in aging cerebral cortex. *Anat. Embryol.*, 1975, *148*, 279-301.

II

FACTS AND RESEARCH
IN AGING GUT

REGULATION OF GASTRIC MUCOSAL CELL PROLIFERATION DURING ADVANCING AGE (*)

Adhip P.N. MAJUMDAR (**)

Summary. – Aging is associated with increased incidence of many gastrointestinal (GI) dysfunction, including malignancy. Since the structural and, in turn, the functional integrity of the GI mucosa are maintained by constant renewal of cells, a datailed knowledge of muscosal cell proliferation and regulation of this process should increase our understanding of the normal aging process as well as the many GI dysfunction that represent disorders of tissue growth. In the Fischer-344 rats, we have observed that aging is associated with increased proliferative activity in the gastric mucosa, and that there are substantial (and in some respects paradoxical) age-related changes in musocal responsiveness to many GI hormones/growth factors including gastrin, EGF and bombesin as well as to injury. We have also observed that these changes are accompanied by parallel alterations in tyrosine kinase (Tyr-k) activity and tyrosine-specific phosphorylation of a 55 kDa membrane protein, suggesting that the 55 kDa phosphotyrosine membrane protein may play a critical role in regulating gastric mucosal cell proliferation during aging. (Facts and Research in Gerontology 1992)

Key-words : gastric mucosal, cell, age.

Mucosal cells of the gastrointestinal (GI) tissues undergo a constant and rapid renewal process (1). It is generally accepted that in normal adults, GI mucosal cell populations are maintained by sustained proliferation of the precursor cells and exfoliation of surface cells (2-4). Thus, a stimulation of proliferation is likely to be accompanied by increased cell loss, whereas an opposite picture could be expected when cell multiplication is diminished. Such a process would sustain the delicate balance which is necessary to maintain a constant number of cells in a healthy adult tissue. An error in any part of this process may accelerate or diminish growth resulting in either hyperplasia and/or hypertrophy or atrophy of the organ. Theoretically, therefore, any substance that affects the growth regulatory process is likely to have an

(*) Supported by grants from the VA Medical Research and the NIH (AG 08434).
(**) VA Medical Center and Wayne State University School of Medicine, Allen Park, Michigan 48101 (USA).

influence on the size of the GI mucosa, which in turn may affect the functional properties of the tissue(s).

The structural and functional integrity of the GI mucosa changes at different stages of life. Since they are maintained by constant renewal of cells, an in-depth knowledge of mucosal cell proliferation and regulation of this process at various stages of life is essential for an understanding of the normal aging process as well as many GI diseases that represent disorders of tissue growth (1, 5-8). In view of this, and the fact that aging is associated with increased incidence of many GI dysfunctions including malignancy, prompted us to evaluate in detail the regulation of GI mucosal cell proliferation at later stages of life. In the present communication, I will report some of our recent observations in the gastric mucosa.

Although there is still a dearth of reliable experimental data, the rate of gastric mucosal cell proliferation changes at different stages of life. We have earlier reported that gastric mucosal proliferative activity in rats, as assessed by DNA and protein synthesis and thymidine kinase activity, remains elevated during the first two weeks of postnatal life then decreases over the next 2-3 weeks (9). Despite this fall in proliferative activity between 4 and 5 weeks of life, mucosal DNA content rises dramatically during this period indicating an increase in total mucosal cell populations (9). Thus, when total ^{3}H-thymidine incorporation into mucosal DNA of the whole organ was determined, we observed a progressive rise (in incorporation) with age (9). Taken together, our results show that in spite of the fall in the rate of mucosal DNA synthesis (expressed per unit of DNA), which begins at around 15 days of age in rats, the total number of cells undergoing division rises throughout the first 4-5 weeks of postnatal life resulting in a steady growth of the organ.

In contrast, aging has been found to be associated with atrophy of the gastric mucosa (10-12). We have observed a significant 32 % reduction in mucosal glandular height in 24 mo old Fischer-344 rats when compared with their 4 mo old counterparts (10, Table I). A similar observation has also been made by Hollander et al. (12) in Sprague-Dawley strain of rats. These changes were also accompanied by a significant reduction in mucosal DNA and RNA content (11). In addition, histologic evaluation revealed that the mucosal atrophy in old rats was associated with decrease in gland density (number of glands per cm²) leading to a reduction in the number of glandular epithelial cells of all types (10). Furthermore, the gastric epithelial cells also showed evidence of decreased secretory activity, with decreased number of intracytoplasmic secretory granules and decreased cell size (10). These age-associated alterations in mucosal cells could partly be responsible for the diminished gastric secretion observed in old animals (11, 13, 14).

TABLE I

Gastric mucosal labelling index (LI) and mucosal glandular height in young (4-mo) and aged (24-mo) rats

Age	LI	Glandular height mu/m)
4 mo	2.5 ± 0.3	745 ± 49
24 mo	3.2 ± 0.2*	506 ± 33*

LI was expressed as percent of labelled cells (number of labelled cells × 100/total number of cells per high power focus). Values represent mean ± SE (n = 3 for each group).
* P moins de 0.05, when compared with 4-mo old rats.
Ref. 10, with permission.

Despite the fact that aging was associated with gastric mucosal atrophy, mucosal proliferative activity in 20-24 mo old Fischer-344 rats was found to be higher than in their 4-5 mo old counterparts (10, 15-18). This was evidenced by increased labelling index (Table I), the rate of DNA synthesis (16, 18), thymidine kinase (16, 17) and orni- thine decarboxylase activities (15, 19). Holt and his associates have earlier demons- trated a similar phenomenon in both small and large intestine (20-24). In the aging small intestine, they have observed a greater number of crypt cells relative to villus cell populations (24). This was accompanied by similar cell migration rates (24). This apparent disequilibrium in crypt cell production rate and villus cell number could not be explained by formation of more crypt (20), which led them to suggest that in the small intestine of aged rats, DNA replication was without cytokinesis. A similar explanation could also be offered for our observation in the gastric mucosa in which increased mucosal proliferative activity was not accompanied by a concomitant rise in mucosal growth, but rather aging resulted in atrophy of the tissue (10).

Numerous extra- and intracellular factors are involved in the regulation of GI mucosal cell proliferation at different stages of life. In the present communication, role of some of the extra- and intracellular factors will be described.

Extracellular factors : GI mucosal cell proliferation is known to be under the regu- lation of a number of nutritional and hormonal factors. In general, deprivation of food results in decreased cell proliferation and refeeding reverses the situation (25). Holt and Yeh (22, 23) have compared the effect of fasting and refeeding on small and large intestinal proliferative activity in young (3-4 mo) and aged (24-28 mo) Fischer-344 rats. In the mucosa of both small and large intestine, a 3-day fasting resul- ted in a 40-60 % reduction in proliferative activity (as evidenced by mitotic index) in young rats, whereas in old rats it was decreased by only 10-20 %, when compa- red with the corresponding fed controls (22-23). Although in both age groups refee- ding increased small intestinal proliferative activity, in aged rats this increase was associated with broadening of the proliferative zone (22, 23). Moreover, in fasted aged rats, proliferative responsiveness of the large intestine to food was found to be blun- ted (22-24). The latter observation clearly indicates that nutritional regulation of mucosal cell proliferation is affected by aging.

Age-associated changes in GI mucosal cell proliferation could be secondary to alterations in hormonal influences. Over the past two decades considerable evidence has appeared to show that a number of GI hormones/peptides and, specifically, gas- trin epidermal growth factor (EGF) and bombesin (an amphibian peptide which is structurally and functionally analogous to gastrin releasing peptide – GRP) regu- late mucosal cell proliferation in much of the GI tract including the stomach (26, 27). However, responsiveness of the gastric mucosa to these peptides changes at diffe- rent stages of life. We have earlier reported that in rats, the gastric mucosa becomes responsive to the growth-promoting action of gastrin around the 3rd postnatal week of life (9). At this time the parietal cells also become sensitive to gastrin and secrete acid in response to the hormone (28), when gastrin receptors also appear (28). In contrast, with aging there was a progressive loss of gastric mucosal responsiveness to both acid secretory (11) and growth-promoting (17) actions of gastrin. Although the underlying mechanisms are unknown at present, one possibility could be the loss of functional receptors for gastrin. Singh et al. (29) reported that the number of gastrin binding sites in the gastric mucosa of 24-mo old rats were lower than in their 3- and 6-mo old counterparts. Taken together, the results suggest a relationship between gastrin receptor populations and gastric mucosal responsiveness to gastrin.

EGF, which is structurally and functionally similar to urogastrone, has also been found to regulate GI mucosal cell proliferation (26). Feldman et al. (30) were the first to demonstrate that administration of EGF to suckling mice stimulates gastric and duodenal mucosal ornithine decarboxylase activity. Subsequently, Malo and Menard (31) reported that EGF not only stimulates growth of the proximal, but also of distal small intestine. Similar observations were also made by us and others (32-35). Using an organ culture system, we have demonstrated that EGF stimulates protein and DNA synthesis in both pre- and neonatal rats (32) and ornithine decarboxylase activity in the colonic mucosa of young mature rats (36). These observations not only indicate a direct growth-promoting effect of EGF on both small and large intestinal mucosa, but also shows that the polypeptide may have a role in regulating intestinal mucosal growth from prenatal to adulthood. Like the small intestinal mucosa, the gastric mucosa also responds to the growth-promoting action of EGF. Dembinski and Johnson (34) reported that in 10 day old suckling rats, repeated injections of EGF for 5 days result in a significant increase in gastric mucosal DNA, RNA and proteiri content. We have observed that in unweaned rats, daily injections of EGF at a dose of 20 ug/kg for 7 days significantly stimulated both gastric and small intestinal protein and nucleic acid content (35). Repeated injections of EGF for 2 days also stimulated gastric mucosal DNA synthesis in young mature rats (16). These observations show that the GI mucosa remains responsive to the growth-promoting action of EGF from the late prenatal through early adulthood. To further determine whether GI mucosal responsiveness to EGF might be affected by aging, we have recently examined the changes in growth-related processes in the gastric and colonic mucosa during advancing age following administration of EGF. We have observed that repeated injections of EGF (10 ug/kg) twice a day for 2 days or continuous infusion of the peptide (200 ng/kg/h) for 4 days significantly stimulates gastric mucosal DNA synthesis and thymidine kinase activity as well as colonic mucosal ornithine decarboxylase activity in 4-mo old rats when compared with the saline treated control (16, 37). EGF treatment produced no significant change in these parameters in the gastric mucosa of 8 and 12-mo old rats, but caused a 40-50 % inhibition in 24-mo old animals, when compared with the corresponding control (16). The results suggest that whereas in young rats EGF stimulates GI mucosal growth, in aged animals it exerts an antiproliferative effect.

Like gastrin and EGF, bombesin has been shown to stimulate gastric mucosal cell proliferation in young animals (38-40). To evaluate its role in GI mucosal cell proliferation during aging, we examined the changes in gastric mucosal DNA synthesis and ornithine decarboxylase activity in young (4 mo) and aged (24 mo) old Fischer-344 rats following infusion of bombesin (300 ng/kg/h) for 2 weeks. We observed that whereas in 4 mo old rats bombesin infusion resulted in a significant 2-fold increase in gastric mucosal DNA synthesis and ornithine decarboxylase activity, in aged rats the peptide had no effect (41, 42). Taken together, these observations suggest that some of the regulatory processes (nutritional and hormonal) are affected by aging.

Intracellular factors : Among many intracellular factors, tyrosine kinases (Tyr-k), which phosphorylate tyrosine residues in protein, play an important role in the regulation of cell proliferation and differentiation (43-45). Tyr-k activity is associated with receptors of many growth factors including EGF, insulin, platelet derived growth factor (PDGF), bombesin as well as with products of a number of protooncogenes (46-49). Most of the supporting evidence to implicate Tyr-k in regulating growth and differentiation has been gathered from *in vitro* studies utilizing a variety of cell lines and little is known about their involvement in intact animals. We have recently demonstrated that highly proliferative tissues such as the gastric mucosa possess higher levels of Tyr-k than relatively stable organs like the liver and pancreas (15).

If aging is associated with increased GI mucosal proliferative activity, we postulated that it might also be associated with increased Tyr-k activity in the GI mucosa.

In support of this line of reasoning, we observed that gastric mucosal Tyr-k activity in 22 mo old Fischer-344 rats is 35-70 % higher than in their 2- and 14 mo old counterparts (Fig. 1). These changes were also associated with parallel alterations in ornithine decarboxylase activity (15). Since Tyr-k are known to undergo autophosphorylation and are themselves substrates (43), we also measured tyrosine-specific phosphorylation of proteins and reported increased labelling of membrane protein with apparent molecular mass of 53-55 kDa in the gastric mucosa compared with the liver and pancreas (15). A similar protein has been detected in the rat spleen (50), lymphoma cell line LSTRA (51) and Leydig tumor cells (52). It therefore appears this 53-55 kDa phosphotyrosine membrane protein may play a role in the regulation of cell proliferation. Further support for this suggestion came from the following observations : (a) a comparatively greater stimulation of gastric mucosal proliferative acti-

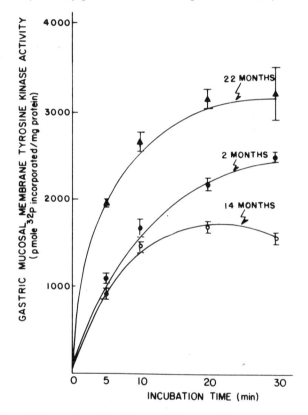

FIG. 1: Time course changes in tyrosine kinase activity in gastric mucosal membranes from 2-, 14- and 22-mo old rats (ref. 15, with permission).

vity in young than in older rats resulting from hypertonic saline-induced injury was associated with parallel alterations in mucosal Tyr-k activity and tyrosine phosphorylation of 55 kDa membrane protein (53) ; (b) the same phenomenon was also observed following administration of EGF, which stimulated gastric mucosal proliferative activity and tyrosine phosphorylation of the 55 kDa membrane protein in young rats, but inhibited these parameters in aged rats (Fig. 2) ; and (c) bombesin-induced stimulation of gastric mucosal proliferative activity in young but not in aged rats was also accompanied by concomitant changes in tyrosine phosphorylation of the 55 kDa membrane protein (42). A similar response was also observed following administration of Captan, a fungicide that produces GI tumors and also stimulates mucosal cell proliferation (54).

Significance of increased Tyr-k activity with resultant rise in tyrosine phosphorylation of membrane proteins including the 55 kDa is not fully understood. However, cellular transformation and neoplasia have been found to be associated with increased phosphotyrosine content. Hunter and Sefton (55) have demonstrated that transformation of chick embryo fibroblasts with Rous sarcoma virus (RSV) produces a 10-fold rise in phosphotyrosine content. Similar observations have been made following transformation of cells with number of other viruses (56, 57). Viral transformation of normal cells also results in increased expression of protooncogenes, and num-

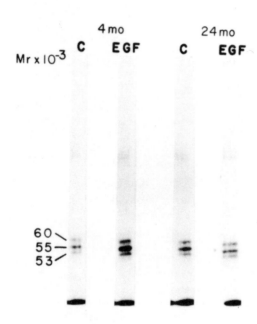

FIG. 2 : Effect of EGF on tyrosine-specific phosphorylation of oxyntic gland mucosal membrane from 4- and 24-mo old rats (ref. 16, with permission).

ber of protooncogene products show Tyr-k activity (48). We have also observed an age-associated rise in Tyr-k activity of pp 60[c-src] and erbB-2 in the gastric mucosa of Fischer-344 rats (unpublished observation). This, together with the finding of an increased mucosal proliferative activity suggests that they may be contributing factors in the development of neoplasia at later stages of life.

REFERENCES

1. LIPKIN (M.) : Proliferation and differentiation of normal and diseased gastrointestinal cells. *In* : Johnson LR, Ed. Physiology of the Gastrointestinal Tract, New York, *Raven Press*, 1987, pp. 255-284.
2. CREAMER (B.), SHORTER (R.G.), BAMFORTH (J.) : The turnover and shedding of epithelial cells. I. The turnover in the gastrointestinal tract. *Gut*, 2, 110-118, 1961.
3. LEBLOND (C.P.), MESSIER (B.) : Renewal of chief cells and goblet cells in the small intestine as shown by radioautography after injection into mice. *Anat. Rec.*, 132, 247-158, 1958.
4. LEBLOND (C.P.), STEVENS (C.E.) : The constant renewal of the intestinal epithelium in the albino rat. *Anat. Rec.*, 100, 357-378, 1948.
5. HERBST (J.J.), BERENSON (M.M.), WISER (W.C.) et al. : Cell proliferation in Barett's esophageal epithelium. *Clin. Res.* 24, 168A, 1976.
6. DESCHNER (E.E.), WINAWER (S.J.), LIPKIN (M.) : Patterns of nucleic acid and protein synthesis in normal human gastric mucosa and atrophic gastritis. *J. Natl Cancer Inst.*, 48, 1567-1574, 1972.
7. WINAWER (S.J.), LIPKIN (M.) : Cell proliferation kinetics in the gastrointestinal tract of man. IV. Cell renewal in the intestinalized gastric mucosa. *Natl Cancer Inst.*, 42, 9-17, 1969.
8. CASTRUP (W.J.), FUCH (K.), PEIPER (H.J.) : Cell renewal of gastric mucosa in Zollinger-Ellison Syndrome. *Acta Hepatogastroenterol.* (Stuttg.), 22, 40-43, 1975.
9. MAJUMDAR (A.P.N.), JOHNSON (L.R.) : Gastric mucosal cell proliferation during development and effects of pentagastrin. *Am. J. Physiol.*, 242, G 135-G 139, 1982.
10. MAJUMDAR (A.P.N.), JASTI (S.), HATFIELD (J.S.) et al. : Morphological and biochemical changes in gastric mucosa of aging rats. *Dig. Dis. Sci.*, 35, 1364-1370, 1990.
11. MAITRA (R.S.), EDGERTON (E.A.), MAJUMDAR (A.P.N.) : Gastric secretion during aging in pyloric-ligated rats and effects of pentagastrin. *Exp. Gerontol.*, 23, 46-472, 1988.
12. HOLLANDER (D.), TRANAWSKI (A.), STACHURA (J.) et al. : Morphologic changes in gastric mucosa of aging rats. *Dig. Dis. Sci.*, 34, 1692-1700, 1989.
13. BARAN (J.H.) : Studies of basal and peak acid output with an augmented histamine meal. *Gut*, 4, 136-144, 1963.
14. BORGSTROM (S.), EMAS (S.), LILIJA (B.) et al. : Acid response to pentagastrin in relation to age and body stature in male and female ulcer patients. *Scand. J. Gastroenterol.*, 8, 209-216, 1976.
15. MAJUMDAR (A.P.N.), EDGERTON (E.A.), ARLOW (F.L.) : Gastric mucosal tyrosine kinase activity during aging and its relationship to cell proliferation in rats. *Biochim. Biophys. Acta*, 976, 97-105, 1988.
16. MAJUMDAR (A.P.N.), ARLOW (F.L.) : Aging : altered responsiveness of gastric mucosa to epidermal growth factor. *Am. J. Physiol.*, 257, G 554-G 560, 1989.
17. MAJUMDAR (A.P.N.), EDGERTON (E.A.), DAYAL (Y.), MURTHY (S.N.S.) : Gastrin : levels and trophic action during advancing age. *Am. J. Physiol.*, 254, G 538-G 542, 1988.
18. MAJUMDAR (A.P.N.) DUBICK (M.A.) : The aging gastrointestinal tract : cell proliferation and nutritional adaptation. *Prog. Food. Nutr. Sci.*, 13, 139-160, 1989.
19. EDGERTON (E.A.), FLIGIEL (S.E.G.), MOSHIER (J.A.) et al. : Effect of gastric mucosal injury on ornithine decarboxylase in young and aged rats. *Exp. Gerontol.*, 26, 45-55, 1991.
20. HOLT (P.R.), PASCAL (R.R.), KOTLER (D.P.) : Effect of aging upon small intestinal structure in the Fischer rat. *J. Gerontol.*, 39, 642-647, 1984.
21. HOLT (P.R.), TIERNEY (A.R.), KOTLER (D.P.) : Delayed enzyme expression : a defect of aging rat gut. *Gastroenterology*, 89, 1026-1034, 1985.
22. HOLT (P.R.), YEH (K.Y.) : Small intestinal crypt cell proliferation rates are increased in senescent rats. *J. Gerontol.*, 44, B9-14, 1989.
23. HOLT (P.R.), YEH (K.Y.) : Colonic proliferation is increased in senescent rats. *Gastroenterology*, 95, 1556-1563, 1988.
24. HOLT (P.R.), YEH (K.Y.), KOTLER (D.P.) : Altered controls of proliferation in proximal small intestine of the senescent rat. *Proc. Natl Acad. Sci.*, (USA), 85, 2771-2775, 1988.
25. MAJUMDAR (A.P.N.) : Regulation of gastric mucosal DNA synthesis during fasting and refeeding in rats. *Digestion*, 27, 36-43, 1983.
26. JOHNSON (L.R.) : Regulation of gastrointestinal growth. *In* : Johnson (L.R.), Ed. Physiology of the Gastrointestinal Tract. New York, 1987, pp. 301-333.
27. MAJUMDAR (A.P.N.) : Growth and maturation of the gastric mucosa. *In* : Growth of the Gastrointestinal Tract ; Gastrointestinal Hormones and Growth Factors. New York, *CRC Press*, 1990, pp. 119-130.
28. TAKEUCHI (K.), PEITSCH (W.), JOHNSON (L.R.) : Mucosal gastrin receptor. V. Development in newborn rats. *Am. J. Physiol.*, 242, G 163-G 169, 1981.
29. SINGH (P.), RAE-VENTER (B.), TOWNSEND (C.M.) Jr. et al. : Gastrin receptor in normal and malignant gastrointestinal mucosa : age-associated changes. *Am. J. Physiol.*, 249, G 761-G 769, 1985.
30. FELDMAN (E.J.), AURES (D.), GROSSMAN (M.) : Epidermal growth factor stimulates ornithine decarboxylase activity in the digestive tract of mouse. *Proc. Soc. Exp. Biol. Med.*, 159, 400-402, 1978.
31. MALO (C.), MENARD (D.) : Influence of epidermal growth factor on the development of suckling mouse intestinal mucosa. *Gastroenterology*, 83, 28-35, 1982.

32. CONTEAS (C.N.), DeMORROW (J.M.), MAJUMDAR (A.P.N.) : Effect of epidermal growth factor on growth and maturation of fetal and neonatal rat small intestine in organ culture. *Experientia*, 42, 950-952, 1986.

33. O'LOUGHLIN (E.V.), CHUNG (M.), HOLLENBERG (M.) et al. : Effect of epidermal growth factor on ontogeny of the gastrointestinal tract. *Am. J. Physiol.*, 249, G 674-G 678, 1985.

34. DEMBINSKI (A.B.), JOHNSON (L.R.) : Effect of epidermal growth factor on the development of rat gastric mucosa. *Endocrinology*, 116, 90-94, 1985.

35. MAJUMDAR (A.P.N.) : Postnatal undernutrition : Effect of epidermal growth factor on growth and function of the gastrointestinal tract in rats. *J. Pediatr. Gastroenterol. Nutr.*, 3, 618-625, 1984.

36. ARLOW (F.L.), WALCZAK (S.M.), MOSHIER (J.A.), MAJUMDAR (A.P.N.) : Gastrin and epidermal growth factor induction of ornithine decarboxylase in rat colonic explants. *Life Sci.*, 46, 777-784, 1990.

37. ARLOW (F.L.), EDGERTON (E.A.), MAJUMDAR (A.P.N.) : The influence of epidermal growth factor on the aging colon. *Am. J. Gastroenterol.*, 82, A 962, 1987.

38. LEHY (T.), PUCCIO (F.) : Influence of bombesin on gastrointestinal and pancreatic cell growth in adult and suckling animals. *Ann. N.Y. Acad. Sci.*, 547, 255-267, 1988.

39. LEHY (T.), ACCARY (D.), LABEILLE (D.) et al. : Chronic administration of bombesin stimulates antral gastrin cell proliferation in the rat. *Gastroenterology*, 84, 914-919, 1983.

40. PUCCIO (F.), LEHY (T.) : Bombesin ingestion stimulates epithelial digestive cell proliferation in suckling rats. *Am. J. Physiol.*, 256, G 328-G 334, 1989.

41. MAJUMDAR (A.P.N.), TUREAUD (J.) : Differential activation of gastric mucosal pp. 60 [c-src], pp. 185 [-neu] and EGF-receptor (EGF-R) associated tyrosine kinases by bombesin in young and aged rats : relationship to cell proliferation. *Gastroenterology*, 100, A 553, 1991.

42. TUREAUD (J.), MAJUMDAR (A.P.N.) : Aging, diminished responsiveness of gastric mucosal ornithine decarboxylase (ODC) to bombesin *in vitro*. *Gastroenterology* 100, A 551, 1991.

43. HUNTER (T.), COOPER (J.A.) : Protein tyrosine kinases. *Ann. Rev. Biochem.*, 54, 897-930, 1985.

44. YARDEN (Y.) : Growth factor receptor tyrosine kinases. *Ann. Rev. Biochem.*, 57, 443-487, 1988.

45. ADAMSON (E.D.) : Oncogenes in development. *Development*, 99, 449-471, 1987.

46. KASUGA (M.), YAMAGUCHI-FUJITA (Y.), BLITHE (D.L.) et al. : Tyrosine-specific protein kinase activity is associated with the purified insulin receptor. *Proc. Natl Acad. Sci.* (USA), 80, 2137-2141, 1983.

47. EK (B.), HELDIN (C.H.) : Characterization of a tyrosine-specific kinase activity in human fibroblast membrane stimulated by platelet-derived growth factor. *J. Biol. Chem.*, 257, 1048-1049, 1982.

48. LAND (H.), PARADA (L.F.), WEINBERG (R.A.) : Cellular oncogenes and multistep carcinogenesis. *Science*, 22, 771-778, 1983.

49. BLACKSHEAR (P.R.) : Converging and diverging pathways in polypeptide hormone action. *Clin. Res.*, 37, 554-563, 1989.

50. SWARUP (G.), DASGUPTA (J.D.), GARBERS (D.L.) : Tyrosine protein kinase activity of rat spleen and other tissues. *J. Biol. Chem.*, 258, 10341-10347, 1983.

51. CASNELLIE (J.E.), HARRISON (M.L.), PIKE (L.J.) et al. : Phosphorylation of synthetic peptides by a tyrosine protein kinase from the particulate fraction of a lymphoma cell line. *Proc. Natl Acad. Sci.* (USA), 79, 282-286, 1982.

52. DANGOTT (L.J.), PUETT (D.), MELNER (M.H.) : Characterization of protein tyrosine activity in murine Leydig tumor cells. *Biochim. Biophys. Acta*, 886, 187-194, 1986.

53. MAJUMDAR (A.P.N.), MOSHIER (J.A.), ARLOW (E.L.) et al. : Biochemical changes in the gastric mucosa after injury in young and aged rats. *Biochim. Biophys. Acta*, 992, 35-40, 1989.

54. WAHBY (M.), SHELEF (L.A.), LUK (G.D.), MAJUMDAR (A.P.N.) : Induction of gastric mucosal cell proliferation by the fungicide captan : role of tyrosine kinases. *Toxicol. Lett.*, 54, 189-198, 1990.

55. HUNTER (T.), SEFTON (B.M.) : The transforming gene product of Rous sarcoma virus phosphorylates tyrosine. *Proc. Natl Acad. Sci.* (USA), 77, 1311-1315, 180.

56. COOPER (J.A.), HUNTER (T.) : Changes in protein phosphorylation in Rous sarcoma virus transformed chicken embryo cells. *Mol. Cell. Biol.*, 1, 165-178, 1981.

57. KAWAI (S.), YOSHIDA (M.), SEGAWA (K.) et al. : Characterization of Y73, an atrian sarcoma virus : a unique transforming gene and its product, a phosphopolyprotein with protein tyrosine kinase activity. *Proc. Natl Acad. Sci.*, (USA), 77, 6199-6203, 1980.

GASTRO-INTESTINAL PEPTIDES
AND AGING [1]

John E. MORLEY (*)

Summary. – *Numerous changes in gastrointestinal peptides occur with age. Amylin may play a role in the pathogenesis of diabetes mellitus. A lack of the opioid feeding drive and an excessive satiety effect of cholecystokinin play a role in the pathogenesis of the anorexia of aging. Peripherally released CCK acts through ascending vagal fibers to enhance memory.* (Facts and Research in Gerontology 1992).

Key-words : *CCK, aging, anorexia gastrointestinal peptides, nutrition.*

The aging process is associated with changes in gut mobility, secretion, and absorption. Many elderly persons suffer from decreased absorption of complex carbohydrates, calcium, and possibly other nutrients. Vitamin B12 deficiency occurs in approximately 5 % of persons older than 80 years, and gastric achlorhydria is present in 1 in 4 older persons. Many also have a decreased secretion of bicarbonate, lipase, and amylase in response to a combined secretin and cerulein infusion (1). With advancing age, there is a slight delay in stomach emptying and a decrease in small intestine contractions, and, in those over 80 years of age, multiple changes in esophageal motility increase the possibility of developing aspiration pneumonia. These normal physiological changes in gut function interact with common disease processes, such as diabetes mellitus and Parkinsonism, and with decreased physical activity and immobility syndromes, to produce a variety of pathological syndromes that effect the gastrointestinal tract.

Research in recent years has shown that, with advancing age, there are numerous alterations in secretion and receptor activity of gastrointestinal peptides. In general, aging results in an increase in gastrointestinal peptide levels that appears to be secondary to a decrease in receptor function. There is a decrease in the number of cholecystokinin (CCK) receptors on pancreatic acinar with advancing age (2). Thus, CCK levels are increased in response to a decrease in the ability of CCK to stimulate

(*) Geriatric Research Education and Clinical Center, St. Louis VA Medical Center. Dammert Professor of Gerontology, Department of Medicine, St. Louis University, St. Louis, Missouri (U.S.A.).

(1) Reproduced from Peptide Therapy Index and Review, vol. III n° 1, 1991. The US Government holds the copyright to this work.

exocrine pancreatic secretion and gallibladder contraction (3). Motilin levels are also increased presumably secondary to the delayed gastric emptying seen with advancing age (4). Somatostatin levels are increased in persons aged 76 to 90 years, but there is a loss of circadian rhythm in older persons and less of a response to a test meal (5).

Hyperglycemia in aging is predominantly due to a postreceptor defect to insulin that results in decreased glucose clearance, but there is also a decreased second phase insulin release in response to carbohydrate, which aggravates the situation (6). Amylin is a newly isolated pancreatic islet hormone that inhibits the insulin effect on muscle and on hepatic glycogenolysis. Amylin also decreases second phase insulin secretion (7). As such, it may play an important role in the pathogenesis of the hyperglycemia of aging amylin is also a potent anorectic peptide. The lipolytic and ketogenic (but not the hyperglycemic) response to glucagon are significantly reduced in older persons (8). These alterations in the response to glucagon may play an important role in the development of the classical hyperosmolar-hyperglycemic coma seen in the elderly.

ANOREXIA OF AGING

Protein energy malnutrition occurs commonly in older persons. There are a variety of physiologic and pathologic reasons for this decreased food intake (9). Alteration in the appreciation of the hedonic qualities of food due to decreased taste and smell, depression, and anorexia secondary to medication ingestion (i.e., digoxin) play a significant role. An important neurotransmitter involved in the feeding drive to ingest fatty foods is the endogenous opioid, dynorphin (10). This opioid feeding drive is markedly attenuated in older animals (11). Also many older individuals complain of early satiety. Recently, Silver et al. (12) have demonstrated that the CCK, which acts as a satiety hormone by terminating food ingestion, is more potent at inhibiting food intake in older animals. Taken together, these studies suggest that altered peptide activity plays an important role in the pathogenesis of the anorexia of aging.

MEMORY, FOOD INTAKE AND CCK

Impaired cognition has been associated with malnutrition in older persons (13). When an older person ingests a meal immediately after learning a task, they have better recall of the learned material than if they delayed eating for some time. When mice are taught to learn a simple T-maze aversive task, they have better recall of the task 7 days later if they are fed immediately after learning, rather than 2 hours after learning (14). When CCK is administered intraperitoneally it also enhances the memory of mice for aversive tasks by stimulating ascending fibers in the vagus, which carry messages to the midbrain and from there to the amygdala. The meal-induced enhancement of memory can be reversed by administration of a CCK-antagonist, suggesting that the release of CCK in response to a meal plays a physiological role in memory modulation (15).

MEAL ASSOCIATED HYPOTENSION

There is a decrease in postprandial blood pressure in both healthy and frail older persons (16). This can result in dizziness, syncope, and falls. This blood pressure decrease is seen after glucose loads but not after fat or protein loads and the effect is less marked with cold meals ; the effect of cold does not appear to be mediated through substance P release (18). The cause is uncertain but appears to be associated with the increase in norepinephrine levels that occurs with advancing age. It has been suggested that vasoactive gastrointestinal hormones may play a role in meal associated hypotension by producing vasodilatation of the splanchnic blood vessels. Neither vasoactive intestinal peptide (17), nor insulin (19) was found to play an important role in glucose-induced hypotension.

Other gastrointestinal peptides such as calcitonin gene-related peptide, neurotensin, amylin, and bradykinin remain putative candidates for producing this hypotensive effect. In addition, the hypotensive effect of a meal is often prolonged for 2 to 3 hours. It is possible that excessive release of atrionatriuretic peptide plays a role in this meal-associated hypotension, because it is known that such a hormone is released following ingestion of a meal.

Significantly, administration of caffeine (20) and the somatostatin analog, octreotide (21) have been shown to prevent meal-associated hypotension.

REFERENCES

1. VELLAS B. et al. : *Int. J. Pancreatol*, 1988, *6*, 497.
2. POSTON G.J. et al. : *Mech. Age Develop.*, 1988, *46*, 59.
3. KHALIL T. et al. : *Surgery*, 1985, *98*, 423.
4. BONORA G. et al. : *J. Gerontol.*, 1986, *41*, 723.
5. ROLANDI E. et al. : *J. Gerontol.*, 1987, *33*, 296.
6. MORLEY J.E., KAISER F.E. : *Clin. Geriatr. Med.*, 1990, *6*, 693.
7. LEIGHTON B., COOPER G.J.S. : *Nature*, 1988, *335*, 632.
8. PAOLISSO G. et al. : *Diabetologia*, 1990, *33*, 272.
9. MORLEY J.E., SILVER A.G. : *Neurobiol. Aging*, 1988, *9*, 9.
10. MORLEY J.E. : *Endocrinol. Rev.*, 1987, *8*, 256.
11. GOSNELL B.A. et al. : *Life Sci.*, 1983, *32*, 2793.
12. SILVER A.J. et al. : *Peptides*, 1988, *9*, 221.
13. GOODWIN J.S. et al. : *J.A.M.A.*, 1983, *249*, 2917.
14. FLOOD J.F. et al. : *Science*, 1987, *236*, 832.
15. FLOOD J.F., MORLEY J.E. : *Peptides*, 1989, *10*, 809.
16. LIPSITZ L.A. et al. : *N. Engl. J. Med.*, 1983, *309*, 81.
17. JANSSEN R.W.M.M. et al. : *Eur. J. Clin. Invest.*, 1990, *20*, 192.
18. KUIPERS H.M.M. et al. : *J. Am. Geriatr. Soc.*, 1991, *39*, 181.
19. JANSSEN R.W.M.M. et al. : *Am. J. Cardiol.*, 1987, *60*, 1087.
20. HESELTINE D. et al. : *J. Am. Geriatr. Soc.*, 1991, *39*, 160.
21. JANSSEN R.W.M.M. et al. : *J. Clin. Endocrinol. Metab.*, 1989, *68*, 752.

NEWS ON AGING GUT

We present here the abstracts of articles published in the international editions of Facts and Research in Gerontology 1992. Reprint are available to the authors (see contributors directory) or to Serdi : 29, rue de Saint-Pétersbourg, 75008 Paris.

1 - RECENT ADVANCES ON THE FATE OF THE EXOCRINE PANCREAS DURING AGING :
J. Moreau

Summary. – Exocrine pancreatic function plays a major role in digestion process. Thus, its place in the nutritional status of elderly people has to be highly considered. However most of previous data have been dedicated to endocrine rather than exocrine pancreatic functions. Involution of pancreatic enzymatic and bicarbonates secretions have been demonstrated among people over 70 years of age and particularly when malnutrition was present. Tubeless tests as pancreolauryl test could be used instead of classical intubation tests that are less suitable for these patients. Disturbances of post-prandial secretion of hormonal peptides, mainly cholecystokinin, have been recently described in elderly. Wether this was due to undernutrition or to aging per se is still debated. Finally, the lack of adaptation to malnutrition and/or to renutrition represents the main characteristic of the involution of exocrine pancreatic function during aging. From a clinical stand point, acute pancreatitis in aged people is mainly from biliary origin. Endoscopic sphincterotomy is now recognized as best therapeutic approach for these patients. The incidence of chronic pancreatitis is largely under estimated in elderly. This is mainly due to the fact that these cases of chronic pancreatitis are usually painless. However this diagnosis has to be considered in aged people with diabetes and diarrhea (or steatorrhea). Indeed, it seems difficult to clearly separate the histopathologic pattern of the natural involution of pancreas during aging from lesions observed in patients with moderate chronic pancreatitis. At last, the hypothesis of a pancreatic carcinoma must not be neglected in every aged people with unexplained impaired clinical conditions. Recent findings regarding the fate of exocrine pancreas allow to individualize significant functional or pathological modifications during aging. The therapeutic implications of these findings are currently under investigation. (Facts and Research in Gerontology 1992)

Key-words : exocrin pancreas, aging, nutrition, cholecystokinin.

2 - INTESTINE ADAPTATIVE RESPONSE ALTERATIONS AFTER NUTRITIONAL STRESS DURING AGING : F. Raul, M. Reville

Summary. – Adaptive responses of brush border hydrolases and crypt cell proliferation rate were measured in the jejunum of young adult (4 month old, n = 30) and senescent (28 month old, n = 30) male Wistar rats. Responses were measured after rats were deprived of food and then refed for 18 h with a normoprotein diet (17 % protein) or an isoenergetic high protein diet (70 % protein). In order to evaluate the proliferation rate of jejunal and ileal epithelial cells, tritiated thymidine was administered i.p. to young adult and senescent rats at the end of the starvation period. Cells were sequentially isolated along the villus-crypt axis 18 h after refeeding the normoprotein diet. The young rats deprived of food, then refed for 18 h with the high protein diet exhibited better body weight recovery than the older animals. In the jejunum, sucrase and lactase activities were similar in both age groups when the animals were refed with the normoprotein diet. Refeeding the high protein diet caused a better recovery of sucrase activity and a stimulation of lactase activity in young animals relative to senescent rats. In the aged rats, sucrase and lactase activities in the jejunum remained significantly lower after refeeding both diets. Compared with nourished controls, aged rats showed enzyme activity to be completely restored in the ileum. The high protein diet increased aminopeptidase activity in the jejunum and ileum of young rats, in contrast to the senescent rats in which the increase of enzyme activity was restricted to the ileum. The cell migration rate from crypt base to villus tip was reduced in the jejunum of aged rats after refeeding, but no age-related changes were observed in the ileum. Our results indicate that the jejunum of senescent rats exhibits reduced adaptive capability in response to nutritional stress that may be partly compensated by enhanced ileal functions. (Facts and Research in Gerontology 1992)

Key-words : hydrolase, small intestine, aging, diet, rats.

SELECTION OF LITERATURE

1 - EXOCRINE PANCREAS AND AGING : J. Moreau

1. VELLAS (B.), BALAS (D.), MOREAU (J.), et al. : Exocrine pancreatic secretion in the elderly. *Int. J. Pancreatol.*, 1988, 3, 497-502.
2. VELLAS (B.J.), BALAS (D.), LAFONT (C.) et al. : Adaptative response of pancreatic and intestinal function to nutritional intake in the aged. *J. Am. Geriatr. Soc.*, 1990, 38, 254-258.
3. MORLEY (J.E.) : Anorexia in the elderly. *Neurobiol. Aging*, 1988, 9, 9-16.
4. STUBBS (R.S.), STABILE (B.E.) : Role of cholecystokinin in pancreatic exocrine response to intraluminal amino acid and fat. *Am. J. physiol.*, 1985, 248, G 347-G 352.
5. ADELMAN (R.C.) : Loss of adaptative mechanisms during aging. *Fed. Proc.*, 1979, 38, 1968-1971.

2 - SMALL INTESTINE AND AGING : F. Raul, M. Reville

1. VELLAS (B.), BALAS (D.) : Modification de la digestion et de l'absorption en fonction du vieillissement. *In :* L'Année Gérontologique, 1988, Paris, *Maloine*, 171-181.
2 THOMSON (A.B.R.) and KELLAN (M.) : The aging gut. *Can. J. Physiol. Pharmacol.*, 1986, 64, 30-38.
3. MESSER (M.), DAHLQVIST (A.) : A one step ultramicromethod for the assay of intestinal disaccharidases. *Analyt. Biochem.*, 1966, 14, 376-392.
4. KOLDOVSKY (O.), ASP (N.G.), DAHLQVIST (A.) : A method for the separate assay of neutral and acid-ß-galactosidase in homogenates of rat small intestinal mucosa. *Analyt. Biochem.*, 1969, 27, 409-418.
5. MAROUX (S.), LOUVARD (D.), BARATTI (J.) : The aminopeptidase from hog intestinal brush border. *Biochim. Biophys. Acta*, 1973, 321, 282-295.
6. RAUL (F.), SIMON (P.), KEDINGER (M.) and HAFFEN (K.) : Intestinal enzyme activities in isolated villus and crypt cells during postnatal development of the rat. *Cell. Tiss. Res.*, 1977, 176, 167-178.
7. WILLIAMSON (R.C.N.) and CHIR (M.) : Intestinal adaptation. Mechanisms of control. *N. Engl. J. Med.*, 1978, 298, 1444-1450.
8. RAUL (F.), GOSSE (F.), DOFFOEL (M.), DARMENTON (P.), WESSELY (J.-Y.) : Age-related increase of brush border enzyme activities along the small intestine. *Gut*, 1988, 29, 1557-1563.
9. GODA (T.), RAUL (F.), GOSSE (F.) and KOLDOVSKY (O.) : Short-term effect of a high-protein, low-carbohydrate diet on the degradation of sucrase-isomaltase in adult rat jejunoileum. *Am. J. Physiol.*, 1988, 254, G907-G912.

10. KIRCHNER (F.R.), BYBEE (J.W.) and OSBORNE (J.W.) : The influence of rat age on crypt cell kinetics after partial resection of the small intestine. *Proc. Soc. Exp. Biol. Med.,* 1978, 157, 572-575.
11. GUIDET (M.), VELLAS (B.), BALAS (D.) : Vieillissement cellulaire : bases moléculaires. *In :* L'Année Gérontologique, 1987, Paris, *Maloine,* 5-18.
12. HOLT (P.R.), TIERNEY (A.R.), KOTLER (D.P.) : Delayed enzyme expression : a defect of aging gut. *Gastroenterology,* 1978, 75, 847-855.
13. WILLIAMSON (R.C.N.), CHIR (M.) : Intestinal adaptation. Structural functional and cytokinetic changes. *N. Engl. J. Med.,* 1978, 298, 1393-1402.
14. FRY (R.J.M.), LESHER (S.) and KOHN (H.) : Influence of age on the transit of cells of the mouse intestinal epithelium, III. *J. Lab. Invest.,* 1962, 11, 289-293.
15. LESHER (S.), SACHER (G.A.) : Effects of age on cell proliferation in mouse duodenal crypts. *Exp. Gerontol.,* 1968, 3, 211-217.
16. HOLT (P.R.), KOTLER (D.P.), PASCAL (R.R.) : A simple method for determining epithelial cell turnover in small intestine. Studies in young and aging rat gut. *Gastroenterology,* 1983, 84, 69-74.
17. HOLT (P.R.), YEH (K.Y.) and KOTLER (D.P.) : Altered controls of proliferation in proximal small intestine of the senescent rat. *Proc. Nat. Acad. Sci.,* (U.S.A.), 1988, 85, 2771-2775.
18. GOODLAD (R.A.), WRIGHT (N.A.) : Changes in intestinal cell proliferation, absorptive capacity and structure in young, adult and old rats. *J. Anat.,* 1990, 173, 109-118.

III

FACTS AND RESEARCH
IN NUTRITION AND AGING

NOTES ON DIETARY INTAKE DATA IN THE ELDERLY

Wija A. van STAVEREN, Jan BUREMA, Lisette (C) P.G.M. DE GROOT, Laura E. VORRIPS (*)

Summary. – Dietary intake data are fundamental to research and clinical practice in the elderly. There are, however, doubts on the accuracy of methods collecting these data. This paper reviews the methodology of food consumption studies in the elderly : the design, the collection of data, the conversion of foods into nutrients and the interpretation of data with the help of recommended dietary intakes. Furthermore the main outcomes of reports on energy and nutrient intake in the elderly have been discussed. It is concluded that hardly any published survey of elderly people living in their own home have revealed a substantial prevalence of malnutrition. However, in many studies the response rate was rather poor. Inadequate intakes of nutrients are most likely to occur for calcium, zinc, potassium, magnesium, vitamin B6 and folates. Surveys conducted in longterm care institutions demonstrated that malnutrition is a very serious problem among the elderly. (Facts and Research in Gerontology 1992)

Key-words : elderly, dietary methods, food composition tables, recommended dierary intakes, malnutrition.

INTRODUCTION

Dietary intake data are fundamental to research and clinical practice in the elderly. First, information obtained with dietary surveys in terms of energy and nutrients can be related to data on the nutritional status and health. Secondly, the data might be useful for nutritional education programmes and food planning. Recently Horwath (1) has reviewed the international literature concerning the dietary intake of representative groups of elderly people to get more insight in what these people do eat. Up to 1989 he found 16 studies based on a random sample of a population, only ten of which achieved a response rate above 60 %. Other problems he encounte-

(*) Department of Human Nutrition, Wageningen Agricultural University, The Netherlands.

Correspondence to : W.A. van Staveren, Department of Human Nutrition, Wageningen Agricultural University, P.O. Box 8129, 6700 EV Wageningen, The Netherlands.

red in comparing data of various publications were differences in design, methods and interpretation of data.

Design of surveys

In comparing dietary intake data of different study groups, possible effects of cohort, period and time should be considered. In a literature review mainly based on cross-sectional studies such effects cannot be taken into account since only adequately developed longitudinal designs may allow for these effects. Lack of adequate studies from which differences in dietary patterns between centres in Europe can be deduced was one of the main incentives for the Euronut-Seneca concerted action. This study conducted in 19 centres in 12 countries in Europe, has a design which allows for calculation of the above mentioned effects (2). Data of this study will become available in the 3rd supplement of the European Journal of Clinical nutrition 1991 (Table 1).

TABLE 1

PUBLICATIONS ON THE VALIDITY AND REPRODUCIBILITY
OF THE 24-HOUR RECALL.

Author	Reference method	Age years	N	Sex
Validity				
Steen (3)	24 hour Urine-N-excretion	70	182	m
Caliendo (4)	observations		89	f + m
Evans (5)	observations	65-94	60	f + m
Gersovitz (6)	observations	60 +	65	f + m
Madden (7)	observations	60 +	76	f + m
Campbell (8)	menu list	65 +	100	m
			100	f
Reproducibility				
Bazarre (9)	repeated	60 +	17	m
	interviews		30	f

Validity of dietary assessment methods

Few studies have been published on the validity of dietary assessment methods. Table 1 gives examples of validity and reproducibility studies of the 24-hour recall. From these studies it is clear that the 24-hour recall has been shown to grossly underestimate dietary intake and has thus been concluded to be unreliable for the measurement of individual intake and, according to some investigators, also group intake. Decline in short term memory with age may make recall methods particularly unreliable with elderly people. Better results have been shown with the dietary history (Table 2), which has been validated against 24-hour urine nitrogen excretion (3).

In the Euronut-Seneca study an adapted dietary history including a 3-day estimated record and a food frequency list showed good comparison with results of a 3-day weighed record (13). British surveys have placed heavy reliance on the use of a 7-day weighed record. However, a recent nationwide study in British adults showed low mean energy intakes of 1600-1700 kcal or 6.7 - 7.1 MJ for all female age groups including the elderly. For women with body weight equal to the average of 66 kg, basic metabolic rate (BMR) and dietary induced thermogenesis (DIT) were calculated by Durnin (14) to cost about 1450 kcal or 6.1 MJ, thus leaving only 160 kcal or 0.6 MJ for other activities during the day. According to Durnin this would be a highly undesirable situation. Therefore in this study the 7-day weighed record was suspected to underestimate the habitual dietary intake.

TABLE 2

PUBLICATIONS ON THE VALIDITY AND REPRODUCIBILITY
OF THE DIETARY HISTORY METHOD.

Author	Reference method	Age years	N	Sex
Validity				
Steen (3)	24 hour Urine-	70	74	m
	N-excretion		63	f
Mahalko (10)	Various blood-tests	55-95	18	m
Reproducibility				
Bazarre (9)	test − retest	60 +	17	m
	interviews		30	f
O'Hanlo (11)	test − retest	60 - 96	85	f + m
Retrospective				
dietary history				
Bakkum (12)	current versus	69-76	18	m
	retrospective	78-93	22	f

In a recent study Brown et al. explored the use of a novel videotape method for dietary assessment (15). In this approach cafetaria trays with the foods selected by study participants are photographed at a videocamera station equipped with visual reference standards to assist researchers in quantitating food items. Videotaping required less than 10 seconds and quantitations about 2 minutes. Nutrient intakes were estimated using a computer program. According to the initial validating studies the videotape method seems very promising : it allows for rapid data collection, it is noninvasive and relatively convenient for subjects and investigators. Furthermore it does not depend on memory, and dietary analysis appears to be sufficiently accurate for many research questions. Whether this method can also be used in non-institutionalised elderly people has not yet been demonstrated.

Conversion of foods into energy and nutrient intake

For conversion of foods into energy and nutrients the use of the local nutrient data base or food composition table is recommended, because differences in the contents of (manufactured or other) foods may be anticipated between countries or regions. It should be recognised, however, that many differences between these tables are due to different systems of analysis and sampling procedures or to different factors applied to convert analysed values to nutrients. Sources of inconsistences between tables are :
- conversion of macronutrients into energy ;
- conversion factors for nitrogen into protein ;
- determination of carbohydrates, and data available on polysaccharides and mono- and disaccharides ;
- determination of dietary fibre ;
- partitioning of fatty acids in saturated fatty acids, mono-unsaturated and poly-unsaturated fatty acids ;
- the units in which fatty acids are expressed, e.g. in g fat/100 g fat or in g fatty acids/100 g fat ;
- the use of retinol equivalents.

As part of the Euronut-Seneca concerted action the effect of differences in food composition tables on the assessment of dietary intake was checked by analysing a sample of food intake data from three countries. The data from Hungary, Norway and Portugal were converted in energy and macronutrients by the local table as well as the Dutch nutrient composition data base. For identification of foods the Eurocode was used, which can be linked to all European nutrient data bases (16). The test was not conducted for micronutrients, because it was hypothesised that major true or biological differences between similar foods in various countries would occur in the micronutrients. The resulting differences found for the macronutrients calculated on either of the two ways were less than 10 % of the values found with the local table.

Interpretation of data : the use of recommended daily dietary intakes

The assessment of nutritional adequacy in populations is commonly based on a comparison of dietary intake data with a set of recommended intakes. Most of these recommendations are derived from limited experimental data almost invariably collected on young adults. Their relevance to elderly people with changed absorptive and metabolic capacities is unclear for many nutrients. Recommended daily intakes may differ widely between countries. The second supplement of the European Journal of Clinical Nutrition in 1990 deals with this subjects (17). Table 3 is just an example of variability in recommendations for one nutrient.

TABLE 3   RECOMMENDATIONS FOR VITAMIN D1
INTAKE PER DAY FOR ELDERLY PEOPLE IN VARIOUS COUNTRIES*
Source (Trichopoulou 1990, 17)

Country	Age in years	Males	Females
Australia	> 65	0.9	0.7
Germany	> 65	1.3	1.1
Ireland	65 - 74 > 70	1.6 1.6	1.3 1.3
Italy	> 60	1.2	0.8
Netherlands	> 65	1.0	1.0
Nordic countries	61 - 75 > 75	1.4 1.2	1.2 1.2

(*) Purpose and bases for recommendations also differ per country ; see Ref. 18.

Dietary intake distributions may be evaluated against recommended levels or more conservative criteria, such as 70 % of recommended intake. An alternative and more appropriate approach to assess dietary inadequacy does not utilize recommended intakes but, instead, estimates of mean requirements. If multiple daily intake data allow for removal of within-subject variation, the prevalence of inadequate nutrient intake may be assessed from the adjusted distribution of intakes. In addition, rather than taking a cut-off point for average requirement, the probability approach introduced by Beaton (19) allows for a distribution of requirements. In table 4 the results of the various calculations are presented for vitamin B6 in a Dutch sample over 65 years of age.

TABLE 4

APPARENT PREVALENCE OF INADEQUATE INTAKE OF VITAMINE B6
IN DUTCH ELDERLY (> 65 yr)

Approach	Males	Females
Observed intake (48-h record) less than 1 mg/day	(%) 13	(%) 27
After adjustment for within-subject variation	4	14
Probability approach	7	19

* Data based on Dutch National Food consumption Survery, (20), 1988.

Reports of energy and nutrient intake

Decreased energy expenditure in the elderly as a result of declining levels of physical activity and reduction in BMR is reflected in lower recommended daily energy intakes for the older age groups. Many studies have shown that there is indeed a decrease in energy intake with aging. In table 5 results of the Dutch National Food Consumption Survey are presented. These cross-sectional data suggest that energy intake decreases with increasing age. Note that the data of the over nineties are from separate studies and may therefore suffer from a lack of comparability to the other age groups. However, the decreasing trend is confirmed in a study with a longitudinal design conducted with only male subjects (22). Reduced physical activity might have a larger impact on energy requirements than aging per se. Voorrips et al. (23) examined food consumption and nutritional status in an apparently healthy active group and a sedentary group of women aged 65 years and over. She found that mean energy intake did hardly differ between the groups, while mean body weight and body mass index (BMI) was significantly different. In addition, the physical active group tended to have a diet more conform the Dutch Dietary Guidelines than the sedentary group.

TABLE 5

ENERGY INTAKE IN VARIOUS AGE CATEGORIES IN MJ

Age/years	Males		Females	
	n	mean	n	mean
22 – 49[1] 50 – 64[1] 65 +[1]	1 296 431 227	11.9 10.7 10.3	1 286 460 261	8.8 8.1 7.9
90 +[2]	18	8.0	22	7.9

1 : Source : Dutch National Food Consumption Survey, 1988 (20).
2 : Source : Danner, 1977 (21).

Hardly any published survey of elderly people living in their own home have revealed a substantial prevalence of malnutrition (1). However, in many studies the response rate was rather poor. In the Euronut-Seneca study, results of a non-responders questionnaire indicated that non-responders in general are less educated and perceive themselves as less healthier than responders (24). Several studies suggest that inadequate diets of elderly people are most likely due to low intakes of calcium, zinc, potassium, magnesium, vitamin B6 and folates. In industrialized countries fat, refined carbohydrate, and sodium intakes are above the recommended levels, whereas complex carbohydrate and dietary fibre intakes are below (1). As is the case in younger people, supplements are most frequently used by elderly subjects who have a healthy diet and do not need the supplements (25).

Surveys conducted in long-term care institutions have demonstrated that malnutrition is a very serious problem among elderly who are unable to feed themselves. Change in weight is a sensitive indicator (26).

It is a common belief that the elderly are reluctant to dietary change and therefore nutrition education for this group is likely to be ineffective. However, those studies which have addressed this question, have found that the proportion of elderly men and women making dietary changes is the same or even more than in younger adults (1). These changes are often made for health reasons or for convenience. Elderly people are more often concerned about their health than younger adults are and the findings of several studies suggest that older age groups are likely to be receptive to appropriate nutrition education programmes.

REFERENCES

1. HORWATH C.C. : Dietary Intake Studies in Elderly People. *In :* Bourne G.H., World review of Nutrition and Dietetics (59). Impact of Nutrition on Health and Disease. *Karger,* 1989.
2. DE GROOT C.P.G.M., VAN STAVEREN W.A. : Nutrition and the Elderly. A European Collaborative Study in Cooperation with the — World Health Organisation (WHO-SPRA) — International Union of Nutritional Sciences (IUNS) — Committee on Geriatric Nutrition. Manual of Operations, Euronut report 11. *Wageningen,* 1988.
3. STEEN B., ISAKSSON B., SVANSBERG A. : Intake of energy and nutrients and meal habits in 70-year old males and females in Gothenburg, Sweden. A population study. *Acta Med. Scand.,* 1977, 611 (suppl.), 39-86.
4. CALIENDO M.A. : Validity of the 24-hour recall to determine dietary status of the elderly in an extended care facility. *J. Nutr. for the Elderly,* 1981, 1, 57-66.
5. EVANS H.K., GINES J.D. : Dietary recall method comparison for hospitalized elderly subjects. *J. Am. Dietet. Assoc.,* 1985, 85, 202-205.
6. GERSOVITZ M., MADDEN J.P., SMICIKLAS-WRIGHT H. : Validity of the 24-hour recall and seven-day record for group comparisons. *J. Am. Dietet. Assoc.,* 1978, 73, 48-55.
7. MADDEN J.P., GOODMAN S.J., GUTHRIE H.A. : Validity of the 24-hour recall. *J. Am. Dietet. Assoc.,* 1976, 68, 143-147.
8. CAMPBELL V.A., DODDS M.L. : Collecting dietary information from groups of older people. *J. Am. Dietet. Assoc.,* 1967, 51, 29-33.
9. BAZARRE T.L., YUHAS J.A. : Comparative evaluation of methods of collecting food intake data for cancer epidemiology studies. *Nutrition and Cancer,* 1983, 5, 201-214.
10. MAHALKO J.R., JOHNSON L.K., GALLAGHAR S.K., MILNE D.B. : Comparison of dietary histories and seven-day food records in a nutritional assessment of older adults. *Am. J. Clin. Nutr.,* 1985, 42, 542-553.
11. O'HANLON P., KOHRS M.B. : Dietary studies of older Americans. *Am. J. Clin. Nutr.,* 1978, 31, 1257-1269.
12. BAKKUM A., BLOEMBERG B., VAN STAVEREN W.A., VERSCHUREN M., WEST C.E. : The relative validity of a retrospective estimate of food consumption based on a current dietary history and a food frequency list. *Nutrition and Cancer,* 1988, 11, 41-53.
13. NES M., VAN STAVEREN W.A., ZAJKAS G., INELMEN E., MOREIRAS-VARELA O. : Validity of the dietary history method un 2x in elderly subjects. *Eur. J. Clin. Nutr.,* 1991, 45 suppl. 3, 97-104.
14. DURNIN J.V.G.A. : Energy metabolism in the elderly (in preparation).
15. BROWN J., THARP T.M., DAHLBERG-LUBY E.M. et al. : Videotape dietary assessment : Validity, reliability and comparison of results with 24-hour dietary recalls from elderly women in retirement home. *Am. J. Diet. Assoc.,* 1990, 90, 1675-1679.
16. ARAB L., WITTLER M., SCHETTLER G. : European food composition tables in translation. *Heidelberg : Springer Verlag,* 1987, 155 pages.
17. TRICHOPOULOU A., VASSILAKOS T. : Recommended dietary intakes in the European Community member States : an overview. *Eur. J. Clin. Nutr.,* 1990, 44 (suppl. 2), 51-126.
18. TRICHOPOULOU A. (Ed.) : Recommended dietary intakes in the EEC : scientific evidence and public health considerations. *Eur. J. Clin. Nutr.,* 1990, 44 (suppl. 2), 1-125.
19. BEATON G.H. : Nutrient requirements and population data. *Proc. Nutr. Soc.,* 1988, 47, 63-78.
20. Wat eet Nederland. Resultaten van de voedselconsumptiepeiling 1987-1988, Ministry of Public Health and Culture, 1988.
21. DANNER S.A. : Methusela's Secret. Cardiovascular Health in the tenth decade. *Thesis,* Amsterdam, 1977.
22. KROMHOUT D. : Energy intake, energy expenditure, and smoking in relation to body fatness : the Zutphen study. *Am. J. Clin. Nutr.,* 1988, 47, 668-674.
23. VOORRIPS L.E., VAN STAVEREN W.A., HAUTVAST J.G.J.A. : Are physically active women in a better nutritional condition than their sedentary peers ? 1991. *Eur. J. Clin. Nutr.,* 1991, in press.
24. VAN 'THOF M.A., HAUTVAST J.G.A.J., SCHROLL M., VLACHONIKOLIS I.G. : Euronut - SENECA : Design, methods and participation. *Eur. J. Clin. Nutr.,* 1991, 45, suppl. 3, 5-22.
25. GRAY G.E., PAGANINI-HILL A., ROSS R.K. : Dietary intake and nutrient supplement use in a Southern Californian retirement community. *Am. J. Clin. Nutr.,* 1983, 38, 122.
26. ROE D.A. : Geriatric Nutrition. *Clinics in Geriatric Medicine,* 1990, 6, 319-334.

NEW APPROACHES TO THE ASSESSMENT OF BODY COMPOSITION IN ELDERLY PERSONS

Richard N. BAUMGARTNER (*)

INTRODUCTION

It is readily observed that significant changes occur qualitatively in the body composition of aging individuals : stature decreases, body fat increases and redistributes from the limbs to the trunk, muscle tone declines, skin texture changes, edema is more common, bones are more brittle and fracture easily, and so on. There is little doubt that these changes have important health related effects. Changes in body composition during aging are probably associated with declines in organ function, metabolism, nutrient intake and utilization, physical activity, and may determine ability to withstand and recover from traumatic and disease stresses (1). It is very difficult, for both conceptual and technical reasons, to quantify accurately changes in body composition in elderly persons so that their statistical relationship with these underlying factors can be studied. As a result, there is limited information regarding these changes or a clear understanding of their relationship to subsequent health in elderly persons (2).

BODY COMPOSITION METHODOLOGY

Methods of analyzing body composition can be arranged in a hierarchy of four levels according to degrees of invasiveness and of accuracy as shown in figure 1 (3). The highest level, with maximum invasiveness and accuracy, is physico-chemical analysis of body tissues from cadaver dissection or from biopsies. There are very few such *level 1* studies (4-7), nonetheless our most fundamental knowledge of the relative weights, proportions, densities, and chemistry of elemental body constituents is derived from these studies. At *level 2* are techniques of *in vivo* quantification of specific chemicals or anatomical structures. These techniques, which include neutron activaton (NA), magnetic resonance imaging (MRI) and spectroscopy (MRS), and dual-energy absorptiometry (DEA), are relatively new and require expensive, sophis-

(*) Clinical Nutrition Laboratory University of New Mexico School of Medicine, Albuquerque, NM 87131.

Presented at Symposium de Recherche en Nutrition et Gérontologie : Modèles de Dénutrition chez la Personne Agée, 5 et 6 juin 1991 Toulouse, France.

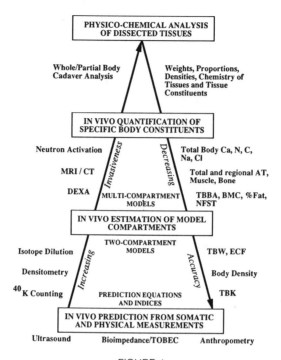

FIGURE 1

The hierarchy of body composition methods.
(based on Heymsfield et al., 1989 ; ref. 3)

ticated instrumentation that is not readily accessible. The quantities obtained by these highly precise methods, however, must be validated against data from *level 1* studies. For example, adipose tissue, muscle, and other areas from cross-sectional MRI images are validated against corresponding measurements from frozen tissue slices (8). Total body calcium (TBCa) from NA and total body bone mineral (TBBM) from DEA are validated against ashed bone (9).

The methods at *level 3* estimate two or more components of body composition using models that require assumptions regarding the densities, proportions, or ratios of various measured constituents. Most *in vivo* body composition analysis has been limited to two-compartment models that divide body mass into fat (or adipose) and fat-free (or lean) fractions. As illustrated in figure 2, a variety of more complex chemical and anatomical models that are more realistic physiologically can be employed given new advances in technology. These " classic " methods require the assumption of certain constants in the composition of the fat-free mass (FFM). For example, the densitometric method assumes that the density of the FFM is a constant 1.10 g/cc ; the total body water method assumes a constant level of hydration of FFM (73.2 %) ; and, the ^{40}K method assumes sex-specific constants for the concentration of potassium in FFM (2.5 g/kg in men, and 2.3 g/kg in women) [10]. Three-compartment models can be achieved by a combination of methods, i.e. densitometry + total body water, but these have been seldom employed in the past. New technology such as NA and DEA now makes possible the development of models with up to

6 compartments, including protein, glycogen, osseous and non-osseous cell mineral masses, and intra- and extra-cellular fluid volumes. Assumptions established from higher level measurements are still necessary ; for example, estimation of total body protein (P) requires the measurement of total body nitrogen (TBN) from NA and assumes that 98 % of N is in P and that P is 16 % N (11).

Level 4 includes methods that measure somatic or physical properties of the body that are correlated with and can be used to predict various components of body composition when calibrated statistically against criterion measurements from a higher level method. The validity of the criterion measurements is important, since errors at the higher levels will be propagated to and often magnified at the lower levels. For instance, an equation for predicting % body fat from skinfold thicknesses will contain technical errors of measurement of the skinfolds as well as error (or bias) propagated from the method used to establish the criterion measurements, e.g. densitometry or total body water. A second problem is the "sample-specificity" paradox. That is, predictive equations usually lose accuracy when applied to data sets substantially different than the ones from which they were developed.

METHODS FOR STUDYING ELDERLY PERSONS

Present knowledge of the complex changes that occur with age in body composition indicates that multicompartmental models are needed for accurate estimation of body composition in elderly persons. The basic assumptions of the "classic" two-compartment models are age-dependent and biased estimates are obtained when they are applied to elderly subjects (3, 12).

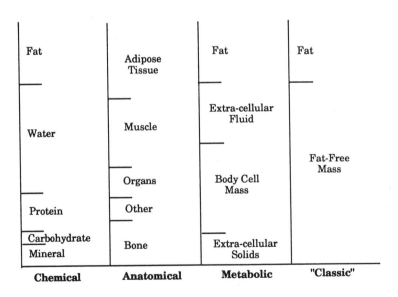

FIGURE 2

Models of body composition.

Elderly women as well as men are likely to have lower values for fat-free density than 1.10 g/cc as a result of loss of mineral from bone with age. Although total body water may decrease on the average with aging (13), the hydration of the FFM may increase in many resulting in further decreases in fat-free density. Figure 3 shows that differences between estimates of % body fat from 2 and 4 compartment models are correlated significantly with hydration of the FFM in elderly men and women. The box in the figure outlines the expected "normal" range for the aqueous fraction of FFM in young adults, 0.70 - 0.75, and the amount of difference that may be attributed to pure measurement error, ± 2 %. Clearly, many subjects have levels of hydration of the FFM considerably in excess of 0.75 and the range is 2 fold greater than expected. The result is an average systematic overestimation by the 2 compartment method of 3 % body fat, greater than could be attributed to technical error. "Overhydration" of the FFM in elderly persons is most likely due to excess extra-cellular fluid in proportion to intra-cellular fluid and may be associated with declining renal function.

Potassium is lost both in absolute and relative terms from skeletal muscle with aging. The decrease with age in the K content of FFM is shown in figure 4. The amounts and rates of decrease have not been established clearly for different ethnic groups or each sex (14). The physiological significance of this decline is not entirely clear either, although it believed to reflect loss of mainly skeletal muscle mass with aging. The use of age and sex-specific means may help reduce some systematic bias when calculating FFM from TBK, however considerable error will remain if variability in TBK/FFM increases with age. In fact, "age-adjusted equations" for any of the "classic" two-compartment models are not likely to improve estimation if variability in body composition increases with age (15).

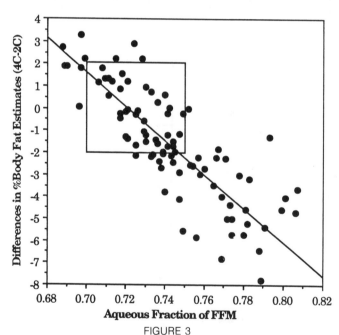

FIGURE 3

Association of differences between 2 and 4 compartment model estimates
of % body fat and hydration of the fat-free mass.
(data from Baumgartner et al., 1991 ; ref. 12)

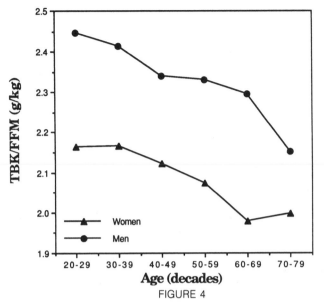

FIGURE 4

Decline with age in potassium content of fat-free mass.
(data from Cohn et al., 1980 ; ref. 11)

Recently, we reported the development of a 4 compartment model based on measurements of body density (Db), total body bone ash (TBBA) from DEA, and total body water (TBW) from tritium dilution (16). These measurements were used to estimate aqueous, mineral, protein, and fat fractions of total body mass. The estimates from this model, now referred to as the SLR (St. Luke's-Roosevelt) model (17), compared favorably to those from a more complex and expensive 5 compartment NA model. The minimum error of estimation of % body fat using the SLR model was calculated to be 1.6 %. The majority of this error was considered to be due to the technical error of measurement of total body water. In application to elderly subjects the total error should be expected to be slightly larger, 2 %, because a greater proportion of elderly than young adults will have difficulty performing underwater weighing and body density determinations will contain greater technical error. This is still less, however, than the average error (4-5 %) that might be expected from a two-compartmental model based on body density only (18).

Clearly, *level 4* prediction equations cannot have errors of prediction equal to or less than the criterion methods. Since the accuracy of the criterion measurements is rarely considered in the statistical derivation of prediction equations by multiple regression methods, the accuracy of the equations is generally overstated. Recently, we showed that an equation calibrated against criterion values from a 2 compartment body density model systematically over-predicted % BF by 1.7 % compared to an equation calibrated against the SLR 4 compartment model (12). The standard error of estimation of the 2C equation was 5 % body fat. Thus, the actual **average** error of the equation should be considered to be at least 6.7 % (i.e. 5 % + 1.7 %). In this context it is important to note that there was an **average systematic difference** between estimates of % body fat from the NA and SLR models of 1.4 %, but some **individual differences** were as great as 6 %. The "uncertainty principal" applies to all body composition methods and accuracy is always relative.

Some body composition methods become increasingly unreliable when applied to elderly subjects (e.g. densitometry as described above) or cannot be applied at all. "Passive" methods that do not require the subject to stand or to participate in the measurement process are desireable. With the exception of densitometry, most level 2 and 3 "criterion" methods are of this kind. The most widely applied *level 4* method, however, is anthropometry which is conventionally performed while the participants stand. Recumbent methods have been developed recently that can be applied regardless of an individual's ability to stand or stand erect (19). Bioelectric impedance analysis (BIA) is a new *level 4* method that is suitable for use in clinical and epidemiologic assessments of elderly populations also because it is " passive " as well as relatively inexpensive, reliable, and portable. The usefulness of BIA in elderly subjects, however, is not well established. The method measures the resistance of the body to a very low amplitude (800 *mu* A), fixed frequency (50 kHz) electric current. The amount of resistance is considered to be proportional to the concentration of free electrolytes in the body water and is used most directly to predict the TBW. Since most of the body water is contained in the FFM, the method can be used to predict this component also. The measured resistance must be standardized against some measure of body size, usually stature or length, and predictions are improved by the inclusion of additional anthropometric measurements (20).

No studies to date have combined recumbent anthropometry with BIA in equations for predicting body composition in elderly populations. Figure 5 shows the correlation of FFM with arm length [2]/arm resistance in a sample of elderly men and women from the New Mexico Aging Process Study. BIA is believed to be sensitive to factors such as cell-membrane permeability, electrolyte imbalances, and the distribution of water between intra- and extra-cellular spaces and between adipose and non-adipose tissues. Potassium loss in elderly subjects may affect cell membrane properties (21), and several studies have shown that the ratio ECF : ICF increases with age over 60 y (13). The effects of these age-related changes on BIA is not well studied.

There are basically two ways of using *level 4* measurements in body composition assessments : (a) to derive prediction equations ; and, (b) to derive indices that are correlated with certain components. Although considerable work has been done in developing prediction equations for younger adults, few are available for elderly populations (12, 22, 23), and none to-date have used recumbent measurements. Indices such as Quetelet's Index (W/S^2, or "body mass index") and the waist/hip circumference ratio are used widely to grade level of fatness and fat distribution, respectively, in clinical and population studies. It does not seem to be well appreciated, however, that changes with aging in body composition, muscle tone, and posture will greatly reduce the sensitivity of these indices when applied to elderly persons. Arm muscle (+ bone) area (AMBA), calculated from anthropometric measurements of arm circumference and skinfold thickness, has been endorsed as a simple index of protein stores and "reference data" for elderly persons have been published (24-26). Heymsfield and associates demonstrated that AMBA significantly overestimates the actual area measured from computed tomography scans by an average of 10-12 % in a sample of young and middle-aged adults (27). Figure 6 compares AMBA from anthropometry with actual area from MRI scans, expressed as percents of total arm area, for 25 elderly men and women from the New Mexico Aging Process Study. In this sample, AMBA overestimated actual area by an average of 50 % and the error increased as a function of body fatness (28).

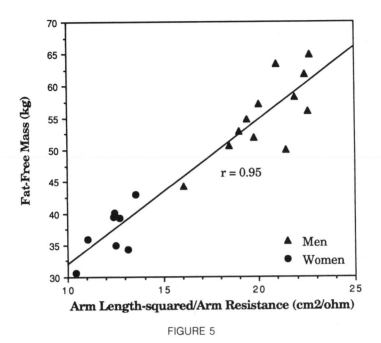

FIGURE 5

Prediction of fat-free mass from arm lenght²/arm resistance in elderly men and women :
New Mexico Aging Process Study.

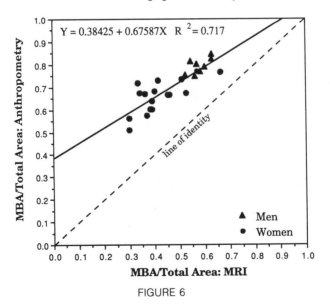

FIGURE 6

Systematic difference between arm muscle-bone areas (MBA) from anthropometry
and actual areas from MRI scans in elderly men and women : New Mexico Aging Process Study.

FUTURE DIRECTIONS IN BODY COMPOSITION ANALYSIS OF ELDERLY PERSONS

Components of body composition other than fat or fat-free mass can be estimated or predicted using new technology that have better clinical significance with regard to the nutritional status and health of elderly persons. These include total body protein (P), skeletal muscle mass (SMM), intra-abdominal fat mass (IAF), and the ratio of extra- to intra-cellular fluids (ECF : ICF). The use of NA to determine P was noted above. Heymsfield et al. (29) recently demonstrated the use of DEA to estimate SMM. IAF can be estimated directly from CT or MRI scans, as shown in figure 7. Theoretically it is possible to develop equations for predicting P, SMM, and IAF from combinations of anthropometry and BIA. Jenin and associates (30) demonstrated the potential several years ago for estimating ECF : ICF using bioelectric resistance at low and high frequencies, and there has been renewed interest in this potential with the recent introduction of multifrequency analyzers.

Most studies of body composition in the elderly have been cross-sectional, of select samples, and have not included many subjects older than 75 y. Information is very scarce for persons over 85 years of age, who are the fastest growing segment of the population. Longitudinal studies of relatively healthy elderly populations are needed to distinguish normal from abnormal age changes in body composition. Large cross-sectional studies of representative samples are needed to provide reference data. Data for regional body composition are needed because of the redistribution of body fat and the losses of muscle and bone. These studies should use innovative methods and the latest technology in ensure accuracy. The increased variability in whole body composition with aging necessitates the use of multicompartmental models in which estimates are based on measurements of two or more components to provide accurate estimates.

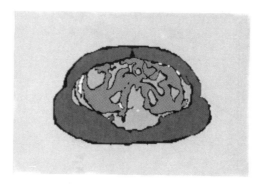

FIGURE 7

Cross-sectional MRI image of abdomen at level of umbilicus showing delineation of intra-abdominal and subcutaneous adipose tissue areas : New Mexico Aging Process Study.

REFERENCES

1. KUCZMARSKI R.J. : Need for body composition information in elderly subjects. *Am. J. Clin. Nutr.*, 1989, 50, 1150-1158.
2. CHUMLEA W.C., BAUMGARTNER R.N. : Status of anthropometry and body composition data in elderly subjects. *Am. J. Clin. Nutr.*, 1989, 50, 1158-1166.
3. HEYMSFIELD S.B., WANG J.,· LICHTMAN S., KAMEN Y., KEHAYIAS J., PIERSON R.N. : Body composition in elderly subjects : a critical appraisal of clinical methodology. *Am. J. Clin. Nutr.*, 1989, 5, 1167-1175.
4. FORBES R.M., COOPER A.R., MITCHELL H.H. : The composition of the adult human body as deter-. mined by chemical analysis. *J. Biol. Chem.*, 1953, 302, 359-66.
5. MITCHELL J., KEYS A., ANDERSON J.T., GRANDE F. : Density of fat and bone mineral of mammalian body. *Metabolism*, 1960, 9, 472-7.
6. WIDDOWSON E.M., MCCANCE R.A., SPRAY C.M. : The chemical composition of the human body. *Clin. Sci.*, 1951, 10, 113-25.
7. MARTIN A.D. : An anatomical basis for assessing human body composition : evidence from 25 dissections. Doctoral Dissertation, *Simon Fraser University*, British Columbia (Canada), 1984.
8. FULLER M.F., FOSTER M.A., HUTCHINSON J.M.S. : Estimation of body fat by nuclear magnetic resonance imaging. *Proc. Nutr. Soc.*, 1985, 44, 108A.
9. MAZESS R.B., PEPPLER W.W., CHESTNUT C.H. et al. : Total body bone mineral and lean body mass by dual-photon absorptiometry. II. Comparison with total body calcium by neutron activation analysis. *Calcif. Tissue Int.*, 1981, 33, 361-3.
10. LUKASKI H.C. : Methods for the assessment of human body composition : traditional and new. *Am. J. Clin. Nutr.*, 1987, 46, 537-556.
11. COHN S.H., VARTSKY D., YASUMURA S. et al. : Compartmental body composition based on total-body nitrogen, potassium, and calcium. *Am. J. Physiol.*, 1980, 239, E524-30.
12. BAUMGARTNER R.N., HEYMSFIELD S.B., LICHTMAN S. et al. : Body composition in elderly people : effect of criterion estimates on predictive equations. *Am. J. Clin. Nutr.*, 1991, 53.
13. SCHOELLER D.A. : Changes in total body water with age. *Am. J. Clin. Nutr.*, 1989, 5, 1176-1181.
14. FLYNN M.A., NOLPH G.B., BAKER A.S., MARTIN W.M., KRAUSE G. : Total body potassium in aging humans : a longitudinal study. *Am. J. Clin. Nutr.*, 1989, 50, 713-717.
15. DEURENBERG P., WESTRATE J.A., VAN DER KOOY K. : Is an adaptation of Siri's formula for the calculation of body fat percentage from body density in the elderly necessary ? *Eur. J. Clin. Nutr.*. 1989, 43, 559-568.
16. HEYMSFIELD S.B., LICHTMAN S., BAUMGARTNER R.N. et al. : Body composition of humans : comparison of two improved four-compartment models that differ in expense, technical complexity, and radiation exposure. *Am. J. Clin. Nutr.*, 1990, 52, 52-8.
17. HEYMSFIELD S.B., WAKI M. : Body composition in humans : advances in the development of multicompartment chemical models. *Nutr. Rev.*, 1991, 49, 97-108.
18. SIRI W.E. : Body composition from fluid spaces and density : analysis of methods. In Brozek J., Henschel A., eds. Techniques for measuring body composition. Washington, D.C. : *National Academy Press*, 1961, 61, 223-44.
19. CHUMLEA W.C., ROCHE A.F. : Nutritional assessment in the elderly through anthropometry. *Columbus, OH : Ross Laboratories*, 1987.
20. BAUMGARTNER R.N., CHUMLEA W.C., ROCHE A.F. : Impedance for body composition. In : Pandolf, K.B. ed., *Exerc. Sport Sci. Rev.*, Vol. 18. *Baltimore : Williams and Wilkins*, 1990, 193-224.
21. PIERSON R.N., WANG J. : The quality of the lean body mass : implications for clinical medicine. In : Ellis K.J., Yasumura S., Morgan W.D. eds, *In Vivo Body Composition Studies*. London, Eng. : *Inst. Phys. Sci., Med.*, 1987, 123-130.
22. DEURENBERG P., VAN DER KOOY K., EVERS P., HULSCHOF T. : Assessment of body composition by bioelectrical impedance in a population aged over 60 y. *Am. J. Clin. Nutr.*, 1990, 51, 3-6.
23. SVENDSEN O.L., HAARBO J., HEITMANN B.L. et al. : Measurement of body fat in elderly subjects by dual-energy x-ray absorptiometry, bioelectric impedance, and anthropometry. *Am. J. Clin. Nutr.*, 1991, 53, 1117-1123.
24. MCEVOY A.W., JAMES O.F.W. : Anthropometric indices in normal elderly subjects. *Age and Ageing*, 1982, 11, 97-100.
25. FRISANCHO A.R. : New standards of weight and body composition by frame size and height for assessment of nutritional status of adults and the elderly. *Am. J. Clin. Nutr.*, 1984, 40, 808-819.
26. CHUMLEA W.C., ROCHE A.F., MUKHERJEE D. : Some anthropometric indice of body composition in elderly adults. *J. Gerontology*, 1986, 41, 36-39.
27. HEYMSFIELD S.B., MCMANUS C., SMITH J. et al. : Anthropometric measurement of muscle mass : revised equations for calculating bone-free arm muscle area. *Am. J. Clin. Nutr.*, 1982, 36, 680-90.
28. BAUMGARTNER R.N., RHYNE R.L., TROOP C., WAYNE S., GARRY P.J. : Assessment of regional body composition in the elderly by magnetic resonance imaging. *Am. J. Clin. Nutr.*, 1991, 53, P-13.

29. HEYMSFIELD S.B., SMITH R., AULET M. et al. : Appendicular skeletal muscle mass : measurement by dual-photon absorptiometry. *Am. J. Clin. Nutr.*, 1990, 52, 214-218.
30. JENIN P., LENOIR J., ROULLET C., THOMASSET A.L., DUCROT H. : Determination of body fluid compartments by electrical impedance measurements. *Aviat. Space Environ. Med.*, 1975, 46, 152-155.

VITAMIN REQUIREMENTS IN OLD AGE

Robert M. RUSSELL (*)

Summary. – Low dietary intakes account for much of the poor vitamin nutriture reported among various elderly population groups. Despite many problems in assessing vitamin nutriture in the elderly, it appears that the 1989 United States RDAs are appropriate to apply to elderly population groups for many vitamins (e.g. vitamin E, thiamin, riboflavin, ascorbic acid). However, there is evidence that the US RDAs for vitamins D B6 and B12 may be too low due to specific age related changes in the metabolism of these vitamins. On the other hand, requirements in the elderly may be lower for vitamin A. Further research is needed in order to develop specific dietary recommendations over the adult life span. (Facts and Research in Gerontology 1992)

Key-words : nutrition, elderly, vitamin A, vitamin D, vitamin B6, vitamin B12, dietary requirement.

INTRODUCTION

This paper will focus on vitamin requirements in old age, but specifically on certain vitamins for which there is some experimental evidence that the requirement is different for the older person than for the younger adult person. There are only three vitamins for which there is any age adjustment in the 1989 United States Recommended Dietary Allowances (RDAs) in the adult age span : thiamineniacin and riboflavin (1). For these vitamins, there are slight decreases for older adults males as compared to younger adult males. It should be noted that the cut-off for defining elderly in the 1989 United States RDAs is 51 years and older. This is not because the US Food and Nutrition Board believes the requirement for any one vitamin is the same for a 90 year old person as for a 50 year old person, but rather because there is a profound lack of experimental evidence for what vitamin requirements should be in old age.

If one applies the full 1989 RDAs to the US elderly population (as sampled in the US Health and Nutrition Examination Survey – HANES – which is carried out periodically by the NIH and the National Centre for Health Statistics), it becomes clear that almost no one in the oldest age decade studied (65-75 years old) meets the

(*) USDA, Human Nutrition Research Center on Aging at Tufts University, Boston (USA).

Address for correspondence : Dr. R.M. Russell, USDA, Human Nutrition Research Center on Aging at Tufts University, 711 Washington Street, Boston, Massachussets 02111 (USA).

1989 American RDA for any one vitamin. Bowman and Rosenberg found that significant percentages of elderly individuals (up to 50 %) were not meeting even two thirds of the RDA requirement for many vitamins, such as thiamine, riboflavin, niacin, and vitamin C (2). This either means that older Americans are eating very poorly, or that the standards being applied are inappropriate to use for the older age groups.

From a recent review, there is evidence that the 1989 US RDAs are too low for the elderly for vitamin B6, vitamin D and vitamin B12 (3). On the other hand, the 1989 RDAs are probably too high for vitamin A. We either have little evidence or no data on other vitamins.

Three vitamins for which there is evidence of an altered requirement in old age will now be examined : vitamin D, vitamin A and vitamin B12.

Vitamin D

Vitamin D is stressed, particularly in Northern Europe, as being a vitamin frequently deficient in the older person (4, 5, 6). It has been shown that older adults have lower levels of serum 1,25-dihydroxyvitamin D (the most active form of the vitamin) than do young adults (7). What is the explanation for this ? First of all, an elderly person's skin is less able to synthesize vitamin D upon ultraviolet light exposure than a younger person's skin (8). There is therefore less substrate (*i.e.* 25-hydroxyvitamin D) to be activated by the kidney. Also older people are less likely to go out in the sunlight than younger people. Further, in the four winter months in Boston, which is at about the same latitude as Madrid, absolutely no synthesis of vitamin D can take place, since the UV light is angled and weak (9). As one gets to more northerly climates, such as in England and Sweden, there is even more of a problem. In this situation, the dietary intake of vitamin D becomes an important issue. A second problem with regard to vitamin D metabolism in aging is the lower actual synthesis of 1,25-dihydroxyvitamin D by the aged kidney. Twenty-five hydroxy-vitamin D is activated to 1,25-dihydroxyvitamin D in the kidney under the influence of parathyroid hormone. In one study by Slovik et al., parathyroid hormone was infused in young adult people and in osteoporotic old people, and serum 1,25-dihydroxyvitamin D levels were measured subsequently for several hours (10). A very nice rise in serum 1,25-dihydroxyvitamin D took place in the young people upon parathyroid infusion, while in the old people the curve remained relatively flat. Thus, older kidneys are less responsive to parathyroid hormone for synthesizing the active form of the vitamin.

The question comes up : can one push the older kidney to synthesize more 1,25-dihydroxyvitamin D by just providing more substrate (i.e. the 25 hydroxy precursor). The answer appears to be yes. That is, for older people who have low or low-normal levels of 25-hydroxyvitamin D circulating in their blood, 1,25-dihydroxyvitamin D levels can rise if more vitamin D is provided (11). Thus, the age-related defect in synthesizing 1,25-dihydroxyvitamin D by the kidney is only relative ; by providing more substrate, a substantial proportion of elderly people, may achieve a rise in the metabolically active form of the vitamin. These above discussed studies provide the evidence that there is probably a higher dietary requirement for vitamin D in old age, although it is not known exactly how much more vitamin D an elderly person will need to eat.

Vitamin A

For vitamin A, the opposite may be true, i.e. the requirement for the older person may be lower than for the younger adult. In the United States the 1989 RDA for vitamin A is 1 000 microgram retinol equivalents (RE) in males and 800 RE in females. In the US HANES survey, almost 50 % of elderly individuals between the ages of 65 and 75 do not meet even two thirds of the RDA standard for vitamin A dietary intake (2).

Autopsy studies have been done in the US on liver levels of vitamin A (the liver is the main storage organ for this vitamin). Although most of the older people in the autopsy studies had chronic diseases, their liver levels of vitamin A compare favorably to those of the younger people who died mainly of accidental deaths (12). When one reflects on the fact that elderly people are eating poorly with regard to vitamin A (HANES) and yet they are still able to maintain their liver levels of vitamin A, one may conclude that the US standards for dietary vitamin A are probably set too high one reason in this is that vitamin A absorption improves with advancing age (13). In rats, ranging from a few months old up 40 months old, vitamin A uptake from perfused intestinal segments increased in direct proportion to the animal's age.

In the human, one cannot easily examine the absorption of afat-soluble vitamin directly due to the necessity of doing lymph duct cannulations ; but vitamin A tolerance curves have been performed, giving to old people and young adult people the same amount of vitamin A (14). In the older group, the peak height and area under the vitamin A tolerance curves were statistically significantly greater than in the younger people. A tolerance curve is made up of two components : an absorptive component and a clearance component. Thus, this difference could either reflect increased absorption of vitamin A in the older people, as was seen in the rats, or a decreased ability of the liver to clear the vitamin from the circulation. Vitamin A clearance by the liver has been studied (15). Older and younger people were fed high fat, vitamin A rich meals. Four hours after the meal, a unit of blood was taken, plasmaphoresis performed, and the red cells were then given back to the individual. After reinfusion of the now vitamin A-rich chylomicrons and chylomicron remnants, a rapid and frequent sampling of blood was performed to describe « fall-off » curve (i.e. a clearance curve) of the vitamin. It was found that the residence-time of a newly administered vitamin A molecule (retinyl ester) is twice as long in the older person as in the younger person. Thus, it is estimated that an older person has one half of the ability to clear vitamin A from the circulation than does the younger person. So, what one sees with vitamin A may not only be a problem of increased absorption but also a decreased ability of the liver to clear it from the circulation. These experiments provide an explanation of why the 1989 RDA for vitamin A in the US is probably set too high for the older person. They also reveal something about the possible dangers of chronic supplementation with this vitamin in the older person.

Vitamin A circulates in two forms in the blood : one is retinol bound to retinol binding protein and the other is retinyl esters associated with lipoproteins. The alcohol form, when bound to retinol-binding protein, is not toxic. Retinyl esters are potentially toxic in that they may be converted to free (i.e. unbound) retinol and then nonspecifically delivered to cell membranes. Frequency distributions of serum retinol in old people are exactly the same – whether they are users of multi-vitamin supplements containing vitamin A in the US RDA dosage or are non-users of the vitamin (16). However, if one looks at retinyl esters, one finds that in the elderly people who take multivitamins containing vitamin A, the frequency distribution shifts toward the right, i.e., there are several individuals, who have serum retinyl ester values in the toxic range. In a survey just recently completed, every older person who had a level of serum retinyl esters above 20 micrograms/dl, also had abnormal liver function tests (17).

Vitamin B12

In order to understand the possible effects of age on vitamin B12 requirements, one must first understand atrophic gastritis, a silent condition associated with aging resulting in hypo- or achlorhydria. This entity affects a large group of elderly people. In Boston, among people 60-69 years old, 24 % of individuals have atrophic gastritis ; in the 70 to 79 year old group, it affects 32 %, and in individuals over 80, almost 40 % are affected (18).

Atrophic gastritis may be diagnosed in several ways : a tube may be placed in the stomach and pentagastrin or histamine stimulation can be done, or endoscopy with gastric biopsy can be done. However, serum markers reflective of atrophic gastritis have now been developed, and these can be used as an epidemiologic tool. Absolute values for serum pepsinogens I and II and their ratio (less than 2.9) have been shown to be excellent markers for atrophic gastritis and gastric atrophy (19). They correlate well with histologic findings and with gastric function test results (19).

The physiologic consequences of atrophic gastritis are slower gastric emptying and decreased intrinsic factor secretion, intrinsic factor being the protein synthesized and secreted by the stomach which is necessary for the absorption of vitamin B12. In mild to moderate atrophic gastritis, intrinsic factor is still secreted in sufficient amounts so that vitamin B12 malabsorption does not come about by this mechanism.

However, in atrophic gastritis, there are two other problems : first of all, there is bacterial overgrowth, not only in the stomach but in the small intestine (20). This is due to the relative lack of gastric acid which normally kills swallowed bacteria. Also there is increased gastric and proximal small intestinal pH. The bioavailability of vitamin B12 appears to depend in part on an acid pH in the stomach (2).

Vitamin B12, when ingested, is bound to food proteins. These food proteins must be cleaved off the vitamin B12 molecule, by the action of acid and pepsin, so that the vitamin can then bind up with the so-called R-binder proteins which are secreted by the stomach and in the saliva. Once these R-binders bind to vitamin B12, the complex migrates down into the proximal small bowel where the pancreatic enzymes digest the R-binder. Only then is vitamin B12 free to bind up to its final binder, intrinsic factor. The vitamin B12 – intrinsic factor complex then migrates down to the terminal ileum. The receptors in the ileum recognize the intrinsic factor, and vitamin B12 is incorporated into the gut epithelial cell and absorbed. If the very first step of this whole train of events is interrupted, that is, the food protein cannot be digested off of the vitamin B12 molecule, then none of the rest can happen.

In atrophic gastritis there is less acid and less pepsin being secreted by the stomach ; so one mechanism whereby vitamin B12 deficiency can come about in individuals with atrophic gastritis is by the inhability to digest food protein from the vitamin. King et al. studied people with atrophic gastritis, who secreted almost no acid on stimulation, but who had normal Schilling tests (21). However, when the vitamin B12 was first bound to chicken serum protein, and then fed to these individuals, none could absorb the vitamin normally. Moreover, when given the protein-bound vitamin with intrinsic factor, which would increase absorption if the problem were due to the lack of intrinsic factor, absorption did not improve at all. However, when they gave it with acid, the patients began to show some improvement in vitamin B12 absorption – and when given with acid plus pepsin, further improvement was seen. One individual failed to improve protein-bound vitamin B12 absorption despite added acid and pepsin, and this may have been due to bacterial uptake of the vitamin-protein complex in the small intestine. So, there are two principal mechanisms in mild-moderate atrophic gastritis, by which food vitamin B12 bioavailability may be reduced : the inability to digest protein off the B12 molecule and bacterial overgrowth (22). We estimate that about 20 % of vitamin B12 deficiency comes about in the elderly US population due to atrophic gastritis, by one and or the other of these two mechanisms. These individuals may need a higher vitamin B12 intake.

CONCLUSION

Although some work has been done on whether dietary requirements in the aged human are different from that of the younger adult human, it will be years before firm age specific recommendations can be made for older people with regard to individual nutrients. Also, it is very likely that the older age group will need to be split into several age categories (e.g. 70-80, 80-90, etc.). Nevertheless, it is hoped that after learning more about dietary requirements in the elderly, this knowledge will be applied so that function can be preserved as long as possible over an individual's life span.

REFERENCES

1. Recommended Dietary Allowances, Tenth Edition. *Nat. Acad. Sc.*, Washington, DC, 1989.
2. BOWMAN B.B., ROSENBERG I.H. : Assessment of the nutritional status of the elderly. *Am. J. Clin. Nutr.*, 1982, 35, 1142-51.
3. SUTER P.M., RUSSELL R.M. : Vitamin requirements of the elderly. *Am. J. Clin. Nutr.*, 1987, 45, 501-12.
4. GARY P.J., GOODWIN J.S., HUNT W.C. : Nutritional status in a healthy population : dietary and supplemental intakes. *Am. J. Clin. Nutr.*, 1982, 36, 319-31.
5. LUND B., SORENSEN O.H. : Measurement of 25-hydroxyvitamin D in serum and its relation to sunshine, age and vitamin D intake in the Danish population. *Scand. J. Clin. Lab. Invest.*, 1979, 39, 23-30.
6. PARFITT A.M., GALLAGHER J.C., HEANEY R.P., JOHNSTON C.C., NEER R., WHEDON G.D. : Vitamin D and bone health in the elderly. *Am. J. Clin. Nutr.*, 1982, 36, 1014-31.
7. MUNRO H.N., SUTER P.M., RUSSELL R.M. : Nutritional Requirements of the Elderly. *Ann. Rev. Nutr.*, 1987, 7, 23-49.
8. MACLAUGHLIN J., HOLICK M.F. : Aging decreases the capacity of human skin to produce vitamin D3. *J. Clin. Invest.*, 1985, 76, 1536-38.
9. WEBB A.R., KLINE L., HOLICK M.F. : Influence of season and latitude on the cutaneous synthesis of vitamin D3 : exposure to winter sunlight in Boston and Edmonton will not promote vitamin D3 synthesis in human skin. *J. Clin. Endocrin. Metab.*, 1988, 67, 373-378.
10. SLOVIK D.M., ADAMS J.S., NEER R.M., HOLICK M.F., POTTS Jr. J.T. : Deficient production of 1,25-dihydroxyvitamin D in elderly osteoporotic patients. *New Eng. J. Med.*, 1981, 305, 372-374.
11. FRANCIS R.M., PEACOCK M., STORER J., DAVIES A.E.J., BROWN W.B., NORDIN B.E.C. : Calcium malabsorption in the elderly : the effect of treatment with oral 25-hydroxyvitamin D3. *Eur. J. Clin. Invest.*, 1983, 13, 391-6.
12. VAUGHN MITCHELL G., YOUNG M. and SEWARD C.R. : Vitamin A and carotene levels of a selected population in metropolitan Washington, D.C. *The American Journal of Clinical Nutrition*, 26 september 1973, pp. 992-997. Printed in U.S.A.
13. HOLLANDER D., MORGAN D. : Aging : its influence on vitamin A intestinal absorption *in vivo* by the rat. *Exp. Gerontol.*, 1979, 14, 301-5.
14. KRASINSKI S.D., RUSSELL R.M., DALLAL G.E., DUTTA S.D. : Aging changes vitamin A absorption characteristics. *Gastroenterology*, 1985, 88, 1715 (Abstr.).
15. KRASINSKI S.D., RUSSELL R.M., SCHAEFER E. : Delayed plasma clearance of chylomicron-retinyl esters in the elderly. *Gastroenterology*, 1987, 92 (5), 1803 (Abstr.).
16. RUSSELL R.M. : « Malabsorption and Aging ». In : Aging in Liver and Gastro-Intestinal Tract, edited by L. Bianchi, P. Holt, O.F.W. James, R.N. Butler. *Kluwer Academic Publishers*, Hingham, M.A., 1988, 297-307.
17. KRASINSKI S.D., RUSSELL R.M., OTRADOVEC C.L., SADOWSKI J.A., STUART H.C., JACOB R.A., MCGANDY R.B. : Relationship of vitamin A and vitamin E intake to fasting plasma retinol, retinol-binding protein, retinyl esters, carotene, alpha-tocopherol, and cholesterol among elderly people and young adults : increased plasma retinyl esters among vitamin A - supplement users. *Am. J. Clin. Nutr.*, 1989, 49, 112-20.
18. KRASINSKI S.D., RUSSELL R.M., SAMLOFF M., JACOB R.A., DALLAL G.E., MCGANDY R.B., HARTZ S.C. : Fundic atrophic gastritis in an elderly population. Effect on hemoglobin and several serum nutritional indicators. *American Geriatrics Society*, 1986, 34, 800-806.
19. SAMLOFF I.M., VARIS K., IHAMAKI T., SIURALA M., ROTTER J.I. : Relationships among serum pepsinogen I, serum pepsinogen II, and gastric mucosal histology. *Gastroenterology*, 1982, 83, 204-209.

20. RUSSELL N., KRASINSKI S.D., SAMLOFF N.I., JACOB R.A., HARTZ S.C., BROVENDER S.R. : Folic acid malabsorption in atrophic gastritis. Possible compensation by bacterial folate synthesis. *Gastroenterology*, 1986, 91, 1476-1482.
21. KING C.E., LEIBACH J., TOSKES P.P. : Clinically significant vitamin B12 deficiency secondary to malabsorption of protein-bound vitamin B12. *Dig. Dis. Sci.*, 1979, 24, 397-402.
22. SUTER (P.M.), GOLNER (B.B.), RUSSEL (R.M.) : Reversal of protein-bound vitamin B12 malabsorption with antibiotics in atrophic gastritis. *Gastroenterology*, 1991, 101, 1039-1045.

ARE THE NUTRITIONAL REQUIREMENTS OF THE ELDERLY DIFFERENT FROM THOSE OF YOUNG INDIVIDUALS ? ZINC AS AN EXAMPLE

Y. GUIGOZ (*)

Summary. – In this review, we consider the changes in cellular zinc uptake with age, dietary zinc intake, and balance studies and the influence of zinc supplementation on cellular immune functions, in an attempt to define the zinc requirements of the elderly. In the elderly zinc intake varies between 9-13 and 6-10 mg/day for males and females respectively, suggesting a potential for marginal zinc deficiencies. Zinc balance studies indicate a reduced zinc absorption in the elderly, with simultaneous reduction in endogenous losses. Hence healthy elderly may be in positive balance on dietary intake as low as 8 mg Zn/day. However the stress of chronic disease probably increases the dietary requirement to maintain the zinc pool size. Zinc supplementation seems to be able to correct T-lymphocyte dysfunction in zinc deficient elderly. However, in a long term study, no positive effect of zinc supplementation on delayed dermal hypersensitivity was observed. To define the specific requirements, the elderly population should therefore be divided into 3 groups : a) the elderly in good health, for whom the nutritional requirements (at least for zinc) do not differ much from those for young adults ; b) the elderly under stress (social or acute diseases), for whom requirements seem to be momentarily increased ; and c) the elderly persons with chronic diseases (poor nutritional status), for whom requirements might be increased and supplementation might be necessary. (Facts and Research in Gerontology 1992)

Key-words : zinc, nutrition, elderly.

INTRODUCTION

The physiological changes of ageing, including perceptual, endocrine, gastro-intestinal, cardiovascular, renal and muscular changes, may affect nutritional needs. Nutrition may act in different ways (1). Firstly nutritional and other habits of adulthood may contribute to decrease the age-related loss of tissue function (e.g. osteo-

(*) Nestlé Ltd Research Centre, Nestec Ltd, Vers-chez-les-Blanc, CH-1000, Lausanne 26, Switzerland.

porosis). Secondly chronic degenerative diseases, such as cardiovascular and cancer, appear to be influenced by nutrition. Finally since the elderly eat less, the intake of some nutrients may fall below that of the recommended dietary allowances. These recommended dietary allowances (RDA) are the daily intakes of nutrients believed to meet the nutritional needs of the healthy population and do not consider disease states or the other prevalent problems. From nutrition surveys, there is evidence that some elderly sub-populations have an increased risk of nutritional deficiencies, since they fail to meet the RDA.

GENERAL ASPECTS OF ZINC

Zinc is an essential trace element, it is a constituant of many metallo-enzymes and is required for important metabolic processes. Dietary surveys have shown zinc intake to be low in the elderly, indicating a potential for marginal zinc deficiencies (2, 3). However, reliable methodology to assess zinc status is still lacking (4, 5). Zinc deficiency is associated with a variety of functional consequences (6) and in the elderly, mild deficiency (low intracellular zinc levels) may be associated with impaired cellular immune function (7). Dietary zinc has also been suggested as having a role in the oxygen free-radical defense (8).

Total body content of zinc is normally 2-3 g for a 70 kg man, of which 60 % is in skeletal muscle, 30 % in bone, 4 % in liver and a free exchangeable pool of 0.1 % in plasma (table 1, [9, 10]). Reported normal mean plasma values are between 71 and 110 ug/dl (10.9 - 16.8 µmol/L) [table 3] and values less than 70 ug/dl (10.7 µmol/L) are considered low [11, 12]. Many factors such as stress or inflammation however are known to influence plasma zinc levels [13].

The recommended dietary intakes in the U.S. for zinc are 15 and 12 mg/day respectively for men and women over 51 years of age [14]. Meat is the most significant source of zinc, providing over a third of the intake. However, milk, milk products and cereals are also important sources [15, 16]. Zinc absorption is affected by the presence of fibre and phytate in the diet [17] and an allowance of a 5 % decreased absorption is made for the presence of these components in food [18]. Western diets provide approximately 5 mg zinc/1000 kcal [18-20]. Excess zinc intake decreases immunological functions [21] and can induce copper deficiency [22, 23]. A provisional maximally tolerated intake of 1 mg zinc/kg body weight has been set by the FAO/WHO (table 1) [24].

TABLE 1

SELECTED DATA RELEVANT TO ZINC
(adapted from [9, 10, 12, 18, 24].

Total body content	2.5 g
Skeletal muscle	60 %
Bone	30 %
Skin	6 %
Liver	4 %
Blood plasma	0.1 %
Minimal requirement to replace endogenous losses	2.5 mg/d
U.S. RDA for male	15 mg/d
Daily intake	8-10 mg/d
Maximal tolerable intake or	70 mg/d
Safety standard	1 mg/kg body weight/d
Normal serum levels	10.7-18.4 Umol/l
	85-110 ug/dl
Low serum levels	< 70 ug/dl

CELLULAR ZINC UPTAKE AND AGING

Decreased tissue zinc uptake was suggested by its altered cellular metabolism during aging : decreased capacity for zinc accumulation in cultured aging fibroblasts [25] and in aged rat adipocytes *in vitro* (26) (figure 1) can give rise to increased levels in the plasma to maintain tissue concentration.

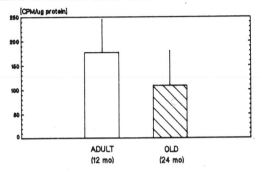

Accumulation of zinc by human fibroblasts in culture
(adapted from Sugarman and Munro [25])

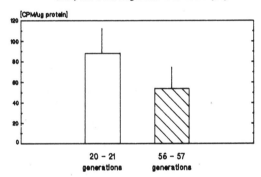

Accumulation of zinc by rat hepatocytes in culture
(Guigoz Y. et al., manuscript in preparation)

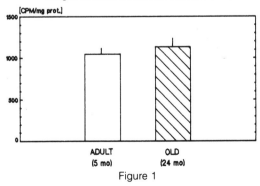

Figure 1

⁶⁵ Zn accumulation after 60 minutes incubation

The liver is central to zinc metabolism, and accounts for the major initial accumulation of newly absorbed zinc [27]. The systemic metabolism of zinc is influenced by many hormonal factors, and correlates with hormonal regulation of metallothionein (28). The capacity of rat liver parenchymal cells to take up zinc is maintained with age (figure 1). Regulation of zinc metabolism and that of metallothionein has been reported to change in parallel (29). Induction of metallothionein-I mRNA by hormones (dexamethasone and glucagon) is however impaired in cells from aged rats, while zinc treatment induced a 4 fold increase in metallothionein-I mRNA (Guigoz Y. et al., manuscript in preparation). These results indicate a possible impairment of hormonal regulation of metallothionein with age, which suggests that under stressful conditions (such as exercise or inflammation) cellular zinc metabolism could be,impaired. Zinc uptake is saturable (30) but the level of saturation appears similar in both adult and aged rat cells. Results of long term accumulation indicate that hepatocytes of aged rats show the same rate of exchange with the intracellular pool as those of adult animals.

These results suggest that nutrient uptake at the cellular level depends on tissue source and that the cells directly involved in zinc homeostasis, such as hepatocytes, seem to maintain normal metabolism except perhaps under stress.

DIETARY INTAKE OF ZINC BY THE ELDERLY

Estimated zinc consumptions are 9-13 and 6-10 mg/day for men and women respectively (table 3 [33-42]), whereas the recommended dietary intake (RDA or recommended intake, RDI) of zinc is 15 mg/day for adult males over 51 in the US [14] and 12 mg/day for the elderly over 75 years in Canada [18] (see table 2 for other countries [31, 32]). The energy intake (approx. 1 900 kcal/day for men and 1 500 kcal/day for women) is the main cause of the difference between men and women. The proportion of low intakes (below 2/3 of the RDA) is of 35 % for elderly males of 60-69 years of age, 44 % for those between 70-79 years and 60 % for those over 80 years, in a population where the mean dietary zinc intake was 12.9, 12.6 and 10.8 mg/day respectively (35). Zinc intake in the elderly parallels that of the caloric consumption and decreases with age (35), whereas the RDA stays high. Even on these low intakes of zinc (7-11.0 mg/day) normal serum values of 10.9 – 16.7 umols are found, suggesting that there is adequate zinc status (table 3) [34, 36-38, 42]. In the Boston study on the institutionalized elderly (36), less than 5 % of patients had serum zinc lower than 10.7 umol/l, which is the cutoff point generally used for risk of zinc deficiency (12).

TABLE 2
RECOMMENDED DIETARY INTAKE AROUND THE WORLD
(adapted from Truswell et al., *Nutr. Abstr. Rev.*, 1983 [31])

	Age [years]	Energy [kcal/d]	Zinc [mg/d]
Australia (1970)	60 – 69	2 020	12 – 16
Canada (1990)	75 +	2 000	12
Czechoslovakia (1981)	75 +	2 100	8
Germany (RDA, 1980)	65 +	2 200	12
Italy (1978)	70 +	2 100	15
Spain (1980)	70 +	2 100	15
Uruguay (1977)	70 +	2 100	15
U.S.A. (1989)	51 +	2 300	15
	25 – 50	2 900	15
RDA Europe (1990)	20 – 59		8 – 12

TABLE 3

ZINC AND ENERGY CONSUMPTION OF ELDERLY MEN AND WOMEN

	Age [years]	Living status	Energy [kcal/d]	Zinc [mg/d]	Serum Zn [umol/l]	Reference
Men	+ 60	Free living	2 073	9.3		Hunt W.C. et al., 1983, [33]
	+ 64	Free living		9.2	13.0	Swanson C.A. et al., 1988, [34]
	60-69	Free living	1 997	12.9		
	70-79		1 811	12.6		McGandy R.B. et al., 1986, [35]
	+ 80		1 792	10.8		
	+ 60 (72)	Nursing home	1 923	11.0	14.7	Sahyoun N.R. et al., 1988, [36]
Men & Women	+ 60 (82)	Geriatric unit		8.9	10.9	Stafford W. et al., 1988, [37]
	+ 69 (82)			7.8	12.7	
	+ 70 (79)	Housebound		6.6	11.3	Bunker V.W. et al., 1987, [38]
Women	55-85	Nursing home	2 007	8.0		Roesch K. et al., 1984, [39]
	+ 80 (91)	Nursing home	1 311	6.0		Barr S.I. et al., 1983 [40]
	+ 60 (72)	Free living	1 653	8.0		Garry P.J. et al., 1982 [41]
	60-69	Free living	1 512	10.6		
	70-79		1 469	9.7		McGandy R.B. et al., 1986 [35]
	+ 80		1 497	10.0		
	+ 60 (75)	Nursing home	1 719	10.0	14.8	Sahyoun N.R. et al., 1988 [36]
	70 (+ 58)	Free living	1 596	10.1	16.7	Gibson R.S. et al., 1985 [42]

In most studies, the percentage of women with an average intake below 2/3 of the RDA was much higher (36, 37, 41). However, the RDA standards have now been changed for women from 15 to 12 mg/day, and as a result only 58 % are considered to be below the new level, as compared with 73 % previously (16).

In summary, energy intake seems to be the important factor affecting zinc intake (43), which is about 10-12 mg daily for men and 7-9 mg daily for women (20, 43). The RDA are presently 15 mg and 12 mg for men and women, respectively, in the U.S. (18), or the more recently proposed levels of 8-12 mg/day in Europe (32).

ZINC BALANCE STUDIES

Zinc homeostasis is maintained by changes in both absorption and excretion. Balance studies are good indicators of the amount of zinc needed to maintain the body zinc pool size (43). Changes in zinc intake mainly induce changes in zinc absorption and endogeneous faecal excretion (44, 45). Adaptation has been shown to occur in young adults because they were able to maintain positive balance at intakes of 5.5 mg/d (or even as low as 3.6 mg/d), when their former intake was 16.5 mg/d (46) (or 8.3 mg/d [47]). Percentage absorption increases at lower zinc intake (table 4) [45, 48]. Approximately 4 mg of absorbed zinc is required to replace the endogenous losses of healthy young men (47, 49, 50).

At zinc intakes of 15.5 mg/d, healthy elderly men show a decrease in absorption compared to young adults, 18 % compared to 33 % (table 4) [51]. The elderly were however in positive balance since the reduction in absorption correlated with the reduction in total endogenous losses (table 5) [51]. These results suggests a possible reduction in zinc requirements for the healthy elderly. This is confirmed in studies of healthy elderly who remained in positive balance at zinc intakes of 7.8 mg/d [52] or 8.8 mg/d (table 6) [53], 50-60 % of the RDA, without biochemical signs of zinc deficiency.

TABLE 4

ZINC ABSORPTION
(adapted from Turnlund et al., 1986 [51], and Jackson et al., 1984 [48])

	Adult 22-30 yr (n = 6)	Elderly 65-74 yr (n = 4-6)
		Dietary zinc 15.5 mg/d
Urinary zinc	0.94	0.85 mg/d
Fecal zinc	14.1	14.6 mg/d
Zinc balance	0.4	0.1 mg/d
Zinc absorption	33.0 %	18.1 %

Adult, 29 yr (n = 1)	Dietary zinc [mg/d]		
	7	15	30
Urinary zinc	0.63	0.60	0.70 mg/d
Fecal zinc	6.8	14.4	30.2 mg/d
Zinc absorption	47 %	32 %	21 %

TABLE 5

ZINC ABSORPTION AND ENDOGENOUS LOSSES
(adapted from Turnlund et al., 1986 [51]

	Adult 22-30 yr (n = 6)	Elderly 65-74 yr (n = 4-6)
		Dietary zinc 15.5 mg/d
Absorbed zinc	5.1	2.8 mg/d
Endogenous fecal zinc	3.8	1.9 mg/d
Total endogenous losses	4.7	2.7 mg/d

TABLE 6

ZINC ABSORPTION AND RETENTION
(adapted from Bunker et al., 1982 [54] & 1987 [38])

	Healthy 72-85 yr (n = 10)	Housebound 70-85 yr (n = 20)
Zinc intake	8.8	5.9 mg/d
Urinary zinc	0.33	0.46 mg/d
Fecal zinc	8.2	6.5 mg/d
Net absorption	0.6	− 0.6 mg/d
Retention	0.2	− 1.0 mg/d

The housebound chronically ill elderly show reduced food consumption compared to healthy elderly, with the same zinc density in the diet, approximately 4.3 mg/1 000 kcal (38). They were in negative zinc balance which cannot be completely explained by the reduction in zinc intake compared to healthy adults (table 6). It could possibly be explained by the difference in nitrogen balance, since the healthy elderly were in positive nitrogen balance (54) while the housebound chronically ill were in negative balance (55). Nitrogen balance correlates with zinc balance (51) and the increased nitrogen loss from muscle probably increased zinc losses from the muscle pool (38).

In conclusion, healthy elderly men can be in positive zinc balance even at the low intake levels reported. However, housebound chronically ill or hospitalized elderly (56), probably have increased requirements for zinc due to their reduction in food intake and their chronic catabolic state.

ZINC SUPPLEMENTATION AND IMMUNE RESPONSE

Zinc is essential for immune function and is also important in cellular and humoral immunity (57, 58). Other nutrients, such as vitamin A, essential fatty acids or vitamin B6, however, also play important roles in immune responses (59). Aging is mainly associated with a decrease in T-cell functions, such as decline in production and response to interleukin-2, with little or no changes in humoral immune response (60).

An impaired lymphocyte production of interleukin-2 has been observed in the elderly with mild zinc deficiency (normal plasma zinc and low lymphocyte zinc content), whereas elderly with normal zinc levels had interleukin-2 production similar to adult controls (61). Short term (4.5 months) oral supplementation of zinc (60 mg/d) of anergic, zinc deficient elderly corrected their immune deficit to the values similar to their non-deficient age-matched controls (62). Using delayed dermal hypersensitivity test, dependent on T-cell functions, Bogden et al. (63-65) have shown a high prevalence of anergy (41 % of the subjects) and prevalence of responders to only one skin antigen (29 % of the subjects) at a zinc intake of 8.7 mg/d and 7.1 mg/d for men and women respectively (63). On short term (3 months) zinc supplementation, 15 mg/d or 100 mg/d, no changes related to zinc supplementation were observed in delayed dermal hypersensitivity, or in the improvement in lymphocyte proliferative response in a small number of subjects (64). With long-term supplementation (one year), 15 mg zinc/d + placebo (containing vitamins and minerals without zinc), 100 mg zinc/d + placebo or placebo only, there was a progressive improvement in delayed dermal hypersensitive response for all groups with a significantly better improvement in the placebo, multivitamin/mineral supplement group (figure 2) [65]. These results indicate a beneficial effect of multivitamin/mineral supplements in the elderly and a deleterious effect of high dosage of zinc (100 mg/d).

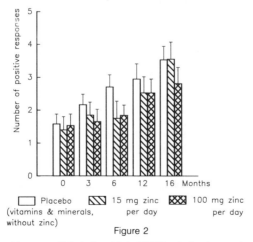

Figure 2

Delayed dermal hypersensitivity in the elderly (60-89 yrs) after 1 year of supplementation with zinc (15 or 100 mg/d) together with vitamins & minerals (from 0-12 months) (adapted from Bagden et al. [65])

The improvement of immune function might not be only dependent on zinc, but correction of protein-energy malnutrition seems to be more important in the long-term (66, 67).

ASSESSMENT OF ZINC STATUS

One of the problems in detecting zinc deficiency is that the methodology available is still relatively insensitive. Recent reviews have discussed the pros and cons of the methods available (68-70). In this section only plasma or serum zinc, metallo-thionein and leukocyte zinc content will be considered as possible indicators of zinc status.

Plasma or serum zinc are the most commonly used parameters to determine zinc status, and with severe zinc deficiency they are low (68). However zinc is rapidly redistributed to the liver during stress, inflammation or infection, mainly under the influence of cytokines (71). Metallothionein measurement has been proposed as a useful marker of zinc status, to differentiate between reduced pool size (low plasma/serum zinc and low plasma metallothionein) and tissue redistribution (low plasma zinc and high plasma metallothionein) [69, 72]. Furthermore erythrocyte metallothionein has been suggested as diagnosis for zinc status, since it responds to changes in zinc intake (73), and is not affected by stress or infection (74). However, further studies are needed before metallothionein can be used as a routine marker of zinc status in man. Another marker of zinc status which needs further investigation is the zinc content of polymorphonuclear cells, since it seems not to be affected by inflammation and stress (75). However its separation from monocytes is somewhat difficult for routine analysis (76). A potential future marker of zinc status might be thymulin, a zinc dependent thymic hormone, which is low in zinc deficiency, and could be used as a functional test (59, 70). Direct assay of thymulin level is, however, not yet available.

In summary, plasma metallothionein measurement as a complement to plasma/serum zinc levels would be the easiest method for assessing zinc status, while awaiting better biochemical indices or routine uses of immune responses, such as delayed hypersentivity response (77).

DIETARY RECOMMENDATIONS

With the physiological changes associated with aging, the appearance of chronic diseases and the resulting medication, the aged population is very heterogenous. With respect to zinc, chronic disease mag increase the requirements. The impact of drugs on the nutrient requirements is relatively unknown, but some drugs can induce specific nutrient deficiency in the elderly (78). Physiological changes related with aging might influence specific nutrients, such as decreased absorption of zinc or increased absorption of vitamine A and ß-carotene, linked with slower clearance of retinyl esters from the circulation (79), or decreased zinc excretion (51). Therefore it seems more prudent to identify requirements for the elderly taking into account three different categories (80) :

1) healthy elderly, for whom the requirements are probably similar to young adults ;

2) acutely ill elderly, with increased requirements, in response to the stress of an acute illness ; and

3) chronically ill elderly, who have a lower dietary intake and an increased need for specific nutrients as suggested by their increased lean body mass loss.

For this last group of elderly vitamin/mineral supplementation under the supervision of a physician (81) is wise (66, 67).

Further studies are however strongly needed to determine the specific requirements of the elderly, since there is some indication that requirements of certain nutrients might be higher in healthy elderly, such as vitamin B6 (82). Nutritional advice and dietary education is probably a better way to improve the nutritional status of the elderly, since dietary intakes are generally low in the elderly. Finally, an increased attention to the nutritional problems of the elderly is necessary since they are at higher risk of malnutrition, and early nutrition intervention is more appropriate.

REFERENCES

1. GUIGOZ (Y.) and MUNRO (H.N.) : Nutrition and aging. In : « Handbook of the biology of aging » (Finch C.E. & Schneider E.L., editors), 2nd ed., Van Nostrand-Reinhold, Princeton, New Jersey, 1985, pp. 878-893.
2. HUTTON (C.W.) and HAYES-DAVIS (R.B.) : Assessment of the zinc nutritional status of selected elderly subjects. J. Am. Diet. Assoc., 82, 148-153, 1983.
3. WAGNER (P.A.) : Zinc nutriture in the elderly. Geriatrics, 40, 111-125, 1985.
4. CLEMENS (R.A.) and BROWN (R.C.) : Biochemical methods for assessing the vitamin and mineral nutritional status of the elderly. Food Technol., 40, 71-81, 1986.
5. PILCH (S.M.) and SENTI (F.R.) : Analysis of zinc data from the second national health and nutrition examination survey (NHANES II). J. Nutr., 115, 1393-1397, 1985.
6. McCLAIN (C.J.), KASARKIS (E.J.) and ALLEN (J.J.) : Functional consequences of zinc deficiency. Progr. Food Nutr. Sci., 9, 185-226, 1985.
·7. KAPLAN (J.), HESS (J.W.) and PRASAD (A.S.) : Impaired interleukin-2 production in the elderly. Association with mild zinc deficiency. J. Trace Elements Exp. Med., 1, 3-8, 1988.
8. TAYLOR (C.G.) and BRAY (T.M.) : Effect of hyperoxia on oxygen free radical defense enzymes in the lung of zinc-deficient rats. J. Nutr. 121, 460-466, 1991.
9. JACKSON (M.J.) : Physiology of zinc. General aspects. In : Zinc in Human Biology, Mills (C.F.), ed., Springer-Verlag, Berlin Heidelberg, pp. 1-14, 1989.
10. JANGHORBANI (M.) and TING (B.T.G.) : Stable isotope methods for studies of mineral/trace elements metabolism. J. Nutr. Biochem., 1, 4-19, 1990.
11. GIBSON (R.S.) : Assessment of trace element status in humans. Prog. Food Nutr. Sci., 13, 67-111, 1989.
12. IYENGAR (V.) and WOITTIEZ (J.) : Trace elements in human clinical specimens ; evaluation of literature data to identify reference values., Clin. Chem., 34, 474-481, 1988.
13. GOODE (H.F.), KELLEHER (J.) and WALKER (B.E.) : The effects of acute infection on indices of zinc status. Clin. Nutr., 10, 55-59, 1991.
14. Committee on Dietary Allowances, Food and Nutrition Board, National Research Council, 1989. Recommended Dietary Allowances, 10th edition. National Academy Press, Washington, D.C.
15. HAZELL (T.) : Minerals in foods : dietary sources, chemical forms, interaction, bioavailability. World Rev. Nutr. Diet., 46, 1-123, 1985.
16. PENNINGTON (J.A.T.) and YOUNG (B.E.) : Total diet study nutritional elements, 1982-1989. Am. J. Diet. Ass., 91, 179-183, 1991.
17. TORRE (M.), RODRIGUEZ (A.R.) and SAURA-CALIXTO (F.) : Effects of dietary fiber and phytic acid on mineral availability. Crit. Rev. Food Sci. Nutr., 1, 1-22, 1991.
18. Scientific Review Committee : Nutrition Recommendations. The report of the scientific review committee 1990. Minister of National Health and Welfare (Canada).
19. COUZY (F.), AUBREE (E.), MAGLIOLA (C.) and MARESCHI (J.P.) : Average mineral and trace element content in daily adjusted (DAM) of French adults. J. Trace Elem. Electrolytes Health Dis., 2, 79-83, 1988.
20. MOSER-VEILLON (P.B.) : Zinc consumption patterns ad dietary recommendations. J. Am. Diet. Ass., 90, 1089-193, 1990.
21. CHANDRA (R.K.) : Excess intake impairs immune responses. J. Am. Med. Ass., 252, 1443-1446, 1984.
22. O'DELL (B.L.) : Mineral interactions relevant to nutrient to nutrient requirements. J. Nutr. 119, 1832-1838, 1989.
23. FOSMIRE (G.J.) : Zinc toxicity. Am. J. Clin. Nutr. 51, 225-227, 1990.
24. FOX (M.R.S.) : zinc excess. In : zinc in human biology (MILLS C.F., ed.). Springer-Verlag, Berlin Heidelberg, pp. 1-14, 1989.
25. SUGARMAN (B.) and MUNRO (H.N.) : Altered accumulation of zinc by aging human fibroblasts in culture. Life Sci., 26, 915-920, 1980.
26. SUGARMAN (B.) and MUNRO (H.N.) : Altered (65Zn) chloride accumulation by aged rats' adipocytes in vitro. J. Nutr., 110, 2317-2320, 1985.

27. COUSINS (R.J.) : Absorption, transport, and hepatic metabolism of copper and zinc. Special reference to metallothionein and ceruloplasmin. *Physiol. Rev.,* 65, 238-309.
28. BREMNER (I.) and MAY (P.M.) : Systemic interactions of zinc. *In :* zinc in human biology (Mills C.F., ed.), Springer-Verlag, Berlin Heidelberg, pp. 95-108, 1989.
29. COUSINS (R.J.), DUNN (M.A.), LEINART (A.S.), YEDINAK (R.C.) and DI SILVESTRO (R.A.) : Coordinate regulation of zinc metabolism and metallothionein gene expression in rats. *Am. J. Physiol.,* 251, E688-E694, 1986.
30. PATTISON (S.E.) and COUSINS (R.J.) : Kinetic of zinc uptake and exchange by primary cultures of rat hepatocytes. *Am. J. Physiol.,* 250, E677-E685, 1986.
31. TRUSWELL (A.S.), IRWIN (T.), BEATON (G.H.), SUZUE (R.), HAENEL (H.), HEDJA (S.), HOU (X.C.), LEVEILLE (G.), MORAVA (E.), PEDERSEN (J.) and STEPHEN (J.M.L.) : Recommended intakes around the world. A report by committee 1/5 of the International Union of Nutritional Sciences. *Nutr. Abstr. Rev.* 53, 1075-1119, 1983.
32. Report of workshops organised by the Nutrition Working Group of International Life Science Institute (I.L.S.I.) Europe. Recommended daily amounts of vitamins and minerals in Europe. *Nutr. Abstr. Rev.,* 60, 827-842, 1990.
33. HUNT (W.C.), LEONARD (A.G.), GARRY (P.J.) and GOODWIN (J.S.) : Components of variance in dietary data for elderly population. *Nutr. Res.,* 3, 433-444, 1983.
34. SWANSON (C.A.), MANSOURIAN (R.), DIRREN (H.) and RAPIN (C.H.) : Zinc status of healthy elderly adults, response to supplementation. *Am. J. Clin. Nutr.* 48, 343-349, 1988.
35. McGANDY (R.B.), RUSSELL (R.M.), HARTZ (S.C.), JACOB (R.A.), TANNENBAUM (S.), PETERS (H.), SAHYOUN (N.) and OTRADOVEC (C.L.) : Nutritional status survey of healthy noninstitutionalized elderly. Energy and nutrient intakes from three-day diet records and nutrient supplements. *Nutr. Res.,* 6, 785-798, 1986.
36. SAHYOUN (N.), OTRADOVEC (C.L.), HARTZ (S.C.), JACOB (R.A.), PETERS (H.), RUSSELL (R.M.) and McGANDY (R.B.) : Dietary intakes and biochemical indicators of nutritional status in an elderly, institutionalized population. *Am. J. Clin. Nutr.,* 47, 524-533, 1988.
37. STAFFORD (W.), SMITH (R.G.), LEWIS (S.J.), HENERY (E.), STEPHEN (P.J.), RAFFERTY (J.), SIMPSON (G.K.), BELLS (P.C.) and O'RORKE (K.) : A study of zinc status of elderly institutionalized patients. *Age & Ageing* 17, 42-48, 1988.
38. BUNKER (V.W.), HINKS (L.J.), STANSFIELD (M.F.), LAWSON (M.S.) and CLAYTON (B.E.) : Metabolic balance studies for zinc and copper in housebound elderly people and the relationship between zinc balance and leukocyte zinc concentrations. *Am. J. Clin. Nutr.* 46, 353-359, 1987.
39. ROESCH (K.), PATTERSON (C.) and REILLY (C.) : Daily copper, zinc and iron intake of elderly patients in a nursing home. *Proc. Nutr. Soc.* 9, 132, 1984.
40. BARR (S.I.), CHRYSOMILIDES (S.A.), WILLIS (E.J.) and BEATTIE (B.L.) : Nutrient intakes of the old elderly ; a study of female residents of a long-term care facility. *Nutr. Res.* 3, 417-431, 1983.
41. GARRY (P.J.), GOODWIN (J.S.), HUNT (W.C.), HOOPER (E.M.) and LEONARD (A.G.) : Nutritional status in a healthy elderly population, dietary and supplemental intakes. *Am. J. Clin. Nutr.* 36, 319-331, 1982.
42. GIBSON (R.S.), MARTINEZ (O.B.) and MacDONALD (A.C.) : The zinc, copper, and selenium status of selected sample of canadian elderly women. *J. Gerontol.* 40, 296-302, 1985.
43. MERTZ (W.) : Use and misuse of balance studies. *J. Nutr.* 117, 1811-1813, 1987.
44. WASTNEY (M.E.), AAMODT (R.L.), RUMBLE (W.F.) and HENKIN (R.I.) : Kinetic analysis of zinc metabolism and its regulation in normal humans. *Am. J. Physiol.* 251, R 398-R 408, 1986.
45. TAYLOR (C.M.), BACON (J.R.), AGGETT (P.J.) and BREMNER (I.) : Homeostatic regulation of zinc absorption and endogenous losses in zinc-deprived men. *Am. J. Clin. Nutr.* 53, 755-763, 1991.
46. WADA (L.), TURNLUND (J.R.) and KING (J.C.) : Zinc utilization in young men fed adequate and low zinc intakes. *J. Nutr.* 115, 1345-1354, 1985.
47. MILNE (D.B.), CANFIELD (W.K.), MAHALKO (J.R.) and SANDSTEAD (H.H.) : Effect of dietary zinc on whole body surface loss of zinc ; impact on estimation of zinc retention by balance method. *Am. J. Clin. Nutr.* 38, 181-186, 1983.
48. JACKSON (M.J.), JONES (D.A.), EDWARDS (R.H.T.), SWAINBANK (I.G.) and COLEMAN (M.L.) : Zinc homeostasis in man ; studies using a new stable isotope-dilution technique. *Br. J. Nutr.* 51, 199-208, 1984.
49. KING (J.C.) : Assessment of techniques for determining human zinc requirements. *J. Am. Diet. Ass.,* 86, 1523-1528, 1986.
50. BAER (M.T.) and KING (J.C.) : Tissue zinc levels and zinc excretion during experimental zinc depletion in young men. *Am. J. Clin. Nutr.* 39, 556-570, 1984.
51. TURNLUND (J.R.), DURKIN (N.), COSTA (F.) and MARGEN (S.) : Stable isotope studies of zinc absorption and retention in young and elderly men. *J. Nutr.* 116, 1239-1247, 1986.
52. BURKE (D.B.), DeMICCO (F.J.), TAPER (L.J.) and RITCHEY (S.J.) : Copper and zinc utilization in elderly adults. *J. Gerontol.* 36, 558-563, 1981.
53. BUNKER (V.W.), HINKS (L.J.), LAWSON (M.S.) and CLAYTON (B.E.) : Assessment of zinc and copper status of healthy elderly people using metabolic balance studies and measurement of leucocyte concentrations. *Am. J. Clin. Nutr.* 40, 1096-1102, 1984.

54. BUNKER (V.W.), LAWSON (M.S.), DELVES (H.T.) and CLAYTON (B.E.) : Metabolic balance studies for zinc and nitrogen in healthy elderly subjects. *Hum. Nutr. Clin. Nutr. 36C,* 213-221, 1982.

55. BUNKER (V.W.), LAWSON (M.S.), STANSFIELD (M.F.) and CLAYTON (B.E.) : Nitrogen balance studies in apparently healthy elderly people and those who are housebound. *Br. J. Nutr. 57,* 211-221, 1987.

56. THOMAS (A.J.), BUNKER (V.W.), HINKS (L.J.), SODHA (N.), MULLEE (M.A.) and CLAYTON (B.E.) : Energy, protein and copper status of twenty-one elderly inpatients ; analysed dietary intake and biochemical indices. *Br. J. Nutr. 59,* 181-191, 1988.

57. FRAKER (P.J.), GERSHWIN (M.E.), GOOD (R.A.) and PRASAD (A.) : Interrelationships between zinc and immune function. *Fed. Proc. 45,* 1474-1479, 1986.

58. KRUSE-JARRES (J.D.) : The significance of zinc for humoral and cellular immunity. *J. Trace Elem. Electrolytes Health Dis. 3,* 1-8, 1989.

59. CHANDRA (R.K.) : 1990 McCollum Award Lecture. Nutrition and immunity : lessons from the past and new insights into future. *Am. J. Clin. Nutr. 53,* 1087-1101, 1991.

60. MILLER (R.A.) : Aging and the immune response. *In :* Handbook of the biology of aging, third edition. Schneider (E.L.) and Rowe (J.W.), editors, *Academic Press,* San Diego, pp. 157-180, 1990.

61. KAPLAN (J.), HESS (J.W.) and PRASAD (A.S.) : Impaired interleukin-2 production in the elderly : association with mild zinc deficiency. *J. Trace Elem. Exper. Med. 1,* 3-8, 1988.

62. COSSACK (Z.T.) : T-lymphocyte dysfunction in the elderly associated with zinc deficiency and subnormal nucleoside phosphorylase activity ; effect of zinc supplementation. *Eur. J. Cancer Clin. Oncol. 25,* 973-976, 1989.

63. BOGDEN (J.D.), OLESKE (J.M., MUNVES (E.M.), LAVENHAR (M.A.), BRUENING (K.S.), KEMP (F.W.), HOLDING (K.J.), DENNY (T.N.) and LOURIA (D.B.) : Zinc and immuno competence in the elderly : baseline data on zinc nutritive and immunity in un supplemented subjects. *Am. J. Clin. Nutr. 46,* 101-109, 1987.

64. BOGDEN (J.D.), OLESKE (J.M.), LAVENHAR (M.A.), MUNVES (E.M.), KEMP (F.W.), BRUENING (K.S.), HOLDING (K.J.), DENNY (T.N.), GUARINO (M.A.), KRIEGER (L.M.) and HOLLAND (B.K.) : Zinc and immunocompetence in elderly people ; effects of zinc supplementation for 3 months. *Am. J. Clin. Nutr. 48,* 655-663, 1988.

65. BOGDEN (J.D.), OLESKE (J.M.), LAVENHAR (M.A.), MUNVES (E.M.), KEMP (F.W.), BRUENING (K.S.), HOLDING (K.J.), DENNY (T.N.), GUARINO (M.A.) and HOLLAND (B.K.) : Effects of one year of supplementation with zinc and other micronutrients on cellular immunity in the elderly. *J. Am. Coll. Nutr., 9,* 214-225, 1990.

66. CHANDRA (R.K.) : Nutritional regulation of immunity and risk of infection in old age. *Immunology 67,* 141-147, 1989.

67. LESOURD (B.), FAVRE-BERRONE (M.), THIOLLET (M.), GAUDEL (M.), MELANI (M.), PIETTE (F.) and MOULIAS (R.) : Action immunostimulante d'une supplémentation orale complète chez des sujets âgés dénutris. *Age et Nutr. 1,* 41-51, 1990.

68. GIBSON (R.E.) : Assessment of trace element status in humans. *Prog. Food Nutr. Sci. 13,* 67-111, 1989.

69. KING (J.C.) : Assessment of zinc status. *J. Nutr. 120,* 1474-1479, 1990.

70. THOMPSON (R.P.H.) : Assessment of zinc status. *Proc. Nutr. Soc. 50,* 19-28, 1991.

71. COUSINS (R.J.) and LEINART (A.S.) : Tissue-specific regulation of zinc metabolism and metallothionein genes by interleukin-1. *FASEB J. 2,* 2884-2890, 1988.

72. BREMNER (I.) : Interactions between metallothionein and trace elements. *Prog. Food Nutr. Sci. 11,* 1-37, 1987.

73. GRIDER (A.), BAILEY (L.B.) and COUSINS (R.J.) : Erythrocyte metallothionein as an index of zinc status in humans. *Proc. Natl. Acad. Sci. USA 87,* 1259-1262, 1990.

74. BREMNER (I.), MORRISON (J.N.), WOOD (A.M.) and ARTHUR (J.R.) : Effects of changes in dietary zinc, copper and selenium and of endotoxin administration on metallothionein I concentrations in blood cells and urine in the rat. *J. Nutr. 117,* 1595-1602, 1987.

75. GOODE (H.F.), KELLEHER (J.) and WALKER (B.E.) : The effects of acute infection on indices of zinc status. *Clin. Nutr. 10,* 55-59, 1991.

76. GOODE (H.F.), KELLEHER (J.) and WALKER (B.E.) : Zinc concentrations in pure populations of peripheral blood neutrophils, lymphocytes and monocytes. *Ann. Clin. Biochem., 26,* 89-95, 1989.

77. RUZ (M.), CAVAN (K.R.), BETTGER (W.), THOMPSON (L.), BERRY (M.) and GIBSON (R.S.) : Development of a dietary model for the study of mild zinc deficiency in humans and evaluation of some biochemical and functional indices of zinc status. *Am. J. Clin. Nutr. 53,* 1295-1303, 1991.

78. ROE (D.E.) : Drug-nutrient interactions in the elderly. *In :* Nutrition, aging and the elderly. Munro (H.N.) and Danford (D.E.), editors. *Plenum Press,* New York, pp. 363-384, 1989.

79. Anonymous : Processing of dietary retinoids is slowed in the elderly. *Nutr. Rev. 49,* 116-119, 1991.

80. VELLAS (B.-J.) and ALBAREDE (J.-L.) : Nutrient requirements of the elderly. *In :* L'Année Gérontologique 1990. Albarède (J.-L.), Vellas (P.) and Rouzaud (D.), editors, *Maloine,* Paris, 1990, pp. 101-113.

81. Coucil of Scientific Affairs : Vitamin preparations as dietary supplements and as therapeutic agents. *JAMA 257,* 1929-1936, 1987.

82. RIBAYA-MERCADO (J.D.), RUSSELL (R.M.), SAHYOUN (N.), MORROW (F.D.) and GERSHOFF (S.N.) : Vitamin B6 requirements of the elderly men and women. *J. Nutr. 121,* 1062-1074, 1991.

TECHNIQUES AND INDICATIONS OF PERCUTANEOUS ENDOSCOPIC GASTROSTOMY IN THE ELDERLY

H. WERNER, B. KARK (*)

Summary. – Malnutrition and undernutrition in the elderly are common problems in Geriatric Medicine. Many of these patients need enteral or parenteral feeding often for extended periods to supply sufficient nutrients and calories. Parenteral feeding via central venous line or enteral feeding by nasogastric tube are widely applicated methods of artificial nutrition. Their use however is limited by the risk of severe complications or they are poorly tolerated by patients. Percutaneous endoscopic gastrostomy (PEG) is an alternative method of enteral nutrition which is indicated in elderly patients who are unwilling or unable to consume sufficient calories to meet their metabolic demands. We report our experience with PEG in 113 patients 65 yrs plus. In our opinion PEG has proved to be a safe and simple method of tube placement for enteral feeding, if contraindications and handling guidelines are carefully observed. PEG is well tolerated by the old patients and is easy to handle for carers and nursing staff. Feeding by PEG is feasable at home or in nursing homes so that patients can be discharged with PEG tube to their own surroundings or to nursing homes. As PEG is an invasive therapy the decision of implantation has to be made up for each individual patient according to medical standards and with highest respect of the old patient's personality and life circumstances. If ethical issues are carefully taken into consideration PEG is not a method of senseless life prolongation but a method which can help the patient to overcome a disabling condition and improve his quality of life. (Facts and Research in Gerontology 1992)

Key-words : aging, undernutrition, enteral feeding, percutaneous endoscopic gastrostomy.

INTRODUCTION

Malnutrition and undernutrition of elderly patients are common problems in geriatric medicine. The causes of this condition vary widely and are most often due to

(*) Städtische Kliniken Frankfurt-Höchst, Frankfurt/Main (Germany). D 6370, Oberdursel.

severe physical disability such as stroke, decreased mobility or tumor, to mental disabilities or ignorance or to social problems such as social isolation, loneliness or poverty.

Alcohol consumption and/or drugs may contribute to malnutrition (1).

The first concern in elderly people with nutritional problems must be the correct diagnosis and treatment of the underlying disease whenever this is possible.

According to a British survey about 3 % of the elderly population suffer from mal- or undernutrition (2).

Prevalence of malnutrition is difficult to determine. Clinical setting and functional status can influence prevalence rates (3). In hospitalized elderly subjects prevalence rates of malnutrition rank from 26 % in a British study of medical patients to 43 % in a study of medical inpatients at the University of Alabama (2).

In all geriatric units one can find the cachectic old patient with multipathology who is admitted to hospital because of an additional acute condition. The patient is depleted of nutritional reserves, he refuses to eat and to drink and his condition deteriorates rapidly from day to day.

These patients are predisposed to infections and to develop pressure sores. In addition, anorectic patients are too weak and frail for mobilisation and can therefore often not be rehabilitated. They are at great risk to loose their competence, to become dependent and not able to live on their own.

Old patients undergoing major surgery, suffering from chronic wasting disease or other chronic conditions need more proteins than healthy elderly subjects. Survivors in longitudinal studies, who maintained a good health over the years of observation, continued to eat well, whereas poor health was associated with poor nutritional status (4).

Elderly patients, who are unable to take sufficient oral alimentation require effective means to supply nutrients often for extended periods.

For a short time parenteral feeding via peripheral vein or central venous line is a useful method, especially for patients in acute metabolic stress such as major surgical interventions (1).

This method however carries the risk of severe complications such as catheter thrombosis, catheter sepsis and dislocation (5).

Longtime enteral feeding via nasoenteral tube is complicated by nasopharyngeal and esophageal ulceration. Nasoenteral tubes are poorly tolerated by patients, which is confirmed by high rates of dislodgement due to tubes being pulled out or falling out (6).

Surgical gastrostomies have been associated with significant morbidity and are quite costly (7).

This contribution focuses on percutaneous endoscopic gastrostomy (PEG), a method of enteral nutrition which was originally developed about 10 years ago for patients with cancer or severe neurologic diseases. It is only a few years ago that geriatricians discovered PEG for their patients (8, 9).

This method of longterm feeding in elderly patients has been used since more than 2 years at the Department of Geriatric Medicine at Hoechst Hospital in Frankfurt.

TECHNICAL ASPECTS

The basic procedure was developed by Ponsky and Gauderer in 1981 (10). It was slightly modified during the last years and we use a prefab PEG-set which was developed by Keymling (11) and which is produced by Fresenius Company, Oberursel. The tube is made of polyurethan with a diameter of 2.9 mm (9 Ch).

After general intravenous sedation (5 mg Midazolam) gastroscopy is performed with the patient in a supine or semisupine position. A brief endoscopic examination is done to insure that no significant pathology is present in the esophagus, stomach and duodenum. The stomach is then inflated with air so that the anterior gastric wall is apposed to the anterior abdominal wall.

With the room lights dimmed, the light of the instrument is transluminating the abdominal wall. This is the point where after local anesthesia and a small incision a percutaneous cannula is thrust into the stomach. The metal stylet is removed and a silk thread is inserted through the cannula into the stomach and then grasped endoscopically with the biopsy forceps.

The gastroscope is now removed together with the biopsy forceps and the guiding silk thread. The latter is fixed to the top of the feeding tube, which is then pulled by hand traction at the percutaneous end of the silk thread through mouth, esophagus, stomach and abdominal wall. The intragastric tip of the tube carries a flexible disc, which is brought up against the gastric mucosa to avoid dislocation of the tube.

When we started with PEG more than two years ago we performed a second gastroscopy to verify the intragastric position of the tube. Today we do not think it is necessary.

The feeding tube is not sutured to the skin. Instead of this a flexible disc like the intragastric one is put to the exit site of the tube to hold it in position. A clamp is now slipped over the tube and a Luer lock stuck to the end of it.

The procedure takes not more than 15 – 20 min. Two doctors and a nurse are needed. One doctor is doing the gastroscopy, the other the abdominal puncture. The nurse is monitoring the patient's vital functions.

Antibiotic prophylaxis (1 g Cefazolin) is given routinely in most patients 30 min before starting the procedure as recommended by Naresh and co-workers (12). By doing this we could achieve a considerable reduction of local wound infection and had no clinically evident peritonitis.

Feeding can be started with tea immediately after placement of the tube.

PATIENTS (Table 1)

In our hospital we performed 148 PEGs following this method. 113 (76 %) of our patients were 65 and over (mean age 78,4), 35 (24 %) under the age of 65.

TABLE I : PATIENTS

– 148 PEGs   64 % females   36 % males
– 113 PEGs (76 %) in patients 65 yrs plus (mean age 78.4)
–   35 PEGs (24 %) in patients under 65 yrs (mean age 52.4)

INDICATIONS FOR PEG IN GERIATRIC MEDICINE (Table 2)

In general PEG is indicated in old patients who are unwilling or unable to consume sufficient calories to meet their metabolic demands and who have an otherwise normal functioning gastrointestinal tract.

The first indication group includes patients who are unwilling to take adequate nutrients because they are too frail and too weak, or because they suffer from loss of appetite or severe depression. In some cases several of these factors contribute to inadequate nutrition.

In 35 % of our patients PEG was implanted for this indication.

The second indication group consists of patients who are not able to eat adequately. 67 % of our patients in this group had a stroke with swallowing dysfunction. In these patients PEG is extremely useful, because undernutrition hinders successful

TABLE 2 : INDICATIONS FOR PEG

PATIENTS UNWILLING TO EAT

- WEAKNESS, FRAILTY, AFTER MAJOR SURGERY
- LOSS OF APPETITE
- CACHEXIA
- SEVERE MENTAL DISORDERS

PATIENTS UNABLE TO EAT

- STROKE
- SWALLOWING DYSFUNCTION
- NEUROLOGIC DISORDERS
- SEVERE CONFUSION/DEMENTIA
- LONGLASTING COMA
- MALIGNANT DISEASE (TUMOR OF PHARYNX, ESOPHAGUS)

stroke rehabilitation and swallowing function can be trained simultaneously by oral feeding. Once the swallowing function is completely restored, PEG tube can be removed any time. If swallowing dysfunction turns out to be irreversible, nutritional status of the patient can be maintained by longterm feeding via PEG.

17 % of the second group had malignant tumors, most of them tumors of the tongue or pharynx and a few tumors of the esophagus provided that the tumor could be passed by the gastroscope.

Other indications were longlasting coma, severe dementing illness, other neurologic disorders, i.e. hypoxic brain damage, severe Parkinson syndrome.

CONTRAINDICATIONS (Table 3)

PEG should not be done if translumination of the abdominal wall cannot be achieved. In two cases we interrupted the procedure because of this problem. We gave these patients a laxative and PEG was successfully repeated two days later. In 7 patients with tumors of the upper gastrointestinal tract the tumor could not be passed endoscopically, so PEG could not be performed. In all other patients PEG tube could be successfully implanted. The decision for PEG should be made up before the tumor completely obstructs the pharynx or esophagus.

Other contraindications for PEG are the acute abdomen of any etiology, gastrointestinal bleeding, bleeding disorders, gastric cancer and vomiting refractory to therapy.

Gastric or duodenal ulcer is in our opinion not a contraindication for PEG. This is confirmed by other authors (13).

TABLE 3 : CONTRAINDICATIONS FOR PEG

– TRANSLUMINATION NOT ACHIEVED – ACUTE ABDOMEN OF ANY ETIOLOGY – BLEEDING DISORDERS – GASTROINTESTINAL BLEEDING – INVASIVE GASTRIC CANCER – VOMITING REFRACTORY TO THERAPY

COMPLICATIONS (Table 4)

The overall procedure related complications in our patient group come to about 24 %. Most of these were minor complications like wound erythema and/or secretion at the site of insertion. In none of these cases it was necessary to remove the tube. All peristomal wound infections were successfully treated by careful dressing and topical Providone iodine.

Local infections could be significantly reduced by routine administration of antibiotic prophylaxis.

Pneumoperitoneum was observed in three patients, although the rate of this phenomenon might be greater if x-ray of the abdomen would be performed in every patient. Pneumoperitoneum is created by gastroscopic air insufflation in association with percutaneous puncture of the stomach (14). It is a minor complication which has no clinical consequences.

In our patient group no bleeding complication or important hematoma occured.

We did not observe aspiration after PEG. This complication occurs in about 1 % according to other authors (8, 11). Feeding the patient in an upright or semi-upright

TABLE 4 : COMPLICATIONS (n = 113)

(OVERALL COMPLICATIONS 23.9 %)	
– LOCAL INFECTION	12
– PNEUMOPERITONEUM	3
– PERITONITIS	1
– BLEEDING COMPLICATIONS	0
– LOCAL HEMATOMA	0
– DISLOCATION OF THE TUBE	3
– ASPIRATION	0
– OCCLUSION OF THE TUBE	3
– DIARRHEA	6
– PROCEDURE RELATED DEATH	0

position and pump controlled running in of the nutrition fluid can avoid this complication to a great extent.

Diarrhea occured in 5 patients. This problem is in most cases caused by inadvertantly too rapid running of the nutrition fluid. Pump controlled running in can solve this problem. In case of diarrhea feeding should be stopped for one day and then restarted cautiously.

Occlusion of the tube occured in two patients, one could be reopened, the other had to be replaced. Occlusion can be avoided by regular and careful rinsing of the tube with water or tea.

Two patients − both of them confused − removed the tube which was replaced without any problems.

One patient had a local peritonitis, which was not diagnosed clinically but at autopsy. The patient died because of intracerebral bleeding. The pathologist noticed local inflammation and fibrin at the site of the puncture. This phenomenon reflects perhaps more the desired effect of fibrous connection of parietal and visceral peritoneum and is not what the clinician calls an acute peritonitis.

One of the younger patients with pharynx tumor had a cardiac arrest after getting the intravenous sedation but before starting the procedure. Reanimation was not successful. In our elderly patient group we had no procedure related death, but 28 % of these patients died during hospital attendance because of their severe underlying disease.

BENEFITS OF PEG FOR ELDERLY PATIENTS (Table 5)

39 % of our patients were discharged to their homes, 10 % to a nursing home. In all these cases relatives and/or nurses were instructed how to handle the PEG tube, which is easy to learn. Our oldest patient, a 88 year old lady, was discharged to a nursing home, with PEG. Her condition stabilized, she began to take food orally and PEG could be removed 5 months later.

We observe one patient with irreversible swallowing dysfunction after stroke, who got a PEG tube in January 1990. She is keeping well at home and is nursed by her husband.

Patients tolerate PEG much better than nasogastric tubes, not only because PEG does not irritate the nasopharyngeal area, but also because PEG is not visible and this cosmetic aspect is important for the patient living at home or in a nursing home.

TABLE 5 : ADVANTAGES OF PEG

- PEG MAKES SUPPLY OF CALORIES, PROTEINS AND FLUIDS POSSIBLE
- ORAL FEEDING CAN BE TRAINED SIMULTANEOUSLY
- PEG CAN BE REMOVED ANY TIME
- PATIENTS CAN BE DISCHARGED WITH PEG TO THEIR HOME OR NURSING HOME
- PEG IS BETTER TOLERATED THAN NASOGASTRIC TUBES
- PEG HAS LESS COMPLICATIONS THAN CENTRAL VENOUS CATHETER
- HANDLING OF PEG IS SIMPLE AND FEASABLE FOR NURSING STAFF, CARING RELATIVES AND FOR PATIENTS
- PEG IS HIGHLY ACCEPTED BY CARERS AND PATIENTS
- PEG IS A SIMPLE AND COST EFFECTIVE PROCEDURE

DISADVANTAGES OF PEG (Table 6)

PEG is an invasive procedure, which has a certain rate of complications.

It is a method of artificial nutrition which cannot replace normal eating and particularly the epicurean joy and pleasure which is related to a delicious meal. Undoubtedly feeding via PEG puts considerable psychological strain on the patient.

TABLE 6 : DISADVANTAGES OF PEG

```
– INVASIVE PROCEDURE WITH COMPLICATIONS
– ARTIFICIAL METHOD OF NUTRITION
```

GUIDELINES FOR HANDLING OF THE PEG

Table 7 gives practical guidelines for handling of the PEG tube. Most problems coming up in the course of feeding via PEG can be avoided by careful and skilled handling and nursing of the tube.

TABLE 7 : GUIDELINES FOR HANDLING OF PEG

```
– START NUTRITION WITH TEA
– FEEDING WITH THE PATIENT IN UPRIGHT/SEMIUPRIGHT POSITION
– NUTRITION FLUID SHOULD BE WARMED UP
– SLOW RUNNING OF THE NUTRITION FLUID
  (Approx. 500 ml/6 hs by pump)
– REGULAR RINSING OF THE TUBE WITH WATER OR TEA
– DAILY REPLACEMENT OF THE LEAD
– CAREFUL ORAL HYGIENE TO AVOID STOMATITIS OR DENTAL LESIONS
– IN CASE OF DIARRHEA
     – ONLY TEA
     – NUTRITION FLUID TOO COLD ?
     – RUNNING IN TOO FAST ?
     – BACTERIAL CONTAMINATION ?
– DRUGS CAN BE GIVEN VIA PEG
```

ETHICAL ISSUES RELATED TO THE USE OF PEG IN GERIATRIC MEDICINE

When the Geriatrician applies invasive therapies to his patients, a debate arises automatically if such therapies are sensible and justified in old patients. This is also the case with PEG.

For this procedure the same high professional standards must be applicated as for other invasive procedures.

The patient must give informed consent.

If his ability of decision making is not given, the relatives of the patient must be consulted. If this is not possible the geriatrician has to make up his decision for implanting PEG in each individual patient according to medical standards and with highest respect of the patient's personality and likely wishes, his circumstances of life and the underlying disease.

If these ethical issues are carefully taken into consideration, PEG is not a method of senseless life prolongation but a method which can help the patient to overcome a disabling condition ; it can help to relieve suffering ; it can help to keep the old patient in his familiar surroundings being cared by his relatives or by a community nurse ; it can contribute to restore or at least to improve the patient's mobility ; it can support his rehabilitation ; it can contribute to the old patient's well-being and joy of life.

Taking all these points into account, PEG can improve the old patient's life quality.

REFERENCES

1. LETSOU (A.P.), PRICE (L.S.) : Health, aging and nutrition. An overview. In : *Clinics in Geriatric Medicine*, 3, 2, 1987.
2. CAPE (R.D.T.) : Malnutrition, weight loss and anorexia. In : *The Merck Manual of Geriatrics*. Rahway, N.J., 1990.
3. BECK (J.C.), Ed. : Geriatric review syllabus, 1989-1990. Program. *Am. Ger. Soc.*, New York, NY 1989.
4. CAPE (R.D.T.) : Nutrition and the elderly. In : Cape (R.D.T.), Coe (R.M.), Rossmann (I.) (eds) : Fundamentals of geriatric medicine. *Raven Press*, New York, 1983.
5. CLEMENT (Th.), LEMBCKE (B.) : Enterale Sondenernährung und perkutane endoskopische Gastrostomie (PEG). *Inn. Med.*, 18, 1991, 48.
6. MEER (J.A.) : Inadvertent dislodgement of nasoenteral feeding tubes. Incidence and prevention. *JPEN*, 11, 1987, 187.
7. KIRBY (D.F.) CRAIG (R.M.) et al. : Percutaneous endoscopic gastrostomies. A prospective evaluation and review of the literature. *JPEN*, 10, 1986, 155.
8. HONNETH (J.), NEHEN (H.G.) : PEG - effiziente Methode für die enterale Langzeiternährung. *Geriatrie Praxis*, 2, 1990, 56.
9. WERNER (H.) : PEG in der Geriatrie. Lecture given at the 3. Annual Meeting of the Deutsche Gesellschaft für Geriatrie in Hannover, 1989.
10. PONSKY (J.L.), GAUDERER (M.W.L.) : Percutaneous endoscopic gastrostomy. A nonoperative technique for feeding gastrostomy. *Gastrointest. Endosc.*, 27, 1981, 9.
11. KEYMLING (M.) : Perkutane endoskopisch kontrollierte Gastrostomie. *Z. Gastroenterologie* (Suppl. 2), 27, 1989, 65.
12. NARESH (K.J.), LARSON (D.E.) et al. : Antibiotic prophylaxis for percutaneous endoscopic gastrostomy. *Ann. Intern. Med.*, 107, 1987, 824.
13. KEYMLING (M.) : personal communication.
14. FOUTCH (P.G.) HAYNES (W.C.) et al. : Percutaneous endoscopic gastrostomy (PEG). *J. Clin. Gastroenterol.*, 8 (1) ; 1986, 10.

NEWS IN GERONTOLOGY
AND NUTRITION

We present here the abstracts of articles published in the international editions of Facts and Research in Gerontology 1992. Reprint are available to the authors (see contributors directory) or to Serdi : 29, rue de Saint-Pétersbourg, 75008 Paris.

1 - PROTEINO-ENERGY MALNUTRITION IN THE ELDERLY : EPIDEMIOLOGICAL DATA :
E. Alix, J.-M. Vetel

Summary. *– Nutrititional status in elderly free living, acute or long stay wards has been reviewed, to establish prevalence. Various problems are analysed by the authors, especially the instruments of assessment, which are of a poor sensitivity and specificity. Dietetic assessment shows low rates of reliability, anthropometric measurements depend on the clinician's experience and are inappropriate to evaluate variation dependent to duration. Biological assays for nutritional assessment are available, but clinicians need elderly « standards ». In term of energy intake, well being ambulatory elderly show a small prevalence for undernutrition but elderly inpatients, in acute care wards as well as in long stay wards, are in the opposite frequently undernourished (50 %). The goal itself of the long stay wards is to support mixed and complex pathology (i.e. cancer, chronic infection, or various disease acting on nutritionnal status). Treatment of such illness need several answers, as different as nutritional help by tube feeding or endoscopic gastrostomy in some cases, care for depression, dietetic enjoyment or time for social worker to help eating the most dependent veteran. The authors insist on the fact that the experience of a long stay wards cannot be extended to all institutions having in charge elderly inpatients, and that each of these institutions has first to evaluate their own nutritional problems before answering to the question of treatment. In this domain experience cannot be exported.*
(Facts and Research in Gerontology 1992)

Key-words : *epidemiology, undernutrition, elderly.*

2 - CRITICAL STUDY ON THE VALIDITY OF THE PROTEIN-ENERGY MALNUTRITION MARKERS IN THE ELDERLY : G. Debry, A. Tebi, C. Jeandel, N. Chau, G. Cuny

Summary. *– Protein energy malnutrition markers are used for detection of incipient malnutrition, for diagnosis of evolutive malnutrition or chronological assessment of nutrition improvement during therapeutic refeeding. The various dietetic, clinical, anthropometric and biological markers are of varying sensitivity and specificity. The markers' predictive value depends on how they are associated. If severe malnutrition is easy to diagnose, moderate or incipient malnutrition is often difficult to establish. The significant dispersion in the protein energy malnutrition prevalences observed during surveys both amongst the general population and in hospitals or institutions can be explained, for one part, by the difficulty in establishing the diagnose,* *but above all by the great variability in the concerned age groups, the diversity in the used markers and the heterogeneity in the values being chosen for determination of the decision thresholds. Identification of markers with a high-probability incipient protein energy malnutrition prediction rate would really be useful both for the practician and for the elderly, since this would, by simple measures, save the psychological, sociological and economic cost of hospitalization. These data are developed using a personal study as a basis. (Facts and Research in Gerontology 1992)*

Key-words : *Malnutrition, markers, plasma protein, trace element, aged.*

3 - IMPEDANCEMETRY AND THE ELDERLY SUBJECT OR HOW TO PRACTICALLY MEASURE BODY COMPOSITION AND WATER CONTENT IN THE ELDERLY :
M. Ferry, A. Boulier, B. Lesourd, A.-L. Thomasset

Summary. – *Evaluation of the nutritional status and the state of health in the elderly requires quantification of body composition and body water. The human organism could theoretically be divided into two parts, one being biologically hightly active : lean body mass, the other one being less active but constituting an energy reserve : body fat (BF). The best part of the body composition weight is held by water (body total water content : TWC). In spite of their significance, body composition and water content are rarely measured. Such defaulting, even more serious in Geriatrics, is mostly due to technical problems of practical feasibility. Different methods for body composition evaluation have, indeed, been developed. Some of them (hydrostatic densiometry, volumetric densiometry, potassium 40, biphotonic absorbtion), being very accurate are, unfortunately, very unwieldy and others, easier to use for medical purposes (anthropometry, skinfolds), lack precision. Bio-electric impedance is a quick and simple method for untraumatic, reproducible quantification of body water content. It is as accurate as densimetry. This is the process employed for quantification of the body composition in healthy elderly. We used Thomasset's technique on the apparatus developed by Boulier. This technique, using two needle electrodes and two frequencies (5 KHz, 1 MHz), allows assessment both of extra-cellular (ECF) and intra-cellular (ICF) water content. The other technique, in contrast, only using one frequency (50 Khz) and 4 skin-adhesive electrodes, only permits assessment of the total water content (TWC). The former, furthermore, uses intradermic needles, thereby avoiding possible errors that may arise from alterations in the skin resistor current (due to dehydrated, thin, thick or even pachydermic skin). For purposes of comparison, we simultaneously used impedancemetry and anthropometry. Our test population was composed of 100 healthy, home-living elderly, all aged from 71 to 76. On a population of this age group, the measurements using impedancemetry amplify not only the decrease in LBM and TWC and the increase in BF, but also the decrease in ICF, being reflected in LBH. Despite a few minor technical problems (which methodology investigations will promptly solve), such measurements by impedancemetry are the only technique for quick, simple, reliable, precise, non-invading, low-cost evaluation of body compartment, body water content and body composition. The two-electrode/two-frequency technique, in our opinion, appears as the one best suited for geriatric studies. Impedancemetry, therefore deserves development for use on elderly patients in whom water-related alterations are very quick and threatening.* (Facts and Research in Gerontology 1992)

Key-words : *Body composition, aging, bioelectric impedance.*

4 - ENTERAL NUTRITION IN THE ELDERLY : X. Hébuterne et P. Rampal

Summary. – *Malnutrition is common in elderly hospitalized patients, and several studies have demonstrated that malnutrition is aggravated in the hospital environment ; this justifies early nutritional support to these patients. Two distinct situations can be envisaged : 1. The elderly patient hospitalized for an acute medical or surgical problem which risks degenerating into nutritional marasmus : this can be prevented by early enteral nutrition ; 2. The elderly patient with an incurable, progressive pathology for whom enteral nutrition raises difficult medical and ethical problems ; the anticipated benefits and potential risks of such therapy must be carefully evaluated. In practice, particular caution is required with enteral nutrition for elderly subjects. Use of fine-bore nasogastric feeding tubes and pumps for administration can reduce the severe esophageal and pulmonary complications which are particularly frequent in this population. Commercial polymeric enteral diets appear as the most suitable ; excessive caloric supplies are not only useless but also dangerous. Cyclic administration of nutrients during the night is justified in ambulatory patients as it permits physical activity and efficient oral nutrition. However, it also requires an increase in the rate of administration ; this can be compensated for by using well-tolerated hypercaloric products. In the elderly, home enteral nutrition is a good alternative to hospitalization. Finally, while enteral nutrition is effective for elderly subjects, it apparently has to be pursued for longer periods than in younger patients to achieve similar results ; this is probably due to less effective use of nutrients by elderly subjects.*
(Facts and Research in Gerontology 1992)

Key-words *: enteral nutrition, malnutrition, elderly, aging, home enteral nutrition, physical activity.*

5 - ANTHROPOMETRIC MEASURES IN ELDERLY PERSONS LIVING IN EUROPE :
B. Vellas, W.-C. Chumlea, F. Beziat, A. Ghisolfi-Marque, S. Guo, J. Conceicao, M. Sedeuilh, R. Dufetelle, J.-L. Albarede

Summary. *– Taking and recording anthropometric measures as part of the nutritional assessment of the elderly are important parts of health care. Nutritional anthropometry provides information about body stores of fat and muscle. These noninvasive measurements are used to evaluate nutritional status and to monitor the effects of nutritional intervention. Nutritional anthropometric assessment of an elderly person can be improved by the use of recumbent measurements because problems associated with mobility do not affect this method of collecting measurements. Anthropometric reference data for elderly persons living in U.S. have been published. However, no similar set of reference data (with recumbent measurements) is available for persons aged 75 years and older living in Europe. To fill this gap, data were collected from 163 men and 329 women aged 60 to 94 years. All subjects were ambulatory Caucasian, free living at home. Trained observer collected data on seven nutritional anthropometric measurements : 1) stature, 2) weight, 3) knee height, 4) mid-arm circumference, 5) calf circumference, 6) triceps skinfold, 7) subscapular skinfold.*
(Facts and Research in Gerontology 1992)

Key-words *: anthropometry, elderly, nutrition, healthy elderly persons.*

SELECTION OF LITERATURE

1 - MALNUTRITION : EPIDEMIOLIGICAL DATA : E. Alix, J.-M. Vetel

1. DEBRY G. : La malnutrition protéino-énergétique des personnes âgées. *R.P.*, 1986, 36, 617-626.
2. CHUMLEA W.C., VELLAS B., ROCHE A.F., GUO S., STEINBAUGH M. : Particularité et intérêt des mesures anthropométriques du statut nutritionnel des personnes âgées. *Age et Nutrition*, 1990, 1, 7-12.
3. BURR M.L., PHILLIPS K.M. : Anthropometric norms in the elderly. *Brit. J. Nutr.*, 1984, 51, 165-169.
4. CZAJKA-NARINS D.M., TSUI J., BESS-KOHRS M.B., NORDSTROM J.A. : Anthropometric indices of a non-institutionalized elderly population. *Age et Nutrition*, 1991, 2, 95-103.
5. HEYMSFIELD S.B., MCMANUS C., SMITH J., STEVENS V., NIXON D.W. : Anthropometric measurement of muscle mass : revised equations for calculating bone-free arm muscle area. *Am. J. Clin. Nutr.*, 1982, 36, 680-690.
6. PAPIN A., ALIX E., VETEL J.M. : Standards anthropométriques et biologiques de l'état nutritionnel de la personne âgée. *Méd. et Hyg.*, 1988, 46, 1515-1523.
7. INGENBLEEK Y., CARPENTIER Y.A. : A prognostic inflammatory and nutritional index scoring critically ill patients. *Internat. J. Vit. Nutr. Res.*, 1985, 55, 91-101.
8. BROCKER P., BRIGNOLE-BAUDOIN, LODS J.C. : Evaluation nutritionnelle du sujet âgé : intérêt du dosage de la triiodothyronine totale. *Sem. Hôp. Paris*, 1988, 64, 1943-1952.
9. MUNRO H.N., MCGANDY R.B., HARTZ S.C., RUSSELL R.M., JACOB R.A., OTRADOVEC C.L. : Proteine nutriture of a group of free-living elderly. *Am. J. Clin. Nutr.*, 1987, 47, 524-533.
10. LECERF J.M., COLVEZ A., HATTON M.F., LEBRUN Th., SAILLY J.C., SALOMEZ J.L., SAMAILLE J., ZYLBERBERG G. : Statut biologique d'une population âgée vivant à domicile. *Sem. Hôp. Paris*, 1990, 23, 1387-1395.
11. MANCIET G., GALLET P., EMERIAU J.P., BOISNIER A., BORDE C. et ANGIBAULT R. : La dénutrition protéino-énergétique chez les patients âgés : enquête prospective dans un service de médecine interne à propos de 400 observations. *Rev. Franç. Endocrinol. Clin.*, 1983, 24, 3225-3236.
12. RAPIN Ch.H., BRUYERE A., ROMAGNOLI A., WEIL R., FEUZ A. et JUNOD J.P. : L'alimentation des personnes âgées. *Méd. Hyg.*, 1985, 43, 3517-3522.
13. RIETSCH M.P., PICAND B., ABY M.A. et KUNTZMANN F. : Equilibre alimentaire « apparent » et malnutrition « clinique et biologique » de la personne âgée : à propos d'une étude prospective effectuée auprès de 283 patients hospitalisés. *Méd. Hyg.*, 1989, 47, 1488-1496.
14. ALIX E., DROUARD-COGNE M., CHRETIENNEAU P., BAGUELIN D., PAPIN A., VETEL J.M. : Etat nutritionnel des personnes âgées de plus de 65 ans admises en médecine aiguë gériatrique. *Conc. Méd.*, 1991, 113, 300-303.
15. WEINSER R.L., HUNCKER E.M., KRUMDIECK C.L., BUTTERWORTH C.E. : Hospital malnutrition : a prospective evaluation of general medical patients during the course of hospitalisation. *Am. J. Clin. Nutr.*, 1979, 32, 418-426.
16. BISTRIAN : Prevalence of malnutrition in general medical patients. *J.A.M.A.*, 1976, 235, 1567-1570.
17. BROCKER P., HOGU N., LODS J.C. : Carences en folates chez les sujets hospitalisés : fréquence, clinique, traitement et résultats thérapeutiques. *Rev. Gériatr.*, 1985, 4, 167-171.
18. BECK H., FORETTE F., HENRY J.F., KEET J., CHERQUI G., VIGNALOU J. : L'alimentation des personnes âgées à l'hôpital-hospice d'Ivry. *Rev. Fr. Diét.*, 1975, 19, 5-12.
19. BONNEAU G., MOREAU D., BOUSSIOUX I., DE TARDY DE MONTRAVEL M., BOGGIO V. et KLEPPING J. : Consommation alimentaire spontanée des personnes âgées séjournant en hospice. *Cah. Nutr. Diét.*, 1983, XVIII, 157-166.
20. COLUCCI R.A., BELLS S., BLACKBURN : Nutritional problems of institutionalised and free-living elderly. *Compr. ther.*, 1987, 13, 20-28.
21. ELMSTAHL S., STEEN B. : Hospital nutrition in geriatric long-term care medicine : II. Effects of dietary supplements. *Age Ageing*, 1987, 16, 73-80.
22. HERCBERG S., SOUSTRE Y., GALAN P., BETZI C., ROUDIER M. : Apports alimentaires d'une population de sujets âgés hospitalisés en long séjour. *Rev. Gériatr.*, 1984, 9 (5), 253-256.
23. RUDMAN D., FELLER A.G. : Protein-calorie undernutrition in the nursing home. *J. Am. Geriatr. Soc.*, 1989, 37, 173-183.
24. SIEBENS H., TRUPE E., SIEBENS A., COOK F., ANSHEN S., HANAUER R., OSTER G. : Correlates and consequences of eating dependency in institutionalized elderly. *J.A.G.S.*, 1986, 34, 192-198.
25. SILVER A.J., MORLEY J.E., STROME L.S. et al. : Nutritional status in an academic nursing home. *J. Amer. Geriatr. Soc.*, 1988, 37, 487-491.
26. COUSIN A., ROUSSEL-GARETT S., DILLON J.C. : La dénutrition protéino-énergétique de la personne âgée : recherche de critères biologiques. *Méd. Nutr.*, 1985, 6, 407-412.
27. KEMM J.R., ALLOCK J. : The distribution of supposed indicators of nutritional status in elderly patients. *Age Ageing*, 1984, 13, 21-28.

28. PINCHCOVSKY D.G.D., KAMANSKI M.V. Jr : Incidence of protein-calorie malnutrition in the nursing home population. *J. Am. Coll. Nutr.,* 1987, 6, 109-112.
29. SCHRIJVER J., BRAM W.C. et al. : Biochemical evaluation of the vitamin and iron status of apparently healthy dutch free living elderly population. *Internat. J. Vit. Nutr. Res.,* 1985, 55, 337-349.
30. ROUDIER M., HERCBERG S., SOUSTRE Y., GALAN P., KADOUCHE J., ABRAMOVITCZ C. : Statuts en fer et en folates d'une population de sujets âgés vivant en hôpital gériatrique de long séjour. *Cah. Nutr. Diét.,* 1984, 1, 27-29.
31. CONGY F., CLAVEL J.P., DEVILLECHABROLLE A., GERBET D., MARESCOT M.R., MOULIAS R. : Le zinc plasmatique chez le sujet âgé institutionnalisé : corrélation avec d'autres marqueurs nutritionnels et immunologiques. *Sem. des Hôp.,* 1983, 45, 3105-3108.
32. IEHL-ROBERT M., DOUCHIN L., BECKER M., IEHL L., DUPOND J.L. : Les carences en zinc en gériatrie : à propos d'une étude prospective chez 100 personnes âgées. *Actualités gérontologiques de l'Est,* 1985 (Specia éditeur).
33. DAVIES M., MAWER E.B., HANN S.T., TAYLOR J.L. : Seasonal changes in the biochemical indices of vitamin D deficiency in the elderly. *Age Ageing,* 1986, 15, 77-83.
34. SEM S.W., SJOEN R.J., TRYGG K., PERDERSEN J. : Vitamin D status of two groups of elderly in Oslo. *Compr. Gerontol.,* 1987, 3, 126-130.
35. TOSS G., SORBO B. : Serum concentration of 25-Dihydroxy Vitamine D and vitamine D binding protein in elderly people : effects of institutionalisation, protein energy malnutrition, and inflamation. *Acta Medic. Scand.,* 1986, 3, 273-277.
36. ABALAN F., SUBRA G., PICARD M., BOUEILH : Fréquence des déficiences en vitamines B12 ou en acide folique chez des patients admis en géronto-psychiatrie. *L'encéphale,* 1984, X, 9-12.
37. GREER A., MACBRIDE D.H., SHENKIN A. : Comparison of the nutritional status of new and long term patients in a psycho-geriatric unit. *British Journal of Psychiatry,* 1986, 12, 738-741.
38. VIR S.C., LOVE A.H. : Vitamine B6 status of institutionalised and non-institutionalised aged. *Int. J. Vit. Nutr. Res.,* 1977, 4, 364-372.
39. GUILLAND J.C., BERESKI-REGUIG, LEQUEU B., MOREAU D., KLEPPING J. et RICHARD D. : Evaluation of pyridoxine intake and pyridoxine status among aged institutionalised people. *Internat. J. Vit. Res.,* 1984, 54, 185-193.
40. BROSSEAU P., SABLONNIERE B. : Carences en folates du sujet âgé : influence du mode d'alimentation. *Méd. et Nutr.,* 1988, 24, 79-82.
41. ITOH R., YAMADA K., OKA J., ECHIZEN H. : Biochemical assessment of vitamin status in healthy elderly japanese : relationships between intakes and biochemical measures of thiamine, riboflavine, and ascorbic acid. *Nut. Report. Intern.,* 1989, 3, 509-519.
42. FERRY (M.), LESOURD (B.) : « Euronut » : situation en France, Congrès international : Nutrition et qualité de vie de la personne âgée « des années à savourer » CMU Genève, octobre 1991.

2 - BIOELECTRIC IMPEDANCE : M. Ferry, A. Boulier, B. Lesourd, A.L. Thomasset

1. PACE J., RATHBUN F.N. : Studies on body composition. The determination of total body fat by means of the body specific gravity. *J. Biol. Chem.,* 1945, 158, 667-676.
2. BEHNKE A.R., OSSEMAN E.F., WELHAM W.C. : Lean body mass. *Arch. Intern. Med.,* 1953, 91, 585-601.
3. FORBES G., GALLUP P.J., HURH J.B. : Estimation of total body fat from potassium 40 content. *Science,* 1961, 133, 101.
4. MOORE F.D., OLESEN K.H., McMURREY J.D., PARKER H.V., BALL M.R., BOYDEN C.M. : The body cell mass and its supporting environment. *Philadelphia, P.A. : W.B. Saunders,* 1963.
5. BROZEK J., GRANDE F., ANDERSON J.T., KEYS A. : Densitometric analysis of body composition : revision of some quantitative assumptions. *Ann. N.Y. Acad. Sci.,* 1963, 110, 113-140.
6. MOORE F.D. and coll. : The body cell mass. Body composition in health and diseases Philadelphia P.A., *W.B. Saunders,* 1963.
7. THOMASSET A.L. : Propriétés bio-électriques des tissus, mesures par impédance. *Lyon Médical,* 1962, 207, 107-118.
8. NYBOER J. : Percent body fat measured by four terminal bioelectrical impedance and body density methods in college freshman. *Proceed. 5th ICEBI,* Tokyo, 1981.
9. DURNIN J.V.G.A., VOMERSLY J. : Body fat assessed from total body density and its estimation from skinfold thickness : measurements on 481 men and women aged from 16 to 72 years. *Br. J. Nutr.,* 1974, 32, 77-97.
10. JACKSON A.S., POLLOCK M.L. : Generalized equations for predicting body density of men. *Br. J. Nutr.,* 1978, 40, 497-504.
11. JACKSON A.S., POLLOCK M.L., WARD A. : Generalized equations for predicting body density of women. *Med. Sci., Sports Exercise,* 1980, 12, 3, 175-182.
12. CHUMLEA C.W., BAUMGARTNER R.N. : Status of anthropometry and body composition data in elderly subjects. *Am. J. Clin. Nutr.,* 1989, 50, 1158-1166.

13. KUCZMARSKI R.J. : Need for body composition information in elderly subjects. *Am. J. Clin. Nutr.*, 1989, 50, 1150-1157.
14. FRICKE J. : A mathematical treatment of the electric conductivity and capacity of disperse system. The electric conductibility of a suspension of homogeneous spheroid. *Physical Rev.*, 1924, 24, 575.
15. THOMASSET A.L. and coll. : Appréciation de la situation électrolytique tissulaire par le rapport des impédances globales du corps humain en basse et haute fréquences. *Rev. Méd. Aéronaut. Spat.*, 1973, 46, 312-315.
16. CHUMLEA W.C., ROCHE A.F., WEBB P. : Body size, subcutaneous fatness and total body fat in older adults. *Int. J. of Obesity*, 1984, 8, 311-317.
17. BOULIER A., FRICKER J., THOMASSET A.L., APPELBAUM M. : Fat free mass estimation by the two electrod impedance method. *Am. J. Clin. Nutr.*, 1990, 52, 581-585.
18. SCHOELLER D.A. : Changes in total body water with age. *Am. J. Clin. Nutr.*, 1989, 50, 1176-1181.
19. SEGAL K.R., GUTIN B., PRESTA E. et al. : Estimation of human body composition by electrical impedance methods : a comparative study. *J. Appl. Physiol.*, 1985, 58, 1565-1571.
20. LUKASKI H.C., BOLONCHUK W.W., HALL C.B. et al. : Validation of the bioelectric impedance method to assess human body composition. *J. Appl. Physiol.*, 1986, 60, 1327-1332.
21. CHUMLEA W.C., BAUMGARTNER R.N., ROCHE A.F. : Specific resistivity used to estimate fat-free mass from segmental body measures of bioelectric impedance. *Am. J. Clin. Nutr.*, 1988, 48, 7-15.
22. ROCHE A.F., CHUMLEA W.C., GUO S. : Estimation of body composition from impedance. *Med. Sc. Sports Exerc.*, 1987, 19, 2 Suppl., 539.
23. DEURENBERG P., VAN DER KOOY K., EVERS P., HULSCHOF T. : Assessment of body composition by bioelectrical impedance in a population aged over 60 y. *Am. J. Clin. Nutr.*, 1990, 51, 3-6.

3 - ANTHROPOMETRIC MEASURES : B. Vellas, W.C. Chumlea, F. Béziat, A. Ghisolfi-Marque, S. Guo, J. Conceicao, M. Sedeuilh, R. Dufetelle, J.-L. Albarede

1.   CHUMLEA W.C., ROCHE A.F., STEINBAUGH M.L., MUKHERJEE D. : Errors of measurement for methods of recumbent nutritional anthropometry in the elderly. *J. Nutr. Elderly*, 1985, 5, 3-7.
2.   CHUMLEA W.C., ROCHE A.F., MUKHERJEE D. : Some anthropometric indices of body composition for the elderly. *J. Geront.*, 1986, 41, 36-39.
3.   LOHMAN T.G., ROCHE A.F., MARTORELL R. : Anthropometric Standardization Manual. *Human Kinetic Books*, Illinois, 1988.
4.   VELLAS B., ALBARÈDE J.L. : Nutrition et vieillissement. *Editions Maloine*, Paris, 1988, 156 p.
5.   CHUMLEA W.C., VELLAS B.J., ROCHE A.F., GUO S., STEINBAUGH M. : Particularités et Intérêt des mesures anthropométriques du statut nutritionnel des personnes âgées. *Age et nutrition*, 1990, 1, 7-12.
6.   National Center for Health Statistic : Disability and Health : Characteristics of Persons by limitation of activity and Assessed Health Status. United States, 1984-1988. Advance Data from Vital and Health Statistics of the National Center for Health Statistics, 1991, 12, 197.
7.   VELLAS B., GARRY P.J., WAYNE S., ALBAREDE J.L. et al. : A Comparative Study of Falls between Europe (Toulouse, France) and US (Albuquerque, NM). To be publish in Epidemiology of Falls in the Elderly. Y. Christen, B. Vellas, L. Rubenstein, M. Toupet. J.L. Albarède eds. *Elsevier*, Publisher.
8.   GARRY P.J., RHYNE R.L., HALIOA L., NICHOLSON C. : Changes in dietary patterns over a 6 year period in an elderly population. *Annals of the New-York Academy of Sciences*, 1989, 561, 104-112.
9.   GARRY P.J., GOODWIN J.S., HUNT W.C., HOOPER E.M., LEONARD A.G. : Nutritional Status in a healthy elderly population ; dietary and supplemental intakes. *Am. J. Clin. Nutr*, 1982, 36, 319-331.
10. VELLAS B.J., WAYNE S.J., HUNT W.C., CHUMLEA W.C., VANDERJAGT D.J., GARRY P.J. : Une étude longitudinale du vieillissement : L'Aging Process Study of New-Mexico. *L'Année Gérontologique*, 1991, 5, 105-119.
11. VELLAS B.J., ALBARÈDE J.L., GARRY P.J. : Diseases and aging, Patterns of Morbidity with Age, Relationships between aging and age-related diseases. *Am. J. Clin. Nutr.*, In Press.
12. CHUMLEA W.C., ROCHE A.F., STEINBAUGH M.L. : Estimating Stature as a clinical measurement of ageing. *J. Am. Geriatr. Soc.*, 1985, 33, 116-120.
13. CHUMLEA W.C., GUO S., ROCHE A.F., STEINBAUGH M.L. : Prediction of body weight for the nonambulatory elderly from anthropometry. *J. Am. Diet. Assoc.*, 1988, 88, 564-8.

4 - ENTERAL NUTRITION IN THE ELDERLY : X. Hébuterne et P. Rampal

1.   MASLOW K. : Total parenteral nutrition and tube feeding for elderly patients : findings of an OTA study. *J.P.E.N.*, 1988, 12, 425-432.
2.   BENNEGARD K., LINDMARK K., WICKSTROM I., SCHERSTEN T., LUNDHOLM K.A. : Comparative study of the efficiency of intragastric and parenteral nutrition in man. *Am. J. Clin. Nutr*, 1984, 40, 752-757.
3.   LE PARCO J.C. : La nutrition entérale chez les sujets âgés. *Ann. Gastroentérol. Hépatol.*, 1988, 24, 305-306.

4. CHERNOFF R., LIPSCHITZ D. : Enteral feeding and the geriatric patient. In : Enteral and tube feeding. Rombeau J.L. and Caldwell M.D. (ed.), *W.B. Saunders Company,* 1990, 386-399.
5. VELLAS B., BALLAS D., GUIDET M. et al. : Vieillissement du tube digestif chez la personne âgée. *Nutr. Clin. Metab.,* 1989, 3, 77-80.
6. SIMKO V., MICHAEL S. : Absortive capacity for dietary fat in elderly patients with debilitating disorders. *Arch. Intern. Med.,* 1989, 149, 557-560.
7. BASTOW M.D. : Complications of enteral nutrition. *Gut,* 1986, 27, 51-57.
8. TOMAIOLO P.P., ENMAN S., KRAUS V. : Preventing and treating malnutrition in the elderly. *J.P.E.N.,* 1981, 5, 46-48.
9. LIPSCHITZ D.A., MITCHELL C.O. : The correctability of the nutritional, immune, and hematopoietic manifestations of protein calorie malnutrition in the elderly. *J. Am. Coll. Nutr.,* 1982, 1, 17-25.
10. KAMINSKI M.V.T., NASR N.J., FREED B.A., SRIRAM K. : The efficacy of nutritional support in the elderly. *J. Am. Coll. Nutr.,* 1982, 1, 35-40.
11. HÉBUTERNE X., ROUSTAN F., RAMPAL P. : Alimentation entérale cyclique (AECy) chez le sujet âgé dénutri. *Nutr. Clin. Metab.,* 1990, 4, 35.
12. JALLUT D., TAPPY L., KOHUT M. et al. : Energy balance in elderly patients after surgery for a femoral neck fracture. *J.P.E.N.,* 1990, 14, 563-568.
13. BASTOW M.D., RAWLING J., ALLISON S.P. : Undernutrition, hypothermia and injury in elderly women with fractured femur ; an injury response to altered metabolism ? *Lancet,* 1983, i, 143-146.
14. WEINSIER R.L., HUNKER E.M., KRUMDIECK C.L. et al. : Hospital malnutrition : a prospective evaluation of general medical patients during the course of hospitalization. *Am. J. Clin. Nutr.,* 1979, 32, 418-426.
15. DELMI M., RAPIN C.H., BENGOA J.M. et al. : Dietary supplementation in elderly patients with fractured neck of the femur. *Lancet,* 1990, 335, 1013-1016.
16. BASTOW M.D., RAWLINGS J., ALLISON S.P. : Benefits of supplementary tube feeding after fractured neck of femur : a randomised controlled trial. *Br. Med. J.,* 1983, 287, 1589-1592.
17. SULLIVAN D.H., MORIARTY M.S., CHERNOFF R., LIPSCHITZ D.A. : Patterns of care : an analysis of the quality of nutritional care routinely provided to the elderly hospitalized veterans. *J.P.E.N.,* 1989, 13, 249-254.
18. KAMATH S.K., LAWLER M., SMITH A.E. et al. : Hospital malnutrition : a 33-hospital screening study. *J. Am. Diet. Assoc.,* 1977, 86, 203-206.
19. APELGREN K.N., ROMBEAU J.L., MILLER R.A. et al. : Malnutrition in veterans administration surgical patients. *Arch. Surg.,* 1981, 116, 1059-1061.
20. CIOCON J.O., SILVERSTONE F.A., GRAVER L.M., FOLEY C.J. : Tube feedings in elderly patients. Indications, benefits and complications. *Arch. Intern. Med.,* 1988, 148, 429-433.
21. PECK A., COHEN C.E., MULVIHILL M.N. : Long-term enteral feeding of aged demented nursing home patients. *J. Am. Geriatr. Soc.,* 1990, 38, 1195-1198.
22. QUILL T.E. : Utilization of naso-gastric feeding tubes in a group of chronically ill, elderly patients in a community hospital. *Arch. Intern. Med.,* 1989, 149, 1937-1941.
23. LA PUMA J., BRENT G.A. : Feeding the demented elderly. *N. Engl. J. Med.,* 1984, 311, 1383-1384.
24. MEER J.A. : Benefits and burdens of tube feeding and physical restrains. *Arch. Intern. Med.,* 1990, 150, 694.
25. LO B., DORNBRAND L. : Guiding the hand that feeds. *N. Engl. J. Med.,* 1984, 311, 402-404.
26. LEE M.P., HARFORD W.V. : Utilization of percutaneous endoscopic gastrostomy in chronically ill elderly patients. *Arch. Int. Med.,* 1990, 150, 2204-2206.
27. KIRBY D.F., CRAIG R.M., TSANG T.K., PLOTNICK B.H. : Percutaneous endoscopic gastrostomy ; a prospective evaluation and review of the literature. *J.P.E.N.,* 1986, 10, 155-159.
28. COGEN R., WEINRYB J. : Aspiration pneumonia in nursing home patients fed via gastrostomy tubes. *Am. J. Gastroenterol.,* 1989, 84, 1509-1512.
29. POMERANTZ M.A., SALOMON J., DUNN R. : Permanent gastrostomy as a solution to some nutritional problems in the elderly. *J. Am. Geriatr. Soc.,* 1980, 28, 104-107.
30. CAMPBELL-TAYLOR I., FISHER R.H. : The clinical case against tube feeding in palliative care of the elderly. *J. Am. Geriatr. Soc.,* 1987, 35, 1100-1104.
31. SILK D.B.A. : Toward the optimization of enteral nutrition. *Clin. Nutr.,* 1987, 6, 61-74.
32. GASTINNE H., CANARD J.M., PILLEGAND B. et al. : Œsophagites au cours de la ventilation artificielle. *Presse Méd.,* 1982, 41, 3029-3032.
33. BURDIN M., LABAYLE D., GIRARDIN J. et al. : Les œsophagites induites par les sondes nasogastriques d'alimentation chez les patients soumis à une ventilation mécanique prolongée : influence de la position demi-assise. *Réan. Soins intens. Méd. Urg.,* 1986, 2, 165-168.
34. RAMPAL P. : Œsophagites sur sonde : la pathogénie n'est pas univoque. *Réan. Soins intens. Méd. Urg.,* 1989, 5, 161-162.
35. CARRIÈRE D., HÉBUTERNE X., MONTOYA M.L., RAMPAL P. : Le reflux gastro-œsophagien au cours de l'alimentation entérale continue. Etude pHmétrique de longue durée. *Gastroentérol. Clin. Biol.,* 1988, 12, 178-179.

36. RAMPAL P., HÉBUTERNE X., ROUSTAN F., LUNDY P. : Complications digestives et respiratoires de l'alimentation entérale continue. *Ann. Gastroentérol. Hépatol.,* 1988, 24, 297-300.
37. OLIVARES L., SEGORIA A., REFUELLA J. : Tube feeding and lethal aspiration in neurological patients : a review of 720 autopsy cases. *Stroke,* 1974, 5, 654-657.
38. SCHROEDER P., FISHER D., VOLZ M., PALOUCEK J. : Microbial contamination of enteral feeding solutions in a community hospital. *J.P.E.N.,* 1983, 7, 364-368.
39. DE LEEUW I.H., VANDEWOUDE M.F. : Bacterial contamination of enteral diets. *Gut,* 1986, 27, 56-57.
40. SILK D.B.A. : Diet formulation and choice of enteral diet. *Gut,* 1986, 27, 40-46.
41. FELLER A.G., CAINDEC N., RUDMAN I.W., RUDMAN D. : Effects of three liquid diets on nutrition-sensitive plasma proteins of tube-fed elderly men. *J. Am. Geriatr. Soc.,* 1990, 38, 663-668.
42. KLEIBEUKER J.H., BOERSMA-VAN EK. W. : Acute effects of continuous nasogastric tube feeding on gastric function : comparison of a polymeric and nonpolymeric formula. *J.P.E.N.,* 1991, 15, 80-84.
43. SILK D.B.A. : Fibre and enteral nutrition. *Gut,* 1989, 30, 246-264.
44. REES R.G.P., COOPER T.M., BEETHAM R., FROST P.G., SILK D.B.A. : Influence of energy and nitrogen contents of enteral diets on nitrogen balance : a double blind prospective controlled trial. *Gut,* 1989, 30, 123-129.
45. SOLOMON S.M., KIRBY D.F. : The refeeding syndrome : a review. *J.P.E.N.,* 1990, 14, 90-97.

IV

FACTS AND RESEARCH
IN PHARMACOLOGY
THERAPEUTIC
AND AGING

ADVANCES AND CONTROVERSIES IN THE PREVENTION AND TREATMENT OF PROSTATE CANCER

Lodovico BALDUCCI (1), Andy TROTTI (2), Julio M. Pow-Sang (3)

Adenocarcinoma of the prostate is the most common malignancy and the second cause of cancer death in men over 65 (1-3). Also, protracted and disabling morbidity makes prostate cancer a serious threat to the quality of life of older men. New modalities of diagnosis and treatment may improve control of prostate cancer in the near future, but at present the benefits of these advances are controversial (2-6).

We explore three areas of controversy which are of interest to the practitioner of geriatrics : screening asymptomatic persons for prostate cancer, management of localized disease and superiority of combined androgen blockade over castration in metastatic cancer. As background we will review epidemiology, etiology and pathogenesis of prostate cancer.

EPIDEMIOLOGY, ETIOLOGY, AND PATHOGENESIS

Incidence and age-specific mortality of prostate cancer increase with age (1-3). Autopsy studies have shown that 50 % of men aged 70 and over harbor prostate cancer (2, 5, 7). Seemingly, with the aging of the general population, occult prostate cancer will have more opportunities to become manifest.

It is difficult to define predisposing factors for a very common disease affecting older persons (3, 8). Of those factors which have been identified (Table 1), race is the strongest, and family history has been gaining more attention.

The incidence of prostate cancer in blacks is approximately twofold that in whites, in the USA and in South Africa (3, 6). It is not clear whether the incidence of the disease is really increased or instead whether prostate cancer is more aggressive and consequently more likely to become symptomatic in blacks.

1. Professor of Medicine, University of South Florida College of Medicine, Chief, Oncology Section, James A. Haley Veterans Hospital, Tampa, Florida.
2. Assistant Professor of Medicine, Radiation Oncology, H. Lee Moffitt Cancer Center and Research Institute, Tampa, Florida.
3. Assistant Professor of Surgery, Department of Urology, H. Lee Moffitt Cancer Center and Research Institute, Tampa, Florida.

TABLE 1

Potential Risk Factors for Prostate Cancer

Race*.
Family History*.

Androgenic stimulation
    Serum Testosterone Levels
    Duration and intensity of sexual life.

Pharmacologic administration of androgens

Diet
    Low intake of carotenoids and retinoids.
    High intake of fatty acids.

Cigarette smoking.

* Established risk factors.
  Hypothetical risk factors.

Recent research has showed that the relative risk of prostate cancer is increased by a factor of 2.8 in a person with a first degree relative affected by the disease and by a factor of 6.2 when both a first and a second degree relative have prostate cancer (8-10). These data strongly suggesting a familial predisposition to prostate cancer, should be interpreted with some caution. It is not impossible that men with prostate cancer in their families undergo more thorough investigation. Thus, an apparent increased incidence of prostate cancer may result from enhanced diagnostic effort.

The influence of sexual activity on the pathogenesis of prostate cancer is not clear (5). Castration at a young age prevents prostate cancer both in humans and in experimental animals, indicating the need for normal sexual development. Some authors have tried to link prostate cancer and serum testosterone levels, with inconclusive results (1, 5). This is not surprising, as serum testosterone levels do not reflect the androgenic production of a lifetime, nor do they account for individual variations in concentrations of « sex hormone binding globulin » which modulates the biologic activity of testosterone (11). Other authors have tried to link the incidence of prostate cancer and the duration and the intensity of one's sexual life, also with inconclusive results (5). These data are indeed difficult to evaluate due to recollection bias and to the intimate nature of the information.

Although reports of prostate cancer during androgen therapy are anecdotical (12-13), this connection is worrysome and needs further investigation. One of the authors (L. B.), witnessed the development of prostate cancer in two men receiving high dose decadurabolin for aplastic anemia and in a multiple myeloma patient treated for impotence with long-acting testosterone preparation.

The evidence that diets low in carotenoids, retinoids, and fiber, and rich in fatty acids may favor prostate cancer is circumstantial at best and founded mainly on comparisons of the incidence of prostate cancer in different countries (14-16).

The intervention of different etiologic factors and the complex interaction of these factors is not surprising. It has been calculated that the pathogenesis of prostate cancer may involve as many as twelve carcinogenic stages and each of these stages may be susceptible to different environmental influences (17).

The growth of prostate cancer is hormone-dependent in part, as castration causes temporary tumor regression (18). The main hormonal effector, dihydrotestosterone (DHT), is synthesized in the tumor, mostly from testicular testosterone, and in a smallest portion from weak adrenal androgens (figure 1). It has been hypothesized –

but it has never been proved – that DHT of adrenal origin may support the growth of prostate cancer after castration. This hypothesis is the basis for combined androgen blockade in metastatic disease (5).

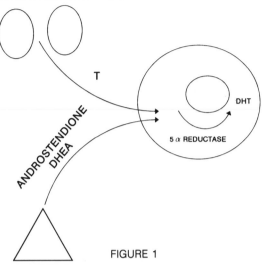

FIGURE 1

Sources of dihydistestosterone (DHT) testicular testosterone and adrenal weak androgens.

The mechanism of noplastic stimulation by DHT has not been clarified. An attractive hypothesis holds DHT to cause oncogene activation (19). Possible targets of androgenic activity are the k-ras oncogene, which encodes transforming growth factor alpha (TGF-alpha), and the HER/2 oncogene, encoding the epithelial growth factor receptor (20-22). Also the c-myc oncogene which was found amplified in several prostate cancers, may represent a target of DHT (23).

PREVENTION OF PROSTATE CANCER

Primary prevention

Primary prevention of cancer implies avoidance of environmental carcinogens or interruption of carcinogenesis. In the case of prostate cancer, the only effective prevention is castration at an early age, a much worse threat to one's quality of life than cancer itself (18). The development of non-steroidal antiandrogens, such as flutamide and nilutimide, presents a new opportunity to study chemoprevention of prostate cancer. Flutamide prevents cancer in experimental models. This drug inhibits the peripheral effects of DHT without diminishing a person's sexual drive. Chemoprevention of breast cancer with estrogen antagonists is being studied both in the United Kingdom and the USA. Chemoprevention of prostate cancer with androgen antagonists appears an achievable goal worthy exploring in a prospective trial.

Secondary prevention

Whereas primary prevention of prostate cancer is only a theoretical possibility, secondary prevention appears more realistic (4). Secondary prevention involves screening asymptomatic persons for cancer. The goal of screening is diagnosis of cancer localized to the prostate and amenable to cure with local treatment, either surgery or radiation therapy (24-25). In discussing screening it is important to address three issues : accuracy, impact on cancer specific mortality, and risks.

Three screening modalities are currently employed : digital rectal examination (DRE), transrectal ultrasound of the prostate (TRUS) and serum levels of prostate specific antigen (PSA) [4, 26]. The detection rate of prostate cancer is improved by any of these tests, when used alone or in combination (Table 2) [27-30]. Catalona et al. (30) studied men with evidence of prostatic disease ; not surprisingly, both sensitivity and PV+ of diagnostic tests were higher than in studies involving asymptomatic persons. Both TRUS and PSA may detect lesions which escape DRE, due to small volume or deep location, and therefore are more sensitive than DRE. Cancer volumes as small as 2cc are detectable with TRUS, but the sensitivity of the test increases with tumor volume (30). The accuracy of PSA increases with the serum levels (30) : 22 % of patients with levels of 4-9 ng/ul and 68 % of those with levels $\geq$ 10 ng/ul had prostate cancer. However, the higher PSA levels generally revealed locally advanced tumors of low curability, which defeats the purpose of screening. It is not clear whether combining TRUS and PSA improves the tumor detection rate. In men with clinical evidence of prostatic disease (30) the majority of tumors were detected by combining DRE and PSA, and the main function of TRUS was to guide the bioptic needle.

The effectiveness of screening is proved by a reduction in cancer-related mortality (4, 24-25). Other end points, such as increased detection rates of early cancer or increased survival since diagnosis of cancer are not acceptable. The interpretation of these end points is confused by three potential biases : overdetection, length- and lead-time bias. Overdetection bias implies that a number of cancers diagnosed at screening might have never become clinically manifest. Overdetection bias is very likely in the case of prostate cancer, given the discrepancy betwen clinical and autoptic incidence, as it may be calculated that only one twentieth of all neoplasms develop into clinical disease (7.31-32).

TABLE 2

Accuracy of DRE, TRUS, and PSA in Comparative Trials

	DRE	TRUS	PSA	
Sensitivity	• 34	• 68	–	(29)
	• 17	–	• 49	(27)
	• 43	• 47	• 68	(28)
	• 86	• 92	• 79	(30) *
Specificity	• 97	• 94	–	(29)
	• 63	–	• 94	(27)
	• 92	• 96	• 90	(28)
	• 44	• 27	• 59	(30) *
PV +	• 21	• 34	–	(29)
	• 12	–	• 46	(27)
	• 30	• 18	• 30	(28)
	• 21	• 21	• 49	(30) *
PV –	• 96	• 98	–	(29)
	• 64	–	• 95	(27)
	• 58	• 43	• 64	(30) *

PV + = Predictive Value Positive.
PV – = Predictive Value Negative.
* This study evaluated patients with symptoms or signs related to the prostate.

Length time bias implies that only neoplasms of low growth rate and low malignancy, whose early detection does not improve curability, are identified at screening. Lead time bias implies that the time during which a person is aware to have cancer, rather than the overall survival, is more prolonged in persons whose cancer has been diagnosed at screening. So far, only screening of asymptomatic persons with DRE has been evaluated in prospective clinical trials, and has not produced an appreciable decrement of cancer-related deaths (4, 33-34). Prospective trials of screening asymptomatic men with PSA are in course in the nordic countries (35) and are considered in the USA (4).

Prospective trials are necessary, because screening is not a riskless endeavor. In addition to the pain and sorrow that false positive results may cause, treatment of early prostate cancer may involve a mortality rate as high as 1 % and a substantial incidence of serious complications, including erectile impotence, urinary incontinence, small bowel obstruction and chronic cystitis (5, 36). It has been calculated that if all men over 50 in the USA underwent screening and radical prostatectomy for early prostate cancer, the number of surgical deaths would be comparable to the number of lives saved by early detection (37). Another important consideration is the cost of screening. In a time of costly technologic advances, rationing of health care with the most effective allotment of limited resources has become imperative (38). Whereas criteria for resource allocation are controversial, those strategies yielding the highest net saving in years of quality life should receive highest priority. In addition to the screening procedure, cost of screening involves the cost of diagnostic tests to confirm a suspicious result, the cost of treatment and of its complications (38).

Another factor which may diminish the benefits of screening, is the natural history of localized prostate cancer. This has been studied by investigators, who delayed treatment until disease progression in Sweden and in the United Kingdom (39-41). Over a ten year follow up, two thirds of the patients have developed more advanced disease, but < 10 % have died of prostate cancer (39). These mortality figures are comparable to those of patients receiving immediate treatment. In particular, the life expectancy of men aged 70 and older was not different from that of age-matched controls without prostate cancer (40-41) [figure 2].

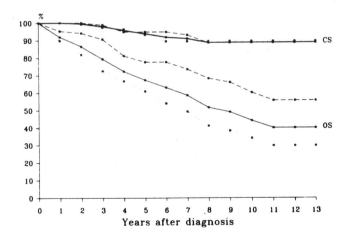

FIGURE 2

Survival of patients with prostate cancer treated expectantly (from reference 41).

In conclusion, it is questionable whether the increased detection rate of early prostate cancer may be translated into reduced mortality. Seemingly, screening may be
most beneficial to men at increased risk of prostate cancer and with a life expectancy longer than ten years. In view of potential risks and substantial costs, however,
screening should not be implemented in practice until completion of ongoing clinical trials.

MANAGEMENT OF PROSTATE CANCER

General Principles

The management of prostate cancer varies with the stage of the disease (table
3). Current staging systems are clinical. When surgically staged, approximately 25 %
of patients with stages A2-B tumors and 50 % of those with stage C tumors have
neoplastic involvement of pelvic lymph nodes (1, 5). Clinical staging of prostate cancer involves determination of levels of prostatic specific antigen and alkaline phosphatase in the serum, bone scintigraphy and abdominal CT. When assessment of
pelvic disease is necessary, MRI is the procedure of choice, as lymphangiography,
ultrasonography, and computerized tomography have poor sensitivity for pelvic lesions
(42).

We will focus our discussion on two areas of major controversy : management of
localized disease (stages A2 and B) and management of metastatic cancer.

TABLE 3

Stages of Prostate Cancer and Related Treatment Options

Stage	Description	Treatment
A	No clinical evidence of tumor. Diagnosis at TURP.	
A1	Well differentiated tumor involving < 5 % of the specimen.	Observation
A2	Poorly differentiated tumor and/or tumor involving ≥ 5 % of the specimen.	Surgery - Radiation Observation
B	Palpable Nodule.	
B1	Nodule 1.5 cm in diameter and involving a single lobule.	Surgery Radiation
B2	Nodule involving two lobules and/or 1.5 cm in diameter.	Observation
C	Involvement of periprostatic structures (seminal vesicles, bladder floor).	Radiation - Surgery Observation
D	Metastatic Disease.	
D1	Metastasis to pelvic lymph nodes.	Observation - Hormonal treatment - Surgery Radiation
D2	Metastases to retroperitoneal lymphatics and extralymphatic metastases.	Hormonal Treatment

Management of Localized Disease

The controversy related to localized disease hinges on two questions : Is any form of treatment necessary ? If treatment is necessary, which therapeutic option – surgery or radiation therapy – is preferable ?

Several studies indicate that the course of localized prostate cancer is predicted by the tumor grade (i.e. degree of histologic differentiation) [39-43]. Well differentiated cancer is a slowly progressive disease, unlikely to cause patient death or distressing symptoms during the first 8-10 years since diagnosis while poorly differentiated carcinoma is an aggressive disease experiencing early metastatic spread and almost invariably leading to death within 5 years. The Veterans Administration Cooperative Uro-oncology Group (VACURG) compared radical prostatectomy and observation in a prospective randomized study of 142 patients. After 15 years of follow up, the survivals of the two groups were similar (43). This interesting trial was fraught by several problems, which might have unbalanced the randomization (44). These included : high proportion (more than one third) of non evaluable patients ; different mean age of the two groups of subjects, failure to employ bone scintigraphy in the initial staging, failure to stratify patients for prognostic factors which were unknown at the time, such as tumor grade and levels of serum acide phosphatase. Because of these flaws in study design one cannot infer that prostatectomy and observation are equivalent. One may safely conclude, however, that the survival and quality of life of the majority of patients with localized prostate cancer is preserved without treatment for a prolonged period of time. The same conclusion was reached in three studies exploring the natural history of prostate cancer in patients managed expectantly (i.e. treatment was instituted upon disease progression rather than at diagnosis) [39-41].

On the basis of these results, persons with a life expectancy of ten years or less, with well differentiated tumor, may be managed expectantly, while those with poorly differentiated cancer should undergo immediate treatment. One cannot overemphasize the importance of close observation of persons whose treatment is delayed. The histologic grade may vary in different tumor areas, and undetected islands of poorly differentiated and highly aggressive disease may be present in neoplasms which appear well differentiated at needle biopsy (45).

For patients requiring treatment, the choice is between surgery and radiation therapy. Only a prospective and randomized study of these treatment modalities has been performed, and the results were inconclusive due to small patient number, inadequate follow up and randomization imbalance (46). Comparison of large series of patients treated with radiation therapy or with retropubic prostatectomy shows the survival and disease free survival to be similar after five, ten and fifteen years of follow-up (table 4) [5, 36, 38]. Presumably, the radiation series were negatively weighed by patients at high surgical risk because of poor general conditions. As the therapeutic results are similar, the selection of treatment is based on considerations of quality of life and cost (Table 4). The risk of postsurgical erectile impotence has substantially decreased in the last decade, since the advent of the nerve sparing procedure (47). This operation, first described by Walsh, may preserve the erection in as many as 75 % of men under 60, but the results are less predictable in older persons. The effects of erectile impotence on the quality of life of older men, may be mitigated by two factors. First, at least two studies have shown that loss of sexual activity is not a significant threat to the quality of life of the majority of men aged 70 and older, nor a deterrent to treatment (48-50). Second, neurogenic impotence from lesion of the « nervi erigentes » (which make the erection possible) does not compromise the penile sensations related to arousal and orgasm, which are carried by the pudendal nerve. Thus, for the patients who desire it, a satisfactory sexual life may be restored by penile implants or by the external application of negative pressure (51-52).

TABLE 4

End Results of Surgery and Radiotherapy in Stages A2 and B Prostate Cancer

	Surgery	Radiotherapy
Survival		
5 years	83-95 %	76-95 %
10 years	62-78 %	56-82 %
15 years	30-67 %	37 %
Disease Free Survival		
5 years	68-90 %	46-100 %
10 years	48-70 %	39 - 71 %
15 years	25-51 %	ND
Complications		
Impotence	30-40 %	7-41 %
Incontinence	5 %	0 - 3 %
Stress incontinence	5 %	0 - 1 %
Urethral Stenosis	1 - 9 %	4.5 - 9 %
Bowel Stenosis	5 %	5 -14 %
Cystitis	−	5 -10 %
Mortality	0.5 - 1 %	ND
Cost ( )		
Primary Treatment	$ 14,969.00	$ 5,090.00
Treatment and Complications	$ 17,457.00*	$ 9,418.00*

ND = No Data

(*) The cost of management of individual complications was multiplied by the risk of that complication as given in table 4.

Recent advances in radiation therapy may reduce the risk of complications and minimize the inconvenience of daily clinic visits. Several groups are developing new brachytherapy (implant) techniques, including CT or ultrasound guided perineal templates for more precise seed localization, new isotopes with shorter half-lives (palladium), and high dose rate systems. The value of these technical changes is under investigations.

In conclusion, during the last decades, newly developed surgery and radiation techniques have made the treatment of localized prostate cancer safer and possibly more effective. The therapeutic results of both treatment modalities appear equivalent and the treatment choice is based on the patient acceptance of the risk of different therapeutic complications as well as of the costs of different treatment modalities.

MANAGEMENT OF METASTATIC PROSTATE CANCER

Treatment with single agent

The primary management of metastatic prostate cancer is hormonal, with a subjective response rate as high as 80 % (6, 54-55). Several therapeutic options are listed in table 5. Castration is the time-honored treatment of metastatic prostate cancer. Orchiectomy is a simple, safe and effective procedure, indicated when regular intake of medications by patients is unreliable, due to impaired cognitive function or inadequate social support. The use of estrogens in the USA has been largely abandoned due to the risk of complications, which include deep vein thrombosis, fluid retention, congestive heart failure and cholestatic jaundice. The incidence of these complications is dose-related. They are seen in approximately 30 % of patients treated with 3 mg of diethylstilbestrol (DES) daily or equivalent doses of other compounds. High estrogen doses may not be necessary, however. At least two studies have shown that 1 mg daily of DES is as effective, and virtually complication free. A main advantage of estrogen is low cost.

Luteinizing Hormone Releasing Hormone (LH-RH) analogs have opposite effects depending on the administration schedule. During cyclic administration these compounds stimulate, and during daily administration they inhibit gonadal steroidogenesis. The mechanism of castration is unclear and may involve down regulation of pituitary receptors for LH-RH, pituitary exhaustion, and unbalanced synthesis of LH alpha and beta chains. These compounds are available as depot preparations, which obviates the inconvenience of daily injections. The main side effects of LH-RH analogs is the occurrences of hot flushes, which respond to transdermal clonidine (56).

One should be aware, however, that these medications may stimulate tumor growth during the first 7-14 days of treatment, due to an initial spate of testosterone secretion. This potentially fatal complication is avoided by the simultaneous administration of antiandrogens.

Ketoconazole, at the dose of 400 mg thrice a day, causes an universal and rapid inhibition of steroidogenesis. This effect is valuable for life-threatening conditions, such as lymphangitic lung metastases, disseminated intravascular coagulation, obstructive renal failure and impending spinal cord compression, when orchiectomy cannot be performed. Adrenal steroids should be supplemented to prevent adrenal crises. Long term treatment with ketoconazole has not been adequately studied and may be less safe than other forms of castration. In addition to adrenal failure, ketoconazole may cause gastrointestinal upset and hepatitis. An almost universal consequence of castration is impotence from suppression of libido.

Antiandrogens comprehend a number of drugs of unrelated chemical structures, with the common characteristic to offset the peripheral effects of DHT. For practical purposes, antiandrogens have been divided into steroidals and non-steroidals. Unlike non-steroidals, steroidal antiandrogens inhibit the secretion of gonadotropins and thus may prevent resistance of the tumor to hormonal treatment from increased concentration of androgen receptors.

Cyproterone, which is as effective as castration in terms of therapeutic response, time to progression and survival, may cause deep vein thrombosis, fluid retention and impotence. Flutamide, the prototype of non-steroidal antiandrogens, has not been adequately studied as a single agent. The main use of this compound, at present, is in combined androgen blockade. Flutamide is particularly attractive, due to low risk of complications. These include gynecomastia, diarrhea and occasionally hepatitis. The sexual function has been preserved in the majority of patients treated with flutamide as single agent new paragraph. Estramustine phosphate is a combination of nornitrogen mustard and estradiol bound by a carbamate link. This synthetic product was designed for selective tumor toxicity : in the original plan, the hormonal moiety would have been bound by the hormonal receptor of the tumor and thus would have favored the entrance of the alkylating moiety into the tumor cell. The actual mechanism of action is not clear, but estramustine phosphate is clearly active against prostate cancer. In terms of therapeutic response, time to disease progression and survival, estramustine phosphate is comparable to castration. According to at least one study, estramustine phosphate is more effective than estrogen in delaying disease progression (57). The main advantage of this compound is preservation of sexual function in a number of patients. The main disadvantage is high incidence of complications related both to the estrogenic and the alkylating component. These include deep vein thrombosis, fluid retention, nausea, vomiting, and myelotoxicity. This toxicity profile makes estramustine a valuable agent for sexually active individuals in good general condition.

The Combined Androgen Blockade (CAB) Controversy

CAB involves castration and simultaneous administration of an antiandrogen, and is aimed to suppress the androgenic effects both of testicular and of adrenal origin (5, 58-60). Whereas uncontrolled studies of CAB suggested that this form of treatment was superior to simple castration in terms of therapeutic response, freedom from progression and survival, randomized trials comparing CAB and castration were inconclusive (table 5). Of particular interest was the intergroup study which contained the largest number of patients. This study showed an overall modest benefit in terms of FFP and survival for patients treated with CAB (64). When the results were analyzed according to specific prognostic factors, such as performance status and number of bony metastases, the benefits were more marked for patients with 3 bony lesions and in better performance status (58). Although it has been criticized for not stratifying patients according to pretreatment serum testosterone levels, which predicts response to hormonal treatment (66), this trial represents the best controlled and the most mature study of CAB and castration involving the largest patient number and provides convincing evidence that CAB is beneficial in selected situations. A more recent trial comparing leuprolide and CAB with leuprolide and anandron, has included serum testosterone levels as stratification criteria and has confirmed the results of the intergroup study (65). We can only speculate as to why several other trials failed to show the benefits of CAB. As a general principle, different results are not unexpected in clinical trials involving the geriatric population, with a high degree of intrinsic diversity. Possibly, negative trials involved patients with more advanced disease or patients with more limited life expectancy. Negative trials are important as they alert us to the fact that the benefits of treatment are not universal, but may be limited to selected groups of older individuals, a conclusion supported by the analysis of the intergroup study itself.

TABLE 5

Treatment Options for Metastatic Prostate Cancer

A. Castration.
   Orchiectomy
   Estrogens
   LH-RH analogs
   Ketoconazole

B. Antiandrogens.
   1. Steroidals
      Cyproterone Acetate.
      Megestrol Acetate.

   2. Non-Steroidals.
      Flutamide
      Nilutimide

C. Estramustine Phosphate (Emcyt)

D. Combined Androgen Blockade

Other areas of controversy

Other areas of controversy involve treatment of locally advanced (stage C) prostate cancer, use of adjuvant hormonal therapy in local (stage A2 and B) and locally advanced (stage C) disease and the advantages of CAB over estramustine phosphate in metastatic cancer (67). These issues are important but are largely speculative. The treatment of stage C prostate cancer is currently by radiation, and surgery or hormonal therapy are experimental. Likewise, adjuvant hormonal therapy should be considered experimental until a survival benefit is proved in randomized trials. Given the limited indications of estramustine phosphate, a comparison of this drug and CAB is probably not of general interest.

TABLE 6

Results of Recent Prospective Trials Comparing CAB and Castration

Author(s) (treatment modalities)	RR	FFP (months)	Survival (months)
Robinson (61) n = 351 Orchiectomy Orchiectomy + CPA 150 mg qd DES 1 mg qd	– – –	23 24 22	nr nr nr
Lunglmayr et al. (62) n = 568 Zoladex Zoladex + Flutamide	77 % 79 %	nr nr	nr nr
Fourcade et al. (63) n = 291 Zoladex Zoladex and Flutamide	79 % 75 %	17 14	nd nd
Crawford et al. (64) n = 626 Leuprolide Leuprolide + Flutamide	– –	14 * 16.5	28.3 * 35.6
Janckegt et al. (65) n = 457 Leuprolide Leuprolide + Anandron	24 % ⧸ * 41 % ⧸	14.9* 19	23.6* 28.2

⧸ Complete Remissions only
(*) Significant for p < 0.05

CPA = cyproterone. RR = Response Rate. FFP = Freedom From Progression. n = evaluable patient. nr = not reported. nd = no difference.

CONCLUSION

The incidence and mortality of prostate cancer are increasing in the older population. The practitioner of geriatrics is likely to get involved in the prevention and treatment of this disease.

Whereas screening asymptomatic persons may reduce the risk of prostate cancer related deaths, it is premature and potentially harmful to implement screening in clinical practice until ongoing trials have been completed new paragraph. Treatment of localized prostate cancer with surgery or radiotherapy yields similar results and the choice should be based on the preferences of individual patients.

In individuals with a life expectancy ≤ 10 years and well differentiated tumors, close observation is a viable option new paragraph. In metastatic prostate cancer, CAB is superior to castration in highly motivated patients with good performance status and small tumor load. In other patients the extra cost and the inconvenience of combined treatment may not be worthy the marginal benefits.

REFERENCES

1. SILVERBERG (E.), BORING (C.C.), SQUIRES (T.S.) : Cancer statistics. *Ca* 40, 9-28, 1990.
2. GITTES (R.F.) : Carcinoma of the prostate. *N. Eng. J. Med.*, 314, 236-245, 1991.
3. MUIR (C.S.), NECTOUX (J.), STASZEWSKI (J.) : The epidemiology of prostatic cancer. *Acta Oncologica*, 30, 133-140, 1991.
4. GERBER (G.S.), CHODAK (G.W.) : Routine screening for cancer of the prostate. *J. Ntl Cancer Inst.*, 83, 329-338, 1991.

5. BALDUCCI (L.), KHANSUR (T.), SMITH (T.), HARDY (C.) : Prostate cancer, a model of cancer in the elderly. *Arch. Gerontol. Geriatr.*, 8, 165-187, 1989.
6. BALDUCCI (L.), PARKER (M.), HESCOCK (H.), TANTRANOND (P.), SEXTON (W.) : Systemic management of prostate cancer. *Am. J. Med. Sci.*, 299, 185-192, 1990.
7. WHITMORE (W.F.) : Natural history of low grade prostate cancer and the impact of early detectioin. *Urol. Clin. N. Am.*, 17, 689-698, 1990.
8. MEIKLE (W.), SMITH (J.A.) : Epidemiology of prostate cancer. *Urol. Clin. N. Am.*, 17, 709-718, 1990.
9. STEINBERG (G.D.), CARTER (B.S.), BEATY (T.H.), CHILDS (B.), WALSH (P.C.) : Family history and the risk of prostate cancer. *Prostate*, 17, 337-347, 1990.
10. KEETCH (D.W.), CATALONA (W.J.) : Familial aspects of prostate cancer. *J. Urol.*, 145 (4), 250 A, 1991.
11. SEGAL (K.R.), DUNAIR (A.), GUTIN (B.), ALBU (J.), NYMAN (A.), PI-SUNYER (F.X.) : Body composition, not body weight, is related to cardiovascular disease risk factors and sex hormone levels in men. *J. Clin. Invest.*, 80, 1050-1055, 1987.
12. JACKSON (J.A.), WAXMAN (J.), SPIEKERMAN (A.M.) : Prostatic complications of testosterone replacement therapy. *Arch. Int. Méd.*, 149, 2365-2366, 1989.
13. BARDIN (C.W.), SWERDLOFF (R.S.), SANTEN (R.J.) : Androgens, risks and benefits. *J. Clin. Endocrinol. Met.*, 73, 4-7, 1991.
14. LEMARCHAND (L.), HALKIN (J.H.), KOLONEL (L.N.), WILKENS (L.R.) : Vegetable and fruit consumption in relation to prostate cancer in Hawaii : A re-evaluation of the effect of dietary beta carotene. *Am. J. Epidemiol.*, 133, 215-219, 1991.
15. PUSATERI (D.J.), ROTH (W.T.), ROSS (J.K.), SEULTZ (T.D.) : Dietary and hormonal evaluation of men at different risks for prostate cancer. Plasma and fecal hormone-nutrient interrelationships. *Am. J. Clin. Nutr.*, 51, 371-377, 1990.
16. HSING (A.W.), McLAUGHLIN (J.K.), SCHUMAN (L.M.), BJELKE (E.), GRIDLEY (G.), WACHOLDER (S.), CHIEN (H.T.), BLOT (W.J.) : Diet, tobacco use, and fatal prostate cancer. Results from the Lutheran Brotherhood Cohort Study. *Cancer Res.*, 50, 6836-6840, 1990.
17. ANISIMOV (W.N.) : Age as a factor of risk in multistage carcinogenesis. In BALDUCCI (L.), LYMAN (G.H.), ERSHLER (W.) : Geriatric Oncology, *J.B. Lippincott*, 1991 (in press).
18. MOON (T.D.), SLOANE (B.B.) : Prostatic adenocarcinoma. *Carcinogenesis and Growth*, 37, 55-65, 1989.
19. HOFER (D.R.), SHERWOOD (E.R.), BROMBERG (W.D.), MENDELSOHN (J.), LEE (C.), KOZLOWSKI (J.M.) : Autonomous growth of androgen-independent human prostatic carcinoma cells. Roles of transforming growth factor alpha. *Cancer Res.*, 51, 2780-2785, 1991.
20. CARTER (B.S.), EPSTEIN (J.I.), ISAACS (W.B.) : Ras gene mutations in human prostate cancer. *Cancer Res.*, 50, 6830-6832, 1990.
21. THOMPSON (T.C.) : Growth factors and oncogenes in prostate cancer. *Cancer Cells*, 2, 345-354, 1990.
22. WARE (J.L.), MAYGARDEN (S.J.), KOONTZ (W.W.), STROM (S.C.) : Immunohistochemical detection of c-erbB-2 protein in human benign and neoplastic prostate. *Human Pathol.*, 22, 254-258, 1991.
23. SHALKEN (J.A.), BUSSEMAKERS (M.J.), DEBRUYNE (F.M.) : Oncogene expression in prostate cancer. *Prog. Clin. Biol. Res.*, 357, 97-105, 1990.
24. ROBIE (P.W.) : Cancer screening in the elderly. *J. Am. Ger. Soc.*, 37, 888-893, 1989.
25. BALDUCCI (L.) : Practical screening for malignancies. *Hospital Med.*, 27, 8, 44-52, 1991.
26. OESTERLING (E.) : Prostate specific antigen. A critical assessment of the most useful tumor marker for adenocarcinoma of the prostate. *J. Urol.*, 145, 907-923, 1991.
27. STONE (N.N.), LAZAN (D.), CLEJAN (S.), MOON (T.), MULHOLLAND (G.), GOMELLA (L.), CHODAC (G.), DOBBS (R.), CRAWFORD (E.D.) : Comparison of digital rectal exam and prostate specific antigen. Biopsy results from prostate cancer awareness week 1989. *J. Urol.* 145, 4, 250 A, 1991.
28. TEILLAC (P.), BRON (J.), TOBOLSKI (F.), CUSSENOT (O.), LESOURD (A.), LEROY (M.), TOUBERT (M.E.), BROCHERIOU (C.), LAVAL-JEANTET (M.), LEDUC (A.) : Detection of cancer of the prostate. A study of 600 cases. *Ann. Urol.*, 24, 37-41, 1990.
29. LEE (F.), LITTRUP (P.J.), TORP-PEDERSEN (S.T.), METTLIN (C.), McHUGH (T.A.), GRAY (J.M.), KUMASAKE (G.H.), McLEARY (R.D.) : Prostate cancer. Comparision of transrectal ultrasound and digital rectal examination for screening. *Radiology*, 168, 389-394, 1988.
30. CATALONA (W.J.), SMITH (D.S.), RATLIFF (T.L.), DODDS (K.M.), COPLEN (D.E.), YUAN (J.J.J.), PETROS (J.A.), ANDROILE (G.L.) : Measurement of prostate-specific antigen in serum as a screening test for prostate cancer. *N. Engl. J. Med.*, 324, 1156-1161, 1991.
31. BUSCH (C.) : The natural history of prostatic carcinoma. *Scand. J. Urol. Nephrol.*, Suppl., 110, 23-29, 1988.
32. VILLERS (A.A.), McNEAL (J.E.), FREIMA (F.S.), STAMEY (T.A.) : Development of prostatic carcinoma. *Acta Oncol.*, 30, 145-151, 1991.
33. FRIEDMAN (G.D.), HIATT (R.A.), QUESENBERRY (G.P.), SELBY (J.V.) : Case-control study of screening for prostatic cancer by digital rectal examinations. *The Lancet*, 337, 1526-1529, 1991.
34. VARENHORST (E.), PEDERSEN (K.V.), CARLSSON (P.), BERGLUND (K.) LOFMAN (O.) : Screening for carcinoma of the prostate in a randomly selected population using duplicate digital rectal examination. *Acta Oncol.*, 30, 273-275, 1991.

35. IVERSEN (P.), TORP-PEDERSEN (S.T.) : Screening for prostatic cancer. Investigational models. *Acta Oncol.*, 30, 281-284, 1991.
36. LANGE (P.H.) : Controversies in the management of apparently localized carcinoma of prostate. *Urology* 24, 4, 13-18, 1989.
37. CHODAK (G.W.) : Early detection and screening for prostatic cancer. *Urology* 24, 4, 10-12, 1989.
38. OPTENBERG (S.A.), THOMPSON (I.M.) : Economics of screening for carcinoma of the prostate. *Urol. Clin. N. Am.*, 17, 719-738, 1990.
39. GEORGE (N.J.R.) : Natural history of localized prostate cancer managed by conservative therapy alone. *Lancet*, 2, 494-497, 1988.
40. ADOLFSSON (J.), CARSTENSEN (J.) : Natural course of clinically localized prostate adenocarcinoma in men less than 70 years old. *J. Urol.*, 146, 96-98, 1991.
41. JOHANSSON (J.E.), ANDERSON (S.O.) : Deferred treatment in localized prostate cancer. *Acta Oncol.*, 30, 2221-224, 1991.
42. DERSHAW (D.D.), PANICEK (D.M.) : Imaging of invasive bladder cancer. *Sem. Oncol.*, 17, 544-550, 1990.
43. MADSEN (P.O.), GRAVERSEN (P.H.), GASSER (T.C.), CORLE (D.K.) : Treatment of localized prostatic cancer. Radical prostatectomy vs placebo. A 15 years follow-up. *S. and J. Urol. Nephrol.*, Suppl., 110, 95-100, 1988.
44. BYAR (D.P.), CORLE (D.K.) : VACURG randomized trial of radical prostatectomy for Stages I and II prostate cancer. *Urology*, 17 (suppl.), 7-10, 1981.
45. WHITMORE (W.F.) : Locoregional prostatic cancer. Advances in management. *Cancer*, 65, 667-674, 1990.
46. BYHARDT (R.W.), JENSEN (R.), ROSWIT (B.), GREENLAW (R.H.), NAG (S.), STEPHANI (S.), WOODWARK (K.) : Radical surgery versus radiotherapy for adenocarcinoma of the prostate. *J. Urol.* 129, 1205-1206, 1983.
47. CATALONA (W.J.) : Patient selection for, results of and impact on tumor resection of potency-sparing radical prostatectomy. *Urol. Clin. N. Am.*, 17, 819-826, 1990.
48. FOUSSA (S.B.), AARONSON (N.K.) NEWLING (D.), VAN CANGH (P.J.), DENIS (L.), KURTH (K.H.), DEPAUW (M.) : Quality of life and treatment of hormone resistant metastatic prostate cancer. *Europ. J. Cancer* 26, 1133-1136, 1990.
49. SINGER (P.A.), TASCH (E.S.), STOCKING (C.), RUBIN (S.), SIEGLER (M.), WEICHSELBAUM (R.) : Sex or survival. Trade offs between quality and quantity of life. *J. Clin Oncol.*, 9, 328-334, 1991.
50. KELLY (K.), JOHNSON (A.), HOFFMAN (S.), BALDUCCI (L.) : Assessment of individual preferences for alternative clinical outcomes (utilities) in older patients. Reliability and validity. *J. Am. Ger. Soc.*, 39, 8, A 30, 1991.
51. KRANE (R.J.), GOLDSTEIN (I.) SAENZ DE TEJADA (I.) : Impotence. *N. Engl. J. Med.*, 321, 1648-1659, 1989.
52. BLASKO (J.C.), RAGDE (H.), GRIMM (P.D.) : Transperineal ultrasound-guided implantation of the prostate. Morbidity and complications. *Scand J. Urol. Nephrol.* Suppl., 137, 1991.
53. NORI (D.), DONATH (D.), HILARIS (B.S.), OSIAN (A.), ZELEFSKY (M.), WALLNER (K.), WHITMORE (W.F.), FUKS (Z.) : Precision transperineal brachytherapy in the treatment of early prostate cancer. *Endocrine Ther. Hypertherma Oncol.*, 6, 119-130, 1990.
54. JOHANSSON (J.E.), ANDERSSON (S.O.), HOLEMBERG (L.), BERSTROM (R.) : Primary orchiectomy versus estrogen therapy in advanced prostatic cancer. A randomized study. *J. Urol.*, 145, 519-523, 1991.
55. McCONNELL (J.D.) : Physiologic basis of endocrine therapy for prostatic cancer. *Urol. Clin. N. Am.*, 18, 1-14, 1991.
56. PARRA (R.O.), GREGORY (J.G.) : Treatment of post orchiectomy hot flashes with transdermal administration of clonidine. *J. Urol.*, 143, 753-754, 1990.
57. BENSON (R.E.), GILL (G.M.) : Estramustine phosphate compared with diethylstilbestrol. A randomized double-blind crossover trial for Stage D prostate Cancer. *Am. J. Clin. Oncol.*, 9, 341-351, 1986.
58. CRAWFORD (D.E.), NABORS (W.L.) : Total androgen ablation. American experience. *Urol. Clin. N. Am.*, 17, 55-64, 1991.
59. DENIS (L.), SMITH (P.), CARNEIRO DE MOURA (J.L.), NEWLING (D.), BONO (A.), KEUPPENS (F.), MAHLER (C.), ROBINSON (M.), SYLVESTER (R.), DE PAUW (M.), VERMEYLEN (K.), ONGENE (P.) : Total androgen ablation. European experience. *Urol. Clin. N. Am.*, 17, 65-74, 1991.
60. BELAND (G.), ELHILALI (M.), FRADET (Y.), LAROCHE (B.), RAMSEY (E.W.), TRACHTENBERG (J.), VENNER (P.M.), TEWARI (H.D.) : Total androgen ablation. Canadian experience. *Urol. Clin. N. Am.*, 17, 75-82, 1991.
61. ROBINSON (M.R.G.) : Complete androgen blockade. The EORTC experience comparing orchiectomy versus orchiectomy plus cyprotene acetate vs low dose stilboestrol in the treatment of metastatic carcinoma of the prostate. *Prog. Clin. Biol. Res.*, 223, 383-390, 1989.
62. LUNGLIMAYR (G.) : Zoladex versus zoladex plus flutamide in the treatment of advanced prostate cancer. *Prog. Clin. Biol. Res.*, 303, 145-151, 1989.
63. FOURCADE (R.D.), CARIOU (G.), COLOBY (P.), COLOMBEL (P.), COULANGE (C.), GRISE (P.), MANGIN (P.), SORET (J.Y.), POTERRE (M.) : Total androgen blockade in the treatment of advanced prostatic carcinoma. Final report of a double blind study using zoladex and flutamide. *J. Urol.* 145, 4, 426 A, 1991.

64. CRAWFORD (E.D.), EISENBERGER (M.A.), McLEOD (D.G.), SPAULDING (J.T.), BENSON (R.), DORR (F.A.), BLUMENSTEIN (B.A.), DAVIS (M.A.), GOODMAN (P.J.) : A controlled trial of leuprolide with and without flutamide in prostatic carcinoma. *N. Engl. J. Med.*, 321, 419-424, 1989.
65. JANCKEGT (R.A.), DELMORAL (P.F.), ABBOU (C.), BRACKEN (L.B.), BARTOLETTI (R.), HANN (L.B.), BRISSET (J.M.), DESILVA (F.C.), CHISHOLM (G.D.), CRAWFORD (E.D.), FRICK (J.), GOEDHALS (L.), KNONAGEL (H.), VENNER (B.), DEBROYN (F.M.J.) : Efficacy and tolerance of total androgen blockade with anandron and orchiectomy. A double blind placebo controlled multicenter study. *J. Urol.*, 145, 4, 425 A, 1991.
66. SOLOWAY (M.S.) : The importance of prognostic factors in advanced prostate cancer. *Cancer,* 66, 1017-1032, 1990.
67. BALDUCCI (L.), TROTTI (A.), POW-SANG (J.M.) : Controversies in the Management of Prostate Cancer. *In* BALDUCCI (L.), LYMAN (G.H.), ERSHLER (W.) : Geriatric Oncology, *Lippincott (J.B.) (In press)* 1991.

SPECIFICITIES
OF THERAPEUTIC RESEARCH
IN PRECLINICAL
AND CLINICAL GERONTOLOGY

Lucien STERU (*), Jean-Marie VETEL (**)

Elderly patients take between 25 % and 50 % of total drug consumption (1, 2). In terms of combined therapies, the elderly consume 80 % of all such treatment regimens. Moreover, the elderly patient population comprises an increasing political and consumer force, therefore guiding research efforts to meet their specific needs. This last point illustrates that an important part of future drug development should focus on research of the elderly patient. Nevertheless, even if the political or marketing incentives to conduct such research are apparent, the methodology and the practical aspects have a deserved reputation of being difficult and methods are seldom as satisfactory as those for equivalent drug development in the adult (by adult we mean non-aged population).

The approach of this article is to abstract from general preclinical and clinical drug development methods particular characteristics for the elderly patient. Our aims are to draw the attention of persons involved in clinical research, both clinical investigators and from the pharmaceutical industry to the main difficulties, particularities or precautions to be addressed in this field of therapeutic research.

Drug development in the elderly has two main purposes: (a) *drug discovery for diseases specifically occurring in the elderly patient:* we can cite as examples a drug to slow down or disrupt the evolution of Alzheimer dementia, or to help patients recover the use of their memory and attention faculties; or a drug to help the lens of the eye retrieve its transparency in cataract; (b) *assessing safety of drugs of general use in the fragile and polypathologic* (1) *aging subject.* For this second orientation, the reassessment of the benefit-risk ratio in the elderly is crucial, although theoritical models may be helpful for the prediction of safety in the context of various types of polypathology.

(*) President and CEO, Institute for the Technical Evaluation of Medicines (I.T.E.M.; Contract Clinical Research, Paris) (France).
(**) Chairman, Department of Gerontology, Centre Hospitalier, Le Mans (France).

Correspondence to : Dr L. Stéru, I.T.E.M. (Institute for the Technical Evaluation of Medicines), 93, avenue de Fontainebleau, 94276 Le Kremlin-Bicêtre cédex (France). Tél. : + 33 (1) 45.21.45.46.

(1) Polypathology refers to several concomitant diseases in the same patient.

Research in adults focuses on an improvement in functional endpoints. In the elderly patient, the current trend is to focus on decreased morbidity and, hopefully, on improved quality of life. We would argue that specific research for the elderly patient should be undertaken, in full recognition of the background factors of this population, in particular the high inter-individual heterogeneity and the fragility of these patients. Heterogeneity stems from a combination of concomitant diseases, treated or not, leading to various clinical pictures and to different levels of patient fragility.

In view of the absence of consensus or reference on how to address the difficulties and constraints of clinical and preclinical research in the elderly subject, we were concerned in not giving a too personal opinion on these issues. Therefore, we interviewed ten experts in animal research, geriatrics and other medical specialties with experience in clinical trials in elderly patients. These experts (see « acknowledgements ») kindly answered a semi-standardized interview sharing their practical experience. The facts and opinions provided here result therefore from the literature, but also from the interviews carried. They are given and compiled under the sole responsibility of the authors, who tried to remain as close as possible to the realities in the « field ».

We first will review some key issues in preclinical research in animal models and in toxicology, and then turn to the practical conduct of clinical research in elderly subjects.

PRECLINICAL RESEARCH RELATED TO AGEING STUDIES

Pre-clinical research in gerontology has two main objectives. The first is **pharmacological,** aiming to model diseases associated with ageing to discover drugs for these disorders. The other is **toxicological,** trying to predict the safety of new drugs in the elderly.

Animal models of ageing disorders

These models aim at mimicking the global disease or features of it which can be a target for drug effect. These models can involve young or old animals. There are two main limits to modeling. One is the knowledge of the mechanisms involved in the pathology, limiting, when they are not comprehensive, the predictive value of the model. The other limit is the extrapolability of the model. It is difficult to extrapolate from rodents to man, it is even more difficult to extrapolate from the healthy young animal in a test situation to the aged and diseased human.

In a recent review, Duprat (3) defines the following requirements for an animal model. The model of human disease must be (a) precisely defined, allowing extrapolation; (b) easily available (spontaneous occurrence frequent in selected species, or good reproducibility for surgically or biochemically modified animals); (c) exist in several species or at least in a multiparous one; (d) the duration of the changes should be long enough to allow its practical use; (e) compatible with laboratory use (housing and handling conditions practical, easy sampling, reasonable cost).

To define the aged animal model, the same author defines the criteria for an aged animal, accepted mainly for rodents: (a) the life-span should be accurately known in standardized laboratory conditions; (b) the 50% survival point should be calculable; (c) multiple pathology should be present.

We will not comment on the surgical modifications mimicking human diseases (e. g. parkinsonism) or other accelerated ageing models, *in vivo* or *ex vivo*. About aged animals for pharmacological research, the conditions listed make it clear that very few possibilities are offered: in practice, rodents (rats and mice) are the most used model. It is theoretically attractive to think of non-human primates for extrapolation reasons, but the cost a 20 year old monkey and the low number of available animals make this idea very unpractical.

Rats are the most often used species for experiments with aged animals. One generally considers that they are « old » after 20 months, the maximal life-span being 24-32 months. The consequence is that housing is long and difficult with the risk of mortality worsened by epidemics and other incidents. A major consequence is the cost, increasing from an average of US$10 for a young adult rat to $100 for an animal aged 20-22 months, fit for « aged animal » models.

The cost of the animals, the necessity of careful experiment planning (stocks in breeding centres are not unlimited) tend to reduce the number of subjects per group. But the polypathology often present induces a heterogeneity (like in clinical trials in elderly patients) which requires sufficient animals for statistical power.

Several models can be quoted (3) such as aged female rats as model of bone loss in relation with ovarian hormone deficiency, aged female Chinese hamsters as model of endomyometrial tumours and aged male beagle dogs as model of benign prostatic hypertrophy.

To illustrate the approach of an active field for pharmacological research, we will take the example of research in cognitive enhancing drugs. Despite the poor definition of this pharmacological class (4), research is most active in this field, and various behavioural research strategies are available (5).

Bartus et al. (6) have elaborated 5 criteria for the development of animal models of ageing: (a) the behaviour measured should display natural age-related deficits; (b) similarities should exist between that behaviour and relevant symptoms in aged humans; (c) species selected should share age-related neuro-chemical/neurological changes with some of those observed in humans, especially those that correlate with the behavioural deficit measured; (d) if a behavioural deficit is artificially induced in younger subjects, concomitant changes in central nervous system (CNS) function should mimic some of those known to exist in aged subjects; (e) some of the drugs shown to improve geriatric behaviour in clinical trials should also produce positive effects in the animal model.

The last point represents the major difficulties due to the fact that no reference compound are available to validate the predictive value of tests.

Simple learning models such as passive avoidance can show significant modifications related to ageing, and are practical for screening drugs which may compensate age-related deficits. Complex learning models test different memory functions (e.g « working memory » models and « reference memory » as explored in the radial maze, « spatial memory » as explored in the water maze, delayed responses in operand conditioning paradigms, etc.). Complex models are more time consuming (up to several weeks) but generally provide data which can be more readily interpreted. Preclinical development strategies must therefore combine screening procedures and complex profiling tests for the selection of compounds for use as potential « cognition enhancers ».

It is important that these models posses behavioural validity, since they cannot be validated using drugs. As there is no drug with proven efficacy in man for cognitive impairment, animal models must provide a convincing rationale for pursuing the development of candidate compounds in man. This is necessary both for the pharmaceutical industry, considering the investment for such a development, and for the clinical investigator, who will invest his or her limited resources in such a clinical program.

Toxicology in aged animals

Toxicology studies in aged animals aim to achieve a better prediction of the tolerance of new drugs in the elderly before clinical development. The rationale is that in many cases, safety issues, such as therapeutic ratio (well tolerated dose/active dose) of the drug is a main decision-making element in the development of a drug in indications frequent in the elderly. Therefore the prediction of poor tolerance or safety in the elderly could « kill » a drug before clinical programs have become too far advanced.

A recent overview by Hollander et al. (7) raised important issues. This kind of toxicological research is limited because of the previously mentioned difficulties in obtaining aged animals (mainly rats), and because there is no legal requirement for such data. One issue discussed is when to conduct such studies. Should it become a frequent procedure for drugs with potential life-time use or should it be restricted to special cases for « problem solving »? The methodology for such studies is not very different from toxicology testing in young animals, except the cost and practicalities. Nevertheless, there seems to be a current temptation to follow the predictions of these models, although the extrapolability from rat to man is not simple. This is even more complicated than in usual toxicology, because aged rats have a polypathology which differs from man, and which can lead to confusing conclusions, e. g. there is a frequent renal pathology resulting in proteinuria the interpretation of which is often difficult.

The results of such toxicological studies in aged animals may improve the present practice, especially when coupled with comprehensive human studies.

In conclusion, pharmacology and possibly toxicology in aged animals or in models which mimic ageing in man can help better selection of the drugs for clinical development in man. The extrapolation to man, i. e. the predictive value of these tests raises many difficulties, thus requiring multiple models and experiments before a drug profile appears. However, in some cases, animal pharmacology is the only rationale to stop or pursue the critical reading by the clinical investigators of the preclinical elements presented: *it takes a solid preclinical rationale to engage a geriatric department for months or years in a clinical trial...*

ABOUT CLINICAL RESEARCH IN ELDERLY SUBJECTS

Clinical research without individual direct therapeutic benefit

This category is defined by the French Law on bio-medical research and distinguishes this type of research (often called clinical pharmacology and pharmacokinetics, or « phase I ») from therapeutic research (with individual therapeutic benefit), where the patient participates in a trial but is at the same time under medical. No individual direct therapeutic benefit can comprise a « healthy » subject or a « symptomatic volunteer », having a disease but undergoing « manœuvres » (numerous blood sampling, arterial blood pressure measurements, etc.) which do not aim at the patient's direct care.

All interviewed experts agreed that there is no ethical concern in paying, in the same way one does for a young adult, an elderly volunteer, provided that the investigator is certain of the ability of the person undergoing the research to give a fully informed, free and conscious consent. An interesting remark concerned the increased difficulty in convincing elderly subjects to participate in these trials. Lack of curiosity? Lower attraction for the payment? Hesitation to take chances? Whatever the reasons, elderly volunteers are more difficult to find and « maintain » than young adults in clinical research without direct therapeutic benefit.

The study of pharmacokinetic parameters for a given drug in the elderly is important since numerous factors are reported to be different in the elderly and to possibly interfere with drug kinetics and action profile. Spilker (8) summarizes the general consensus of pharmacokinetic observations of medicines in the elderly in table 1 and by the following points: (a) with most medicines there is no age-related change in either the rate or the extent of absorption; a decrease may be observed with some drugs such as digoxin; (b) the volume of distribution of lipophilic medicines (such as diazepam) often increases with age, with the relative increase in body fat; no consistent pattern of change is found for plasma protein binding or volume of distribution for most medicines; (c) medicines affected by conjugation processes are not generally metabolized differently in the elderly, but medicines that undergo oxidation may have reduced hepatic clearance; (d) renal excretion of medicines often decreases with age (but not always, as commented below).

TABLE 1

FACTORS THAT MAY AFFECT PHARMACOKINETICS IN THE ELDERLY
(from Spilker B. : Guide to Clinical Trials, p. 660 [7]).

A. ABSORPTION
  1. Diminished acid secretion in the stomach
  2. Reduced gastric motility and increased gastric emptying time
  3. Decreased splanchnic blood flow
  4. Decreased intestinal surface area
  5. Decreased active transport system for monosaccharides
  6. Increased duodenal diverticula

B. DISTRIBUTION
  1. Decreased lean body mass
  2. Decreased total body water
  3. Smaller total body mass
  4. Plasma albumin decreases
  5. Increased fat is present
  6. Decreased cardiac output

C. METABOLISM
  1. Decreased liver size
  2. Decreased ratio of liver weight to body weight
  3. Decreased hepatic blood flow
  4. Decreased number of functional liver cells
  5. Decreased clearance of highly excreted medicines given i.v.
  6. Decreased enzyme activity for some medicines
  7. Enzyme may be « resistant » to induction.

D. RENAL ELIMINATION
  1. Glomerular filtration rate decreases (creatinine clearance falls)
  2. Decreased renal blood flow
  3. Renal tubular excretory function decreases
  4. Renal tubular secretory function decreases
  5. Renal mass decreases.

The clinicians' use of these data is however less clear, since claims are made that they do not notice visible differences, except for renal elimination, for which they have easy measurement methods and scales to adapt posology. Absorption is in practice seldom clinically relevant. Distribution is to be considered for undernourished patients with hypoalbuminemia, when the considered drug has a high ratio of protein binding. Liver function can be assessed but the usual routine tests are ineffective and more specialised tests are not usual since the drug fate is seldom modified.

Beside these changes, impaired homoeostasis is one important factor of fragility in the elderly. It is reported (8) that there are possible changes in receptor sensitivity: « the elderly are generally more sensitive to certain medicines (e. g. warfarin) and less sensitive to others (e. g. propanolol) ». The consequences of impaired homoeostasis can be related to drug-induced hypothermia, orthostatic hypotension (with its risk of falling) and confusion.

In conclusion, the heterogeneity in the functional deficits of the elderly, the lack of predictive value of the impairment of one organ or system to the others, the poor correlation between chronological age and so-called « physiological age » render impossible the establishment of an adequate index for predicting the changes occurring in a particular elderly individual. Pharmacokinetic data are thus a necessary prerequisite before undertaking clinical research in the elderly.

Which pharmacokinetic data should be studied and how?

Experts agree on the fact that these data are to be generated in priority for compounds where the therapeutic ratio is narrow, and/or which may threaten the homoeostasis in the patients. More generally, frequently used drugs in elderly patients should be studied for pharmacokinetic parameters. In particular it is essential to assess the CNS activity of compounds which are often responsible for confusion and/or neurological adverse reactions and which increase the risk of falling.

These data should be available before clinical programs in patients are commenced, especially when the therapeutic ratio is predicted to be narrow.

The selection of these subjects and the description of their vital functions are of major importance.

In a recently issued « Guide-line for the Study of Drugs Likely to be Used in the Elderly » (13), the Food and Drug Administration (FDA) insists on the evaluation of potential pharmacokinetic differences related to age itself or age-associated conditions, such as renal impairment, high blood pressure or multiple drug therapy. Apart from the formal pharmacokinetic studies, to answer questions about specific subgroups, a screening procedure or a « pharmacokinetic screen » may be used to identify subgroups of patients in whom the drug has unusual pharmacokinetic characteristics even where no such groups are suspected. A pharmacokinetic screen consists of obtaining, for all or most patients in phases II and III trials, a small number of steady-state blood level determinations, in order to assess the variability of blood concentrations of a drug. According to the guide-lines, even one or two such measurements can answer a number of simple but important questions, provided that the trial includes a full range of patients in terms of age, sex, race, weight, body composition, concomitant illness, smoking and alcohol consumption and the use of concomitant drugs. This can help determine whether the elderly differ from adults, and whether the possible differences are the result of age alone or other age associated-conditions. In the elderly population, the presence of outliers indicates the need to conduct further trials to explore the relationship of dose, blood levels and patient characteristics. An outlier is defined as a patient with a tenfold or greater difference in plasma level than expected (8).

Studies in renal failure patients should be conducted when this is in the preferential elimination path of the compound. In our opinion it is not necessary to study patients who are both aged *and* suffering from renal failure since it is only the renal function which is assessed. For drugs with significant hepatic metabolism, especially drugs undergoing oxidation, special pharmacokinetic studies should be carried out to look for genetic variability in metabolism, or drug-drug interaction. The same Guide-line (as quoted by *Scrip*), recommends that specific interaction studies should be carried out in cases where the therapeutic ratio is low and the chance of concomitant therapy or illness is great. The studies needed, decided on a case-by-case basis, could comprise an evaluation of digoxin interaction, a review of the effects of hepatic enzyme inducers (e. g. phenobarbital) and inhibitors (e. g. cimetidine) for those drugs which undergo extensive hepatic metabolism, together with studies to determine whether a drug which is extensively bound to protein is displaced by another drug (e. g. displacement of warfarin by NSAIDs).

On clinical trial conduct with elderly patients

How to define the « geriatric » patient population when heterogeneity increases with age?

The consequences of ageing on physical and cognitive impairment result from a continuous process, uneven in its inter-individual progress. There is no satisfactory definition of a geriatric population. Is a « geriatric » subject a person over 65, the official retirement age in most countries? If between 60 and the early 70s (« young old » or « senior adult »), few pathologies are generally present, impairments due to ageing will generally occur from the age of 75, involving all body systems, accelerated or caused by various diseases (treated or untreated), but also by the lifestyle and habits. This geriatric population « constitutes the broad spectrum of subjects ranging from the totally independent suffering from only minor ailments and who live alone in the community, to the mildly dependent who rely upon day care or day hospital, to the bed-ridden polymedicated, institutionalized, demented patients » (2).

Polypathology is a keyword for elderly, but to consider one by one the different diseases of the elderly patient is not acceptable. Nor is the widespread belief that there is a « normal » decline of certain organs, such as renal function. It has been shown (9, 10) that ageing does not necessarily lead to functional renal insufficiency. The same kind of results have been found for cardiac output (11).

Various concomitant pathologies may occur in the same individual, pathologies which may exist in the adult or be specific to ageing. The clinical picture is therefore complicated and unpredictable. One should consider not only the pathological deficits, but also: **compensated deficits** (i.e. silent or compatible with tests in the normal adult range) which may decompensate in the presence of a moderate disturbing factor (e.g. concomitant disease, stress, nutritive imbalance, adverse drug reaction or drug-drug interaction). This may, in a clinical trial, result in an iatrogenic cascade of adverse reactions. The phenomenon illustrated here results in the increased **fragility** of the elderly patients.

Heterogeneity, aggravated by increased fragility, is as important in research as in the normal healthcare of these patients. These considerations determine the precautions to be taken in research in the elderly, as well as the limits of data interpretation and extrapolation.

To compensate for heterogeneity and fragility we would recommend the following precautions:

– study groups with sufficient numbers of patients, to decrease the odds of an imbalance between groups, due to uneven distribution of known or unknown severity factors. Another rationale for larger groups is that the power of the trial may be lower than the calculations resulting from adult experience because of increased dispersion of parameters. As a consequence, it is necessary to include a larger number of elderly patients than adults to reach a given statistical power;

– stratify the research population if some heterogeneity factors predictably influence the results. Such factors can include renal function (affecting drug kinetics), nutritional status (affecting patients recovery capacities, e. g. in pressure wounds studies...). It is important to remain reasonable in the number of stratification groups, knowing that the clinical investigator can hardly handle more than 2 stratification criteria. As one investigator has once stated « Never more stratification criteria than pockets in my white gown! ». Minimisation techniques may appear appealing but inevitably lead to complicated logistics and possible criticisms on the statistical front;

– design follow-up and statistical analysis to take into account the fact that long-term studies will have to accept higher numbers of drop-outs (for intercurrent diseases and treatments occurring which are incompatible with the study, deaths, etc.). Every effort must be made to avoid patients « lost-to-follow-up ». A simple phone call to the relatives, the family or nursing home doctor can sometimes resolve this difficult issue which turns such patients into « early terminators », and threatens the validity of the trial.

Defining a convincing « geriatric patient population »

Some unofficial terms used to describe geriatric patients are the following: « Future old, old adult, young old, old, very old, old old, frail old, too old, *Hors d'Age* ». These terms are a mixed reference to chronologic age and a global assessment of the physiological status. They are more entertaining than accurate, and can be sometimes confusing since no consensus exists. They may, however help communication by explaining to colleagues what kind of patients (in terms of age **and** medical condition) can be considered for particular kinds of study.

A frequent distorting factor in geriatric study reports is the presentation of results from patients « over 65 » (mean, for example, 72) which in fact is similar to an adult population. Authors have described elderly patients included with a diagnosis of « poor nutritional status » and extrapolate study results concerning the nutritional value of a new product. Further analysis reveals that these patients were suffering from terminal cancer, which completely alters the implications of the study, moving out of the geriatric setting, into oncology. Conclusions drawn from an extremely small « coincidental » elderly patient population in a large clinical trial must be made carefully, with the possibility of performing sub-group analysis only when one is sure that the group is representative both in terms of numbers and patient characteristics.

Obviously, the population to be studied depends on the study objectives. If the purpose is to assess benefit/risk ratio in the elderly, or even simply the safety of a drug, geriatricians require a mean of age of 80, with patients whose health is threatened by a pre-existing polypathology, and who have *in addition* the disease for which the investigational drug is prescribed. This is not a powerfully convincing situation for the geriatricians. When the patients are studied in a specialized department (neurology, surgery or cardiology) they are often found to have been in good shape before *the* studied disease occurred, with a minimal threat to their homoeostasis...

In conclusion, the site where the study is conducted will determine the study population, and will be determined by the study objective and phase of research: if the purpose is to assess efficacy in an age-related disease, and the phase is II, a statistically « powerful trial » is required with as few patients as possible, which leads to the selection of « healthy patients », who suffer from nothing but the disease and the investigational treatment. These patients are, depending on the disease, at home or in a nursing home, or consult at an outpatient clinic. In Phase III, more « real world » data is required with fewer « pure » cases. In this case more patients are needed in a pragmatic study design.

If the purpose is « safety » in the frail old, the study should be conducted in a geriatrics department (or nursing home for milder severity), and this is a necessary objective in Phases III and IV.

Ethics and the consent

The French Law on clinical research requires that patients who are not officially placed under guardian responsibility must give their free and written informed consent prior to their inclusion in a clinical trial. Investigators all report considerable difficulties with this procedure:

– time requirement: informing an elderly subject requires approximately about 30 minutes, as opposed to a usual 10-15 minutes generally requested for informing an adult;

– reluctance to sign: elderly patients feel that signing somehow reduces the liability of their doctor (although the contrary is written). The importance placed on this procedure is higher in elderly patients, indeed, reports of patients feeling as though they are signing « their will » have been made;

– difficulties in understanding: cultural barriers, lack of information on the nature and meaningof clinical research is, difficulties in coping with a new situation all create an atmosphere of tension even when physical (sight problems) or cognitive (mild dementia) impairment are not present;

– interactions with other members of their environment: study refusal on the part of the family has been observed or has led to placing conditions on the informed consent. « Keep my grandmother in hospital and I will encourage her to sign »;

– lack of involvement: the patients may sign to participate in the study for simple reasons of wanting to be polite or « nice » to the doctor. Under such conditions, the patient is psychologically not fully involved in the study and is likely to be a poor drug complier or drop out prematurely.

If the patient is demented and has a guardian, it seems very difficult if at all possible to receive the guardian's signature, with the claims that he/she is not trained to protect the patient's health.

In borderline cases (patients with mild cognitive impairment) the value of the « informed » consent may be questionable. This issue is usually described to the ethics committee who assess the ethical and practical aspects of the issue.

Concomitant therapies and compliance

Concomitant medications are often taken by elderly patients, frequently prescribed by several different physicians (General Practitioner, cardiologist and rheumatologist) together with the scenario of various self-medications. It is reported (1) that elderly patients receive in the USA an average of 11 treatments per year and that shortly before hospitalization, they receive an average of 4.5 ± 3.0 medications. It is also reported that the chance of an older patient falling is correlated with the number of drugs taken and that drug associated cognitive impairment is nine times more likely to occur in patients taking more than four prescription medications.

The preparation of the study protocol must bear this background situation of concomitant medications in mind, because immediate pre-study treatment withdrawal can have severe physical and psychological effects. Nevertheless, it is unsatisfactory to assess a patient who receives several drugs, the interactions of which are seldom known. Neither it is satisfactory to assess a patient who may be experiencing a « withdrawal crisis ».

Stability of treatments at baseline can be one solution, which does not however address the interaction issue. A further solution is, if appropriate, to withdraw certain ancillary therapies within a pre-defined period before study inclusion for a baseline assessment. Importantly, the protocol must aim to avoid poor compliers feeling « guilty » which leads to dishonest claims of grug compliance.

Drug compliance is largely influenced by the type of investigational site used in a clinical study. Clearly the hospital or nursing home provides a safe environment to assure a higher degree of drug compliance. Nevertheless, a complex dosing regimen of drops plus tablets in the morning, different drops only at lunchtime and capsules and tablets to be taken in the evening is a frequent drawback of many study protocols in elderly patients, particularly those living alone. Such difficulties can be relatively easily addressed, in particular for patients suffering from dementia or tremor. Practical logistics established thoughtfully can be decisive factors. Blisters market with the day and time, clear reminders, diary cards and even phone calls can considerably help drug compliance.

Prescriptions by another doctor represent another source of compliance difficulties. The investigator must be responsible for contacting all treating physicians to make them aware of the study protocol. The experts interviewed raised an interesting sociological point. It appears that the elderly patient is *a priori* considered incapable of understanding/deciding upon his or her health. The doctor in charge, even if only on emergency call, will take decisions on behalf of the patient more freely than for an adult (hospitalization, surgery, changing treatment...) unless strong opposition is made by the patient. This is often a cause of early termination of trials, i.e. somebody deciding to change treatments and nobody being aware of this decision for many days.

Another interesting contributor to poor compliance is « deconditioning » of drug supplies. Nurses often open capsules, squash tablets to mix them in food. This practice can lead to absorption difficulties and to unblinding of the nature of the treatment i. e. blue tablets versus pink tablets hidden in capsules, and even the investigator may not be aware of this violation.

Study objectives selection and efficacy assessment criteria

Pragmatically clinical trials can be divided into 4 groups (15) :

(a) **Studies aimed at curing the disease :** a long-lasting absence of the disease according to specific criteria. This presumes the existence of objective assessment tools and verifiable hypotheses on the drug's mechanism of action. In the absence of the above, the term « pseudo-specificity » is used to oppose the claims of a curative effect in the elderly. For example, a drug can show a positive effect in elderly patients, without being specific to geriatric populations. An example of this « pseudo-specificity » issue is illustrated (18) in the debate concerning research on cognition enhancers. The U.S. FDA regards positive effects in Alzheimer disease as the only evidence of efficacy of such drugs. Nevertheless, experts consider « age-associated memory impairment » as a sufficiently specific diagnosis to justify approval for an indication.

(b) **Studies aimed at slowing deterioration:** the objectives here are to arrest the evolution of the disease, or to provide prophylactic relief. Here too objective criteria are necessary.

(c) **Studies aimed at treating symptoms:** in this case the objectives are limited and include relief of suffering, whether specific or not.

(d) **Long term assessment of the benefit-risk ratio:** these studies allow the validation of therapeutic strategies.

There can therefore be 4 types of possible objectives for a pragmatic clinical trial:

1) **Immediate efficacy** e. g. lowering blood pressure over 24 hours.

2) **Medium term efficacy** e. g. persistent blood pressure lowering effect over 6 months.

3) **Benefit to be seen in terms of morbidity and/or mortality** e. g. complication of hypertension over 5 years.

4) **Benefits in terms of morbidity or mortality versus decline in quality of life – assessment of the ratios** i.e. what decline in quality of life is the price for a certain benefit of longevity.

The protocol and the inclusion/exclusion criteria are a direct result of these basic decisions. It is clear that the first two of the above categories are considerably easier to study than the latter two. The answers to these latter points are at present mostly proposed as extrapolations instead of proper studies.

The assessment criteria, as required by the generic clinical trial methodology using « decision-making statistical aids », must be divided into « principal » and « ancillary ». The reason being, if two criteria are « principal », unless the issue is stated in the protocol (e.g. both criteria must improve significantly for the drug to be considered active), when the drug improves one and not the other criterion, what has been achieved? Is the drug efficacious and safe? Answers are vague and regulatory authorithies, at best, uncertain.

Criteria used can be objective measures or subjective tests, assessed by the investigator, the nursing team and/or caregivers, and/or by self-assessment on the part of the patient. One should look critically at the meaning of « objective »: reading joint X-rays or biopsy-slides may be « objective » if the reading is done by an expert in blind conditions.

In general, every effort should be made to reduce assessment variability in all possible respects, in order to compensate for the loss of statistical power resulting from a heterogeneous patient population. If rating scales are used, « rating harmonization sessions » must be organized between investigators, for the purposes of commenting upon and reducing differences.

The protocol should be specific on issues such as how and when the « Clinical Global Impression » is assessed in a dementia study. Is extensive information available, including relatives' assessments and psychological tests, or is it simply the investigators' overall opinion that is referred to? All such issues should be clearly stated in the protocol. It may happen that investigators see fit to reject one criterion during the study. Taking, once again, a dementia case as an example, it may be seen that Folstein's Mini-Mental State (MMS) raises relevant problems. A truly demented Nobel Prize-winner may have a MMS of over 25 and not be included, while an undemented illiterate person with a low Intelligence Quota may display a MMS of under 20, and should nevertheless not be considered as demented. Therefore, instead of being « pushed » to « weight » the rating so that the patient fits with the protocol (one knows how sought-after these patients are) a new trend is to allow flexibility within the inclusion criteria range provided that this is documented by the investigator.

Other issues (such as exact assessment session « scenario », sentences said to introduce key elements, etc.) should be specified in an operating manual, if the protocol is too heavy to be easily digested.

Who rates the patient?

The investigator generally rates the main criterion, but there are exceptions. A psychologist often rates particular tests or scales, such as ADAS (Alzheimer Dementia Assessment Scale). A neurologist and/or a psychiatrist may rate other dimensions of CNS functioning. The nursing team or other caregivers, may participate in the rating and the patient may make a self-assessment.

As indicated earlier, other specialists may interpret other specific parameters (such as, imaging, biology, pathology...), and functional indexes.

Assessment interview with and elderly patient

As mentioned above, elderly patients tend to speak more slowly than adults at the same cultural level. This may be the result of a retardation of thought processes, a particular functional dysarthria, or depressive mood. Possibly a mixture of all three. It is wise to respect the individual rhythm of the patient, for otherwise he or she is effectively placed in a failure position. The best approach, then, is to adjust the pace of the interview according to the patient.

A further issue which can lead to an upset patient and a subsequent broken relationship is being unnecessarily offensive. Simple « childish » tests or questions may seem disrespectful or undignified to the patient who may protest (« I'm not senile yet »). Sometimes, of course, this reaction concerns a real inability to respond to the test question. Building an appropriate fruitful relationship takes time and sensitivity.

No consensus can be reached with regard to a reasonable maximum time for the assessment of elderly patients. Some say 20 minutes whilst others maintain that up to two hours may be possible. It is important that the interview should be diverse and varied because, as is unanimously agreed, continuous psychometric testing is exhausting.

On a more practical level it is worth mentioning that should the patient be required to read or draw something, do remind him or her to bring a pair of glasses to the next consultation.

Quality of life in geriatric clinical trials

A recent review by Williams (16) states, « Factors which in earlier years of life at first seem to be optional, become critical in old age for the maintenance of a person's integrity, independence, and autonomy; they become life-or-death matters, figuratively and literally ». We can refer to the subjective assessment (i.e. seen from the patient's point of view) of these matters as « health-related quality of life ».

Autonomy issues determined by medical condition and their treatment are important and constitute a basic component of the quality of life. But assessment of quality of life involves a multifactorial approach, adding to medical and functional aspects also psycho-social consequences.

The tools for measuring quality of life can be general assessments (such as the Nottingham Health Profile, validated in both French and English) or function oriented tools, depending on the predominant disability of the patient population. An inventory is not possible here but some reference books (17) are available on the subject.

Protocol writing and study planning

Feasibility assessment is of paramount importance in all clinical research, but even more so in clinical trials involving the elderly because of the sheer number in of difficulties raised. The worst which can happen take the form of « *armchair protocols* ». Two such protocol types are frequently encountered:

1) Those which set unrealistic criteria, describing an ideal patient who cannot exist

in the real world. The outcome of such trials depends on onsite clinical monitoring. If the monitoring is rigorous and intelligent, no inclusions are to be expected. At this point someone will discover that an error has been made somewhere along the line, will listen to the investigators and will amend the protocol. If, however, the clinical monitoring is pseudo-rigorous and less than intelligent (« Dear investigator, we want all boxes ticked or you will not be paid and will never work in clinical research again »), even the most honourable investigator will be forced towards « a life of crime »... and all boxes will be ticked. At some stage somebody (most likely the statistician) will find this population suspicious, and, inevitably... the drug won't work...

2) The perfectionist's protocol and Case Report Form (CRF). Based on a kind of obsessive-compulsive logic, the best assessment criterion not being entirely proven, this protocol will make use of all possible assessments. The CRF looks like a telephone directory and the completion time does not allow for a second look at the patient. We believe that the available time for CRF completion is, unfortunately, not that elastic. So every added « box » competes with the amount of time allocated to the others and thus dilutes the possible attention given.

Feasibility assessment requires a collaboration between sponsor and investigator(s), based on realism, trust, mutual respect and negotiation. Even when everybody is convinced that it is feasible, experienced professionals know that difficulties will inevitably be encountered. If the study is pronounced **not** feasible, why bother starting at all? Start the next project instead !

Safety and tolerance assessment

Fragility in elderly patients is one of the main reasons for undertaking geriatric trials, so safety and tolerance issues are absolutely essential. Unfortunately: (a) tolerance is integrated in the polypathology of the patient, making it difficult to determine whether a particular symptom is drug-induced or disease-related; (b) concomitant medications make for further confusion; (c) many symptoms of poor tolerance are ambiguous (falling) or are forgotten/hidden by the patient (an episode of confusion, for example, or incontinence); (d) the probability of death is high in this group.

Some experts view the occurrence of some adverse reactions as the result of a number of simultaneously-occurring events, thus imbalancing the homoeostasis of the patient. For example, Drug A alone would not cause confusion, but when coupled with the somatic disease from which the patient suffers (causing impaired nutritional status) and the effects of hospitalization disorganizing the patient's environment could have serious effects. When combined with drug B, which has sedative potential, the patient might experienced dramatic confusion. It is these aspects which complicate the process of tolerance assessment in the elderly.

All geriatricians emphasise the danger of central or peripheral nervous system adverse drug reactions, the reason being that a little confusion or disorientation, dizziness or orthostatic hypotension can lead to a fall with potentially severe consequences for the future of the patient. A fracture necessarily leads to hospitalization, where the patient can become bed-ridden and possibly die. Therefore, the prediction, from the pharmacological data, of a CNS sedative effect and the consequent assessment of such effects in clinical trials is of the utmost importance.

We will not describe the usual procedures for reporting adverse events, but let us underline a fact often poorly understood at study sites: the title of « adverse drug reaction » changed to « adverse event » since « reaction » implies a causality link. Adverse events comprise any adverse incident occurring to the patient, even if the investigator believes it is completely unrelated to the drug. By so defining adverse events the opportunity is given to pool data from different trials and « meta-analyse » in order to detect effects seemingly unrelated to the drug at first sight.

In these studies, the event of death and the occurrence of other incidents are frequent, the reporting procedure for adverse events must be strictly followed.

Logistics of the trial and practical issues which can turn an exciting project into a disaster or a success

The spouse, relatives, next of kin and other caregivers will be involved in the trial: they influence the consent; will help with or antagonize the patient's compliance with the investigational drug and other medications, will assist the patient in travelling to and from assessment visits, and often, are themselves part of the efficacy and tolerance assessment. This leads experienced investigators to build a positive relationship not only with the patient but also with his or her personal network of caregivers.

The family doctor, the specialists and other health professionals will also be involved. If improperly handled, they will not want to know about the trial. At best, they will ignore it and prescribe other therapies often incompatible with trial specifications, and at worst, antagonise the trial, criticising what is done to their patient. It is advisable to build a positive and courteous relationship with the health professionals identified by the patient and leave a document with the patient explaining the basis of the trial in which he/she is participating.

Transportation is an important factor for the patient, especially if disabled. Assistance in this area is vital in order to eliminate an important and seldom identified reason for the early termination of trials. The trial should include a transport budget which can (a) reimburse the patient for taxi rides; (b) arrange regular transportation of the patient with an ambulance service (or sanitary light vehicles); (c) compensate (and motivate) a relative or neighbour of the patient to drive him or her to the assessments. The organisation of these payments is sometimes problematic from the point of view of both accountancy, patient confidentiality and free informed consent. Debates may be raised, but with the help of the investigator, this should not prove insurmountable.

If transporting the subject facilitates compliance on the one hand, on the other it brings further problems. When making a cognitive assessment, one should take into account the fact that « going to town » or to the hospital has a generally disturbing effect on the elderly, which may well impair the test performance.

Although clinical trials are often proposed, (amid complaints that such proposals are too numerous and too urgent), many clinical investigators lack training in the clinical research field. This makes such research even more difficult and weakens the power ot the investigator to convince the sponsor when a question is being debated. Therefore, each trial should be seen as an opportunity to learn more about clinical research.

An important issue is that of time management. Investigators must carefully plan to have the time to assess each patient recruited. It should be borne in mind that the patients are likely to speak more slowly and that questions may have to be repeated frequently. In many protocols, the patient assessment lasts from 40 minutes to 2 hours. This amounts to no more than 2 to 3 patient assessments per half day. The question then presents itself: how many half-days are available for research in the week? This should be a limiting factor in the inclusion of patients. Careful planning is necessary therefore to avoid « jamming » and nervousness.

An interesting technique was suggested by one expert: he waits until 3 to 4 patients are ready for inclusion (in pathologies which allow that of course). Then all patients are included, followed. and « terminated » together. The clear advantage of this method is that research efforts, instead of being scattered, are concentrated over a specific period of time.

Institutional teams (geriatric department, nursing home) share one universal characteristic: too much work, not enough staff. « Research » is frowned upon. They can hardly cope with a normal hard working day without having to shoulder the added burden of the requirements of a protocol. And what is the benefit anyway? Opposition can take the awkward form of moralistic reproaches: the poor old patients suffer enough without useless additional hardships inflicted for the sake of research (i.e. investigators money...). For the sake of smooth cooperation, staff should therefore be actively involved in all aspects of the research, including a financial return on their extra work. The practicalities involved present further difficulties however. If paying nothing to the staff is self-defeating, some investigators warn against directly paying the staff who help research. This raises jealousy and arguments, and sometimes guilty feelings. An elegant solution is to open a special account for « research money » and to use half of it for improving the department space in the interest of the patients (decoration, videos, etc.), and the other half to pay for travelling to congresses and the collective entertainment of the staff. A further solution, more common in the USA than in France, is to hire research staff (« study coordinator », « research nurse », « research psychologist » or even medics, etc.). The integration of such research staff with the hospital staff is essential.

In conclusion, research issues should be debated with the staff, and the investigator should select projects in which his or her interest is convincing enough to be effectively communicated in selling the project to the staff. Honesty and transparency are, here, as in many aspects of management, two principles which can build the collaboration necessary to undertake difficult studies, especially if these are long term. Experts with extensive investigative experience can be identified when they ask 3 questions before accepting the study protocol: (a) does the study sponsor provide a sound and motivating rationale for the compound to justify a clinical programme? (b) is the investigational team able to find an adequate patient population and the necessary time for the project? (c) when the project is completed what will it contribute to the health care of future patients?

A selection of practical issues is summarized in table 2.

TABLE 2

SPECIAL CONSIDERATIONS IN DESIGNING PROTOCOLS
AND CONDUCTING STUDIES IN ELDERLY PATIENTS
(from Spilker B. [12])

1. Use reminder cards, mailings, telephone calls prior to appointements.
2. Arrange for transportation to and from study site.
3. Arrange for periodic reviews to insure patient understanding of protocol requirements.
4. Conduct periodic checks of compliance.
5. Include a sufficient number and frequency of tests of vital status and other safety parameters to insure patient well-being.
6. Avoid rigourous demands which might unduly strain some patients.
7. Involve family members, nursing home staff, or other individuals to provide assistance and observe the patient for relevant signs and symptoms.
8. Consider previous data with the test therapy to determine whether elderly patients are at higher risk of adverse reactions than a younger adult population.

CONCLUSION

Research in the elderly is a growing field both in animal and in clinical drug development. Animal data are often the only rationale for justifying clinical trials, thus deserving a critical appraisal; toxicology in aged animals, necessarily limited by their availability, raises questions of when it should be performed and for which compounds.

Because of the limited availability of geriatricians' time for research projects, due to their considerable work-load within health care, project selection in which the investigational team will be involved for a considerable time must be carefully based on a critical assessment of the rationale for the study.

A critical feasibility analysis must be made at the protocol preparation stage integrating the future investigators and the sponsor, so that the specificities of the study site (which will play a major role in the selection of the patient population) are taken into account. Communication will then be extended to the environment of the patient, the physicians in charge of the patient's ambulatory care and to any other person involved in the trial from whom cooperation will be requested.

The heterogeneity of the population is a key issue to address and the protocol must find a compromise between the definition of homogeneous in inexistent patient groups and an easy inclusion of groups so heteregeneous that the statistical analysis leads to nothing. The logistics of the trial involving the investigator and the sponsor with its study monitoring team must plan for every event, providing provisions for very close documentation, since it cannot avoid numerous drop-outs. The management and reporting of adverse events is of paramount importance, perhaps even more so in research in the elderly.

A discussion of the results must assess the clinical signification as well as statistical significance. This can be integrated into the study protocol by use of clinically relevant criteria, valid in the elderly population.

The motivation for research in elderly patients originates in geriatrician concerns about the pharmaceutical industry presenting adult data for extrapolation in the elderly, which may be possible but are often not a good predictor for elderly profiles.

Geriatricians require as well as regulatory authorities, increasingly also the pharmaceutical industry, to be told what a given drug may bring in the geriatric setting i.e. patients aged over 80 and with concomitant disorders. Geriatricians need to have information on what benefit a given drug brings, in their patient population, at what dose (depending on what factors), the treatment period, with which associated risks and with which safety monitoring. An ideal scenario? We believe it justifies the concerted efforts of sponsors and investigators for geriatric research.

ACKNOWLEDGEMENTS

The authors wish to express their warmest thanks to the following experts who accepted to share their knowledge and experience in the interviews they kindly accepted:

Prof. BOUSSER (Neurologist, Paris)
Prof. DUPONT (geriatrician, Dijon)
Dr DUPRAT (Centre de Recherche MSD-Chibret, Riom, France)
Prof. IMBS (Cardio-renal Medicine and Pharmacology, Strasbourg)
Prof. KUNTZMANN (geriatrician, Strasbourg)
Dr OLLIVIER (geriatrician, Marseille)

Dr PETER (geriatrician, Mulhouse)
Prof. PIETTE (geriatrician, Paris)
Dr PORSOLT (I.T.E.M. - Labo, Le Kremlin-Bicêtre)
Dr VELLAS (geriatrician, Toulouse)
Dr FORETTE (geriatrician, Paris)
Prof. SPILKER (Burroughs Wellcome, U.S.A.)

The authors also wish to thank Ms V. CLEMENTS for the editorial help she kindly provided.

BIBLIOGRAPHY

1. OWENS (N.J.), LARRAT (E.P.), FRETWELL (M.D.) : Improving compliance in the older patient : the role of comprehensive functional assessment. In : Patient Compliance in Medical Practice and Clinical Trials, Cramer J.A., Spilker B. (Eds.), Raven Press, New York, 1991.
2. MORSELLI (P.), GUILLIET (P.) : Drug developments in the elderly : problems and constraints. In : Burley (D.) et al. (eds.) : The Proceedings of the 6th International Meeting of Pharmaceutical Physicians, Brighton, June 1987 ; MacMillan Press, London, 1988.
3. DUPRAT (P.) : Aged animals as model of human disease : an overview. In : XI Proceedings of the « Role and evolution of the laboratory animal in biomedical research on ageing ». 10th IFA-CREDO workshop, May 11-12, 1989, Milan, Italy ; pp. 15-32. Published by Fondation Marcel Merieux, Lyon.
4. PORSOLT (R.D.), STERU (L.) : Cognition enhancers – from Animals to Man. Pharmacopsychiatry, 1990/23 (suppl. II), 99-100.
5. PORSOLT (R.D.), LENEGRE (A.) : The use of aging animals for the study of memory disturbance and its treatment. In : Proceedings of the « Role and evolution of the laboratory animal in biomedical research on ageing). 10th IFA-CREDO workshop, May 11-12, 1989, Milan, Italy ; pp. 95-112. Published by Fondation Marcel Mérieux, Lyon..
6. BARTUS (R.T.), DEAN (R.L.), BEER (B.) : An evaluation of drugs for improving memory in aged monkeys : implications for clinical trials in humans. Psychopharmacol. Bull., 19, 168-184, 1983.
7. HOLLANDER (C.F.), DELORT (P.), DUPRAT (P.) : Toxicology in the older age group. In : Progress in predictive toxicology (D.R. Clayson et al. Eds). Esevier Science Publishers, 1990, pp. 113-142.
8. SPILKER (B.) : Special patient populations. In : Guide to clinical trials, pp. 658-672, Raven Press, New York, 1991.
9. LINDEMAN (R.D.), TOBIN (J.), SHOCK (N.W.) : Longitudinal studies on the rate of decline in renal function with age. J. Am. Geriatr. Soc., 33, 278-285, 1985.
10. LARSSON (M.), JAGENBURG (R.), LANDAHL (S.) : A study of 5-creatinine, ^{51}Cr-EDTA clearance, endogenous creatinine clearance and maximal tubular water reabsorption. Scand. J. Clin. Lab. Invest., 1986, 46, 593-598.
11. RODEHEFFER (R.J.), GERSTENBLITH (G.), BECKER (L.C.), FLEG (J.L.) et al. : Exercise cardiac output is maintained with advancing age in healthy human subjects : cardiac dilatation and increased stroke volume compensate for a diminished heart rate. Circulation, 1984, 69, 203-213.
12. SPILKER (B.) : Conducting studies in special patient populations. In : Guide to Planning and Managing Multiple Clinical Studies : p. 163, Raven Press, New York, 1987.
13. Scrip n° 1499, March 23rd 1990, p. 25.
14. Scrip n° 1655, September 27 1991, p. 4.
15. VETEL (J.M.), MONTASTRUC (J.L.) : L'essai des médicaments en gériatrie. Manuel de Gériatrie Clinique. Duportet, Paris (sous presse).
16. WILLIAMS (T.F.) : Geriatrics : a Perspective on Quality of Life and Care for Older People. In : Quality of Life Assessments in Clinical Trials (B. Spilker Ed.), pp. 217-223, Raven Press, New York, 1990.
17. SPILKER (B.) : Quality of Life Assessments in Clinical Trials (B. Spilker Ed.), pp. 217-223, Raven Press, New York, 1990.
18. LEBER (P.) in : Treatment Development Strategies for Alzheimer's Disease, CROOK (T.), BARTUS (R.T.), FERRIS (F.), GERSHON (S.) [Eds.], Mark Powley Assoc., Connecticut 1985.

NEWS IN PHARMACOLOGY, THERAPEUTIC AND AGING

We present here the abstracts of articles published in the international editions of Facts and Research in Gerontology 1992. Reprint are available to the authors (see contributors directory) or to Serdi : 29, rue de Saint-Pétersbourg, 75008 Paris.

1 - DOPAMINERGIC SYSTEMS AND AGING : A. Nieoullon

Summary. – Measurement of dopamine neuronal markers with aging evidences a marked decrease in dopaminergic transmission. Interestingly, such a decrease in dopaminergic transmission preferentially involves a marked reduction of the D1 and D2 dopaminergic receptors whereas presynaptic markers showed either in humans and animals only a moderate alteration. In fact, more recent data seem to illustrate a rather limited decrease (about 30 %) of the total number of mesencephalic dopaminergic neurons with age, in contradiction with previous studies showing more drastic changes. Taking into consideration the primary role of dopamine in the psychobiologic adaptation at behavioural level, data of biochemical analysis further strongly suggest that alteration of behaviour with aging correlates with a concomitant decrease in central dopaminergic transmission. Such a proposal, however, has to be considered with the view that numerous other neuronal systems can likely contribute with dopamine to behavioural adaptation. However, stimulation of dopaminergic tranmission may actually improve behaviour in aging as shown from pharmacological studies suggesting a primary role of dopaminergic transmission in regulating behaviour. (Facts and Research in Gerontology 1992)

Key-words : Aging, Dopamine.

2 - CLINICAL EXPERIMENTATION : THE ELDERLY SUBJECT : Y. Juillet

Summary. – Drug registration health authorities currently consider that there is a requirement for dedicated studies on the changes that ageing introduces on the use to be made of drugs. Such an assessment is not an easy undertaking since the elderly population is not homogeneous neither as regards their physiological characteristics nor as regards the pathologies liable to be associated with the treated illness. A pragmatic approach, using all data collected during clinical development, will allow to determine whether any particular studies are required for confirmation of the posology, and to specify the optimal conditions for the use of the drug. Whatever the level of information that is to be gained from such studies, prescription of drugs for the aged will always have to be subjects to particular precaution. (Facts and Research in Gerontology 1992)

Key-words : aged populations, drug, pharmacokinetic, clinical trial.

3 - PHARMACOLOGICAL EFFICIENCY OF DRUGS PROPOSED IN PSYCHOBEHAVIORAL TROUBLES OF BRAIN AGEING : A 1992 REVIEW : P. Bustany

Summary. – No general etiological treatment of brain aging was nowadays reported. But the concept of « psychobehavioral troubles of brain ageing » (PTBA) was identified and included as an entity, in fact very polymorphic, in the official rules of prescription of up to 150 drugs in the P.D.R. book. We have to cope with an intense demand from the aged patients and a recognized, real but rather moderate efficiency of these derivates. The difficulty, quite the art, of the prescription remains in a previous acute analysis of the varied symptomes to choose which group of derivates will benefit the patient. A readily but not always easily treated, origin of these PTBA is their iatrogenic revelation by many unrelated drugs (diuretics and anti-hypertension derivates first), very often underestimated in old people. We reviewed there in a synthetic and graduated schema, the different families of compounds which must be evoked for the PTBA treatment, giving for each one, the state of art and the new acquisitions about their efficiency in human or animal collected during this year 1991. The most new molecules, often still under limited investigation were described, together with some more famous compounds for which a new pharmacological use was recognized. So will be discussed : – the obsolete treatments to avoid, often costly, sometimes hazardous for the patient ; – the usual therapeutics, well-known, with a measured effect and, in some cases, really unbased or in full opposition to the newly discovered neurophysiological regulations ; – the neurotransmitter supply, of course indirect, unindicated there as a source of partial and unbalanced effects on a particular system : an action quite out of meaning in the absence of identified dementia ; – the new trophic treatments, often efficient, under investigation, with acute problems of administration, and sometimes recorded as side-effects of Converting-Enzymes-Antagonists and other peptides, ... ; – the scavenger molecules, hard to use in human (hepatotoxicity) but very efficient to prevent many biochemical stigmates of brain aging ; – at least, some varied drugs, not directly and firstly involved in PTBA treatment but for which these fields of indication may be soon officially accepted.
(Facts and Research in Gerontology 1992)

Key-words : Acetylcholine, Aging, Agonist, Behavior, Brain, Dopamine, GABA, Human, Memory, Metabolism, Neuropeptide, Pharmacology, Psychotrope, Review, Vasodilatator.

4 - PREVENTION AND TREATMENT OF OSTEOPOROSES IN 1992 : M.-C. Chapuy, P.-J. Meunier

Summary. – For the treatment of osteoporosis, two approaches can be made to prevent or to reverse bone loss : use of agents which stimulate bone formation or of agents which inhibit bone resorption. In 1992, hormone replacement therapy remains the best suited preventive treatment for postmenopausal osteoporosis, particularly in the early stages. Intranasal salmon calcitonine is an effective alternative. For the treatment of established osteoporosis, sodium fluoride has proven its direct effect on stimulating new bone formation. The doses must be moderate even if a significant proportion of patients does not respond to the therapy. Antiresorptive agents such as bisphosphonates appeared to be efficacious in the treatment and prevention of osteoporosis but their long term benefit and safety are yet to be determined.
(Facts and Research in Gerontology 1992)

Key-words : osteoporosis, 17 ß œstradiol, fluoride, calcitonine, bisphosphonates.

SELECTION OF LITERATURE

1 - DOPAMINERGIC SYSTEMS AND AGING : A. Nieoullon

1. CALNE (D.B.) and PEPPARD (R.F.) : Aging of the nigrostriatal pathway in humans. *Can. J. Neurol. Sci.,* 1987, 14, 424-427.
2. NIEOULLON (A.) : Dopamine et vieillissement cérébral. *Neuropsy.,* 1990, 4, 7-12.
3. GAGE (F.H.) and BJORKLUND (A.) : Neural grafting in the aged rat brain. *Ann. Rev. Physiol.,* 1986, 48, 447-459.
4. GLOWINSKI (J.) : Functional properties ; Introductory remarks. In : *Monoamine innervation of cerebral cortex.* DESCARRIES (L.), READER (T.R.) and JASPER (H.H.) [eds], *Alan R. Liss,* New York, 1984, pp. 229-231.
5. APICELLA (P.), TROUCHE (E.), NIEOULLON (A.), LEGALLET (E.) and DUSTICIER (N.) : Motor impairments and neurochemical changes after unilateral 6-OHDA lesion of the nigrostriatal dopaminergic system in monkeys. *Neuroscience,* 1990, 38, 655-666.
6. LE MOAL (M.) and SIMON (H.) : Mesocorticolimbic dopaminergic network ; functional and regulatory roles. *Physiol. Rev.,* 1991, 71, 155-427.
7. SIMON (H.) and LE MOAL (M.) : Mesencephalic dopaminergic neurons ; functional role. In : *Catecholamines, neuropharmacology and central nervous systems. Theoretical aspects.* USDIN (E.), CARLSON (A.), DAHLSTRÖM (A.) and ENGEL (J.) [eds]. *Alan R. Liss,* New York, 1984, pp. 293-307.
8. SIMON (H.), SCATTON (B.) and LE MOAL (M.) : Dopaminergic A10 neurons are involved in cognitive functions. *Nature,* 1980, 286, 150-151.
9. FOOTE (S.L.) and MORRISON (J.M.) : Extrathalamic modulation of cortical function. *Ann. Rev. Neurosci.,* 1987, 10, 67-95.
10. GOZLAN (H.), DAVAL (G.), VERGE (D.), SPAMPINATO (U.), FATTACCINI (C.M.), GALLISSOT (M.C.), EL MESTIKAWY (S.) and HAMON (M.) : Aging associated changes in serotoninergic and dopaminergic pre- and postsynaptic neurochemical markers in the rat brain. *Neurobiology of Aging,* 1990, 11, 437-449.
11. JOSEPH (J.A.) and ROTH (G.S.) : Upregulation of striatal dopamine receptors and improvement of motor performance in senescence. *Ann. N.Y. Acad. Sci.,* 1988, USA, 515, 355-362.
12. GODEFROY (F.), BASSANT (M.H.), LAMOUR (Y.) and WEIL-FUGAZZA (J.) : Effect of aging on dopamine metabolism in the rat cerebral cortex ; a regional analysis. *J. Neural. Transm.,* 1991, 83, 13-24.
13. VENERO (J.L.), MACHADO (A.) and CANO (J.) : Turnover of dopamine and serotonin and their metabolites in the striatum of aged rats. *J. Neurochem.,* 1991, 56, 1940-1948.
14. GOLDMAN-RAKIC (P.S.) and BROWN (R.M.) : Regional changes of monoamines in cerebral cortex and subcortical structures of aging Rhesus monkey. *Neuroscience,* 1981, 6, 177-187.
15. STRONG (R.), SAMORAJSKI (T.) and GOTTESFELD (Z.) : High-affinity uptake of neurotransmitters in rat neostriatum ; effects of aging. *J. Neurochem.,* 1984, 43, 1766-1768.
16. SHIMIZU (I.) and PRASAD (C.) : Relationship between [3] H-mazindol binding to dopamine uptake site and [3] dopamine uptake in rat striatum during aging. *J. Neurochem.,* 1991, 56, 575-579.
17. GOVONI (S.), RIUS (R.A.), BATTAINI (F.), MAGNONI (M.S.), LUCCHI (L.) and TRABUCCHI (M.) : The central dopaminergic system ; susceptibility to risk factors for accelerated aging. *Gerontology,* 1988, 34, 29-34.
18. FREEMAN (G.B.) and GIBSON (G.E.) : Selective alteration of neurotransmitter release with aging. *Soc. Neurosci. Abstr.,* 1986, 12, 271-275.3.
19. GREGERSON (K.A.) and SELMANOFF (M.) : Changes in the kinetics of [3] H-dopamine from median eminence and striatal synaptosomes during aging. *Endocrinology,* 1990, 126, 228-234.
20. JOSEPH (J.A.), DALTON (T.K.) and HUNT (W.A.) : Age-related decrements in the muscarinic enhancement of K^+-evoked release of endogenous striatal dopamine : an indicator of altered cholinergic-dopaminergic reciprocal inhibitory control in senescence. *Brain Res.,* 1988, 454, 140-148.
21. JOSEPH (J.A.), KOWATCH (M.A.), MAKI (T.) and ROTH (G.S.) : Selective cross-activation/inhibition of second messenger systems and the reduction of age-related deficits in the muscarinic control of dopamine release from perfused rat striata. *Brain Res.,* 1990, 537, 40-48.
22. MAGNONI (M.S.), GOVONI (S.), BATTAINI (F.) and TRABUCCHI (M.) : The aging brain ; protein phosphorylation as a target of changes in neuronal function. *Life Sci.,* 1991, 48, 373-385.
23. HAN (Z.), KUYATT (B.L.), KOCHMANN (K.A.), DE SOUZA (E.B.) and ROTH (G.S.) : Effect of aging on concentrations of D2-receptors-containing neurons in the rat striatum. *Brain Res.,* 1989, 438, 299-307.
24. MORELLI (M.), MENNINI (A.), CAGNOTTO (A.), TOFFANO (G.) and DI CHIARA (G.) : Quantitative autoradiographical analysis of the age-related modulation of central dopamine D1 ad D2 receptors. *Neuroscience,* 1990, 36, 403-410.
25. JOYCE (J.N.), LOESCHEN (S.K.), SAPP (D.W.) and MARSHALL (J.F.) : Age-related regional loss of caudate-putamen dopamine receptors revealed by quantitative autoradiography. *Brain Res.,* 1986, 378, 158-163.

26. GIORGI (O.), PORCEDDU (M.L.), PEPITONI (S.), SERRA (G.P.), TOFFANO (G.) and BIGGIO (G.) : Differential effect of aging on ^{3}H-SCH23390 binding sites in the retina and in distinct areas of the rat brain. *J. Neural. Transm.*, 1990, 82, 157-166.

27. GIORGI (O.), DE MONTIS (G.), PORCEDDU (M.L.), MELE (S.), CALDERINI (G.), TOFFANO (G.) and BIGGIO (G.) : Developmental and age-related changes in D1-dopamine receptors and dopamine content in the rat striatum. *Develop. Brain Res.*, 1987, 35, 283-290.

28. CARLSSON (A.) and WINBLAD (B.) : Influence of age and time interval between death and autopsy on dopamine and 3-methoxytyramine levels in human basal ganglia. *J. Neural. Transm.*, 1976, 38, 271-276.

29. McGEER (E.G.) and McGEER (P.L.) : Age changes in the human for some enzymes associated with metabolism of catecholamines, GABA and acetylcholine. *Adv. Behav. Biol.*, 1975, 16, 287-305.

30. McGEER (P.L.), ITAGAKI (S.), AKIYAMA (H.) and McGEER (E.G.) : Comparison of neuronal loss in Parkinson's disease and aging. In : *Parkinsonism and Aging*. CALNE (D.B.), COMI (G.), CRIPPA (D.), HOROWSKI (R.) and TRABUCCHI (M.) [eds], *Raven Press*, 1989, New York, pp. 25-34.

31. WOLF (M.E.), LE WITT (P.A.), DRAGOVIC (L.J.) and KAPATOS (G.) : Effect of aging on tyrosine hydroxylase protein content and the relative number of dopamine nerve terminals in human caudate. *J. Neurochem.*, 1991, 56, 1191-1200.

32. MARTIN (W.R.W.) and PALMER (M.R.) : The nigrostriatal system in aging and Parkinsonism ; *in vivo* studies with positron emission tomography. In : *Parkinsonism and Aging*. CALNE (D.B.), COMI (G.), CRIPPA (D.), HOROWSKI (R.) and TRABUCCHI (M.) [eds], *Raven Press*, 1989, New York, pp. 165-172.

33. SAWLE (G.V.), COLEBATCH (J.G.), SHAM (A.), BROOKS (D.J.), MARSDEN (C.D.) and FRACKOWIAK (R.S.J.) : Striatal function in normal aging ; implication for Parkinson's disease. *Ann. Neurol.*, 1990, 28, 799-804.

34. MANN (D.M.A.) : Dopamine neurones of the vertebrate brain ; some aspects of anatomy and pathology. In : *The neurobiology of dopamine systems.* WINLOW (W.) and MARKSTEIN (R.) [eds], *Manchester University Press,* Manchester, 1984, pp. 87-103.

35. LANGSTON (J.W.), IRWIN (I.) and FINNEGAN (K.T.) : Using neurotoxicants to study aging and Parkinson's disease. In : *Parkinsonism and Aging*. CALNE (D.B.), COMI (G.), CRIPPA (D.), HOROWSKI (R.) and TRABUCCHI (M.) [eds], *Raven Press*, 1989, New York, pp. 145-153.

36. RINNE (J.O.), LONNBERG (P.) and MARJAMAKI (P.) : Age-dependent decline in human brain dopamine D1 and D2 receptors. *Brain Res.*, 1990, 508, 349-352.

37. SEVERSON (J.A.), MARCUSSON (J.), WINBLAD (B.) and FINCH (C.E.) : Age-correlated loss of dopaminergic binding sites in human basal ganglia. *J. Neurochem.*, 1982, 39, 1623-1631.

38. DE KEYSER (J.), DE BACKER (J.P.), VAUQUELIN (G.) and EBINGER (G.) : The effect of aging on the D1 dopamine receptors in human frontal cortex. *Brain Res.*, 1990, 528, 308-310.

39. DE KEYSER (J.), DE BACKER (J.P.), VAUQUELIN (G.) and EBINGER (G.) : D1 and D2 dopamine receptors in human substantia nigra ; localization and the effect of aging. *J. Neurochem.*, 1990, 56, 1130-1133.

40. WONG (D.,F.), WAGNER (H.), DANNALS (R.), LINKS (J.), FROST (J.), RAVERT (H.), WILSON (A.), ROSENBAUM (A.), GJEDDE (A.), DOUGLASS (K.), PETRONIS (J.), FOLSTEIN (M.), TOUNG (T.), BURNS (D.) and KUHAR (M.) : Effects of age on dopamine and serotonin receptors measured by positron tomography in the living humain brain. *Science*, 1984, 226, 1391-1395.

41. WONG (D.F.) and VILLEMAGNE (V.) : Dopamine D1 and D2 receptors in aging, Parkinson's and other neurodegenerative diseases ; an overview. In : *Parkinsonism and Aging*. CALNE (D.B.), COMI (G.), CRIPPA (D.), HOROWSKI (R.) and TRABUCCHI (M.) [eds], *Raven Press*, 1989, New York, pp. 173-185.

42. LEENDERS (K.L.), PET studies in Parkinson's disease with new agents. In : *Parkinsonism and Aging*. CALNE (D.B.), COMI (G.), CRIPPA (D.), HOROWSKI (R.) and TRABUCCHI (M.) [eds], *Raven Press,* 1989, New York, pp. 187-197.

43. COIRINI (H.), SCHUMACHER (M.), ANGULO (J.A.) and McEWEN (B.S.) : Increase in striatal D2 receptor mRNA after lesions or haloperidol treatment. *Europ. J. Pharmacol.*, 1990, 186, 369-371.

44. AGID (Y.), JAVOY (F.) and GLOWINSKI (J.) : Hyperactivity of remaining dopaminergic neurons after partial destruction of the nigrostriatal dopaminergic system in the rat. *Nature*, 1973, 245, 150-151.

45. SCHULTZ (W.) : Depletion of dopamine in the striatum as an experimental model of parkinsonism ; direct effects and adaptive mechanisms. *Prog. Neurobiol.*, 1982, 18, 121-166.

46. ZIGMOND (M.J.), ABERCROMBIE (E.D.), BERGER (T.W.), GRACE (A.A.) and STRICKER (E.M.) : Compensations after lesions of central dopaminergic neurons ; some clinical and basic implications. *Trends in Neurosciences*, 1990, 13, 290-295.

47. NIEOULLON (A.) : Aspects neurochimiques de la communication interneuronale. *J. Physiol.* (Paris), 1986, 81, 88-109.

48. STRONG (R.), WAYMIRE (J.C.), SAMORAJSKI (T.) and GOTTESFELD (Z.) : Regional analysis of neostriatal cholinergic and dopaminergic receptor binding and tyrosine hydroxylase activity as a function of aging. *Neurochem. Res.*, 1984, 9, 1641-1653.

2 - CLINICAL EXPERIMENTATION : Y. Juillet

1. SWIFT G.C. : Prescribing in old age. *B. M. J.*, 1988, 296, 913-914.
2. CROOKS J. : Rational therapeutics in the elderly. *J. Chron. Dis.*, 1983, 36, 59-65.
3. Guideline for the study of drugs likely to be used in the elderly. U.S. Department of health and human services, Food and Drug Administration, Nov. 1989.
4. Les personnes âgées en France (résultats du recensement de mars 1982). *S.E.S.I. Informations rapides*, n° 35, 1984.
5. Global estimates and projections of population by sex and age. The 1988 Revision, *United Nations*, New York, 1989.
6. Tous les pays du monde (1989). *Population et Société*, 1989, 237, 1-6.
7. Medication for the elderly. *Royal Coll. Phys.*, London, 1984, 18, 3-10.
8. KITLER M.E. : The elderly in clinical trials : regulatory concerns. *Drug Information Journal*, 1989, 23, 123-127.
9. GOSNEY M., TALLIS R. : Prescription of contraindicated and interacting drugs in elderly patients admitted to hospital. *Lancet*, 1984, 564-567.
10. DUBOS G., PROCACCIO J., FERRY M. et coll. : Essai d'évaluation du coût de la pathologie iatrogène en gériatrie. *Lettre Pharmacol.*, 1988, 168-172.
11. RESCHEL W.A. : Disposition of drugs in geriatric patients. *Pharmacy intern.*, 1980, 1, 226-230.
12. MASSOUD N. : Pharmacokinetic considerations in geriatric patients. In : L.Z. Benet et coll., Pharmacokinetic basis of drug treatment, *Raven Press*, New York, 1984.
13. PEYTAVIN G., PICARD O., VAYRE P. et coll. : Influence du vieillissement sur la pharmacocinétique des médicaments chez l'homme. *J. Pharm. Clin.*, 1989, 9, 8-16.
14. GUILLET P., PIETTE F. : Pharmacologie du sujet âgé. *Rev. Prat.*, 1986, 36, 581-592.
15. PUECH A. : Vieillissement et pharmacodynamie des psychotropes. *Psychol. Med.*, 1990, 22, 811-812.
16. BUHLER F.R. : Age and cardiovascular response adaptation : determinant of an antihypertensive treatment concept primarly based on beta-blockers and calcium entry blockers. *Hypertension*, 1983, 5 (Suppl. III), 94-100.
17. BELL J.A., MAY F.E., STEWART R.B. : Clinical research in the elderly. Ethical and methodological considerations. *Drug. Intell. Clin. Pharma.*, 1987, 21, 1002-1007.
18. VETEL J.M., ALIX E., LE PROVOST C.H., DUGAY M. : Problèmes statistiques posés par l'essai du médicament chez le sujet âgé. Quels patients. *E.M.C. Thérap.*, 5, 1985, 25999, 33-34.
19. Essais cliniques du médicament chez les personnes âgées. Note explicative sur la qualité, la sécurité et l'efficacité du médicament à usage humain. *Commission des Communautés Européennes*, 1989, 147-152.
20. BOUVENOT G., PIETTE F. : Les essais thérapeutiques chez le sujet âgé : in Essais thérapeutiques. Mode d'emploi p. 183-187. *INSERM Ed.*, Paris, 1990.
21. TEMPLE R. : Food and drug administration's guidelines for clinical testing of drugs in the elderly. *Drug Inf. J.*, 1985, 19, 483-486.

3 - PHARMACOLOGICAL EFFICIENCY OF DRUGS PROPOSED IN PSYCHOBEHAVIORAL TROUBLES OF BRAIN AGEING : A 1992 REVIEW : P. Bustany

1. HOLLISTER (L.E.) : Survey of Treatment Attempts in Senile Dementia of the Alzheimer Type. *In :* Gottfries (C.G.) Ed. Normal Aging, Alzheimer's Disease and Senile Dementia. *Editions de l'Université de Bruxelles*, 1985, 299-306.
2. GOUDSMIT (E.), LUINE (V.N.), SWAAB (D.F.) : Testosterone Locally Increases Vasopressin Content But Fails to Restore Choline Acetyltransferase Activity in Other Regions in the Senescent Male Rat Brain. *Neurosci. Lett.*, 1990, 112 (2-3), 290-296.
3. SCHONHOFER (P.S.) : Ginkgo-Biloba Extracts. *Lancet*, 1990, 335 (8692), 788-788.
4. BERTONI-FREDDARI (C.), FATTORETTI (P.), CASOLI (T.), MEIERRUGE (W.), ULRICH (J.) : Morphological Adaptive Response of the Synaptic Junctional Zones in the Human Dentate Gyrus During Aging and Alzheimer's Disease. *Brain Res.*, 1990, 517 (1-2), 69-75.
5. FROSTL (W.), MAITRE (L.) : The Families of Cognition Enhancers. *Pharmacopsychiatry*, 1989, 22 (S2), 54-101.
6. FLORIO (J.C.), PALERMONETO (J.) : Effects of Dihydroergotoxine on Some Dopamine-Related Behaviors in Rats. *Gen. Pharmacol.*, 1990, 21 (4), 411-415.
7. FLORIO (T.), VENTRA (C.), RAPANA (A.), SCORZIELLO (A.), COCOZZA DI MONTANARA, MARINO (A.), SCHETTINI (G.) : Dihydroergotamine Treatment Improves Active Avoidance Performance and Increases Dopamine-Stimulated Adenylate Cyclase Activity, in Young and Aged Rats. *Behav. Pharmacol.*, 1991, 2, 31-36.
8. AMENTA (F.), JATON (A.L.), RICCI (A.J.) : Effect of Long Term Hydergine Treatment on the Age-Dependent Loss of Mossy Fibers and of Granule Cells in the Rat Hippocampus. *Arch. Gerontol. Geria.*, 1990, 10 (3), 287-296.

9. THOMPSON (T.L.), FILLEY (C.M.), MITCHELL (W.D.), CULIG (K.M.), LOVERDE (M.), BYYNY (R.L.) : Lack of Efficacy of Hydergine in Patients with Alzheimer's Disease. *New Engl. J. Med.*, 1990, 323, (7), 445-448.

10. POSNER, LANDSBERG : Lack of Efficacy of Hydergine in Alzheimer's Disease. *New Engl. J. Med.*, 1991, 324 (3), 197-197.

11. FILLEY (C.M.), MITCHELL (W.D.), THOMPSON (T.L.), CULIG (K.M.), BYYNY (R.L.), LOVERDE (M.) : Lack of Efficacy of Hydergine in Alzheimer's Disease - Reply. *New Engl. J. Med.*, 1991, 324 (3), 197-198.

12. SCHMIDT (J.), BUCHER (U.) : Influence of Nootropic Drugs on Spontaneous and Apomorphine-Induced Locomotor Activity in Rats. *Biog. Amines*, 1990, 7 (1), 63-69.

13. NICHOLSON (C.D.) : Pharmacology of Nootropics and Metabolically Active Compounds in Relation to Their Use in Dementia. *Psychopharmacology*, 1990, 101 (2), 147-159.

14. PEPEU (G.), SPIGNOLI (G.), GIOVANINI (M.G.), MAGNANI (M.) : The Relationship Between the Behaviorial Effects of Cognition-Enhancing Drugs and Brain Acetylcholine - Nootropic Drugs and Brain Acetylcholine. *Pharmacopsychiatry*, 1989, 22 (S2), 116-119.

15. GAMZU (E.R.), HOOVER (T.M.), GRACON (S.I.), NINTEMAN (M.V.) : Recent Developments in 2-Pyrrolidinone-Containing Nootropics. *Drug Devel. Res.*, 1989, 18 (3), 177-189.

16. PACKARD (M.G.), WHITE (N.M.) : Memory Facilitation Produced by Dopamine Agonist - Role of Receptor Subtype and Mnemonic Requirements. *Pharmacol. Biochem Behav.*, 1989, 33 (3), 511-518.

17. BATTAGLIA (A.) : A Double-Blind Randomized Study of Two Ergot Derivatives in Mild to Moderate Dementia. *Current Therap. Res.*, 1990, 48 (4), 597-612.

18. RICH (K.M.), HOLLOWELL (J.P.) : Flunarizine Protects Neurons from Death After Axotomy or NGF Deprivation. *Science*, 1990, 248 (4961), 1419-1421.

19. SANDIN (M.), JASMIN (S.), LEVERE (T.E.) : Aging and Cognition - Facilitation of Recent Memory in Aged Nonhuman Primates by Nimodipine. *Neurobiol. Aging*, 1990, 11 (5), 573-575.

20. DE JONG (G.I.), DEWEERD (H.), SCHUURMAN (T.), TRABER (J.), LUITEN (P.G.M.) : Microvascular Changes in Aged Rat Forebrain - Effects of Chronic Nimodipine Treatment. *Neurobiol. Aging*, 1990, 11 (4), 381-389.

21. VAN DER ZEE (C.E.E.), SCHUURMAN (T.), VAN DER HOOP (R.G.), TRABER (J.), GISPEN (W.H.) : Beneficial Effect of Nimodipine on Peripheral Nerve Function in Aged Rats. *Neurobiol. Aging*, 1990, 11 (4), 451-456.

22. CARTER (C.J.), LLOYD (K.G.), ZIVKOVIC (B.), SCATTON (B.) : Ifenprodil and S1-82.0715 As Cerebral Antiischemic Agents. 3. Evidence for Antagonistic Effects at the Polyamine Modulatory Site Within the N-Methyl-D-Aspartage Receptor Complex. *J. Pharmacol. Exp. Thert.*, 1990, 253 (2), 475-482.

23. MONAHAN (J.B.), HANDELMANN (G.E.), HOOD (W.F.), CORDI (A.A.) : D-Cycloserine, a Positive Modulator of the N-Methyl-D-Aspartate Receptor, Enhances Performance of Learning Tasks in Rats. *Pharmacol. Biochem. Behav.*, 1989, 34 (3), 649-653.

24. MAYEUX (R.) : Therapeutic Strategies in Alzheimer's Disease. *Neurology*, 1990, 40 (1), 175-180.

25. STAUBLI (U.), KESSLER (M.), LYNCH (G.) : Aniracetam Has Proportionately Smaller Effects on Synapses Expressing Long-Term Potentiation - Evidence That Receptor Changes Subserve LTP. *Psychobiology*, 1990, 18 (4), 377-381.

26. PONZIO (F.), POZZI (O.), BANFI (S.), DORIGOTTI (L.) : Brain Entry and Direct Central Pharmacological Effects of the Nootropic Drug Oxiracetam - Oxiracetam - Brain Entry and Pharmacological Effects. *Pharmacopsychiatry*, 1989, 22 (S2), 111-115.

27. CONSOLO (S.), SALMOIRAGHI (P.), AMOROSO (D.), KOLASA (K.) : Treatment with Oxiracetam or Choline Restores Cholinergic Biochemical and Pharmacological Activities in Striata of Decorticated Rats. *J. Neurochem.*, 1990, 54 (2), 571-577.

28. WULFERT (E.), HANIN (I.), VERLOES (R.) : Facilitation of Calcium-Dependent Cholinergic Function by Ucb L059, a New 2nd Generation Nootropic Agent. *Psychopharmacol. Bull.*, 1989, 25 (3), 498-502.

29. CLAUS (J.J.), LUDWIG (C.), MOHR (E.), GIUFFRA (M.), BLIN (J.), CHASE (T.N.) : Nootropic Drugs in Alzheimer's Disease - Symptomatic Treatment with Pramiracetam. *Neurology*, 1991, 41 (4), 570-574.

30. ITO (I.), TANABE (S.), KOHDA (A.), SUGIYAMA (H.) : Allosteric Potentiation of Quisqualate Receptors by a Nootropic Drug Aniracetam. *J. Physiol.*, 1990, 424 (MAY), 533-543.

31. MONDADORI (C.), PETSCHKE (F.), HAUSLER (A.) : The Effects of Nootropics on Memory. New Aspects for Basic Research. *Pharmacopsychiatry*, 1989, 22 (S2), 102-106.

32. GROSSMANN (W.M.), STANDL (A.), MAY (U.), VANLAAK (H.H.), HIRCHE (H.) : Naftidrofuryl in the Treatment of Mild Senile Dementia. A Double-Blind Study. *Pharmacopsychiatry*, 1990, 23 (6), 265-273.

33. SHERMAN K.A., FRIEDMAN E. : Pre-Synaptic and Post-Synaptic Cholinergic Dysfunction in Aged Rodent Brain Regions. New Findings and an Interpretative Review. *Int. J. Dev. Neurosci.*, 1990, 8 (6), 689-709.

34. BOWEN D.M. : Treatment of Alzheimer's Disease. Molecular Pathology Versus Neurotransmitter-Based Therapy. *Br. J. Psychiatry*, 1990, 157 (9), 327-330.

35. KUMAR V., CALACHE M. : Treatment of Alzheimer's Disease with Cholinergic Drugs. *Int. J. Clin. Pharmacol. Therap. Toxicol.*, 1991, 29 (1), 23-37.

36. ALLAIN H. : Dopamine et vieillissement : bases physiopathologiques du déficit neurobiologique de la post-cinquantaine. *Rev. Prat.*, 1988, 38 (25 Suppl.), 25-28.

37. WEIHMULLER F.B., BRUNO J.P. : Age-Dependent Plasticity in the Dopaminergic Control of Sensori-motor Development. *Behav. Brain Res.*, 1989, 35 (2), 95-109.
38. SCHMIDT J. : Influence of Nootropic Drugs on Apomorphine-Induced Stereotyped Behaviour in Rats. *Biomed. Biochim. Acta*, 1990, 49 (1), 133-136.
39. CLARKSON-SMITH L., HARTLEY A.A. : The Game of Bridge As an Exercise in Working Memory and Reasoning. *J. Gerontol.*, 1990, 45 (6), 233-238.
40. LEVIN E.D., MAC GURK S.R., ROSE J.E., BUTCHER L.L. : Cholinergic-Dopaminergic Interactions in Cognitive Performance. *Behav. Neural. Biol.*, 1990, 54 (3), 271-299.
41. MARKSTEIN R. : Pharmacological Approaches in the Treatment of Senile Dementia. *Eur. Neurol.*, 1989, 29 (S3), 33-41.
42. PIERCEY M.F., LUM J.T. : Electrophysiological Effects of Dopamine Autoreceptor Antagonists, (+)-Aj76 and (+)-Uh232. *Eur. J. Pharmacol.*, 1990, 182 (2), 219-226.
43. JEZIORSKI M., WHITE F.J. : Dopamine Agonists at Repeated Autoreceptor-Selective Doses. Effects upon the Sensitivity of A10-Dopamine Autoreceptors. *Synapse*, 1989, 4 (4), 267-280.
44. SONCRANT T.T. : Age-Associated Functional Impairments of Specific Neurotransmitter Systems. Detection by Pharmacological Brain Metabolism Studies and Criteria for Design of Human Investigations. *Int. J. Clin. Pharmacol. Res.*, 1990, 10 (1-2), 27-47.
45. YAMAZAKI N., KATO K., KURIHARA E., NAGAOKA A. : Cholinergic Drugs Reverse AF64A-Induced Impairment of Passive Avoidance Learning in Rats. *Psychopharmacology*, 1991, 103 (2), 215-222.
46. FITTEN L.J., PERRYMAN K.M., GROSS P.L., FINE H., CUMMINS J., MARSHALL C.J. : Treatment of Alzheimer's Disease with Short-Term and Long-Term Oral Tha and Lecithin. A Double-Blind Study. *Am. J. Psychiatry*, 1990, 147 (2), 239-242.
47. GAUTHIER S., BOUCHARD R., LAMONTAGNE A., BAILEY P., BERGMAN H., RATNER J., TESFAYE Y., SAINTMARTIN M., BACHER Y., CARRIER L., CHARBONNEAU R., CLARFIELD A.M., COLLIER B., DASTOOR D., GAUTHIER L., GERMAIN M., KISSEL C., KRIEGER M., KUSHNIR S., MASSON H., MORIN J.P., NAIR V. : Tetrahydroaminoacridine Lecithin Combination Treatment in Patients with Intermediate-Stage Alzheimer's Disease : Results of a Canadian Double-Blind, Crossover, Multicenter Study. *N. Eng. J. Med.*, 1990, 322 (18), 1272-1276.
48. FRANCIS P.T., BOWEN D.M. : Tacrine, a Drug with Therapeutic Potential for Dementia. Post-Mortem Biochemical Evidence. *Can. J. Neurol. Sci.*, 1989, 16 (4), 504-510.
49. HODGES H., RIBEIRO A.M., GRAY J.A., MARCHBANKS R.M. : Low Dose Tetrahydroaminoacridine (Tha) Improves Cognitive Function But Does Not Affect Brain Acetylcholine in Rats. *Pharmacol. Biochem. Behav.*, 1990, 36 (2), 291-298.
50. MARX J.L. : Alzheimer's Drug Trial Put on Hold. *Science*, 1987, 238, 1041-1042.
51. PETERSON C. : Tetrahydroaminoacridine Increases Acetylcholine Synthesis and Glucose Oxidation by Mouse Brain Slices *In vitro. Neurosci. Lett.*, 1990, 115 (2-3), 274-278.
52. FLOOD J.F., MORLEY J.E. : Pharmacological Enhancement of Long-Term Memory Retention in Old Mice. *J. Gerontol.*, 1990, 45 (3), B101-B104.
53. WHALLEY L.J. : Drug Treatments of Dementia. *Br. J. Psychiatry*, 1989, 155 (11), 595-611.
54. CENNI A., PULITI R., DE REGIS M., VIGGIANI P., SPIGNOLI G. : Pharmacological Properties of a Nootropic Agent of Endogenous Origin : D-Pyroglutamic Acid. *J. Drug. Develop.*, 1988, 1 (3), 157-162.
55. GRIOLI S., LOMEO C., QUATTROPANI M.C., SPIGNOLI G., VILLARDITA C. : Pyroglutamic Acid Improves the Age Associated Memory Impairment. *Fundam. Clin. Pharmacol.*, 1990, 4 (2), 169-173.
56. YONKOV D.I., GEORGIEV V.P. : Cholinergic Influence on Memory Facilitation Induced by Angiotensin-II in Rats. *Neuropeptides*, 1990, 16 (3), 157-162.
57. MANNING-SAYI J., LEONARD B.E. : Studies on the Nootropic Potential of Some Angiotensin Converting Enzyme Inhibitors in the Mouse. *Prog. Neuro. Psychopharmacol. Biol. Psychiatry*, 1989, 13 (6), 953-962.
58. VARON S., HAGG T., FASS B., VAHLSING L., MANTHORPE M. : Neuronotrophic Factors in Cellular Functional and Cognitive Repair of Adult Brain. *Pharmacopsychiatry*, 1989, 22 (S2), 120-124.
59. ANDO S., TANAKA Y. : Synaptic Membrane Aging in the Central Nervous System. *Gerontology*, 1990, 36 (S1), 10-14.
60. ALA T., ROMERO S., KNIGHT F., FELDT K., FREY W.H. : GM-1 Treatment of Alzheimer's Disease. A Pilot Study of Safety and Efficacy. *Arch. Neurol.*, 1990, 47 (10), 1126-1130.
61. DE SIMONE C., CATANIA S., TRINCHIERI V., TZANTZOGLOU S., CALVANI M., BAGIELLA E. : Amelioration of the Depression of HIV-Infected Subjects With L-Acetyl Carnitine Therapy. *J. Drug. Develop.*, 1988, 1 (3), 163-166.
62. NAPOLEONE P., FERRANTE F., GHIRARDI O., RAMACCI M.T., AMENTA F. : Age-Dependent Nerve Cell Loss in the Brain of Sprague-Dawley Rats. Effects of Long Term Acetyl-L-Carnitine Treatment. *Arch. Gerontol. Geriatrics*, 1990, 10 (2), 173-185.
63. LASCHI R., DEGIORGI B., BONVICINI F, CENTURIONE L. : Ultrastructural Aspects of Aging Rat Hippocampus After Long-Term Administration of Acetyl-L-Carnitine. *Int. J. Clin. Pharmacol. Res.*, 1990, 10 (1-2), 59-63.

64. MARKOWSKA A.L., INGRAM D.K., BARNES C.A., SPANGLER E.L., LEMKEN V.J., KAMETANI H., YEE W., OLTON D.S. : Acetyl-1-Carnitine. 1. Effects on Mortality, Pathology and Sensory-Motor Performance in Aging Rats. *Neurobiol. Aging*, 1990, 11 (5), 491-498.
65. BARNES C.A., MARKOWSKA A.L., INGRAM D.K., KAMETANI H., SPANGLER E.L., LEMKEN V.J., OLTON D.S. : Acetyl-1-Carnitine. 2. Effects on Learning and Memory Performance of Aged Rats in Simple and Complex Mazes. *Neurobiol. Aging*, 1990, 11 (5), 499-506.
66. PAVLIK A., PILAR J. : Protection of Cell Proteins Against Free-Radical Attack by Nootropic Drugs. Scavenger Effect of Pyritinol Confirmed by Electron Spin Resonance Spectroscopy. *Neuropharmacology*, 1989, 28 (6), 557-561.
67. BENESOVA O., TEJKALOVA H., KRISTOFIKOVA Z., BINKOVA B., TUCEK S., DLOHOZKOVA N. : The Evaluation of Nootropic Drug Effects in Aging Rats. *Activitas Nervosa Superior*, 1990, 32 (1), 53-55.
68. VOLICER L., CRINO P.B. : Involvement of Free Radicals in Dementia of the Alzheimer Type. A Hypothesis. *Neurobiol. Aging*, 1990, 11 (5), 567-571.
69. KRESYUN V.I., ROZHKOVSKII Y.V. : Molecular-Biochemical Mechanisms of the Action of Nootropic Drugs. *Bull. Exp. Biol. Med.*, 1990, 109 (7), 919-921.
70. KAMEI C., TSUJIMOTO S., TASAKA K. : Effects of Cholinergic Drugs and Cerebral Metabolic Activators on Memory Impairment in Old Rats. *J. Pharmacobio. Dynamics*, 1990, 13 (12), 772-777.
71. TAYLOR J.E. : The Effects of Chronic Oral Ginkgo Biloba Extract Administration on Neurotransmitter Receptor Binding in Young and Aged Fisher 344 Rats. In Agnoli A., Rapin J.R., Eds. Effects of Ginkgo Biloba Extract on Organic Cerebral Impairment. *J. Libbey Eurotext Ltd*, 1985, pp. 31-34.
72. TAILLANDIERJ., AMMAR A., RABOURDIN J.P., RIBEYRE J.P., PICHON J., NIDDAM S., PIERART H. : Traitement des troubles du vieillissement cérébral par l'extrait de Ginkgo biloba. *Presse Méd.*, 1986, 15 (31), 1583-1587.
73. ISRAËL L., DELL'ACCIO E., MARTIN G.M., HUGONOT R. : Extrait de Ginkgo biloba et exercices d'entraînement de la mémoire. Evaluation comparative chez des personnes âgées ambulatoires. *Psychol. Méd.*, 1987, 19 (8), 1431-1439.
74. DELUMEAU J.C., BENTUE-FERRER D., SAIAG B., ALLAIN H. : Clinical Neuropharmacology of Calcium Antagonists. *Fundam. Clin. Pharmacol.*, 1989, 3 (S), S89-S102.
75. BARONE D., SPIGNOLI G. : Investigations on the Binding Properties of the Nootropic Agent Pyroglutamic Acid. *Drug. Exp. Clin. Res.*, 1990, 16 (2), 85-99.
76. HAROUNTUNIAN V., KANOF P.D., TSUBOYAMA G., DAVIS K.L. : Restoration of Cholinomimetic Activity by Clonidine in Cholinergic Plus Noradrenergic Lesioned Rats. *Brain Res.*, 1990, 507 (2), 261-266.
77. MCENTEE W.J., CROOK T.H., JENKYN L.R., PETRIE W., LARRABEE G.J., COFFEY D.J. : Treatment of Age-Associated Memory Impairment with Guanfacine. *Psychopharmacol. Bull.*, 1991, (7), 41-46.
78. KALIVAS P.W., DUFFY P., EBERHARDT H. : Modulation of A10 Dopamine Neurons by Gamma-Aminobutyric Acid Agonists. *J. Pharmacol. Exp. Ther.*, 1990, 253 (2), 858-866.
79. NAKAMURA S. : Antidepressants Induce Regeneration of Catecholaminergic Axon Terminals in the Rat Cerebral Cortex. *Neurosci. Lett.*, 1990, 111 (1-2), 64-68.
80. MANGONI A., GRASSI M.P., FRATTOLA L., PIOLTI R., BASSI S., MOTTA A., MARCONE A., SMIRNE S. : Effects of a MAO-B Inhibitor in the Treatment of Alzheimer's Disease. *Eur. Neurol.*, 1991, 31 (2), 100-107.
81. BARNES J.M., COSTALL B., COUGHLAN J., DOMENEY A.M., GERRARD P.A., KELLY M.E., NAYLOR R.J., ONAIVI E.S., TOMKINS D.M., TYERS M.B. ; The Effects of Ondansetron, a 5-Ht3 Receptor Antagonist, on Cognition in Rodents and Primates. *Pharmacol. Biochem. Behav.*, 1990, 35 (4), 955-962.
82. SARTER M. : Elevation of Local Cerebral Glucose Utilization by the Beta-Carboline ZK-93426. *European J. Pharmacol.*, 1990, 177 (3), 155-162.
83. GOTTFRIES C.G. : Pharmacological Treatment Strategies in Dementia Disorders. *Pharmacopsychiatry*, 1989, 22 (S2), 129-134.
84. HOLLISTER L.E. : Alzheimer's Disease. Is It Worth Treating ? *Drugs*, 1985, 29, 483-488.
85. HERMANN C., STERN R., LOSONZCY M., JAFF S., DAVIDSON M. : Diagnostic and Pharmacological Approaches in Alzheimer's Disease. *Drugs and Aging*, 1991, 1 (2), 144-162.

4 - PREVENTION AND TREATMENT OF OSTEOPOROSES : M.-C. CHAPUY, P.-J. MEUNIER

1. RIGGS B.L., WAHNER H.W., DUNN W.L., MAZESS R.B., OFFORD K.P., MELTON J.L. : Differential changes in bone mineral density of the appendicular and ex. al Skeleton with aging. Relationship to spinal osteoporosis. *J. Clin. Invest.*, 1981, 67, 328-335.
2. RIGGS B.L., MELTON L.J. : Evidence for two distinct syndromes of involutional osteoporosis. *Am. J. Med.*, 1983, 75, 899-901.
3. WASNICH R.D., ROSS P.D., DAVIS J.W. : Osteoporosis current practice and future perpectives. *Trends Endocrinol. Metab.*, 1991, 2, 59-62.
4. CHRISTIANSEN C., RIIS B. : 17 ß œstradiol and continuous norethisterone : a unique treatment for established osteoporosis in elderly women. *J. Clin. Endocrinol. Metab.*, 1990, 71, 836-841.

5. LINDSAY R., TOHME J.F. : Estrogen treatment of patients with established post-menopausal osteo-porosis. *Obstet. Gynecol.*, 1990, 76, 290-901.

6. REGINSTER J.Y., DENIS D., ALBERT A., FRANCHIMONT P. : Assessment of the biological effectiveness of nasal synthetic salmon calcitonin (SSCT) by comparison with intramuscular or pla-cebo injection in normal subjects. *Bone and Mineral*, 1987, 2, 133-138.

7. REGINSTER J.Y., DEROISY R., LECART M.P., SARLET N., LATOUR P., ALBERT A., FRANCHIMONT P. : Rôle des bisphosphonates et de la calcitonine en prévention de l'ostéoporose post-ménopausique. In : La Fracture de l'extrémité supérieure du fémur. L. Simon, *Masson éd.*, Paris, 1991, 315-324.

8. OVERGAARD K., RIIS B.J., CHRISTIANSEN C., HANSEN M.A. : Effect of calcatonin given intrana-sally on early post-menopausal bone loss. *Brit. Med. J.*, 1989, 299, 477-479.

9. MEUNIER P.J., DELMAS P.D., CHAUMET-RIFFAUD P.D., GOZZO I., DUBŒUF F., CHAPUY M.C., GUIGNARD M. : Intranasal salmon calcitonin for prevention of post-menopausal bone loss. A pla-cebo controlled study in 109 women. In : Osteoporosis 1990. C. Christiansen and K. Overgaard Eds, Copenhagen. *Osteopress*, 1990, 1861-1867.

10. CHAPUY M.C., ARLOT M.E., DUBŒUF F., BRUN J., CROUZET B., ARNAUD S., DELMAS P.D., MEUNIER P.J. : Prevention of hip fractures and other non vertebral fractures in elderly women. A prospective double blind controlled trial using vitamin D3 and calcium supplements. *Soumis au Lancet*.

11. MEUNIER P.J. : Sels de fluor et ostéoporose vertébrale. Réexamen d'une controverse. *Revue du Pra-ticien*. Editorial sous presse.

12. MAMELLE N., MEUNIER P.J., DUSAN R. et al. : Risk-benefit ratio of sodium fluoride treatment in primary vertebral osteoporosis. *Lancet*, 1988, ii, 361-365.

13. RIGGS B.L., HODGSON S.F., O'FALLON M.W. et al. : Effect of fluoride treatment on the fracture rate in postmenopausal women with osteoporosis. *N. England J. Med.*, 1990, 322, 802-809.

14. KLEEREKOPER M., PETERSON E.L., NELSON D.A. et al. : A randomized trial of sodium fluoride as a treatment for postmenopausal osteoporosis. *Osteoporosis Int.*, 1991, 1, 155-161.

15. FARLEY S.M., WERGEDAL J.E., FARLEY J.R. et al. : Fluoride decreases spinal fracture rate : a study of over 500 patients. In : Osteoporosis 1990, C. Christiansen and K. Overgaard eds. Copenhagen, *Osteopress*, 1990, 1330-1334.

16. BOIVIN G., GROUSSON B., MEUNIER P.J. : X ray microanalysis of fluoride distribution in microfrac-ture calluses in cancellous iliac bone from osteoporotic patients treated with fluoride and untreated. *J. Bone Min. Res.*, 1991, in press.

17. DELMAS P.D., DUPUIS J., DUBŒUF F., CHAPUY M.C., MEUNIER P.J. : Treatment of vertebral osteo-porosis with disodium monofluorophosphate. Comparison with sodium fluoride. *J. Bone Min. Res.*, 1990, 5, suppl. 1, 143-147.

18. LUFKIN E.G., HODGSON S.F., KOTOWICZ M.A., O'FALLON Wm.-M., WAHNER H.W., RIGGS B.L. : The use of transdermal estrogen treatment in osteoporosis. In : Osteoporosis 1990, C. Christiansen and K. Overgaard eds, Copenhagen, *Osteopress*, 1990, 1995-1998.

19. STORM T., THAMSBORG G., STEINICHE T., GENANT H.K., SORENSEN O.H. : Effect of intermittent cyclical etidronate therapy on bone mass and fracture rate in women with postmenopausal osteopo-rosis. *N. England J. Med.*, 1990, 322, 1265-1271.

20. WATTS N., HARRIS S., GENANT H., WASNICH R., MILLER P., JACKSON R., LICATA A., ROSS P., WOODSON G., YANOVER M., MYSIW W., KOHSE L., RAO M., STEIGER P., RICHMON B., CHES-NUT C. : Intermittent cyclical etidronate treatment of postmenopausal osteoporosis. *N. Engl. J. Med.*, 1990, 323, 73-79.

21. FDC Reports : « The Pink Sheet », 1991, March 11, 1991, 3-4.

22. DAWSON-HUGHES B., DALLAL G., KRALL E., SADOWSKI L., SAHYOUN N., TANNENBAUM S. : A controlled trial of the effect of calcium supplementation on bone density in postmenopausal women. *N. Engl. J. Med.*, 1990, 323, 878-883.

V

FACTS AND RESEARCH IN CLINICAL GERONTOLOGY

PREVALENCE OF DIABETIC RETINOPATHY RELATES TO ADVANCED AGE (*)

Mark J. ROSENTHAL (**), Bruce D. NALIBOFF (***)

Summary. – *Diabetes is most common among older people, but few publications have specifically addressed the impact of age on diabetic complications. The present study examined older men with diabetes to determine the prevalence of two of the most damaging diabetic complications, retinopathy and neuropathy. In order to evaluate contributing factors, multiple risk determinants were also considered including age, duration of illness, type of treatment, metabolic control and obesity. These were each assessed individually and by multifactorial analysis using logistic regression in a population aged 53 to 80 years. Results demonstrate a significant increase in the prevalence of retinopathy with greater age. This correlation with age was independent of the effects of metabolic control, duration of illness, and other risk variables. Age was also related to prevalence of symptomatic peripheral neuropathy. Glycemic control was not as strongly related to retinopathy and neuropathy in these patients. These findings suggest that the increased prevalence of diabetic complications in older persons results from an interaction of diabetes variables and general age related changes.* (Facts and Research in Gerontology 1992)

Key-words : *diabetes, older people, complications, interaction, cost.*

INTRODUCTION

Non-insulin dependent diabetes (NIDDM) afflicts predominantly older people. Indeed, diabetes is the third most widespread life-threatening ailment among older people after atherosclerosis and cancer. However, there have been relatively few publications related to diabetes in the elderly, inspiring one recent author to label this a « neglected area » (1). Nearly one in five people over age 65 has diabetes with

(*) Address correspondence to Dr. Rosenthal, GRECC 11E, Sepulveda VA Medical Center, 16111 Plummer Street, Sepulveda, CA 91343, USA.
(**) Associate Professor of Medicine, Multicampus Division of Geriatric Medicine and Gerontology, UCLA School of Medicine.
(***) Adjunct Associate Professor, Department of Anesthesiology, UCLA School of Medicine.

Acknowledgements : Support for this research was provided by the Veterans Administration Medical Research Program. Portions of the data reported have been previously published in the Journal of the American Geriatric Society, 37, 838-842, 1989.

the highest prevalence in octagenarians (1, 2). Two thirds of all diabetic patients are older than 65 years (1, 3). Moreover mortality rates for diabetics increase with age (4).

Despite this epidemiologic trend, little attention has been paid to the similarities and differences in diabetes complications between older and younger diabetic patients (5). Diabetes in older people was long held to be mild and easy to treat. Nevertheless, the prevalence of some diabetic complications has been reported to increase with age (6-8). Not all studies concur, others have found duration of diabetes and recent glucose control to be more important predictors of complication rates (9, 10). These risk factors are intercorrelated so that it is important to assess both their individual and combined impact on development of diabetic complications (10).

To define better the natural history of diabetes in older persons, a cross-sectional study was undertaken of diabetic patients ranging from 53 to 80 years old. The prevalence of two prominent diabetic complications, retinopathy and neuropathy, was evaluated in subjects of different ages. Potential risk factors for these complications such as duration of diabetes and metabolic control were examined as predictors.

METHODS

Sample. A population of 102 patients with non-insulin dependent (type II) diabetes served as subjects for the study. All subjects were enrolled in one of the diabetes outpatient clinics at the Sepulveda Veterans Administration Medical Center and the measures used were part of the initial screening battery in these clinics.

Measures. Medical history was obtained from each patient. Clinical judgment of the degree of neuropathy was based on the presence of symptoms and signs, gathered from patient interview and examination. Peripheral neuropathy was scored as : (0) no symptoms and, (1) pain or numbness in hands and feet and/or abnormal sensory examination. Retinopathy was assessed by direct ophthalmoscopy by an ophthalmologist after pupillary dilation and rated as (0) absent, (1) non-proliferative retinopathy (greater than one microaneurysm, hemorrhages, or exsudates), or (2) proliferative retinopathy in either eye. Proliferative findings were relatively infrequent, present in only 14.6 % of the sample. Initial analyses did not show any significant differences between the retinopathy types. In light of these findings, all subjects with retinopathy, either non-proliferative or proliferative, were combined for further analysis. Total glycosylated hemoglobin was measured by affinity column chromatography (normal values for our laboratory range from 4.3 to 8.9 %) and used as a measure of metabolic control. Percent ideal weight was determined from height and weight measurements and the Metropolitan Tables (1983). Demographic characteristics of age and duration of diabetes (time since diagnosis) were determined from patient interview and chart review.

Statistical Analyses. Initial analyses examined the prevalence rates of diabetic retinopathy and peripheral neuropathy for four age groupings (under 65 years, n = 22 ; 65-69 years, n = 44 ; 70-74 years, n = 19 ; and over 74 years, n = 16). Multiple logistic regression analysis, which allows for the simultaneous assessment of multiple risk factor variables as predictors of the prevalence for a single complication were then performed using the statistical program BMDP-LR (11). The variables of duration, glycosylated hemoglobin, age, medication type, presence of heart disease, and percent ideal weight were evaluated for their independent association with increasing risk of each of the complications (i.e., the increase in risk associated with that variable if all others were to remain constant). Age was a continuous variable in these analyses. Relative odds ratios, 95 % confidence intervals and chi-square tests were computed (12).

RESULTS

The patient sample is described in Table I. Prevalence rates of retinopathy for the four age groups are shown in Figure 1. The prevalence of retinopathy is dramatically higher in the older age groups as shown in the figure : from less than 10 % for the youngest group up to nearly 80 % for the oldest group. This age effect was confirmed by a chi-square test of linear trend ($X^2 = 17.08$, $p < .001$). There was a comparable trend toward group differences for peripheral neuropathy that almost reached statistical significance ($X^2 = 3.38$, $p = .06$) also shown in Figure 1.

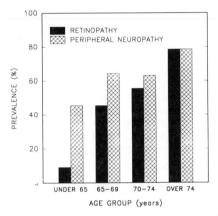

FIGURE 1 : Prevalence of retinopathy and peripheral neuropathy for four age groupings.

TABLE 1 : DESCRIPTION OF SUBJECTS

	Mean	Range
Age (years)	66.6	53 - 80
Time since diagnosis (years)	13.7	1 - 48
Percent Ideal Weight	120 %	80 - 197
Total Glycosylated Hemoglobin	11.6 %	6.4 - 19.5
Treatment		
Diet alone	2.8 %	-
Oral agents	39.6 %	-
Insulin	57.5 %	-
Symptomatic Peripheral Neuropathy	59.6 %	-
Retinopathy		
None	57.3 %	-
Background	28.2 %	-
Proliferative	14.6 %	-

For comparison purposes, a similar analysis of retinopathy prevalence was performed using duration of diabetes which was divided into subgroups as follows : under 6 years - 17.9 %, 6 - 10 years - 42.9 %, 11 - 20 years - 54.5 %, and over 20 years - 63.0 %. Duration was also linearly related to retinopathy although not as strongly as age ($X^2 = 12.0$, $p < .01$).

The results of the multiple logistic regression analyses are summarized in Table 2. Age was significantly associated with the prevalence of both neuropathy and retinopathy when the other potential risk variables were statistically controlled. For example, the odds ratio of 1.25 indicates that a one year increase in age is associated with a 25 % increase in the odds of having retinopathy, if all other predictors remain constant. The standardized coefficient allows for comparisons of the relative importance of each predictor by indicating the change in one logit of risk resulting from a change of one standard deviation in the predictor variable. Larger coefficients indicate greater relative risk.

Glycosylated hemoglobin was also significantly associated with increased prevalence of retinopathy and peripheral neuropathy symptoms. Longer duration of diabetes was not associated independently with retinopathy or peripheral neuropathy when the other variables were included. Percent ideal weight was only associated independently with an increased risk of peripheral neuropathy. The type of medication being used to treat the diabetes was not independently associated with the prevalence of retinopathy or neuropathy. Neither the presence of hypertension or of ischemic heart disease was related to relative risk of diabetic complications.

Since other investigators reported that duration of diabetes was a significant factor in the development of these complications, we examined the univariate association of duration with each complication. When analyzed alone, duration was associated with a significant increase in risk of retinopathy (odds ratio = 1.06, $p < .01$, standardized coefficient = 2.96) and peripheral neuropathy (odds ratio = 1.63, $p < .01$, standardized coefficient = 2.37).

In order to compare our results with previous studies, multiple logistic regression analyses were also performed using age at diagnosis instead of current age. Age at diagnosis ($p < .001$), duration ($p < .001$), and glycosylated hemoglobin ($p < .05$) were associated with increased risk of retinopathy. However, when examined alone, age at diagnosis was not significantly associated with retinopathy prevalence. Hence, current age appears the most parsimonious predictor. Moreover, a significant correlation was found between the presence of retinopathy and of neuropathy, $r = 0.64$, suggesting strongly that they co-exist in this population.

TABLE 2 : MULTIPLE LOGISTIC REGRESSION ANALYSIS
FOR PREDICTING RETINOPATHY AND NEUROPATHY

Variable	Coefficient	Odds Ratio	P Value
Retinopathy			
Age	3.54	1.25	$p < .01$
HbA1	2.08	1.26	$p < .05$
Peripheral Neuropathy			
Age	2.99	1.15	$p < .01$
HbA1	2.58	1.36	$p < .01$

Note. HbA1 = Total glycosylated hemoglobin. Coefficient = standardized coefficient, measures change in the logit of risk resulting from a change of one standard deviation in the predictor variable (16). The odds ratio represents the increase in risk associated with a change of one unit of the predictor variable (see text).

DISCUSSION

The prevalence of diabetic complications, notably retinopathy and peripheral neuropathy, was highest in the oldest diabetic group (see Figure 1). The presence of retinopathy in those over age 70 was exceedingly common. These results suggest a significant association between age per se and the development of several diabetic complications in middle age to older Type II diabetics.

Retinopathy prevalence clearly increased with age across the entire age span (53 to 80 years) examined in this study. In addition, the relationship between age and retinopathy remained after inclusion of various potential moderator variables in the logistical regression, such as duration of illness, metabolic control, and percent ideal weight. Age therefore emerges as a strong and independent risk factor associated with retinopathy in our population.

The findings from previous studies have been inconsistent with regard to the role of aging in complication development. Ballard et al. (13) in two incidence studies of non-insulin dependent diabetes found a positive correlation between age and risk for persistent proteinuria at diagnosis but a negative correlation between age and risk for retinopathy. Knuiman et al. (7) using a design similar to the current study but including in addition, younger patients with insulin-dependent diabetes also found increasing age to be independently associated with increasing risk for renal impairment, macrovascular complications, and sensory neuropathy. Retinopathy prevalence was associated with duration of diabetes but not age. Nathan and coworkers (9) found a higher prevalence of retinopathy in 65 to 74 year old diabetic patients compared to those 55 to 64 years old. In a second study (10), using multiple logistic regression, only duration and recent blood sugar control (glycosylated hemoglobin) emerged as independent predictors of retinopathy prevalence. Population differences may account for these inconsistencies. The overall prevalence rate for retinopathy in the present sample was about 43 % which is higher than the 25 % rate reported by Nathan et al. (10) and the 28 % rate reported by Knuiman et al. (7). The average age for our sample was also somewhat greater than that reported in these two studies.

Several previous studies have suggested that both duration of illness and control (assessed by glycosylated hemoglobin) are related to retinopathy prevalence (7, 10, 14). Our findings also indicate that retinopathy risk is significantly related to both control and duration, but only control remains as a significant predictor (along with age) when other moderator variables are controlled for. Two factors may account for the lack of an independent association between duration and retinopathy. First, in our population with a greater prevalence of retinopathy, especially at the older ages, duration may not be as significant a risk variable for this complication. Another possibility involves the measure of duration used in this study. Although it is the measure typically used in studies of this type, time since diagnosis may be a very imprecise measure of disease chronicity. Type II diabetes probably has a very gradual onset and may not be diagnosed for a substantial period of time (2). Non-diabetic variables such as frequency and thoroughness of routine medical care and existence of other medical problems can greatly affect the timing of diabetes detection for an individual patient. Age and time since diagnosis in our sample were not correlated (r = .01). Therefore the increased risk for retinopathy with older age is not simply due to greater duration of illness. It is possible that error in our duration measure may have led to an underestimate of the importance of this risk variable for these patients. One intriguing possibility which could account for our results is an age related bias in the detection rate of diabetes although this was not found in the NHANES II study (2).

Age was also the strongest predictor of peripheral neuropathy symptoms. Glycosylated hemoglobin and percent ideal weight were associated with peripheral neuropathy symptoms. The strength of the association between age and this complication again appears greater in our sample than in previous studies. Knuiman et al. (7) found age at diagnosis and duration to be the strongest predictors of sensory neuropathy, but not age per se. Nathan et al. (9) reported a greater percentage of sensory neuropathy in their older sample but did not perform comparisons among the risk factors. Age and duration of illness were about equal in terms of their association with hypertension.

Hypertension, reported to be a risk factor for the development of retinopathy among younger diabetics (15), was not significantly correlated with retinopathy in the current study as previously reported for older subjects (9). Although retinopathy was determined by careful exam and peripheral neuropathy primarily by symptom report, these measures were strongly related and had in common a generally increasing incidence with increasing age.

The results of this study suggest that increasing age, of itself, may be a significant factor in the prevalence of diabetic complications in some populations of older diabetic patients. The very high prevalence of retinopathy for the older age groups indicates that careful assessment for complications is especially important for geriatric diabetic groups. Though the pathogenesis of these findings remains to be elucidated, development of retinopathy and other complications among older male diabetics may follow a pattern markedly different from that reported for other age groups.

REFERENCES

1. TATTERSALL (R.B.) : Diabetes in the elderly : a neglected area ? *Diabetologia*, 27, 167-173, 1984.
2. HARRIS (M.I.), HADDEN (W.C.), KNOWLER (W.C.), BENNETT (P.B.) : Prevalence of diabetes and impaired glucose tolerance and plasma glucose levels in U.S. population aged 20-74 yr. *Diabetes*, 36, 523-534, 1987.
3. Data sheet on prevalence and incidence of diabetes in the United States. National Diabetes Group, National Institute of Arthritis, Diabetes, and Digestive and Kidney Diseases, *National Institutes of Health*, 1982.
4. Trends in diabetes mellitus mortality, in Gregg M.B. (ed.) : Morbidity and Mortality Weekly Report, Atlanta, *Centers for Disease Control*, 37, 1988.
5. MORLEY (J.E.), MOORADIAN (A.D.), ROSENTHAL (M.J.), KAISER (F.E.) : Diabetes mellitus in elderly patients. It is different ? *American Journal of Medicine*, 83, 533-542, 1987.
6. DORF (A.), BALLINTINE (E.J.), BENNETT (P.H.), MILLER (M.) : Retinopathy in Pima Indians : relationships to glucose level, duration of diabetes, age a diagnosis of diabetes, and age at examination in a population with a high prevalence of diabetes mellitus. *Diabetes*, 25, 554-560, 1976.
7. KNUIMAN (M.W.), WELBORN (T.A.), McCANN (V.J.), STANTON (K.G.), CONSTABLE (I.J.) : Prevalence of diabetic complications in relation to risk factors. *Diabetes*, 35, 1332-1339, 1986.
8. BALLARD (D.J.), HUMPHREY (L.L.), MELTON (L.J.), FROHNERT (P.P.), CHU (C.P.), O'FALLON (W.M.), PALUMBO (P.J.) : Epidemiology of persistent proteinuria in Type II Diabetes Mellitus. Population-based study in Rochester, Minnesota. *Diabetes*, 37, 405-412, 1988.
9. NATHAN (D.M.), SINGER (D.E.), GODINE (J.E.), PERLMUTER (L.C.) : Non-insulin-dependent diabetes in older patients. Complications and risk factors. *American Journal of Medicine*, 81, 837-842, 1986.
10. NATHAN (D.M.), SINGER (D.E.), GODINE (J.E.), HARRINGTON (C.H.), PERLMUTER (L.C.) : Retinopathy in older Type II diabetics : Association with glucose control. *Diabetes*, 35, 797-801, 1986.
11. DIXON (W.J. (ed.) : BMDP. Berkeley, *University of California Press*, 1983.
12. SCHLESSELMAN (J.J.) : Case-control studies. New York, *Oxford University Press*, 171, 1982.
13. BALLARD (D.J.), MELTON (L.J.), DWYER (M.S.), TRAUTMAN (J.C.), CHU (C.P.), O'FALLON (W.M.), PALUMBO (P.J.) : Risk factors for diabetic retinopathy. A population-based study in Rochester, Minnesota. *Diabetes Care*, 9, 334-342, 1986.
14. PIRART (J.) : Diabetes mellitus and its degenerative complications : a propective study of 4,400 patients observed between 1947 and 1973. *Diabetes Care*, 1, 252-263, 1978.
15. KNOWLER (W.C.), BENNETT (P.H.), BALLINTINE (E.J.) : Increased incidence of retinopathy in diabetics with elevated blood pressure. *New England Journal Medicine*, 302, 645-650, 1980.
16. TRUETT (J.), CORNFIELD (J.), KANNEL (W.) : A multivariate analysis of the risk of coronary heart disease in Framingham. *Journal Chronic Diseases*, 20, 511-517, 1967.

RATES OF HEALTH CARE UTILIZATION OF NIDDM PATIENTS NEW TO ORAL HYPOGLYCEMIC THERAPY (1)

Steven R. GAMBERT (*), **Nancy A. FOX**, (**),
Jake JACOBS (**)

Summary. – *A retrospective study was conducted utilizing a large computerized data base derived from state Medicaid claims to determine rates of diabetic-related emergency room and hospitalization use for NIDDM patients. Two comparisons are made. Patients prescribed hypoglycemic medications before the development of one of the late complications of diabetes are compared with those initiating therapy later. Amongst patients without record of a late complication, comparisons are made between individual drug therapy groups. Glipizide patients were found to have had a significantly lower rate of hospitalization than first-generation patients (29.1 versus 87.3 per 1,000 patients, p = 0.01). No statistically significant differences in emergency room utilization were uncovered. Patients with reported late complications of diabetes utilized emergency room services at nearly five times the rate of those without. The rate of hospitalization was approximately eleven times greater in the late complications group.* (Facts and Research in Gerontology 1992)

Key-words : *diabetes mellitus, cost-effective, NIDDM, health care utilization.*

INTRODUCTION

Health care costs have increased dramatically during the past two decades, creating pressures to minimize costs at all levels in the health care system. One area of great concern is diabetes mellitus. The economic burden resulting from a chronic illness such as diabetes is of major importance in the allocation of health care resources and in the evaluation of health research and treatment programs. A recent study estimated the costs of diabetes in the U.S. at $20.4 billion (1). Inpatient hospitalization costs accounted for one-third of all costs.

(1) Supported by a research grant from Roerig, a division of Pfizer Pharmaceuticals.

(*) Professor of Medicine and Gerontology, New York Medical College, Munger Pavilion, Room 170, Valhalla, New York 10595 (U.S.A.).

(**) Center for Economic Studies in Medicine, Reston, Virginia.

The majority of U.S. diabetes patients have adult onset or non-insulin dependent diabetes mellitus (NIDDM). While many of these patients can control their disease through a diet and exercise program, others require insulin or oral hypoglycemic agents to remain euglycemic. First-generation oral agents, including tolbutamide, chlorpropamide, acetohexamide and tolazamide, have been used for years and, until 1984, were the only oral agents available in the U.S. Second-generation agents, glipizide and glyburide, first became available for use in the United States in mid-1984 and appear to offer certain advantages over first-generation products. One multi-center study reported that 75.3 percent of patients who failed to achieve adequate blood glucose control on first-generation agents were able to be managed on glipizide (2). Lebovitz (3) and Melander (4) reported that clinically significant hypoglycemia occurred less often in patients treated with glipizide compared to those on chlorpropamide or glyburide. Although medication induced side effects and treatment failures can increase the need for medical services and thus health care costs, little is known regarding oral hypoglycemic agent use and rates of health care utilization.

The following reports the results of a retrospective study designed to determine rates of diabetic-related utilization for new-to-therapy NIDDM patients with and without diabetic-related late complications. The focus of this investigation is to investigate differences in diabetic-related emergency room and inpatient hospitalization use the following patient populations : (1) NIDDM patients without late complications by the oral hypoglycemic regimen ; and (2) NIDDM patients with and without diabetic-related late complications.

METHODS

The demographics, medical history and health care utilization patterns of NIDDM patients were studied using computerized data obtained from the Pennsylvania Medicaid program. Although originally created for fiscal and administrative purposes, similar data sources are being frequently utilized for epidemiological research (5-9). The U.S. Food and Drug Administration has adopted state Medicaid data as a potential source for conducting postmarketing drug surveillance studies.

The data source utilized here includes a record of each inpatient hospital stay, emergency room or physician visit and outpatient pharmaceutical prescription reimbursed by the Pennsylvania Medicaid program. Each health care encounter record provides the reason for the medical service, as reported by the health care provider. For medical service encounters, the reason for service is reported utilizing International Classification of Diseases, Ninth Revision — Clinical Modification (ICD-9-CM) (10) diagnosis codes. Encounters for pharmaceuticals (submitted by retail pharmacies) provide a National Drug Code indicating the product dispensed and prescription size. Patient date of birth, sex, race, specific dates of eligibility for Medicaid coverage and place of residence are provided for all Medicaid recipients.

All patients receiving an oral hypoglycemic agent during the two-year period beginning January 1, 1985 were identified. The date the patient received his/her initial oral hypoglycemic prescription during this period was determined. Health care records of these patients were then extracted from the data base for the six-month period prior to their initial hypoglycemic prescription and for the period spanning the receipt of their initial prescription to June 30, 1987, the final date that data were available for this analysis. The patient's precise diabetes disease progression, including duration of diabetes and past level of blood glucose control, is not available in the Medicaid computerized data files used. To ensure a more homogeneous study population of patients at comparable disease states, only those patients who were new to hypoglycemic therapy were included in the study population. New to diabetic therapy patients were defined as those not receiving insulin or an oral agent during the six months prior to receipt of the initial prescription leading to study entry.

Several additional patient entry criteria were used to ensure a more homogeneous study population. All subjects were required to receive oral agent therapy for at least 90 days. Patients were excluded if they received any form of coexisting health insurance, such as Medicare or Workmen's Compensation, to ensure the patient's complete health care history was available for analysis. Patients residing in nursing homes were excluded, as their compliance is often mandated by medical staff. Finally, patients who were pregnant or had a history of alcoholism were excluded, as the diabetic-related care provided to these patients is not typical of NIDDM patients as a whole.

Patients were classified into three therapy groups according to their initially prescribed oral hypoglycemic agent : glipizide, glyburide or first-generation agent. Patients were also classified as to presence of a late complication. Patients receiving outpatient or inpatient treatment for any of the conditions in Figure 1 are considered to

RISK FACTORS	ICD-9-CM CODE
Renal Manifestations	
– Diabetes with renal manifestations	250.4
– Diabetic nephropathy	583.81
– Diabetic nephrosis	581.81
Ophthalmic Manifestations	
– Diabetes with ophthalmic manifestations	250.5
– Diabetic retinopathy	362.0
– Cataracts	366.41
– Glaucoma	365
Neurological Manifestations	
– Diabetes with neurological manifestations	250.6
– Amyotrophy	358.1
– Mononeuropathy	354.0-355.9
– Neurogenic arthropathy	713.5
– Peripheral autonomic neurapthy	337.1
– Polyneurapthy	357.2
Circulatory manifestations	
– Diabetes with peripheral circulatory disorders	250.7
– Gangrene	785.4
– Amputations	885-887, 895-897
– Peripheral angiopathy	443.81
– Ischemic heart disease	410-414
– Hypertension	401
– Stroke	436
– Arteriosclerosis obliterans (ASO)	440
– Other specified manifestations	250.8
– Diabetic bone changes	731.8
– Diabetic ulcer	707.1, 707.8, 707.9
– Unspecified complications	250.9

Figure 1

Late complications of diabetes

have late complications of diabetes. Subjects were exited from further analysis at the first of five occurrences : loss of Medicaid eligibility ; termination of drug therapy ; poor drug compliance (no prescription refilled for a period of sixty days) ; change in medication regimen ; or June 30, 1987, the final date that data were available for analysis.

Diabetic-related health care utilization was defined as those health care encounters reporting the reason for service as diabetes (ICD-9-CM 250), hypoglycemic coma (ICD-9-CM 251.0) or hypoglycemia without coma (ICD-9-CM 251.2). Diabetic-related utilization was determined for outpatient physician, emergency room and inpatient hospitalization services based on the provider and place of service reported.

Utilization data were converted to number of events per 1,000 patients per year. The following control variables were utilized to minimize self-selection between groups : age ; sex ; race ; annual number of outpatient diabetic-related physician visits ; presence of reported hypertension ; and presence of reported obesity.

We compared utilization of services, by drug therapy group, in patients presenting without late complications. Patient demographics, presence of diabetic-related risk factors, outpatient health care utilization and reason for patient drop-out was compared for patients without complications using chisquare analysis and unpaired student T-test (two-sided). To adjust for possible sources of bias from confounders, analysis of covariance was used to compare diabetic-related emergency room and inpatient hospitalization use between drug therapy groups (11).

We then performed a parallel analysis comparing utilization of NIDDM patients presenting with and without complications. Analysis of covariance was used to compare diabetic-related emergency room and inpatient utilization for these two patient groups.

RESULTS

A total of 3,062 NIDDM patients without complications met the established criteria for study entry, consisting of 1,578, 422 and 1,062 patients in the first-generation, glipizide and glyburide groups, respectively. Of the first-generation group, 74 percent received chlorpropamide, 17 percent tolazamide, 7 percent tolbutamide and 2 percent acetohexamide. Table 1 reports patient demography and other health care characteristics. Patients receiving first-generation agents tend to be older (mean 52.8 years) than glipizide (51.0 years, $p < 0.01$) and glyburide patients (51.2 years, $p < 0.01$). Overall, approximately three-quarters of the population was female and approximately 60 percent caucasian. There were no statistical differences in the sex or racial distributions between therapy groups. Glipizide patients averaged more diabetes-related physician visits per year than first-generation patients ($p < 0.01$) and glyburide patients ($p = ns$). Almost half of all glipizide patients were treated for hypertension, compared to 41 percent of first-generation ($p < 0.01$) and 44 percent of glyburide patients ($p = ns$). Additionally, seven percent of glipizide patients were treated for obesity, compared to four percent of first-generation patients ($p < 0.05$) and five percent of glyburide patients ($p = ns$).

There was no significant difference between the mean number of days that first-generation, glipizide and glyburide patients were followed in the study (297, 280, and 295 days, respectively). However, only 28 percent of first-generation patients remained in the study through June 30, 1987, compared to 44 percent of glipizide ($p < 0.05$) and 46 percent of glyburide patients ($p < 0.05$). The most common reason for patient exit was poor compliance ; 26 percent of first-generation agents exhibited a period of poor compliance, compared to 22 percent of glipizide ($p < 0.05$)

and 21 percent of glyburide patients (p < 0.05). The rate of switching to alternative drug therapies was also highest for those initially prescribed first-generation agents (17 percent) versus glipizide (10 percent, p < 0.05) and glyburide patients (7 percent, p < 0.05).

Diabetic-related emergency room use is reported in Figure 2. After adjustment for the control variables, utilization ranged from 48.2 per 1,000 glipizide patients to 92.3 per 1,000 glyburide patients per year. Analysis of covariance indicated no significant difference between study groups.

TABLE 1

PATIENT DEMOGRAPHIC AND OTHER HEALTH CARE CHARACTERISTICS
OF NIDDM PATIENTS WITHOUT DIABETIC-RELATED COMPLICATIONS*

Percentage of Patients	First Generation (n = 1578)	Glipizide (n = 422)	Glyburide (n = 1062)
25 to 44 years	23.1 % +	25.6 %	27.9 %
45 to 64 years	65.0 + I	67.5	62.7
> 65 years	11.9	6.9	9.4
Caucasian	58.2	57.8	62.5
Female	70.6	73.7	73.1
Diabetic-related Outpatient Visits : > 2 visits/year	63.6	58.8	62.8
Treated for Hypertension	40.5 §	48.8	44.0
Treated for Obesity	4.4 I	7. 1	5.5

* Chi-square analysis used for all comparisons.
\+ p < 0.01 vs. glyburide patients.
I p < 0.05 vs. glipizide patients.
§ p < 0.01 vs. glipizide patients.

Figure 3 presents diabetic-related inpatient hospitalization use. Patients receiving glipizide had a significantly lower rate of diabetic-related hospitalizations, compared to first-generation patients (29.1 vs. 87.3 per 1,000 patients per year, p = 0.01). There was no statistical difference between the rate of hospitalization between glipizide and glyburide patients (29.1 vs. 69.9 per 1,000 patients per year, p = 0.10).

A total of 871 NIDDM patients with diabetic-related late complications were identified as meeting established criteria for study entry. Patients with complications tended to be older than patients without complications (mean 53.1 versus 52.0 years, p < 0.01) (Table 2). There were no differences in the sex or racial distributions between these groups. Patients with complications visited the physician due to diabetes more frequently than their counterparts (mean 6.4 versus 3.3 times per year, p < 0.01). More than half of all patients with complications were treated for hypertension, compared to 43 percent of patients without complications (p < 0.01). Twice as many patients with complications were treated for obesity (13 versus 5 percent, p   0.01).

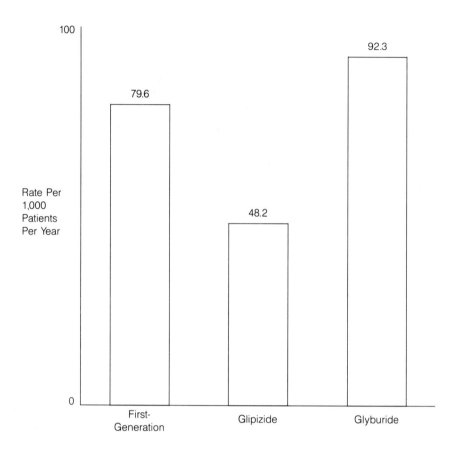

Figure 2

Diabetic-related emergency room utilization of NIDDM patients
without diabetic-related complications

Diabetic-related emergency room and inpatient hospitalization use was significantly greater for patients with complications. The annual rate of diabetic-related emergency utilization was 331.7 per 1,000 patients with complications compared to 71.8 per 1,000 patients without complications (p < 0.01). The annual rate of diabetic-related hospitalization was nearly 12 times as great for patients with complications (1117.7 versus 94.5 per 1,000 patients, p < 0.01).

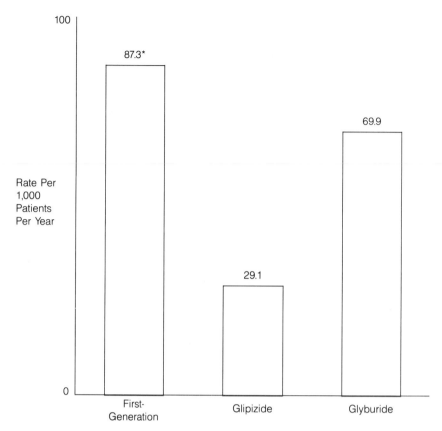

* p < 0.01 vs. glipizide.

Figure 3

Diabetic-related inpatient hospitalization utilization of NIDDM patients
without diabetic-related complications

DISCUSSION

These data suggest that the choice of oral hypoglycemic medication in the treatment of patients with NIDDM may modify patterns of health care utilization. The major
difference noted between NIDDM patients without complications was the rate of hospitalization, with the lowest being for patients treated with glipizide. The differences
in health care utilization may indeed influence the diabetic-related treatment costs.
These data also suggest that early recognition and treatment of NIDDM appears
to be a cost effective health care practice. Patients placed on oral agent therapy only

TABLE 2

COMPARISON OF PATIENT DEMOGRAPHIC
AND OTHER HEALTH CARE CHARACTERISTICS OF NIDDM PATIENTS WITH
AND WITHOUT DIABETIC-RELATED COMPLICATIONS*

Percentage of Patients	Patients Without Complications	Patients With Complications
25 to 44 years	25.1 % +	18.1 %
45 to 64 years	64.5 +	74.7
> 65 years	10.4 +	7.1
Caucasian	71.9	69.9
Female	59.6	61.4
Diabetic-related Outpatient Visits : > 2 visits/year	62.4 +	27.3
Treated for Hypertension	´42.8 +	53.5
Treated for Obesity	5.1 +	13.4

* Chi-square analysis used for all comparisons.
 + $p < 0.01$.

after developing diabetic-related complications utilized a greater number of health care services compared to those treated earlier in the course of their disease.

State Medicaid programs typically reimburse medical providers at a rate much lower than U.S. reimbursement levels. Therefore, estimated prices are utilized to attempt to determine the true societal cost of the medical services provided to the Medicaid population studied. That is, the opportunity cost to society of the services provided to the Medicaid study population is the value of the medical services that cannot be provided because the same resources are not available to treat other patients. Thus, because the medical services provided to the Medicaid study population can be used elsewhere, we use estimated costs to evaluate the value of these resources in such alternative uses. Assuming $100 per emergency room visit and $3500 per inpatient hospitalization (i.e., $500 per day with an average seven day stay), the value of these services is estimated at $313 per first-generation patient, $107 per glipizide patient and $254 per glyburide patient. In addition to personal benefits that most certainly are associated with the decreased rate of hospitalization, cost savings must not be taken lightly, especially in these days of increasing fiscal constraint and limited resources.

Utilizing the same estimated resource values, patients with complications had nearly five times as great emergency room costs ($33 versus $7 per patient) and nearly 12 times as great inpatient hospitalization costs ($3912 versus $333 per patient) compared to NIDDM patients without late complications. Although not able to be measured by this study, early treatment of diabetes is known to retard and even prevent the development of many diabetic-related complications that can impair one's quality of life as well.

Glipizide's short half-life, physiological action and low rate of drug-drug interactions (3) most likely were responsible for its performance in this study population. One must question, however, whether the small but still greater number of physician visits for the glipizide group resulted in better physician follow-up and thus less medication-related problems. The poor compliance for first-generation agents could be responsible for the higher number of diabetic-related hospitalizations.

Unfortunately, patients receiving Medicare benefits were excluded from data analysis. This was necessary to insure accurate and complete data retrieval ; however, persons over 65 years of age make up the highest percentage of diabetics (38 percent) (12) and are known to be at greater risk of drug interactions and sequelae from both hyper- and hypoglycemia.

As with most retrospective studies, not all desired information was available for study patients. For example, state Medicaid data do not provide measures of disease severity, such as duration of diabetes, length of diabetic therapy, use of diet and exercise or results of blood glucose laboratory tests. Therefore, it is impossible to determine whether these factors had a major influence on the rates of utilization reported in this analysis. Additionally, the patients who served in this retrospective study are limited to Pennsylvania Medicaid recipients. The demographic make-up of state Medicaid programs are markedly different than the U.S. population as a whole. Generally, state Medicaid populations tend to be much younger and more female than the U.S. population. For example, approximately 60 percent of Pennsylvania Medicaid patients are under age 20 compared to 37 percent of the U.S. civilian population (13, 14). Therefore, caution should be taken before making inferences from these data to a more heterogenous population.

Our study investigates utilization of patients treated with oral hypoglycemic agents for NIDDM. We are unable to compare our results to patients treated with insulin or who continue on diet and exercise therapy alone. Previous studies have, however, reported excellent results for those persons treated with appropriate oral hypoglycemic agents (2). When the choice is made to use an oral hypoglycemic agent, however, our data suggest that differences may exist between available agents and that this be considered prior to initiating pharmacological intervention.

RÉFÉRENCES

1. The Center for Economic Studies in Medicine. Direct and indirect costs of diabetes in the United States in 1987. Presented at the Council on Health Care Delivery and Public Health during the American Diabetes Association Annual Meeting. *Alexandria : American Diabetes Association*, 1988.
2. OSTMAN J. : Worldwide clinical experience with glipizide : an overview. Glipizide : a worldwide review. *Princeton : Excerpta Medica*, 1984.
3. LEBOVITZ H.E. : Glipizide : a second-generation sulfonylurea hypoglycemic agent. *Pharmacotherapy*, 1985, 5 (2), 63-77.
4. MELANDER A. : Clinical pharmacology of sulfonylureas. *Metabolism : Clinical and Experimental*, 1987, 36 (Suppl. 1), 12-2.
5. RAY W.A., GRIFFIN M.R., SCHAFFNER W. et al. : Psychotropic drug use and the risk of hip fracture. *N. Engl. J. Med.*, 1987, 316, 363-369.
6. STROM B.L., CARSON J.L., MORSE M.L. et al. : The effect of indication on hypersensitivity reactions associated with zomepirac sodium and other nonsteroidal antiinflammatory drugs. *Arthritis Rheum.*, 1987, 30, 1142-1148.
7. CARSON J.L., STROM B.L., MORSE M.L. et al. : The relative gastrointestinal toxicity of the nonsteroidal antiinflammatory drugs. *Arch. Intern. Med.*, 1987, 147, 1054-1059.
8. JACOBS J., KEYSERLING J., BRITTON M. et al. : The total cost of care and the use of pharmaceuticals in the management of rheumatoid arthritis : the Medi-Cal program. *J. Clin. Epidemiol.*, 1988, 41, 215-223.
9. AVORN J., EVERITT D.E., WEISS S. : Increased antidepressant use in patients prescribed ß-blockers. *J.A.M.A.*, 1986, 255, 357-360.
10. Health Care Financing Administration. The international classification of diseases, 9th revision, clinical modification. Washington, D.C. : Department of Health and Human Services, 1980 ; DHHS Publication No. (PHS) 80-1260, vol. 1.

11. SNEDECOR G.W., COCHRAN W.G. : Analysis of covariance. In : Statistical Methods. *6th ed. Ames, Iowa : The Iowa State University Press,* 1967, 419-446.

12. OLSON O.C. : Classification and Epidemiology. In : Diagnosis and Management of Diabetes Mellitus. *2nd ed. New York : Raven Press,* 1978, 1-11.

13. Health Care Financing Administration. Statistical report on medical care : recipients, payments, and services. Washington, D.C. : Department of Health and Human Services, 1987, Form HCFA-2082 (4-80).

14. Bureau of the Census : Current Population Report : U.S. Population Estimates by Age, Sex and Race : 1980 to 1987. Series P-25, No. 1022. Washington, D.C., Bureau of the Census, March, 1988.

AGING AND SEXUALITY

John E. MORLEY (*), Fran E. KAISER (**)

Summary. – *Many older persons remain sexually active. Impotence in older males is morthy due to organise causes. The commonest cause of impotence is vascular disease. Hypogonadism in males often leads to deceneared of libido and may also be associated with decrease muscle strength and osteoporous. Less information is available on sexual dysfunction in older females. Many sexual problems in older females ave related to estrogen dificiency.* (Facts and Research in Gerontology 1992)

> « Charito is more than sixty
> yet her hair is still a dense forest
> and no brassiere holds up the marble cones
> of her high-pointed breasts.
> Her unwrinkled flesh exhales ambrosia
> and myriads of teasing charms.
> Lovers, if you do not run from hot desire,
> enjoy Charito and forget her many decades. »
>
> Philodemus.

Most literature has dealt less kindly with sexuality in older persons than did the Greek poet, Philodemus. Much literature takes the viewpoint espoused by Cephalus in Plato's « The Republic », who commented that « ... in old age, you become quite free of passions of this sort and they leave you in peace ». Other literature stresses the development of impotence with old age and the foolishness of an old man attempting to marry a young woman, such as portrayed in the tale of January who married May in Chaucer's « Merchant's Tale » and was subsequently cuckolded due to his impotence. While some modern literature has started to recognize that pleasure in sexuality does not disappear with advancing age ; (as evidenced by Captain Osborn, finding pleasure in the noises of a young couple making love even though he was in his eighties), most modern literature continues to stereotype older persons as asexual or impotent and, if not, as behaving inappropriately (« the dirty old person » syndrome).

In the last decade, both society and scientists have come to recognize that sexua-

(*) Division of Geriatric Medicine, St. Louis University School of Medicine, St. Louis, MO.
(**) Geriatric Research Education and Clinical Center (GRECC), VA Medical Center, St. Louis, MO.

lity can and does continue as normal behavior into the extremes of old age, and that failure of sexuality relates to disease processes often associated with aging and in some cases to societal attitudes. Clearly, for a number of older persons, maintenance of sexual expression is an important quality of life issue.

Bretschneider and McCoy (1) reported that 30 % of highly healthy 80 to 102 year olds were still sexually active. Other studies have confirmed that a substantial percentage of adults over 70 years of age engage in sexual intercourse (2, 3). Starr and Wiener (2) noted that in females aged 60 to 91, the frequency of sexual intercourse was reported as 1.39 time per week, which was similar to the frequency reported by Kinsey et al. (4) some thirty years earlier for females aged 46 to 50 years.

This chapter will briefly review the prevalence of hypogonadism in older males and its relationship to decreased libido. It will then discuss the causes and management of impotence. Finally, it will discuss sexual function in the aging female.

MALE HYPOGONADISM, DECREASED LIBIDO AND FRAILTY

The major effect of testosterone appears to be on libido, with lesser effects demonstrated on potency. Numerous studies have investigated the relationship of aging and testosterone. Overall, these studies support the concept that aging is associated with a decrease in testosterone levels (5). This is seen more dramatically when bioavailable testosterone (BT, a measure of free and albumin-bound testosterone) is measured. We have reported that just over 50 % of highly healthy males between 50 and 70 years of age have BT levels lower than those observed in young males (6). In that study, hypogonadism occurred equally in men with or without impotence. Most hypogonadal older males have secondary hypogonadism with the luteinizing hormone (LH) levels being low normal.

With advancing age, there is a decrease in Leydig cell number and a decreased testosterone production rate, with blunting of the normal circadian variation in testosterone levels (5). Despite these changes, LH levels are elevated in only a small percentage of older males. This suggests that aging is associated with a hypothalamic-pituitary defect in gonadotropin secretion, as well as with a primary testicular defect. Various studies have found a decrease in pulsatile secretion of GnRH and an impaired secretion of LH in response to GnRH with aging (7). There is also an increase in the ability of testosterone to suppress LH in older persons (8). Estradiol levels are either slightly increased or unaltered with advancing age, and there is a minor increase in circulating prolactin levels (5).

The effect of testosterone on sexuality in older males is poorly explored. In a large group of males aged 41 to 93 years of age, changes in free testosterone appear to play only a minor role in sexual dysfunction (9). Androgen replacement in young hypogonadal males increases normal sexual drive, ejaculation and spontaneous erections (10). In a group of middle-aged males, we found that testosterone enhanced potency and nocturnal penile tumescence compared to when they were receiving saline injections (11).

There is also some evidence that testosterone deficiency may be partially responsible for some of the frailty seen with aging. Testosterone deficiency has been associated with the development of hip fractures (12). Furthermore, testosterone deficiency may also play a role in the decreased muscle strength that may be associated with aging (13). In older males, testosterone therapy has been reported to increase sexual interest and energy, produce better sleep, less depression and an increased hematocrit (14).

Potential side effects of testosterone therapy include prostatic enlargement, stroke (associated with the increase in hematocrit), gynecomastia, water retention leading to hypertension and exacerbation of cardiac failure, and liver dysfunction. Hypercholesterolemia does not appear to be problematic in older persons receiving testosterone. At present, the case for testosterone therapy in older males with hypogonadism is not as clear-cut as is the case for estrogen therapy in postmenopausal females. However, there is increasing evidence that a subgroup of older males may benefit from testosterone replacement therapy. If testosterone therapy is utilized, the patient should be regularly checked for increases in hematocrit, have prostate specific antigen (PSA) measured and have a 6 monthly digital prostate examination.

IMPOTENCE

Impotence is a common problem in older males. One-third of males over 40 years of age with one or more medical conditions will be impotent (15). Approximately half of these patients would like to have something done about their impotence. In older males the cause of impotence is often multifactorial (table I).

The most common cause of impotence in older males is vascular disease involving the penile arteries (16). Diagnosis of vascular disease can be made by measuring the penible blood pressure or by duplex utrasonography. Approximately half of the patients with minor degrees of penile arterial blockage will only have their disease demonstrated after lower limb exercise. This causes redistribution of blood to the buttocks away from a partially obstructed penile artery, i.e. the so-called « pelvic steal syndrome ». It should be recognized that atherosclerotic penile disease may be a harbinger of atherosclerosis in other parts of the body. Older males with impotence based on a vascular etiology have a 23 % chance of developing a myocardial infarction or a stroke over the subsequent 2 to 3 years, compared with only a 4.5 % incidence in impotent patients with normal penile blood pressures (17).

Defects in the tunica albuginea (which occur with increasing frequency with advancing age) lead to venous leakage from the corpora cavernosa. Venous leakage impotence may play a role in from 14 to 54 % of all cases of impotence (18). The diagnosis is suspected when the male is unable to maintain an adequate erection after intracorporeal injection of papaverine or prostaglandin, and diagnosis can be confirmed by either pharmacocavernosography and/or cavernosometry (19).

Elevated prolactin levels result in impotence, and in approximately 1 in 10 of these patients an associated prolactinoma will be found (19). Medications, renal failure and diabetes mellitus (20) are common causes of elevated prolactin levels in older males. Hyper- and hypothyroidism lead to impotence (21). Diabetes mellitus results in impotence either secondary to vascular disease or due to autonomic neuropathy, or a combination of these factors.

Medications play a role in the pathogenesis of impotence in up to 25 % of older males (15). Thiazide diuretics are a common cause of impotence. Most antihypertensive agents have been associated with impotence, though this is much less common with vasodilators, angiotensin converting enzyme inhibitors and calcium channel antagonists. Other pharmacologic causes of impotence include most psychoactive drugs, H-2 antagonists, digoxin, gemfibrozil, corticosteroids, carbonic anhydrase inhibitors and cytotoxic agents (18).

Depression is not a rare cause of impotence in older males, and needs to be carefully sought for by utilizing a screening test such as the Yesavage Geriatric Depression Screen. Depression may be associated with decreased testosterone levels and decreased nocturnal penile tumescence (18). Psychological causes of impotence are responsible for approximately 10 % of impotence in older persons (15). The Widower's syndrome occurs in older males, who having lost a spouse, find themselves being pressed to perform sexually with an older woman whom they have relied on for companionship but may not be attracted to ; or the widower may feel that they have betrayed their deceased partner.

There is also some evidence that testosterone deficiency may be partially responsible for some of the frailty seen with aging. Testosterone deficiency has been associated with the development of hip fractures (12). Furthermore, testosterone deficiency may also play a role in the decreased muscle strength that may be associated with aging (13). In older males, testosterone therapy has been reported to increase sexual interest and energy, produce better sleep, less depression and increase hematocrit (14).

Potential side effects of testosterone therapy include prostatic enlargement, stroke (associated with the increase in hematocrit), gynecomastia, water retention leading to hypertension and exacerbation of cardiac failure, and liver dysfunction. Hypercholesterolemia does not appear to be problematic in older persons receiving testosterone. At present, the case for testosterone therapy in older males with hypogonadism is not as clear-cut as is the case for estrogen therapy in postmenopausal females. However, there is increasing evidence that a subgroup of older males may benefit from testosterone replacement therapy. If testosterone therapy is utilized, the patient should be regularly checked for increases in hematocrit, have prostate specific antigen (PSA) measured and have a 6 monthly digital prostate examination.

IMPOTENCE

Impotence is a common problem in older males. One-third of males over 40 years of age with one or more medical conditions will be impotent (15). Approximately half of these patients would like to have something done about their impotence. In older males the cause of impotence is often multifactorial (table I).

The most common cause of impotence in older males is vascular disease involving the penile arteries (16). Diagnosis of vascular disease can be made by measuring the penible blood pressure or by duplex utrasonography. Approximately half of the patients with minor degrees of penile arterial blockage will only have their disease demonstrated after lower limb exercise. This causes redistribution of blood to the buttocks away from a partially obstructed penile artery, i.e. the so-called « pelvic steal syndrome ». It should be recognized that atherosclerotic penile disease may be a harbinger of atherosclerosis in other parts of the body. Older males with impotence based on a vascular etiology have a 23 % chance of developing a myocardial infarction or a stroke over the subsequent 2 to 3 years, compared with only a 4.5 % incidence in impotent patients with normal penile blood pressures (17).

Defects in the tunica albuginea (which occur with increasing frequency with advancing age) lead to venous leakage from the corpora cavernosa. Venous leakage impotence may play a role in from 14 to 54 % of all cases of impotence (18). The diagnosis is suspected when the male is unable to maintain an adequate erection after intracorporeal injection of papaverine or prostaglandin, and diagnosis can be confirmed by either pharmacocavernosography and/or cavernosometry (19).

Elevated prolactin levels result in impotence, and in approximately 1 in 10 of these patients an associated prolactinoma will be found (19). Medications, renal failure and diabetes mellitus (20) are common causes of elevated prolactin levels in older males. Hyper- and hypothyroidism lead to impotence (21). Diabetes mellitus results in impotence either secondary to vascular disease or due to autonomic neuropathy, or a combination of these factors.

TABLE I

CAUSES OF IMPOTENCE

1. Vascular :	Arterial
	Venous
	Raynaud's phenomenon
2. Central Nervous System :	Stroke
	Tumors
	Multiple sclerosis
	Temporal lobe epilepsy
3. Spinal Cord Disease :	Trauma
	Tumors
4. Peripheral Neuropathy :	Sensory
	Autonomic
5. Endocrine Disorders :	Hypogonadism
	Hyperprolactinemia
	Cushing's disease
	Thyroid disease
	Diabetes mellitus
6. Systemic Disorders :	Renal failure
	Liver disease
	Chronic obstructive pulmonary disease
7. Nutritional Disorders :	Zinc deficiency
	Protein energy malnutrition
8. Medications :	Thiazide diuretics
	Antihypertensive agents
	Digoxin
	Carbonic Anhydrase inhibitors
	Psychoactive agents
	Chemotoxic agents
9. Peyronie's disease	

Medications play a role in the pathogenesis of impotence in up to 25 % of older males (15). Thiazide diuretics are a common cause of impotence. Most antihypertensive agents have been associated with impotence, though this is much less common with vasodilators, angiotensin converting enzyme inhibitors and calcium channel antagonists. Other pharmacologic causes of impotence include most psychoactive drugs, H-2 antagonists, digoxin, gemfibrozil, corticosteroids, carbonic anhydrase inhibitors and cytotoxic agents (18).

Depression is not a rare cause of impotence in older males, and needs to be carefully sought for by utilizing a screening test such as the Yesavage Geriatric Depression Screen. Depression may be associated with decreased testosterone levels and decreased nocturnal penile tumescence (18). Psychological causes of impotence are responsible for approximately 10 % of impotence in older persons (15). The Widower's syndrome occurs in older males, who having lost a spouse, find themselves being pressed to perform sexually with an older woman whom they have relied on for companionship but may not be attracted to ; or the widower may feel that they have betrayed their deceased partner.

A number of therapeutic modalities exist for the treatment of impotence (table II). Of these, three options appear most useful in older persons in whom discontinuation of a medication causing impotence is not possible or desirable and, in whom, treatable causes of impotence, e.g. depression, thyroid disorders, hyperprolactinemia (with bromergocriptine) have been excluded.

Vacuum tumescence (external negative pressure) devices have high acceptability among older persons in stable relationships (22). The device consists of a clear plastic

TABLE II

MANAGEMENT OF IMPOTENCE

1. Vacuum tumescence devices
2. Intracavernosal injections
   - papaverine
   - phentolamine
   - prostaglandin E1
3. Transdermal agents
   - nitroglycerine
   - minoxidil
4. Penile prosthesis
   - semi-rigid
   - inflatible
5. Endocrine
   - testosterone
   - bromergocriptine
   - ? opioid antagonism
6. Discontinue medications
7. Nutritional
   - zinc
8. Surgery for venous leakage
9. Miscellaneous
   - yohimbine
   - oral phentolamine

cylinder that is placed over the penis and is connected to a hand-operated suction pump. This allows the creation of a negative pressure which draws blood into the corpora cavernosa, resulting in the development of a penile erection which can then be maintained by slipping a rubber band or ring over the penile base. The device can also be used in some persons following removal of a penile prosthesis. The major side effects seen with vacuum devices are : premature loss of penile rigidity, pain or discomfort, occasional failure to ejaculate, bruising and/or inconvenience of use.

Intracavernosal injections of a variety of drugs, such as papaverine, phentolamine and/or prostaglandin E1, have been demonstrated to produce excellent quality penile erections (18). Patients can be taught to self-inject at home. Side effects of these agents include priapism, pain, penile bruising, scarring, fibrosis, urethral bleeding and, rarely, hypotension. An alternative to injections may be transdermal administration of vasodilators. While little success has been had with transdermal nitroglycerine, a recent report suggested that minoxidil may enhance intercourse after application to the penis (23).

Implantation of a penile prosthesis remains an important treatment modality for many older males with impotence (21). We prefer the semi-rigid devices to multicomponent inflatible devices because of fewer side-effects and the lesser chance of breakdown. Overall, satisfaction rates with penile prostheses remains at about 80 % provided the recipients are carefully chosen and are appropriately counseled, together with their partner, before the device is implanted.

Impotence is an important quality of life issue for many older couples and some single males. Modern advances allow the satisfactory management of impotence in the vast majority of older males. It is important to carefully listen to and discuss the needs of the impotent male. Where possible, the least invasive management modalities are preferred over those that are more invasive.

FEMALE SEXUALITY

As pointed out in the introduction, sexual intercourse decreases with advancing age in both males and females. In females, one of the common reasons given for this decline is an ill or impotent spouse, or unavailability of a suitable partner (24). Masturbation remains an important sexual outlet for older females, even when in their eighties and nineties (1).

The major sexual problems that may be experienced by older females are lack of libido, failure to achieve orgasm, lack of vaginal lubrication and dyspareunia (24). Management of dyspareunia includes the use of oral or vaginal estrogens (though this may produce unacceptable breast engorgement), water-soluble vaginal lubricants and dilatation of the vagina, usually starting with one finger and progressing to two before intercourse is reinitiated. Vaginal dilatation should be carried out in conjunction with Kegel exercises to strengthen pelvic musculature. In some cases, reassurance and/or the instruction in alternative pleasuring techniques may be all that is necessary.

Decreased libido is often a difficult problem to manage in the immediate post-menopausal or older female. While estrogen replacement improves lubrication and increases both vaginal expansion and blood flow in response to sexual arousal, it appears to have little effect on libido (5). On the other hand, a number of small studies have suggested that a combination of testosterone and estrogen may improve libido (25, 26). However, at present, the use of testosterone for libido enhancement should remain experimental. Depression should always be excluded as a possible cause of diminished libido in older persons.

Incontinence is another important cause of sexual dysfunction in older females, and appropriate management of incontinence may enhance sexual function. Special counseling concerning sexuality and body image may be important for older females following myocardial infarction, mastectomy or the placement of a colostomy or ileostomy, and with any malignancy or chronic disease.

Hysterectomy is a grossly overperformed procedure in the United States when compared to the occurrence of hysterectomies in Europe. Women who truly require hysterectomy should be informed of the advantages and disadvantages of subtotal (leaving the cervix intact) compared to total hysterectomy. Whether subtotal hysterectomy improves sexual enjoyment appears unclear at present.

The effects of aging, and concomitant disease on female sexuality are a complex and as yet poorly explored area. There is little reason to suspect that female sexual changes should be any less complex than those seen in males. There is a great need for more research on the optimal management of sexual problems and sexual health in older females.

SEX, ALZHEIMER'S DISEASE AND LONG TERM CARE SETTINGS

Numerous problems can occur with sexuality when an older person develops Alzheimer's disease or other forms of dementia. Hypersexuality or inappropriate sexual advances may be a problem which requires as much support for the patient's spouse and staff as it does treatment of the patient. It is necessary to explain that the patient is not in control of their behavior and that the major management technique is to firmly discourage, or in some cases, ignore the inappropriate behavior. On the other hand, many spouses are uncertain whether continued intercourse is appropriate in a patient with dementia. In such instances, appropriate discussion with the physician may be helpful. It is important that health care professional remember that spouses of Alzheimer's patients undergo a premature bereavement process and may need help and counseling in their development of new relationships, both with their spouse and with others. A sympathetic, nonjudgmental ear is often the most important tool in our therapeutic armamentarium.

Sexuality does not die when a person enters a nursing home. However, many staff find the expression of sexuality in the nursing home difficult to accept. Staff education regarding the handling of sexual expression in the nursing home is extremely important. Nursing homes should provide « quiet rooms » where sexually active consenting adults can obtain privacy. Unfortunately, many persons find it inhibiting to use « quiet rooms » during conjugal visits, and wherever possible, privacy within the patient's own room should be provided. Some patients may need to view pornographic or « sexy » movies, and this opportunity should be made available if individuals request it. Masturbation also requires privacy. When individuals in nursing homes become romantically linked, a series of complex ethical issues arise. These should be approached by first discerning whether the individuals involved understand their action (this can be the case in some persons with moderate dementia) and then acting in the best (not necessarily the most puritanical) interests of the patient.

CONCLUSION

Sexuality remains an important quality of life issue in older persons. As expressed by Shearer and Shearer (27), « Fun and enjoyment are not luxuries ; they are necessities of mental health. Depending on his or her value system, a person's fun may or may not include sex. There are ample forms of fun without sex ; but sex is a natural body function, and our society has grossly distorted it, especially with the older generation ».

It should be remembered that older persons are products of our society and that homosexual and lesbian relationships may continue into the twilight years. These persons, and all who are sexually active, require counseling on the elements of « safe sex », just as much as a 20-years-old does. In dealing with a patient's sexuality, health care professionals should remain as nonjudgmental as possible, and if they do not feel comfortable dealing with sexual issues, appropriate consultations and referrals should be made.

REFERENCES

1. BRETSCHNEIDER J.A., McCOY N.L. : Sexual interest and behavior in healthy 80 to 102-year olds. *Ann. Sex Behav.*, 1988, 17, 109-129.
2. STARR B.D., WEINER M.B. : On sex and sexuality in the mature years. *Stein and Day,* New York, 1981.
3. DIONKO A.G., BROWN M.B., HARZOG A.R. : Sexual function in the elderly. *Arch. Intern. Med.,* 1990, 150, 197-200.
4. KINSEY A.C., POMEROY W.B., MARTIN C.E. : Sexual behavior in the human female. *W.B. Saunders,* Philadelphia, 1953.
5. MORLEY J.E. : Endocrine factors in geriatric sexuality clinics in Geriatric. *Medicine,* 1991, 7, 85-93.
6. KORENMAN S.G., MOORADIAN A.D. et al. : Secondary hypogonadism in older men : Its relationship to impotence. *J. Clin. Endocrinol. Metab.,* 1990, 71, 963-969.
7. MORLEY J.E., KAISER F.E. : Sexual function with advancing age. *Med. Clin. North Am.,* 1989, 73, 1483-1490.
8. WINTERS S.J., SHERINS R.J., TROEN P. : The gonadotropin-suppressive activity of androgen is increased in elderly men. *Metabolism,* 1984, 33, 1052-1059.

9. DAVIDSON J.M., CHEN J.J., CRAPO C.L. et al. : Hormonal changes and sexual function in aging men. *J. Clin. Endocrinol. Metab.,* 1983, 57, 71-77.
10. DAVIDSON J.M., CARMARGO C.A., SMITH E.R. : Effects of androgen on sexual behavior in hypogonadal men. *J. Clin. Endocrinol. Metab.,* 1979, 48, 955-958.
11. BILLINGTON C.J., MOORADIAN A.D., DAFFY L., LANGE P.M., MORLEY J.E. : Testosterone therapy in impotent patients with normal testosterone. *Clin. Res.,* 1983, 31, 718A.
12. STANLEY H.L., SCHMITT B.P., POSES R.M., DEISS W.P. : Does hypogonadism contribute to the occurrence of a minimal trauma hip fracture in elderly men. *J. Am. Geriatr. Soc.,* 1991, 39, 766-771.
13. GRIGGS R.C., KINGSTON W., JOZEFOWICZ R.F. : Effect of testosterone on muscle mass and muscle protein synthesis. *J. Appl. Physiol.,* 1989, 66, 498-503.
14. HARTNELL J., KORENMAN S.G., VIOSCA S.P. : Results of testosterone enanthate therapy for hypogonadism in older men. *Endocrine Soc. Abstracts no 428,* p. 131, Atlanta, Georgia (72nd Annual Meeting), 1990.
15. SLAG M.F., MORLEY J.E., ELSON M.K. et al. : Impotence in medical clinic outpatients. *J.A.M.A.,* 1983, 249, 1736-1740.
16. KAISER F.E., VIOSCA S.P., MORLEY J.E. et al. : Impotence and aging : clinical and hormonal factors. *J. Am. Geriatr. Soc.,* 1988, 36, 511-519.
17. MORLEY J.E., KORENMAN S.G., KAISER F.E. et al. : Relationship of penile brachial pressure index to myocardial infarction and cerebrovascular accidents in older males. *Am. J. Med.,* 1988, 84, 445-448.
18. MORLEY J.E., KAISER F.E. : Impotence in elderly men. *Drugs and Aging,* In press, 1991.
19. LEONARD M.P., NICKEL C.J., MORALES A. : Hyperprolactinemia and impotence : Why, when and how to investigate. *J. Urol.,* 1989, 142, 992-994.
20. MOORADIAN A.D., MORLEY J.E., BILLINGTON C.J. et al. : Hyperprolactinemia in male diabetics. *Postgrad Med. J.,* 1985, 61, 11-15.
21. MORLEY J.E. : Impotence. *Am. J. Med.,* 1986, 81, 679-695.
22. KORENMAN S.G., VIOSCA S.P., KAISER F.E., MOORADIAN A.D., MORLEY J.E. : Use of a vacuum tumescence device in the management of impotence. *J. Am. Geriatr. Soc.,* 1990, 38, 217-220.
23. CAVALLINI G. : Minoxidil versus nitroglycerin : A prospective double-blind controlled trial in transcutaneous erection facilitation for organic impotence. *J. Urol.,* 1991, 146, 50-53.
24. MORLEY J.E. : Sexual function and the aging female. In : Geriatric Endocrinology, Morley J.E., Korenman S.G. eds., Blackwell Scientific : New Brunswick N.J. In press, 1991.
25. BURGER H., HAILES J., NELSON J. et al. : Effect of combined implants of œstradiol and testosterone on libido in postmenopausal women. *Br. Med. J.,* 1987, 294, 936-937.
26. SHERWIN B.B., GELFAND M.M. : The role of androgen in the maintenance of sexual functioning in oophorectomized women. *Psychosom. Med.,* 1987, 49, 397-409.
27. SHEARER M.R., SHEARER M.L. : Sexuality and sexual counseling in the elderly. *Clin. Obstetr. Gynecol.,* 1977, 20, 197-208.

CARE OF THE ELDERLY
IN NURSING HOMES

Joseph G. OUSLANDER (*)

INTRODUCTION

An American nursing home is an institution that provides health, social and recreational services to chronically ill people who, for a variety of reasons, cannot be managed in their own home. There are several different types of nursing homes in the United States (U.S.), and the number of beds in each facility varies considerably. Because of the way that health and social services are funded, and the regulations imposed on nursing homes by the federal and state governments, nursing homes tend to follow a medical rather than a social model. Thus, most American nursing homes look like and are administered in a manner similar to small acute care hospitals, rather than homes in which skilled nursing, medical and other services are available.

At any one time about 5 %, or 1.5 million, of America's population age 65 and older is in an nursing home. But this is a deceiving statistic, for several reasons. First, the rate of nursing home use varies considerably with age and sex. Among those 65-74 less than 3 % are in a nursing home ; among those 85 and older about 15 % of men and 25 % of women are in a nursing home, and close to half in this age group die in a nursing home or shortly after discharge from a nursing home to an acute care hospital (1). Second, a subgroup of nursing home patients stay for only a short period of time. Thus, the lifetime risk of entering a nursing home is underestimated by the prevalence data cited above ; it is now estimated that Americans have a 25-50 % chance of spending some time in a nursing home (2, 3). Third, for every elderly American in a nursing home, there are two or three with a similar clinical and functional status living at home. The primary factors that determine whether an American enters a nursing home include their medical and functional status, the availability and accessibility of non-institutional community based long term care services, and economic factors (1, 3). Economic factors are critical, and are very different in the U.S. than in countries with a national health program. Thus, in order to understand the American nursing home, one must understand how long term care is financed in the U.S. (4, 5).

(*) Medical Director, Eisenberg Village, Jewish Home for the Aging of Greater Los Angeles. Associate Professor, Multicampus Division of Geriatric Medicine and Gerontology, UCLA School of Medicine.
Address Correspondence to : Joseph G. Ouslander, M.D., Jewish Home for the Aging of Greater Los Angeles - 18855 Victory Boulevard - Reseda, CA 91335 - (818) 774-3051 – Fax (818) 774-3053.

ECONOMIC CONSIDERATIONS

Health care for elderly Americans is funded in four basic ways : 1) private health insurance ; 2) Medicare ; 3) Medicaid, and 4) out-of-pocket expenditures. Though insurance companies are now developing long term care policies, private insurance plays virtually no role in paying for nursing home care in the U.S. at the present time. Medicare is a federally administered health insurance program for the elderly. The vast majority of elderly Americans qualify for basic Medicare coverage at age 65 by contributions they or a spouse have made during their working years. Although most elderly Americans believe that Medicare will pay for nursing home care, it is not until they or a relative needs nursing home care that reality sets in. Less than 2 % of Medicare expenditures go to nursing home care, and less than 3 % of nursing home care is funded by Medicare (3, 4). Medicare will pay for up to 100 days of nursing home care after an acute illness, but only under specific circumstances. In order to qualify for Medicare reimbursement for nursing home care, nursing home admission must follow a three-day stay in an acute care hospital, and the patient must require continuous "skilled" nursing care and/or active rehabilitation with carefully documented potential and progress (6, 7). Patients recovering from a hip fracture or stroke with good rehabilitation potential, and patients with unstable medical conditions will qualify for some Medicare coverage, usually for a few weeks. Patients with dementia and chronic functional disabilities on the other hand are viewed as requiring "custodial" care, and do not qualify for Medicare coverage. Thus, the vast majority of funding for nursing home care comes from Medicaid and out-of-pocket expenditures. Medicaid is a state administered medical welfare program for the poor ; one has to have very limited assets (for example, less than $ 2,000, excluding a house) to qualify. This has created a phenomenon known as "spend down" ; elderly Americans must spend down their assets to pay for nursing home care until they become poor enough to qualify for Medicaid − which will then cover their nursing home care. Because private pay rates for most nursing homes are in the range of $ 2,000 − $ 3,000 per month, spend down occurs quickly for most elderly Americans who enter a nursing home (4). Nursing home care in the U.S. is presently a $ 30 billion industry, and the costs are expected to rise rapidly over the next several decades (3, 4). Thus, it is not surprising that the delivery and costs of long term care have recently become major societal issues for U.S. citizens as well as the politicians that govern the country (4, 5, 8, 9).

CHARACTERISTICS OF NURSING HOMES

In the U.S. there are more nursing home beds than acute care hospital beds. These are between six and seven thousand acute care hospitals with a total of approximately one million beds, and there are over 19,000 nursing homes with over 1.5 million beds (3). Table 1 outlines selected characteristics of nursing homes in the U.S. Three-quarters are run for profit, and a large proportion of these are run by organizations that own several or a chain of nursing homes. Most are under 100 beds in size, and about half are certified as a skilled nursing facility (SNF). The distinction between an SNF and an intermediate care facility (ICF) has been based on the number of hours of skilled nursing available ; the federal government has essentially abolished this distinction (10). Thus, the typical American nursing home is a privately-owned and operated free-standing facility of between 50 and 200 beds. Some nursing homes are hospital-based, occupying an unused ward in an acute care hospital. Others are located on the campus of a multi-level long term care community, such as a "life care" or "continuing care retirement" community. The federal and state governments also operate some nursing homes, including over 100 in the Veterans Administration system that serve veterans of U.S. armed forces.

NURSING HOME STAFF

The key staff in an American nursing home are the administrator, who is responsible for the day-to-day operation of the facility, and the director of nurses, who supervises the bulk of the facility's employees. Most nursing homes have very few registe-

TABLE 1

SELECTED CHARACTERISTICS OF AMERICAN NURSING HOMES.

	Nursing Number	Homes %	Nursing Home Beds %
Total	19,100	100	100
Ownership			
Proprietary	14,300	75	69
Non-Profit	3,800	20	23
Government	1,000	5	8
Affiliation			
Chain	7,900	41	49
Independent	10,000	52	42
Government	1,000	5	8
Unknown	100	1	1
Certification [1]			
Not certified	4,700	24	11
SNF only	3,500	18	19
SNF/ICF	5,700	30	45
ICF only	5,300	28	25
Bed Size			
50	6,300	33	9
50- 99	6,200	33	27
100-199	5,400	28	43
200 +	1,200	6	20

(1) Certification by federal and state government ; SNF : skilled nursing facility ; ICF : intermediate care facility.
After Kane R.A. and Kane R.L., 1987.

red and license nurses ; staff ratios average about one registered nurse for each 50 beds and one licensed vocational nurse for each 25-30 beds. Over 90 % of the hands-on care in American nursing homes is provided by nurse's aides, who are generally poorly educated, frequently do not speak English (especially in some areas of the U.S.), and are poorly paid (generally under $ 5.00 per hour). In small and average size facilities, other members of the multidisciplinary team, including the rehabilitation therapists, social workers, activity therapists, and dietitians are part-time and work under contract, rather than as employees of the nursing home. Ancillary services, such as bioclinical laboratory, x-ray, dentistry and podiatry are also provided by outside contracts. Only in a small number of very large facilities will one find full-time multidisciplinary staff who provide the types of services mentioned above.

NURSING HOME RESIDENTS

Residents of American nursing homes are generally characterized as predominantly elderly women with impaired mobility and dementia. It is true that close to three-quarters of nursing home residents are women and older than 75, over half are non-ambulatory and need assistance in transferring, and over half have some degree of dementia (1). But this type of characterization masks the heterogeneity of the nursing home population. Nursing home residents can be broadly characterized based on their length of stay : "short" (i.e. 1-6 months) vs "long" (2). Short stayers can be subdivided into two groups : those who enter the nursing home for short term rehabilitation after an acute illness (e.g. hip fracture, stroke) ; and patients who are medically unstable or terminally ill who are either quickly discharged to an acute hospital or die in the nursing home. Long stayers can be subdivided into three groups : those with primarily cognitive impairment (e.g. the ambulatory, wandering patient with Alzheimer's disease) ; those with primarily impairments of physical functioning (e.g. the patient with severe arthritis or end-stage heart or lung disease) ; and patients with both cognitive and physical impairments (1, 11). Figure 1 illustrates this subgrouping of the nursing home population. Obviously individuals may move from one subgroup to another when acute illnesses intervene, chronic illness develops or progresses, or cognitive function declines.

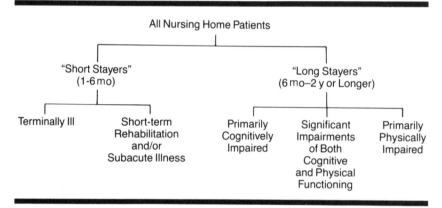

FIGURE 1

Depiction of different types of patients in American nursing homes.
(from Kane, Ouslander and Abrass, 1989)

Conceptualizing nursing home residents in this manner has important implications for the goals of nursing home care, for quality assurance, and even for the structure of the nursing home environment. The goals of caring for a previously healthy individual undergoing rehabilitation after a hip fracture are obviously very different than the goals of caring for a resident with advanced dementia and related behavioral disorders, or the goals of caring for a resident with a terminal malignancy. Similarly, from the perspective of quality assurance, processes and outcomes of care relevant for one subgroup of residents may be inappropriate or irrelevant to another subgroup. From a structural standpoint, many American nursing homes attempt to geographically separate different subgroups of residents. This approach offers many potential advantages when it is feasible : the physical environment can be modified for certain types of residents (e.g. wanderers) ; the staff can be trained and develop expertise in managing specific types of care (e.g. terminal or hospice type care ; or rehabilitative care) ; and residents are often more comfortable when they are around others they can relate to. The latter is especially true for cognitively intact residents who are often very distressed by constant interaction. especially at mealtimes, with residents who have dementia and associated behavioral disorders.

MEDICAL CARE

The goals of medical care in American nursing homes are listed in Table 2. While these goals appropriately focus on several non-medical aspects of care, the increasing acuity of medical conditions of residents in nursing homes and the influence these conditions have on function and quality of life, demand that physicians be intimately involved in nursing home care (11, 12).

TABLE 2

GOALS OF CARE IN AMERICAN NURSING HOMES.

Provide a safe and supportive environment for chronically ill and dependent people. Restore and maintain the highest possible level of functional independence. Preserve individual autonomy. Maximize quality of life, perceived well-being and life satisfaction. Provide comfort and dignity for terminally ill patients and their loved ones. Stabilize and delay progression, whenever possible, of chronic medical conditions. Prevent acute medical and iatrogenic illnesses, and identify and treat them rapidly when they do occur.

After Ouslander, Osterweil and Morley, 1991.

The vast majority of American nursing homes are too small to have a full-time medical staff or even a full-time medical director, although a small proportion of the larger facilities have both. Most facilities have a loosely organized medical staff supervised by a medical director who works part-time for the nursing home and is paid on an hourly, monthly or annual basis (13). Because most American nursing homes are run for profit and have an open medical staff, numerous primary care physicians may be involved in a single nursing home. It is common for dozens of physicians to provide primary care for only a few residents in a small or medium sized facility. This situation can make it difficult for nursing home nursing staff to develop effective communication and rapport with the medical staff, as well as make it difficult for the medical director to monitor policies, procedures and standards for medical care. The role of the primary physician in the American nursing home is to perform a comprehensive medical evaluation at the time of admission, to periodically reassess the resident's progress (visits at 30-60 day intervals are generally required), and to assess acute and subacute changes when they occur (12, 14, 15). Thus, physicians usually visit nursing homes only once or twice a month, depending on the number of residents they have in a given facility. Because physicians are generally not in the nursing home, various regulations and their interpretation result in nursing staff frequently calling physicians to report a variety of problems, such as weight loss, laboratory values, and falls (even when they do not result in injury). In addition, acute changes in residents' conditions are generally reported by telephone, often resulting in transfer of the resident to the emergency ward of an acute care hospital for further evaluation (16, 17). The lack of physician presence in the American nursing home therefore results in many unnecessary phone calls and the overuse of acute care hospital emergency wards for patient evaluation (17). One potential solution to this inefficient way of handling these problems is the involvement of physicians' assistants and/or nurse practitioners (11, 12, 18, 19). They are trained in basic patient care assessment techniques, and generally manage acute and subacute conditions using standard protocols under the supervision of a physician. They may be hired by the nursing home and/or by a physician or a group of physicians, and spend a substantial amount of their time in the nursing home. Nurse practitioners have been shown to play an important role in patient outcomes when employed in selected nursing home settings (20, 21).

Unfortunately, the quality of medical care provided in most American nursing homes is far from optimal (9, 22). Many treatable conditions, such as depression and urinary incontinence, are undiagnosed or misdiagnosed (23, 24, 25, 26) ; documentation in medical records is poor ; and many medications, especially psychotropic drugs and antimicrobials, are overused or misused (27, 28) ; and there is little if any input from psychiatrists or psychologists despite the high prevalence of mental morbidity among nursing home patients (24, 25, 29). There are several factors that contribute to this less than optimal quality of care, including educational, attitudinal and financial. Very few American physicians have had any training in geriatric medicine. Most medical schools have no required geriatric curriculum, and there are less than 1,000 physicians with post graduate training in geriatric medicine (8, 30). Even among the latter, the majority do not spend a lot of time in nursing homes. Only a small proportion of practicing physicians visit nursing homes (31). Many physicians have the same attitude as the American public − the nursing home is the last stop on the way to death, and once in a nursing home there is little that can be done to improve the medical situation. To compound the educational and attitudinal barriers, caring for patients in the nursing home is not a financially rewarding activity. Medicare will generally pay for only one physician nursing home visit a month at a rate significantly lower than that for a hospital or office visit (32). One additional visit may be covered if the resident becomes acutely ill. In addition to the financial disincentive, it is a logistical problem for physicians with busy office and hospital practices to go to the nursing home frequently (31). Thus, there are strong incentives for physicians to not visit nursing homes and to send nursing home residents to acute care hospitals when a patient's condition changes. Admission to an acute care hospital is not only much more expensive than care in the nursing home ; the transfer can be physically and emotionally disruptive for nursing home residents and their families, and the acute care hospital is fraught with iatrogenic hazards for this resident population (such as adverse drug reactions, falls, delirium, pressure sores, etc.) (12, 17, 33, 34). More cost-effective strategies must be developed to care for acute and subacute conditions among residents of nursing homes (3, 4, 35).

In addition to cost-effectiveness, ethical and legal considerations play an important role in decisions about the intensity of care provided to very elderly nursing home residents (36). It is beyond the scope of this article to discuss these considerations in any detail ; however a few key issues will be briefly mentioned. One of the goals of nursing home care is to preserve individual autonomy (Table 2). The high prevalence of dementia among nursing home residents makes this complicated. There are no validated methods of determining when an individual with dementia is no longer capable of making health care decisions for themselves, and no well established standards for surrogate decision makers. Advance directives, such as a durable power of attorney for health care offers a potential solution, by enabling a person, while still capable, to designate a surrogate decision maker and state their preferences in the event of serious illness. The increased use of advance directives and their incorporation into nursing home medical records will hopefully preserve individual autonomy and at the same time help guide physicians in managing serious illnesses that arise in the nursing home setting (11, 37, 38, 39, 40, 41).

FUTURE PERSPECTIVES

Though many American nursing homes provide excellent care, the overall quality of care in this setting must be improved − especially given the projected enormous need for and costs of nursing home care over the next several decades. At least three approaches will be required : changes in the way that nursing home care is financed, education and training, and research. The potential costs of nursing home care in the U.S. over the next several decades are staggering. At the present time the federal government is experimenting with a prospective payment system that would base reimbursement for nursing home care on the resources required to care for specific subgroups of nursing home residents, and the prevalence of the different subgroups in a particular facility (so called "RUGS" or Resource Utilization Groups) [42]. The subgrouping will be based on a standard nationwide set of assessment data that all nursing homes will be required to collect. In theory, RUGS will distribute reimbursement more equitably based on resident's needs. There is one caveat about this reimbursement scheme ; it may create an incentive to keep patients sicker and more dependent to achieve higher reimbursement rates. Appropriate adjustments will have to be incorporated for rehabilitative approaches to care. The government is also considering physician payment reform, which would adjust reimbursement for some physician activities, such as nursing home visits, that are currently under-valued (32). But more than financial changes will be necessary to improve care in American nursing homes. Education in geriatric medicine, gerontology and long term care must increase for physicians, nurses and all other health care professional who care for nursing home patients (8, 43). The U.S. has made great studies in this regard over the last decade, but much more must be done to meet the tremendous needs for adequately trained health professionals over the next several decades (30, 44, 45). Finally, and very importantly, the nursing home must increasingly become a research laboratory (44, 46). A broad range of research is needed. Basic studies will help determine the causes, treatment and prevention of conditions that lead to nursing home admission, such as Alzheimer's disease and osteoporosis. Clinical trials will assist in identifying the most effective strategies for managing common conditions among nursing home residents, such as urinary incontinence, depression, and behavioral disorders associated with dementia. Non-biomedical research is also needed to address issues of quality of life and ethics which are so important in the nursing home population (11, 37, 38, 39, 40, 41). Health services research will help identify methods of defining, measuring, and improving quality of care, and in determining the most cost-effective strategies for managing many aspects of nursing home care (5, 47, 48, 49). Only through this type of multifaceted research will we learn more about caring for the millions of people who will spend some time in an American nursing home over the next several decades.

REFERENCES

1. KANE (R.A.), OUSLANDER (J.G.), ABRASS (I.B.) : *Essentials of Clinical Geriatrics.* 2nd Edition, New York, NY : McGraw-Hill International Book Company, 1989.
2. KEMPER (P.), and MURTAUGH (C.M.) : Lifetime Use of Nursing Home Care. *N. Engl. J. Med.*, 324, 595-600, 1991.
3. KANE (R.A.), KANE (R.L.) : Long-term care. Principles, programs and policies. New York, NY. *Springer-Verlag NY Inc.*, 1987.
4. SOMERS (A.R.) : Long-term care for the elderly and disabled. A new health priority. *N. Engl. J. Med.*, 307, 221-226, 1982.
5. ZWEIBIL (N.R.), CASSEL (C.K.) [eds] : Clinical and policy issues in the care of the nursing home patient. *Clin. Geriatr. Med.*, 4, 471-690, 1988.
6. LOESER (W.D.), DICKSTEIN (E.S.), SCHIAVONE (L.D.) : Medicare coverage in nursing homes. A broken promise. *N. Engl. J. Med.*, 304, 353-355, 1981.

7. SMITS (H.L.), FEDER (J.), SCANLON (W.) : Medicare's nursing home benefit. Variations in interpretation. *N. Engl. J. Med.* 307, 353-356, 1981.
8. American College of Physicians Health and Public Policy Committee. Long Term Care of the Elderly. *Ann. Intern. Med.*, 100, 760-763, 1984.
9. Institute of Medicine : *Improving the Quality of Care in Nursing Homes.* Washington, DC : *National Academy Press,* 1986.
10. Department of Health and Human Services, Health Care Financing Administration. Medicare and Medicaid. Conditions of participation for long-term care facilities ; final rule with requests for comments. *Federal Register,* February 2, 54, 5317-5373, 1989.
11. OUSLANDER (J.G.) : Medical care in the nursing home. *JAMA,* 262, 2582-2589, 1989.
12. OUSLANDER (J.G.), OSTERWEIL (D.), MORLEY (J.) : *Medical Care in the Nursing Home.* New York, NY McGraw-Hill. *International Book Company,* 1991.
13. LEVENSON (S.) [ed.] : *Medical Direction in Long-Term Care.* Owings Mills, MD. *National Health Publishing,* 1988.
14. OUSLANDER (J.G.), MARTIN (S.E.) : Assessment in the nursing home. *Clin. Geriatr. Med.,* 3, 155-174, 1987.
15. LEVENSTEIN (M.R.), OUSLANDER (J.G.), RUBENSTEIN (L.Z.), FORSYTHE (S.B.) : Yield of routine annual laboratory tests in a skilled nursing home population. *JAMA,* 258, 1909-1915, 1987.
16. KAYSER-JONES (J.S.), WIENER (C.L.), BARBACCIA (J.C.) : Factors contributing to the hospitalization of nursing home residents. *Gerontologist.,* 29, 502-510, 1989.
17. RUBENSTEIN (L.Z.), OUSLANDER (J.G.), WIELAND (D.) : Dynamics and clinical implications of the nursing home. Hospital interface. *Clin. Geriatr. Med.,* 4, 471-491, 1988.
18. MARTIN (S.E.), TURNER (C.L.), MENDELSOHN (S.), OUSLANDER (J.G.) : Assessment and initial management of acute medical problems in a nursing home. *In :* Bosker (G.) [ed.] : Principles and practice of acute geriatric medicine, St. Louis, MO : CV Mosby Co, 1989.
19. KANE (R.A.), KANE (R.L.), ARNOLD (S.), GARRARD (J.) et al. : Geriatric nurse practitioners as nursing home employees. Implementing the role. *Gerontologist.,* 28, 469-477, 1988.
20. KANE (R.A.), GARRARD (J.), SKY (L.) et al. : Effects of a geriatric nurse practitioner on process and outcome of nursing home care. *Am. J. Pub. Health.,* 79, 1271-1277, 1989.
21. WIELAND (D.), RUBENSTEIN (L.Z.), OUSLANDER (J.G.), MARTIN (S.E.) : Organizing an academic nursing home : impacts on institutionalized elderly. *JAMA,* 255, 2622-2627, 1986.
22. VLADEK (B.) : Unloving care. The nursing home tragedy. New York, NY. *Basic Books, Inc., Publishers,* 1980.
23. OUSLANDER (J.G.), KANE (R.L.), ABRASS (I.B.) : Urinary incontinence in elderly nursing home patients. *JAMA,* 248, 1194-1198, 1982.
24. BORSON (S.), LIPTZIN (B.), NININGER (J.) et al. : Psychiatry in the nursing home. *Am. J. Psychiatry,* 144, 1412-1418, 1987.
25. ROVNER (B.W.), KAFONEK (S.), PHILLIP (L.) et al. : Prevalence of mental illness in a community nursing home. *Am. J. Psychiatry,* 143, 1446-1449, 1986.
26. ZIMMER (J.G.), BENTLEY (D.W.), VALENTI (W.M.) et al. : Systemic antibiotic use in nursing homes ; a quality assessment. *JAGS,* 34, 703-710, 1986.
27. BEERS (M.), AVORN (J.), SOUMERAI (B.), EVERITT (D.E.) et al. : Psychoactive medication use in intermediate-care facility residents. *JAMA,* 260, 2016-2030, 1988.
28. RAY (W.A.), FEDERSPEIL (C.F.), SCHAFFNER (W.) : A study of antipsychotic drug use in nursing homes. Epidemiologic evidence suggesting misuse. *Am. J. Public Health,* 70, 485-491, 1980.
29. ZIMMER (J.G.), WATSON (N.), TREAT (A.) : Behavioral problems among patients in skilled nursing facilities. *Am. J. Public Health,* 74, 1118-1121, 1984.
30. ROWE (J.W.), GROSSMAN (E.), BOND (E.) : The institute of medicine committee on leadership for academic geriatric medicine. Academic geriatrics for the year 2000. *N. Engl. J. Med.,* 316, 1425-1428, 1984.
31. MITCHELL (J.B.), HEWES (H.T.) : Why won't physicians make nursing home visits ? *Gerontologist,* 26, 650-654, 1986.
32. HSIAO (W.C.), BRAUN (P.), KELLY (N.L.), BECKER (E.R.) : Results, potential effects, and implementation issues of the Resource-Based Relative Value Scale. *JAMA,* 260, 2429-2438, 1988.
33. STEEL (K.), GERTMAN (P.M.), CRESCENZI (C.), ANDERSON (J.) : Iatrogenic illness on a general medical service at a university hospital. *N. Engl. J. Med.,* 1981, 304, 638-642.
34. TRESCH (D.D.), SIMPSON (W.M.), BURTON (J.R.) : Relationship of long-term and acute-care facilities. The problem of patient transfer and continuity of care. *JAGS,* 33, 819-826, 1985.
35. ZIMMER (J.G.), EGGERT (G.M.), TREAT (A.), BRODOWS (B.) : Nursing homes as acute care providers. A pilot study of incentives to reduce hospitalizations. *JAGS,* 36, 124-129, 1988.
36. GLASSER (G.), ZWEIBEL (N.R.), CASSEL (C.K.) : The ethics committee in the nursing home. Results of a national survey. *JAGS,* 36, 150-156, 1988.
37. BESDINE (R.W.) : Decisions to withhold treatment from nursing home residents. *JAGS,* 30, 602-606, 1983.

38. MURPHY (D.J.) : Do-not-resuscitate orders. Time for reappraisal in long-term care institutions. *JAMA,* 260, 2098-2101, 1988.
39. VOLICER (L.), RHEAUME (Y.), BROWN (J.) et al. : Hospice approach to the treatment of patients with advanced dementia of the Alzheimer's type. *JAMA,* 256, 2210-2213, 1986.
40. LYNN (J.) [ed.] : *No Extraordinary Means. The Choice to Forego Life-sustaining Food and Water.* Bloomington. *Indiana University Press,* 1986.
41. UHLMAN (R.F.), CLARK (H.), PEARLMAN (R.A.) et al. : Medical management decisions in nursing home patients. Principles and policy recommendations. *Ann. Intern. Med.,* 106, 879-885, 1987.
42. SCHNEIDER (D.P.), FRIES (B.E.), FOLEY (W.J.) et al. : Case mix for nursing home payment ; resource utilization groups, version II. *Health Care Financing Review,* Annual Supplement, pp. 39-51, 1988.
43. AIKEN (L.H.), MEZEY (M.D.), LYNAUGH (J.E.), BUCK (C.R.) : Teaching nursing homes. Prospects for improving long-term care. *JAGS,* 33, 196-201, 1985.
44. RIESENBERG (D.) : The teaching nursing home. A golden annex to the ivory tower. *JAMA,* 257, 3119-3120, 1987.
45. LIBOW (L.S.) : The teaching nursing home. Past, present and future. *JAGS,* 32, 598-603, 1984.
46. LIPSITZ (L.A.), PLUCHINO (F.C.), WRIGHT (S.M.) : Biomedical research in the nursing home ; methodological issues and subject recruitment results. *JAGS,* 35, 629-634, 1987.
47. CHAMBERS (L.W.) : Promoting long-term care quality assurance. Strategies used in Europe and North America. *Danish Med. Bull.* No. 5, 21-28, Special Supplement Series, 1987.
48. MOHIDE (E.A.), TUGWELL (P.), CAUIFIELD (P.A.) et al. : A randomized trial of quality assurance in nursing homes. *Med. Care,* 26, 554-565, 1988.
49. ZIMMER (J.G.) : Quality assurance. *In :* Katz (P.), Calkins (E.) [eds] : Principles and practice of nursing home care. New York, NY. *Springer Publishing Co. Inc.,* 91-112, 1989.

HYPOCHLORHYDRIA IN THE ELDERLY

Kris V. KOWDLEY (*), Robert M. RUSSELL (**)

INTRODUCTION

Hypochlorhydria, defined as reduced gastric acid production, can be due to a variety of causes, including gastric infection with Helicobactor pylori, medications that block histamine H_2 receptors or block parietal cell H+/K+ ATP-ase, and inflammation/atrophy of the fundic gland mucosa of the stomach (types A and AB gastritis). By one classification, chronic type A gastritis is associated with other autoimmune disorders and occurs more commonly in relatives of patients with thyroid and adrenal diseases. Hypochlorhydria in this condition is related to a decreased parietal cell mass, and is felt to be due to an autoimmune cause. When hypochlorhydria is associated with autoantibodies against parietal cells and intrinsic factor, the subsequent condition is called pernicious anemia. Chronic AB gastritis (involving both the antrum with patchy involvement of the fundus) is not associated with autoimmune disease and is thought to have an environmental etiology (including H pylori infection). In any type of atrophic gastritis, the degree of hypochlorhydria may vary, ranging from a mild decrease in gastric acid production to achlorhydria. However, only in cases of severe atrophy of the parietal cell mucosa (gastric atrophy) is the achlorhydria unresponsive to pharmacologic stimuli.

The most common cause of hypochlorhydria in the elderly is chronic atrophic gastritis. In one study, one-third of a healthy, elderly population met the criteria for atrophic gastritis by screening serum pepsinogen assays (1). Moreover, the prevalence of atrophic gastritis appears to increase with increasing age, from 20 % in the 60-69 year old age group, to over 30 % in those over 80 years old (1).

DIAGNOSIS OF ATROPHIC GASTRITIS

Hypochlorhydria in type A chronic atrophic gastritis is felt to be due, in part, to circulating anti-parietal cell antibodies and a reduced number of chief cells in the fundic gland mucosa. Patchy gastritis of the entire stomach (Type AB) may also result in hypochlorhydria due to loss of parietal cell mass. The reduced chief cell mass

(*) Assistant Professor of Medicine, Case Western Reserve University School of Medicine.
(**) Professor of Medicine and Nutrition Tufts University School of Medicine.

Address correspondence to : Kris V. Kowdley, M.D., Gastroenterology Division, University Hospitals of Cleveland, 2074 Abington Road, Cleveland, Ohio 44106.

can be indirectly measured by the determination of serum levels of pepsinogen A (formerly known as pepsinogen I) and pepsinogen C (formerly pepsinogen II), and by the ratio of pepsinogen A/pepsinogen C. Both these proteins are presurors of pepsins normally produced by chief cells and neck cells of the fundic mucosa ; however, pepsinogen C is also synthesized in other parts of the upper gastrointestinal tract, namely, in the cardia, pylorus and duodenum. Several investigators have shown that the ratio of pepsinogen A/pepsinogen C is the most sensitive screening test for atrophic gastritis involving the fundus of the stomach. Borch and co-workers studied 179 patients with fundic atrophic gastritis, 29 patients with gastric adenocarcinoma, 15 patients status-post total gastrectomy and 50 controls with endoscopically normal stomachs. Pepsinogen determinations were made using radioimmunoassay techniques. Using a discrimination limit of 5.5 for the ratio of pepsinogen A to pepsinogen C, Broch and colleagues detected patients with atrophic gastritis with a sensitivity of 94 % and a specificity of 99 % (2). Similar findings have been reported by Samloff and colleagues (3). They also showed that the ratio of pepsinogen A to pepsinogen C can help make the diagnosis of atrophic gastritis, and moreover that the ratio of pepsinogen A to pepsinogen C correlates with degree of severity of atrophic gastritis (3). In their study, patients with atrophic gastritis could be identified by a pepsinogen A level of less than 20 ng/L, and a pepsinogen A/pepsinogen C ratio of less than 2.9. In comparison, normal subjects had a pepsinogen A/pepsinogen C ratio of 4.0 or greater. In addition to serum pepsinogen assays, other means of making the diagnosis of atrophic gastritis include radiographic, endoscopic, and histologic techniques, as well as tests of gastric secretory function. These are briefly discussed below.

X-ray double-contrast studies of the stomach in chronic atrophic gastritis characteristically reveal decreased mucosal folds in the fundus and body of the stomach, and indicate a thinning of the muscular and glandular portions of the involved stomach (4). Consistent with these observations are the endoscopic findings of visible submucosal vessels through an atrophic gastric mucosal lining ; histologic examination of biopsy specimens reveals decreased numbers of glands containing parietal and chief cells, especially in the fundus, and infiltration by inflammatory cells ; the extent of inflammation may be variable. The superficial epithelium is usually preserved (5). Intestinal or "pseudopyloric" metaplasia of the fundic mucosa may occur in severe atrophic gastritis (5). Physiologic tests of gastric acid production in response to stimulants such as histamine and gastrin can be helpful in evaluating for the presence and extent of gastric atrophy, especially in cases where serum tests are in the borderline range.

CLINICAL AND PHYSIOLOGICAL CONSEQUENCES OF ATROPHIC GASTRITIS

Pernicious Anemia / Intrinsic Factor Deficiency

Pernicious anemia (PA) may occur in some patients with severe atrophic gastritis (type A), and is characterized by the presence of a megaloblastic anemia due to vitamin B_{12} deficiency. The deficiency of this vitamin in PA is the result of impaired secretion of intrinsic factor (IF) by parietal cells. Some patients with this condition have antibodies to parietal cells, and/or intrinsic factor. Both blocking antibodies, which prevent the binding of vitamin B_{12} to intrinsic factor and binding antibodies which inactivate either vitamin B_{12}, intrinsic factor, or the vitamin-IF complex have been described (6).

Gastric Emptying

It has been shown by some investigators that gastric emptying is delayed in elderly subjects compared to younger persons. Others have reported that atrophic gastritis patients have slower gastric emptying of mixed meals than controls (7). If, in fact, atrophic gastritis is associated with delayed gastric emptying, physiological consequences might include adverse effects from drugs that diminish gastric motility, impaired absorption of nutrients, and spuriously abnormal results of tests of absorption. Thus, metabolic tests that employ urine or blood collections might need longer periods of monitoring.

Bacterial Overgrowth of the Small Intestine

Under normal circumstances, the pH of gastric juice is < 3.0, which prevents bacterial overgrowth. Hypo- or achlorhydria in patients with atrophic gastritis frequently results in colonization of the stomach with bacteria. It has been shown that such patients also develop bacterial overgrowth in the proximal small intestine. However, there is evidence that clinically significant fat malabsorption does not occur with bacterial overgrowth seen in the setting of atrophic gastritis (8) ; this is in contrast to blind-loop syndrome or intestinal hypomotility, where anaerobic colonization of the small intestine with bile salt splitting organisms is common. Bacterial overgrowth in atrophic gastritis may also result in bacterial competition for certain micronutrients (e.g. vitamin B_{12}).

Altered Proximal Small Intestine pH

The pH of the proximal small intestine is elevated in patients with atrophic gastritis. Consequences of increased pH in the lumen of the proximal small intestine include diminished activity of digestive enzymes with lower pH optimums, inhibition of active transport mechanisms for vitamins such folic acid with lower pH optimums and incomplete release of nutrients from food complexes (e.g. divalent cations such as zinc from fiber).

Hypochlorhydria and Drug Availability

The bioavailability of certain drugs may be affected by gastric pH. Blum et al. studied 24 healthy male volunteers, 19 to 43 years old, and administered oral fluconazole 200 mg, or ketoconazole 400 mg, with or without cimetidine using a randomized, four-way crossover study design. Two doses of cimetidine 300 mg were given intravenously in bolus form 60 and 30 minutes before the antifungal drug. Gastric pH was monitored continuously via an intragastric radiotelemetry capsule. Three additional 100 mg boluses of cimetidine were administered if gastric pH decreased below 6.0 at any time during the first five hours of the study. Pharmacokinetics were plotted after serum samples were obtained for 24 hours and 144 hours after administration of ketoconazole and fluconazole, respectively (9).

Although there was no significant difference in serum levels of fluconazole when cimetidine was given concomitantly, ketoconazole serum levels were significantly lower with cimetidine than without cimetidine (mean area-under-the-curve 34.1 ± 12.0 µg - h/mL vs 1.7 ± 1.5 µg - h/mL). These data indicate that experimental hypochlorhydria with cimetidine clearly reduces absorption of some oral antifungal agents, but not others. The authors attributed the difference in bioavailability between fluconazole and ketoconazole to the higher pK of fluconazole, and thus, better absorption of fluconazole in the setting of hypochlorhydria. The effect of atrophic gastritis and/or hypochlorhydria on the absorption of other drugs has not been studied extensively. A recent study has demonstrated increased bioavailability of digoxin in hypochlorhydric states (10).

EFFECT OF HYPOCHLORHYDRIA ON ABSORPTION
OF NUTRIENTS AND MINERALS IN ATROPHIC GASTRITIS CALCIUM

Calcium

The absorption of calcium salts is most effective when they are in ionized and soluble forms (4) ; due to the acid secretion by the stomach, most dietary calcium is likely to be ionized and solubilized (in the form of calcium chloride), thus facilitating absorption in the proximal small intestine. Conversely, the absorption of dietary calcium may be diminished in patients with hypochlorhydria. There are varying reports in the literature on the impact of gastric pH on dietary calcium absorption. It has been known that elderly subjects absorb calcium less well than younger persons (1). However, the effect of hypo-achlorhydria on calcium absorption has been controversial. The conflicting results of various studies appear to depend on whether the calcium was given with or without food and on the degree of hypochlorhydria. For example, in one study, achlorhydria was produced with cimetidine, and gastric pHs in these subjects were in the 5 range (11), while in a second study, gastric pH was in the 7 range (12). Knox et al. suggest that gastric acid is required to solubilize calcium salts in the fasting state but is not needed when calcium is taken with food (13). These investigators clearly demonstrated that acid made no difference to calcium bioavailability in normal elderly subjects and subjects with atrophic gastritis as long as the calcium was ingested with a meal.

Vitamin B12 Bioavailability

Normal absorption of vitamin B_{12} or cobalamin occurs in the following manner : the vitamin is first released from its food protein bound forms by pepsins in the stomach. In the stomach, cobalamin is then bound to the so-called R protein of salivary and gastric origin, and transported into the small intestine where pancreatic proteases digest the R-protein (14, 15). Subsequently, free cobalamin binds to intrinsic factor, and is transported in this form to the terminal ileum, where active transport of vitamin B_{12} into the blood takes place (16).

Hypo- or achlorhydria may affect the absorption of cobalamin in several ways. One possible manner by which vitamin B_{12} may be malabsorbed in the setting of achlorhydria is due to lack of intrinsic factor in the setting of severe atrophic gastritis and gastric atrophy (type A) ; prolonged and severe B_{12} deficiency in these patients leads to pernicious anemia. However, most subjects with atrophic gastritis have enough intrinsic factor secretion to ensure normal vitamin B_{12} absorption. Moreover, several investigators have demonstrated that in many patients with atrophic gastritis and achlorhydria, absorption of crystalline vitamin B_{12} is normal, but absorption of protein bound B_{12} is impaired (17, 18). King et al., have shown that absorption of protein-bound vitamin B_{12} in subjects with atrophic gastritis is improved with concurrent administration of acid, implying that the presence of gastric acid is independently important for the absorption of vitamine B_{12} (17). Thus, reduced gastric acid may result in diminished release of protein-bound cobalamin. Finally, B_{12} malabsorption in patients with hypochlorhydria may occur secondary to bacterial overgrowth in the small intestine. It has been shown that bacteria can chemically alter vitamin B_{12} and render it unusable (19). Further, Suter et al. have demonstrated recently that oral tetracycline can correct protein-bound vitamine B_{12} malabsorption in subjects with atrophic gastritis and bacterial overgrowth (20). These data suggest that bacterial overgrowth rather than protein maldigestion is the major cause of vitamin B_{12} malabsorption in persons with atrophic gastritis.

Iron

Iron can be obtained in heme and non-heme forms. Absorption of iron in its heme form is not impaired in atrophic gastritis, and is uninfluenced by acid administration (21, 22, 23). The absorption of non-heme iron in the ferric form, however, is diminished in patients with atrophic gastritis (23) and with cimetidine treatment (24). An acid environment is necessary to dissolve non-heme iron in the ferric form (4), following which the iron can be chelated and delivered to the small intestine for absorption (24).

Folate

Folic acid absorption by the small intestinal mucosa is pH dependent. At a pH that is above or below the optimum of 6.3, folate absorption is diminished. Russell et al., have shown that elderly persons with atrophic gastritis have impaired folate absorption (25). However, folate deficiency is unusual in this group. The proposed explanation for this finding is that the bacteria which colonize the upper small intestine in patients with atrophic gastritis produce folate, and thus prevent folate deficiency from occuring. Other investigators have also shown that groups of patients with bacterial overgrowth due to other causes (e.g. blind loop, etc.) have high serum folate levels (26). Thus, although persons with atrophic gastritis may malabsorb folic acid due to altered small intestinal pH, bacteria that colonize their small intestines may fortuitously compensate for this by synthesizing folate.

CONCLUSION

There are a number of causes of hypochlorhydria in the elderly. Other than medications, the most common cause of hypochlorhydria in elderly persons is chronic atrophic gastritis. Clinical and physiological sequelae of this disorder include bacterial overgrowth of the stomach and small intestine and changes in small intestinal pH ; in addition, alterations in the absorption of various micronutrients may occur, with a subsequently increased risk for malnutrition. The most important micronutrient to be affected in vitamine B_{12}. The availability of serum pepsinogen assays have greatly increased our ability to screen populations at risk for atrophic gastritis. Further research on the mechanisms of atrophic gastritis will advance our understanding of the aging process in the gastrointestinal tract and its consequences.

REFERENCES

1. KRASINSKI (S.D.), RUSSELL (R.M.), SAMLOFF (I.M.), JACOB (R.A.), DALLAL (G.E.), McGANDY (R.B.), HARTZ (S.C.) : Fundic atrophic gastritis in an elderly population : effect on hemoglobin and several serum nutritional indicators. J. Am. Ger. Soc., 1986, 34, 800-806.
2. BORCH (K.), AXELSSON (C.K.), HALGREEN (H.), NIELSON (M.D.), LEDIN (T.), SZESCI (P.B.) : The ratio of pepsinogen A to pepsinogen C : A sensitive test for atrophic gastritis. Scand. J. Gastroenterol., 1989, 24, 870-876.
3. SAMLOFF (I.M.), VARIS (K.), IHAMAKI (T.), SIURALA (M.), ROTTER (J.I.) : Relationships among serum pepsinogen I, serum pepsinogen II and gastric mucosal histology. Gastroenterology, 1982, 83, 204-209.
4. KASSARJIAN (Z.), RUSSELL (R.M.) : Hypochlorhydria. A factor in nutrition. Annu. Rev. Nutr., 1989, 9, 271-285.
5. WEINSTEIN (W.M.) : Gastritis. In : Sleisenger (M.H.), Fordtran (J.S.) [eds] : Gastrointestinal disease. Philadelphia, W.B. Saunders Company, 1989, 4th edition, p. 796.
6. GREEN (L.K.), GRAHAM (D.Y.) : Gastritis in the elderly. Gastroenterol. Clin. North America, 1990, 19, 273-292.
7. DAVIES (W.T.), KIRKPATRICK (J.R.), OWEN (G.M.), SHIELDS (R.) : Gastric emptying in atrophic gastritis and carcinoma of the stomach. Scand. J. Gastroenterol., 1971, 6, 297-301.

8. SIMON (G.L.), GORBACH (S.L.) : Intestinal flora in health and disease. *Gastroenterology*, 1984, 86, 174-193.

9. BLUM (R.A.), D'ANDREA (D.T.), FLORENTINO (B.M.), WILTON (J.H.), HILLIGOS (D.M.), GARDNER (M.J.), HENRY (E.G.), GOLDSTEIN (H.), SCHENTAG (J.J.) : Increased gastric pH and the bioavailability of fluconazole and ketoconazole. *Ann. Int. Med.*, 1991, 114, 755-757.

10. COHEN (A.F.), KROON (R.), SCHOEMAKER (R.), HOOGKAMER (H.), VAN VLIET (A.) : Influence of gastric acidity on the bioavailability of digoxin. *Ann. Int. Med.*, 1991, 115, 540-545.

11. BO-LINN (G.W.), DAVIS (G.R.), BUDRUS (G.R.), MORAWSKI (S.G.), SANTA ANA (C.), FORDTRAN (J.S.) : Evaluation of the importance of gastric acid. *J. Clin. Invest.*, 1984, 73, 640-647.

12. RECKER (R.R.) : Calcium absorption and achlorhydria. *New Eng. J. Med.*, 1985, 313, 70-73.

13. KNOX (T.A.), KASSARJIAN (Z.), DAWSON-HUGHES (B.), GOLNER (B.), DALLAL (G.E.), ARORA (S.), RUSSELL (R.M.) : Calcium absorption in elderly subjects on high and low fiber diets : effects of gastric acidity. *Am. J. Clin. Nutr.*, 1991, 53, 1480-1486.

14. MARCOULLIS (G.), ROTHENBERG (S.P.) : Macromolecules in the assimilation and transport of cobalamin. *In* Lindenbaum J. (ed.) : Nutrition in Hematology, New York, *Churchill Livingstone*, 1983, p. 89.

15. TOSKES (P.P.) : Current concepts of cobalamin (vitamin B_{12}) absorption and malabsorption. *J. Clin. Gastroenterol.*, 1980, 2, 287-297.

16. HOOPER (D.C.), ALPERS (D.H.), BURGER (R.I.), MEHLMAN (C.S.), ALLEN (R.H.) : Characterization of ileal vitamin B_{12} binding using homogeneous human and hog intrinsic factor. *J. Clin. Invest.*, 1973, 52, 3074-3083.

17. KING (C.E.), LEIBACH (J.), TOSKES (P.P.) : Clinically significant vitamin B_{12} deficiency to malabsorption of protein bound vitamin B_{12}. *Dig. Dis. Sci.*, 1979, 24, 397-402.

18. DOSHERHOLMEN (A.), SWAIM (W.R.) : Impaired assimilation of egg Co_{57} vitamin B_{12} in patients with hypochlorhydria and achlorhydria and after gastric resection. *Gastroenterology*, 1973, 64, 913-919.

19. BRANDT (L.J.), BERNSTEIN (L.H.), WAGIE (A.) : Production of vitamin B_{12} analogues in patients with small bowel bacterial overgrowth. *Ann. Intern. Med.*, 1977, 87, 546-551.

20. SUTER (P.M.), GOLNER (B.), GOLDIN (R.), MORROW (F.D.), RUSSELL (R.M.) : Reversal of protein bound vitamin B_{12} malabsorption with antibiotics in atrophic gastritis. *Gastroenterology*, 1991, 101, 1039-1045.

21. PRASAD (A.S.) : Iron. In : Trace elements and iron metabolism. New York, *Plenum*, p. 91.

22. BJORN-RASMUSSEN (E.), HALLBERG (L.), ISAKSSON (B.), ARVIDSSON (B.) : Food iron absorption in man. *J. Clin. Invest.*, 1974, 53, 247-255.

23. JACOBS (P.), BOTHWELL (T.), CHARLTON (R.W.) : Role of hydrochloric acid in iron absorption. *Appl. Phys.*, 1964, 29, 187-188.

24. ALPERS (D.A.) : Absorption of vitamins and divalent minerals. *In* : Sleisenger (M.H.), Fordtran (J.S.) [eds] : Gastrointestinal disease. Philadelphia, *W.B. Saunders Company*, 1989, 4th edition, p. 1057.

25. RUSSELL (R.M.), KRASINSKI (S.D.), SAMLOFF (I.M.), JACOB (R.A.), HARTZ (S.C.) et al. : Folic acid malabsorption in atrophic gastritis. *Gastroenterology*, 1986, 91, 1476-1482.

26. HOFFBRAND (A.V.), TABAQCHALI (S.), MOLIN (D.L.) : High serum folate levels in intestinal blind-loop syndrome. *Lancet*, 1966, 1, 1339-1342.

NEWS IN CLINICAL GERONTOLOGY

We present here the abstracts of articles published in the international editions of Facts and Research in Gerontology 1992. Reprint are available to the authors (see contributors directory) or to Serdi : 29, rue de Saint-Pétersbourg, 75008 Paris.

1 - PARKINSON'S DISEASE : RECENT RESEARCH ADVANCES : F. Boller

Summary. – Parkinson's disease (PD) is the only degenerative disease where treatment provides noticeable improvement. Its etiology is still unknown but we know that it is age-related. It also has complex ties with Alzheimer's disease. A condition resembling PD can be produced in humans and in some animal species by MPP+, a substance derived from Methyl-phenyl-tetrahydropyridine (MPTP). It is however unlikely that PD is always due to exposure to this or other toxic agent. The prevalence of the disease in people aged 60 and over is about 1 %. It is more frequent among whites than among blacks, in males, in Northern states and in non-smokers. It was long thought to have a strong genetic component, but a recent study has shown a low concordance rate among twins. PD affects mainly the brainstem but cortical changes undistinguishable from AD occur in a sizeable percentage of patients. From a biochemical standpoint, the disease affects mainly dopamine, but also noradrenaline, serotonin and acetylcholine. In addition to the classical motor signs (tremor, rigidity, bradykinesia and postural and gait changes) up to 80 % of patients experience, some years after dopaminergic treatment, unpleasant side effects consisting mainly of abnormal movements and marked fluctuations of symptoms which may at times prevent them from moving (« on/off » effect). Most PD patients show neuropsychological changes which in about 30 % of cases correspond to a true dementia. The disease tends to affect mainly memory, the visuo-spatial system and frontal-lobe (« executive ») functions. Linguistic and praxic functions are relatively spared. Depression is also quite common. These cognitive and personality changes are probably mainly due to the lesion of non-dopaminergic systems. In addition to L-DOPA, dopaminergic agonists have become available. Neuronal grafts, consisting either of cells from the adrenal glands or of fetal cells have now been performed in several hundreds of patients in various countries and it is claimed that many patients have benefited from the procedure. (Facts and Research in Gerontology 1992)

Key-words : Parkinson's disease, clinical research, therapy, neuronal grafts.

2 - RESPONSE TO VACCINATION IN THE ELDERLY : F. Denis, S. Ranger, M. Mounier

Summary. – Aging involves modifications in immunity, most of which induce an increase in infections and a decrease in vaccination responses. Two bacterial (Tetanus and Pneumococci) and two viral (Hepatitis B and Influenza) vaccines were studied. The results showed a decreased antiviral response in the elderly, mainly with respect to antibody levels. However, despite this low antibody response, mortality and

morbidity were reduced in vaccined elderly as shown by the protection observed with pneumo-coccal or with influenza vaccines (respectively 60 % and 75 %). These levels were clearly above the percentage of elderly with antibody response. Thus, it appeared that vaccine and aging would be a potential area for research to analyse non-response factors, to correct them and to increase antibody response. These results demonstrated the necessity of studying vaccine response in the concerned population. It seems obvious that the results obtained in young people cannot be translated to the elderly without introducing an significant risk of error.
(Facts and Research in Gerontology 1992)

Key-words : *elderly, vaccines, significant hepatitis B, influenza, tetanus, pneumococci.*

3 - DEPRESSIVE PSEUDODEMENTIA IN THE ELDERLY : A. Donnet, J.-M. Azorin

Summary. – *The term pseudodementia refers to psychiatric conditions not associated with true dementia, which mimic an organic dementing illness. Depression is the commonest cause of pseudodementia in the elderly. Diagnosis and management of depressive pseudodementia are discussed, and systematic treatment of the depression in the elderly is emphasized. In the past ten years, lists of clinical items (Wells' criteria) as well as laboratory tools have been proposed as ancillary diagnostic aids and diagnostic profiles have been suggested both for pseudodementia and dementia. Recently, the reports of Reynolds and Buysse indicate that sleep measurements are a very good index to differentiate pseudodementia and dementia.*
(Facts and Research in Gerontology 1992).

Key-words : *depression, dementia, pseudodementia.*

SELECTION OF LITERATURE

1 - PARKINSON'S DISEASE : F. Boller

1. PARKINSON J. : An Essay on the Shaking Palsy. *Sherwood, Neely and Jones,* London, 1817.
2. LANGSTON J.W. : MPTP : Insights into the etiology of Parkinson's disease. *European Neurology,* 1987, 26, suppl. 1, 2-10.
3. AMADUCCI L., LIPPI A. : The epidemiology of dementia, Alzheimer's disease and Parkinson's disease. In : Handbook of Neuropsychology, Boller F., Grafman J. (eds). *Elsevier,* Amsterdam, 1991, volume 5, chap. 1 : 3-13.
4. KURTZKE J.F., GOLBERG I.D. : Parkinsonism death rates by race, sex and geography. *Neurology,* 1988, 38, 1558-1561.
5. KOLLER W., O'HARA R., WEINER W., LANG A., NUTT J., AGID Y., BONNET A.M., JANKOVIC J. : Relationship of aging to Parkinson's disease. *Advances in Neurology,* 1986, 45, 317-321.
6. WARD C.D. et al. : Parkinson's disease in 65 pairs of twins and in a set of quadruplets. *Neurology,* 1983, 33, 815-824.
7. HOFMAN A., SCHULTE W., TANJA T.A., van DUIJN C.M., HAAXMA R., LAMERIS A.J., OTTEN V.M., SAAN R.J. : History of dementia and Parkinson's disease in 1st-degree relatives of patients with Alzheimer's disease. *Neurology,* 1989, 39, 1589-1592.
8. BOLLER F., MIZUTANI T., ROESSMANN U., GAMBETTI P.L. : Parkinson disease, dementia and Alzheimer disease : Clinico-pathological correlations. *Annals of Neurology,* 1980, 7, 329-335.
9. DUBOIS B., BOLLER F., PILLON B., AGID Y. : Cognitive disorders in Parkinson's disease, Handbook of Neuropsychology, Boller F., Grafman J. (eds). *Elsevier,* Amsterdam, 1991. volume 5, chap. 10, 195-240.
10. McGEER P.L., McGEER E.G., SUSUKI J.S. : Aging and extrapyramidal function. *Archives of Neurology,* 1977, 34, 33-35.

11. DUBOIS B., HAUW J.J., RUBERG M., SERDARU M., JAVOY-AGID F., AGID Y. : Démence et maladie de Parkinson : corrélations biochimiques et anatomocliniques. *Revue Neurologique*, 1985, 141, 184-193.
12. GUILLARD A., FÉNELON G., MAHIEUX F. : Les altérations cognitives au cours de la maladie de Parkinson. *Revue Neurologique*, sous presse.
13. MAYEUX R. : The « serotonin hypothesis » for depression in Parkinson's disease. In : Parkinson's disease : anatomy, pathology and therapy. Streifler M.B., Korczyn A.D., Melamed E., Youndim M.B.H. (eds). *Advances in Neurology*, 1990, 53, 163-166.
14. ALBERT M.L., FELDMAN R.G., WILLIS A.L. : The subcortical dementia of progressive supranuclear palsy. *Journal of Neurology, Neurosurgery and Psychiatry*, 1974, 37, 121-130.
15. RINNE U.K. : Lisuride, a dopamine agonist in the treatment of early Parkins'on's disease. *Neurology*, 1989, 39, 336-339.
16. PINCUS J.H., BARRY K. : Influence of dietary protein on motor fluctuations in Parkinson's disease. *Archives of Neurology*, 1987, 44, 270-272.
17. ADAMS R.D., VICTOR M. : Principles of Neurology. *McGraw Hill*, 4th Edition, New York, 1989.
18. LANDAU W.M. : Pyramid sale in the bucket shop : Datatop bottoms out. *Neurology*, 1990, 40, 1337-1339.
19. KATZMAN R., BJÖRKLUND A., OWMAN C., STENEVI U., WEST K. : Evidence for regeneration axon sprouting of central catecholamine neurons in the rat mesencephalon following electrolytic lesions. *Brain Research*, 1971, 25, 579-596.
20. BJÖRKLUND A., STENEVI U. : Reconstruction of the nigrostriatal dopamine pathway by intracerebral nigral transplants. *Brain Research*, 1979, 177, 555-560.
21. BACKLUND E.O., GRANDBERG P.O., HAMBERGER B. et al. : Transplantation of adrenal medullary tissue to striatum in Parkinsonism : first clinical trials. *Journal of Neurosurgery*, 1985, 62, 169-173.
22. MADRAZO I., DUSCHER-COLIN L.A., DIAZ V., MARTINEZ-MATA J., TORRES C., BECERRIL J.J. : Open microsurgical autograft of adrenal medulla to the right caudate nucleus in two patients with intractable Parkinson's disease. *New England Journal of Medicine*, 1987, 316, 831-834.
23. OSTROSKY-SOLIS F., QUINTANAR L., MADRAZO I., DRUCKER-COLIN R., FRANCO-BOURLAND R., LEON-MEZA V. : Neuropsychological effects of brain autograft of adrenal medullary tissue for the treatment of Parkinson's disease. *Neurology*, 1988, 38, 1442-1450.
24. ZIEGLER M. : La maladie de Parkinson à l'heure des greffes de cellules fœtales. *Le Quotidien du Médecin*, 1990, 15, 4657.
25. BJÖRKLUND A., LINDVALL O., ISACSON O., BRUNDING P., WICTORIN K., STRECKER R.E., CLARKE D.J., DUNNETT S.B. : Mechanisms of action of intracerebral neural implants : studies on nigral and striatal grafts to the lesioned striatum. *Trends in Neuroscience*, 1987, 10, 509.
26. FREED C.R., BREEZE R.E., ROSENBERG N.L., SCHNECK S.A., WELLS T.H., BARRETT J.N., GRAFTON S.T., HUANG S.C., EIDELBERG D., ROTTENBERG D.A. : Transplantation of human fetal dopamine cells for Parkinson's disease. Results at one year. *Archives of Neurology*, 1990, 47, 505-512.
27. DEGOS J.D. : Greffes intracérébrales dans la maladie de Parkinson, un grand remue-ménage. *Revue du Praticien*, 1989, 39, 43-44.

2 - RESPONSE TO VACCINATION IN THE ELDERLY : F. Denis, S. Ranger, M. Mounier

1. AJJAN N. : La vaccination. *Institut Mérieux éd.*, Lyon, 1989.
2. MOULIAS R. : Age et immunité. *Bio. Méd. Pharmathér.*, 1987, 41, 115-121.
3. SALMON D., LEPORT C., VILDE J.L. : Facteurs de sensibilité à l'infection et immunité chez le sujet âgé. *Méd. Mal. Inf.*, 1988, 18, N° spécial, 311-318.
4. SALTZMAN R.L., PETERSON P.K. : Immunodeficiency of the elderly. *Rev. Inf. Dis.*, 1987, 9, 1127-1139.
5. SCHOENBAUM S.C. : Immunization. *In :* Infections in the elderly. R.A. Gleckman and N.M. Gantz Ed. *Little, Brown and Company*, Boston/Toronto, 1983.
6. COOK J.M., GUALDE N., HESSEL L., MOUNIER M., MICHEL J.P., DENIS F., RATINAUD H. : Alterations of the human immune response to the hepatitis B vaccine among the elderly. *Cell. Immunology*, 1987, 109, 89-96.
7. KISHIMOTO S., TOMINO S., MITSUYA H., FUSIWARA H., TSUDA H. : Age-related decline in the *in vitro* and *in vivo* synthesis of anti-tetanus toxoid antibody in humans. *J. Immunol.*, 1980, 125, 2346-2352.
8. PENIN F., BAUSTER C., BURDIN J.C., CUNY G. : Enquête sur l'immunité antitétanique et résultats de la vaccination des sujets non protégés de plus de 60 ans vivant en hébergement médicalisé. *Méd. Hyg.*, 1982, 40, 1856-1870.
9. RUBEN F.L., NAGEL J., FIREMAN P. : Antitoxin responses in the elderly to tetanus-diphteria (TD) immunization. *Amer. J. Epidemiol.*, 1978, 108, 145.
10. CADOZ M., ARMAND J., ARMINJON F., MICHEL J.P., MICHEL M., DENIS F., SCHIFFMAN G. : A new 23 valent pneumococcal vaccine : immunogenicity and reactogenicity in adults. *J. Biol. Standardization*, 1985, 13, 261-265.

11. MICHEL J.P., CADOZ M., DENIS F., HESSEL L., MOUNIER M., SCHIFFMAN G. : Comparaison des réponses immunes au vaccin antipneumococcique 23 valent entre adultes jeunes et personnes âgées. *Méd. Mal. Inf.*, 1988, 18, N° spécial, 406.

12. MICHEL J.P., GAUTHEY L., JEANNET N., HESSEL L. : Les vaccinations indispensables chez les personnes âgées. Trois priorités : les vaccinations antigrippale, antipneumococcique et antitétanique. *Rev. Prat.*, 1990, 96, 9-14.

13. DENIS F., MOUNIER M., HESSEL L., MICHEL J.P., GUALDE N., DUBOIS F., BARIN F., GOUDEAU A. : Hepatitis B vaccination in the elderly. *J. Infect. Dis.*, 1984, 149, 1019.

14. MOUNIER M., DENIS F., HESSEL L., MICHEL J.P., GUALDE N., DUBOIS F., BARIN F., GOUDEAU A. : Epidémiologie de l'hépatite B et réponse à la vaccination spécifique chez le sujet âgé. *Méd. Hyg.*, 1984, 42, 1681-1685.

15. KEREN G., SEGEV S., MORAG A., ZAKAY-RONES Z., BARZILAI A., RUBINSTEIN E. : Failure of influenza vaccination in the aged. *J. Méd. Virol.*, 1988, 25, 85-89.

16. LEVINE M., BEATTLE B.L., MC LEAN D.M. : Comparison ot the one and two dose regimens of influenza vaccine for the elderly men. *C.M.A.J.*, 1987, 137, 722-726.

17. STRASSBURG M.A., GREENLAND S., SORVILLO F.J., LIEB L.E., HABEL L.A. : Influenza in the elderly : report of an outbreak and a review of vaccine effectiveness report. *Vaccine*, 1986, 4, 38-44.

3 - DEPRESSIVE PSEUDODEMENTIA IN THE ELDERLY : A. Donnet, J.-M. Azorin

1. KILOH (L.G) [1961] : Pseudodementia. *Acta Psychiatr. Scand.*, 37, 336-351.

2. WELLS (C.E.) [1979] : Pseudodementia. *Am. J. Psychiatr.*, 136, 7, 895-900.

3. BOURGEOIS (M.) [1987] : Pseudodémence dépressive. In : Diagnostic et traitement de la dépression : *"Quo Vadis ?"*, BIZIERE (K.), GARATTINI (S.), SIMON (P.), [eds.]. Symposium *"Quo Vadis ?"* pp. 227-243. Groupe Sanofi 11-12 mai 1987, Montpellier, France.

4. GOOD (M.I.) [1981] : Pseudodementia and physical findings masking significant psychopathology. *Am. J. Psychiatry*, 138, 6, 811-814.

5. CAINE (E.D.) [1981] : Pseudodementia. Currents concepts and future directions. *Arch. Gen. Psychiatry*, 38, 1359-1364.

6. AZORIN (J.-M.), MATTEI (J.-P.) [1983] : Les pseudo-démences. Problèmes cliniques et pathogéniques. *L'Encéphale*, IX, 175-191.

7. BULBENA (A.), BERRIOS (G.E.) [1986] : Pseudodementia, facts and figures. *Br. J. Psychiatr.*, 148, 87-94.

8. DONNET (A.), HABIB (M.), AZORIN (J.-M.) [1990] : Actualité du concept de pseudodémence. *Rev. Méd. Int.*, XI, 2, 133-141.

9. WERNICKE (C.) [1900] : Grundriss der Psychiatrie in klinischen Vorlesungen. *Thieme*, Leipzig.

10. GARCIA (C.), SANDER (H.J.) [1983] : Pseudohysterische Verhaltensweisen bei endogenen depressionen. *Nervenarzt*, 54, 354-362.

11. SHRABERG (D.) [1978] : The myth of pseudodementia : depression and the aging brain. *Am. J. Psychiatry*, 135, 5, 601-603.

12. FOLSTEIN (M.F.), Mc HUGH (P.R.) [1978] : Dementia syndrome of depression. In : R. KATZMAN et al. (eds), Alzheimer disease : senile dementia and related disorders (Aging vol. 7), *Raven Press*, New York.

13. Mc ALLISTER (T.W.) [1981] : Cognitive functioning in the affective disorders. *Comprehensive Psychiatry*, 22, 6, 572-586.

14. DSM III R [1987] : Diagnostic and statistical manual of mental disorders, 3rd ed. revised. Washington, DC : *American Psychiatric Association*.

15. AZORIN (J.-M.), LIEUTAUD (J.), HABIB (M.) [1986] : Phenomenology of depressive pseudodementias, diagnostic and therapeutic issues. In : Senile dementias, early detection. *Ed. A. Bes. et al.*, John Libbey Eurotext, 477-481.

16. STEEL (H.), FELDMAN (R.G.) [1979] : Diagnosing dementia and its treatable causes. *Geriatrics*, 34, 79-88.

17. YOUNG (R.C.), MANLEY (M.W.), ALEXOPOULOS (G.C.) [1985]. « I don't know » responses in elderly depressives and in dementia. *J. Am. Geriatr. Soc.*, 33, 4, 253-257.

18. AZORIN (J.-M.), DONNET A., HABIB (M.), RÉGIS (H.) [1990] : Critères pour le diagnostic de pseudo-démence dépressive. *L'Encéphale*, XVI, 31-34.

19. REYNOLDS (C.F.), HOCH (C.C.), KUPFER (D.J.), BUYSSE (D.J.), HOUCK (P.R.), STACK (J.A.), CAMP-BELL (D.W.) [1988] : Bedside differentiation of depressive pseudodementia from dementia. *Am. J. Psychiatr.*, 145, 1099-1103.

20. RABINS (P.V.), MERCHANT (A.), NESTADT (G.) [1984] : Criteria for diagnosing reversible dementia, validation by 2-year follow. *B. J. Psychiatr.*, 144, 488-492.

21. NOTT (P.N.), FLEMINGER (J.J.) [1975] : Presenile dementia : the difficulties of early diagnosis. *Acta Psych. Scand.*, 51, 210-217.

22. SMITH (J.S.), KILOH (L.G.) [1981] : The investigation of dementia : results in 200 consecutive admissions. *Lancet*, 1, 824-827.

23. HUBBARD (B.M.), ANDERSON (J.M.) [1981] : Age, senile dementia and ventricular enlargement. *J. Neurol. Neurosurg. Psychiatr.,* 44, 631-635.

24. CARROLL (B.J.), FEINBERG (M.), GREDEN (J.F.), TARIKA (J.), ALBALA (A.A.), HASKETT (R.F.), JAMES (N. Mc I.), KRONFOL (Z.), LOHR (N.), STEINER (M.), DE VIGNE (J.P.), YOUNG (E.) [1981] : A specific laboratory test for the diagnostic of melancolia. *Arch. Gen. Psychiatr.,* 38, 15-22.

25. RUDORFER (M.V.), CLAYTON (P.J.) [1981] : Depression, dementia, and dexamethasone suppression. *Am. J. Psychiatry,* 138, 5, 701.

26. SPAR (J.E.), GERNER (R.) [1982] : Does the dexamethasone test distinguish dementia from depression ? *Am. J. Psychiatry,* 139, 2, 238-241.

27. RASKIND (M.A.), PESKIND (E.R.), HALTER (J.B.), JIMERSON (D.C.) [1984] : Norepinephrine and MHPG levels in CSF and plasma in Alzheimer's disease. *Arch. Gen. Psychiatry,* 41, 343-346.

28. GRUNHAUS (L.), DILSAVER (S.), GREDEN (J.F.), CARROLL (B.J.) [1983] : Depressive pseudodementia. A suggested diagnostic profile. *Biol. Psychiatry,* 18, 2, 215-225.

29. REYNOLDS (C.F.), SPIKER (D.G.), HANIN (I.), KUPFER (D.J.) [1983] : Electroencephalographic sleep, aging, and psychopathology : new data and state of the art. *Biological Psychiatry,* 18, 2, 139-155.

30. REYNOLDS (C.F.), KUPFER (D.J.), HOUCK (P.R.), HOCH (C.C.), STACK (J.A.), BERMAN (S.R.), ZIMMER (B.) [1988] : Reliable discrimination of elderly depressed and demented patients by electroencephalographic sleep data. *Arch. Gen. Psychiatry,* 45, 258-264.

31. BUYSSE (D.J.), REYNOLDS (C.F.), KUPFER (D.J.), HOUCK (P.R.), HOCH (C.C.), STACK (J.A.), BERMAN (S.R.) [1988] : Electroencephalographic sleep in depressive pseudodementia. *Arch. Gen. Psychiatry,* 45, 568-573.

32. DONNET (A.), AZORIN (J.-M.), REGIS (R.) : EEG de sommeil, démence et dépression. In : Comptes rendus du Congrès de Psychiatrie et de Neurologie de langue française. LXXXVIII° session, Lille, 18-23 juin 1990 (à paraître).

33. DELAY (J.), MOREAU (J.) [1944] : Syndrome mélancolique pseudodémentiel chez un lacunaire. Constatation encéphalographique. Action de l'électrochoc. *Ann. Med. Psychol.,* 11, 3, 300-305.

34. BOURGEOIS (M.), HEBERT (A.), MAISONDIEU (J.) [1970] : Les dépressions séniles pseudodémentielles convulsivo-curables. *Ann. Med. Psychol.,* 1, 751-758.

35. KRAL (V.A.) [1982] : Depressive Pseudodemenz und Senile Demenz vom Alzheimer-Typ. *Nervenarzt,* 53, 284-286.

36. SACHDEV (P.S.), SMITH (J.S.), ANGUS-LEPAN (H.), RODRIGUEZ (P.) [1990] : Pseudodementia twelve years on. *J. Neurol. Neurosurg. Psychiatr.,* 53, 254-259.

37. FREEMAN (R.L.), GALABURDA (A.M.), CABAIL (R.D.), GESCHWIND (N.) [1985] : The neurology of depression. *Arch. Neurol.,* 42, 289-291.

38. RABINS (M.A.), PESKIND (E.R.), HALTER (J.B.) [1982] : Norepinephrine and MHPG levels in CSF and plasma in Alzheimer's disease. *Arch. Gen. Psychiatry,* 139, 5, 623-629.

39. FOLSTEIN (M.F.), FOLSTEIN (S.E.), Mc HUGH (P.R.) [1975] : « Mini-mental state » : a practical method for grading the cognitive state of patients for the clinician. *J. Psychiatr. Res.,* 12, 189-198.

40. TARIOT (P.N.), WEINGARTNER (H.) [1986] : A psychobiologic analysis of cognitive failures. *Arch. Gen. Psychiatr.,* 43, 1183-1188.

41. JIMERSON (D.C.) [1987] : Role of dopamine mechanisms in the affective disorders. In : MELTZER (H.P.) [ed.] : Psychopharmacology : the third generation of progress, *Raven Press,* New York, 505-511.

42. EMRICH (H.M.), VON ZERSSEN (D.), KISSLING (W.), MÖLLER (H.J.), WINDORFER (A.) [1980] : Effect of sodium valproate in mania. The GABA hypothesis of affective disorders. *Arch. Psychiatr. Nervenkrank.,* 229, 1-16.

43. JANOWSKY (D.C.), EL-YOUSEF (M.K.), DAVIS (J.M.), SEKERKE (H.J.) [1972] : A cholinergic adrenergic hypothesis of mania and depression. *Lancet,* 2, 632-635.

44. BAXTER (L.E.), PHELPS (M.E.F.), MAZZIOTTA (J.C.), SCHWARTZ (J.M.), GERNER (R.H.), SELIN (C.E.), SUMIDA (R.M.) [1985] : Cerebral metabolic rates for glucose in mood disorders. *Arch. Gen. Psychiatry,* 42, 441-447.

45. POYNTON (A.), BRIDGES (P.K.), BARTLETT (J.R.) [1988] : Resistant bipolar affective disorder treated by stereotactic subcaudate tractotomy. *Br. J. Psychiatry,* 152, 354-358.

VI

FACTS AND RESEARCH IN SOCIAL GERONTOLOGY

NEW APPROACHES
TO FUNCTIONAL ASSESSMENT

David B. REUBEN (*),
Albert L. SIU (*)

Summary. – *Functional status assessment has become an integral part of clinical geriatrics and research on aging. Three levels of physical functioning have been described : basic, intermediate, and advanced. Tasks that are at higher levels are progressively more difficult and usually are guided by personal choice.*

Functional status can be assessed by obtaining information from the patient, a proxy, or by directly observing the patient completing the functional task. Questions and instruments have been validated for each of these methods and examples are provided. The most simple method of assessing function is to integrate functional status questions into the standard medical interview. Self-administered questionnaires have the advantage of providing information about dimensions of function other than physical function without requiring substantial physician time. Direct observation of performance has several advantages but requires a trained observer and props. The choice of an appropriate assessment method must be guided by the purpose of the information being collected and the population being assessed.
(Facts and Research in Gerontology 1992)

Although the clinical importance of functional status has been recognized for more than forty years (Karnofsky, 1949), its emergence as a major theme of clinical geriatrics and research on aging began in the 1960s with some of the pioneering work of Katz and others (Katz, 1970). Since that time functional status assessment has become an established part of the clinical evaluation of the older patient and has become an essential baseline (and frequently outcome) measure in geriatrics research. Functional status can provide important information about the need for assistance in personal care, ability to live independently, and prognosis. Moreover, improvement in functional status is an important goal of therapy that is equally, if not more important than control of the physiologic manifestations of disease.

Please address correspondence to : David B. Reuben, M.D., Multicampus Division of Geriatric Medicine and Gerontology, UCLA School of Medicine 32-144 CHS, 10833 Le Conte Avenue, Los Angeles, CA 90024-1687.

(*) From the Multicampus Division of Geriatric Medicine, UCLA School of Medicine. Dr. Siu is the recipient of a National Institute on Aging Academic Award.

Most simply, functional status can be defined as a person's « ability to perform tasks and fulfill social roles associated with daily living across a broad range of complexity ». Although functional status has been used to refer to a wide range of health dimensions (e.g. mental health, cognition, general health states) in this paper we use a more restrictive definition and refer to only physical, social, and role function. When reporting a patient's physical functional status, it has been customary in geriatrics to refer to capabilities at two general levels of function, basic activities of daily living (BADLs) (Katz) and intermediate (or instrumental) activities of daily living (IADLs) (Lawton). Basic activities of daily living, such as feeding, transferring, toileting, dressing and bathing are items that represent personal care. Intermediate activities of daily living include shopping, doing laundry, taking medications, doing housework, taking public transportation, cooking, telephoning, and managing money. The ability to perform these tasks is perhaps the most important determinant of capability to sustain independent living.

More recently, it has been suggested that another level of more difficult functional tasks, advanced activities of daily living (AADLs) (Reuben, 1989) should also be measured and reported. Advanced activities of daily living include social, occupational, and recreational activities that are voluntary and are intimately related to the quality and enjoyment of life. Compared to BADLs and IADLs, these functions are much more determined by personal choices, aptitude, interests, and beliefs. Many AADLs also tap into more than one dimension ; a tennis match is both a social and physical AADL. Examples of extremely advanced social, occupational, and recreational function, respectively, are travelling overseas, working as a corporate executive, and competitive running. Although many older persons do not participate in such advanced activities, most do function beyond the level of IADL function. This classification of function into these three levels has historical significance and clinical utility ; however, function is probably best regarded as a continuum from most basic to most advanced.

Sources of information about function include self-report, proxy report (e.g. spouse or caregiver) and direct observation. Numerous self-report measures have been described (Kane, 1981), and several (e.g. the Katz Activities of Daily Living [ADL] (Katz) and Lawton-Brody Instrumental Activities of Daily Living [IADL] (Lawton), are commonly used in clinical and research settings. These self-report instruments usually ask patients whether they are capable of performing a task or whether they actually perform the task. Thus, the wording of these questions is often « can you do... ? » or « do you do... » Observer report scales are similar but rely on a proxy to respond for the patient. Usually the proxy is a family member who lives with the patient or a staff person at an institution. The source of information (patient versus proxy) can have an important influence on diagnostic and therapeutic plans. For example, Rubenstein et al. (Rubenstein, 1984) have shown that functional status scores vary depending on the source of information ; patients rate their own function higher than do family or nursing staff. Depending upon who is believed and who is correct, self-report or proxy-report functional information can lead to over or undertreatment of functional impairment. Direct observation requires the presence of an examiner and a cooperative patient. The patient is then lead through various tasks and rated by the examiner according to scale criteria.

The remainder of this paper reviews recent advances in the development and validation of scales to measure physical function in community-dwelling elderly persons and presents options for clinical and research use. We begin with the simplest of measures, those that can be ascertained with a few simple questions in the office ; then describe measures that require formal instruments or questionnaires to be completed ; and conclude with performance based measures of function that require props and personnel to administer.

SIMPLE MEASURES OF FUNCTION THAT CAN BE INCORPORATED INTO THE ROUTINE PATIENT INTERVIEW

During atypical office visit, physicians may not be able to assess function accurately. In a study of twenty-eight New England practices, physicians underestimated their patients functional limitations 35 % of the time (Nelson, 1983). Therefore, every initial assessment of an older patient and periodic follow-up evaluations should ask specific questions about the patient's physical functioning. The clinician may choose to use standardized questions, but more often will use conversational language to assess function. Regardless, of the formality of the questions, the items (tasks) assessed usually fit into one of many scales of physical function.

Hierarchical scales of function are appealing because they are economical with respect to the number of questions that need be asked and can rapidly, and often precisely, place a patient at a functional level from lowest to highest relative to his or her peers. By hierarchical, we mean that a scale meets Guttman criteria (Proctor, 1971) of reliability (scalability and reproducibility) and thereby forms an ordered scale such that persons who can complete the most difficult task can be presumed to be capable of completing all less difficult tasks in the scale. Thus, the patient who can walk a city block does not need to be asked about his ability to dress himself. Spector and colleagues linked basic and intermediate activities of daily living in a hierarchical manner to form a single scale and validated this scale in three community-based samples. Although some of the most advanced items did not always follow the strict hierarchy, their study supported the Guttman reliability of the six-item scale (in descending order of difficulty) : shopping, transportation, bathing, dressing, transferring, and feeding (Spector, 1987).

More recently, we have evaluated the reliability and validity of four hierarchical measures of physical function (Katz ADL, Spector Hierarchical Scale [Spector, 1987], 5-item Older American Research Scale [OARS] [Fillenbaum, 1985], and a modified Rosow-Breslau [Rosow-Breslau, 1966] in 123 elderly subjects seen in four ambulatory settings (Siu, 1990). The vast majority (83 %) were fully independent on the Katz Scale. However, fewer subjects were fully independent on the scales that included IADL items (71 % independent on the Spector Scale and 66 % independent on the OARS Scale). Only 48 % were fully independent on the Rosow-Breslau Scale, which contains more difficult items that would be considered AADLs (heavy work, walking 1/2 mile and climbing stairs). Dependency in the Katz ADL items did not occur in their expected order of frequency, primarily due to the high frequency of incontinence (occurring in 11 %). As a result, maintaining continence, rather than bathing, was the most difficult item on the scale. Although the other three scales (Spector, OARS, and Rosow-Breslau) have either borderline or more acceptable coefficients of scalability (0.57-0.77), errors in the hierarchical order of items occurred in 5-14 % of subjects.

We then combined items from the three scales to create two new scales that span from basic to advanced activities of daily living (Tables 1 and 2) that have high scalability (0.86 and 0.94). Both new scales exhibited very high correlations (0.63 to 0.89) with more established measures of physical function, supporting convergent validity. They had less strong correlations with other related dimensions of health (e.g., cognitive and mental health [0.25-0.32]), supporting discriminant validity. The applicability of these new scales to other populations (e.g., nursing home) and their value in longitudinal studies remains to be demonstrated.

We have also recently created and validated an exercice scale that measures functioning at the AADL level in a hierarchical manner (Reuben, 1990a). Using a community-based probability sample in Boston and Brookline, Massachusetts, we asked three questions modified from the 1984 National Health Interview Supplement

on Aging (ref) and the OARS instrument (ref) to define the level of a person's performance of recreational activities : 1) Do you participate in any active sports such as
swimming, jogging, tennis, bicycling, aerobics, exercise classes, or other activities
that may cause you to work up a sweat or become winded ? 2) How often do you
walk a mile or more at a time, about eight to twelve blocks, without resting ? 3) How

TABLE 1

CHARACTERISTICS OF A 6-ITEM SCALE WITH AN
EXTENDED RANGE OF DISABILITY*

	Site 1	Other Sites	All 4 Sites
Functional status items in decreasing frequency of dependency and the % of subjects dependent in that item			
Strenuous physical activities	58.7	68.9	64.5
Heavy work	39.1	49.2	44.9
Shopping or transportation	26.1	27.9	27.1
Shopping and transportation	21.7	18.0	19.6
Bathing or dressing	17.4	8.2	12.1
Bathing and dressing	10.9	3.3	6.5
Coefficient of reproducibility	0.964	0.967	0.966
Improvement over the Minimum Marginal Reproducibility	0.225	0.197	0.209
Coefficient of scalability	0.861	0.857	0.859

* Selected items missing from 16 subjects.

TABLE 2

CHARACTERISTICS OF A 5-ITEM SCALE WITH AN
EXTENDED RANGE OF DISABILITY*

	Site 1	Other Sites	All 4 Sites
Functional status items in decreasing frequency of dependency and the % of subjects dependent in that item			
Strenuous physical activities	58.3	70.0	64.8
Heavy work	39.6	50.0	45.4
Walking a 1/2 mile	25.0	33.3	29.6
Bathing or dressing	14.6	8.3	11.1
Bathing and dressing	8.3	3.3	5.6
Coefficient of reproducibility	0.983	0.933	0.956
Improvement over the Minimum Marginal Reproducibility	0.242	0.183	0.209
Coefficient of scalability	0.936	0.733	0.825

* Selected items missing from 15 subjects.

often do you walk one-quarter of a mile, about two or three blocks, without resting ? The responses to these three questions were dichotomized to define persons who performed these activities frequently, at least three or four times per week, and those who did not. This level of frequency was selected because persons seeking a protective effect from cardiovascular disease are advised to exercise at least three times a week and by common parlance exercising at this frequency would be termed « regular » exercise. Using these dichotomous variables, subjects were classified into four categories : 1) frequent vigorous exercisers, 2) frequent long walkers, 3) frequent short walkers and 4) persons who did not exercise frequently.

The scale met Guttman criteria for reproducibility and scalability and our findings supported the construct validity of the scale with other measures of health status, mental health, and social functioning. For example, at least 84 % of subjects in each exercise group rated their health as excellent or good compared with 59 % of subjects in the no regular exercise group (p < .001). Mental health index scores were also higher (better function) for exercisers compared to non-exercisers (p < 0.01). For both of these health measures, however, there appeared to be a threshold effect, i.e., progressively increasing exercise levels did not positively affect the health measure.

Of note, not all measures of social function were correlated with level of physical AADL. As expected, we could not demonstrate a difference between groups in participation in the less vigorous social AADLs (entertaining at home and visiting others at their homes) but marked differences between groups could be demonstrated for working at a hobby and traveling, supporting the scale's discriminant validity. Perhaps a lower threshold of AADL level is necessary for preservation of most social activities. On the other hand, advanced social activities of daily living that appear to be the most vigorous (working at a hobby and traveling out of town) were performed more frequently by those at the highest level of physical advanced activity of daily living. The scale also demonstrated some predictive validity in that persons who participated in no regular exercise had higher mortality at the year follow-up compared to those who participated in any of the physical AADLs. Nevertheless, the clinical value of detecting change from one exercise level to another must still be determined.

TABLE 3

QUESTIONS FOR HIERARCHICAL SCALE OF EXERCISE-RELATED AADLs

---

1. Do you frequently (at least three times a week) participate in any active sports such as swimming, jogging, tennis, bicycling, aerobics, exercise classes, or other activities that may cause you to work up a sweat or become winded ?

2. Do you frequently (at least three times a week) walk a mile or more at a time, about eight to twelve blocks, without resting ?

3. Do you frequently (at least three times a week) walk one-quarter of a mile, about two or three blocks, without resting ?

Because of the great diversity in activities pursued at this level, it will be difficult to develop a « universal » scale as has been created for basic activities of daily living. One approach to this problem has been the development of a « patient-specific » Functional Status Index in which the patient is asked at the baseline interview to identify the most strenuous physical activity he or she performs and how much he or she performs on a good day and on a bad day (MacKenzie, 1986). In subsequent interviews, a transition assessment is conducted in which the patient is asked whether he or she has changed in terms of physical activity, whether the person can still do the item identified at baseline, and whether this is the most strenuous activity he or she can do. One limitation of this approach is that it measures only a single aspect of maximal physical function, given patient. Nevertheless, it provides a virtually boundless method of determining a patient's level of function that can be followed as a clinical marker.

Another approach towards the routine incorporation of functional measurements into office practice has been adopted by the Eastern Cooperative Group in developing their COOP Charts that provide pictorial as well as verbal description of responses (Nelson, 1985) for a variety of physical and emotional functions. These may prove simpler for the frail and cognitively impaired and may also be valuable cross-culturally. However, these charts do not provide a detailed picture of specific functional disabilities.

FORMAL INSTRUMENTS OR QUESTIONNAIRES THAT CAN BE COMPLETED IN THE OFFICE

Although the use of formal instruments or questionnaires have been primarily used in research and academic settings for many years, there is good reason to suspect that they may begin to gain more use in clinical settings. First, because they can often be self-administered or administered by a relative or friend, they do not require additional physician time. In fact, they may actually save physicians time. Second, specific scales that measure different dimensions of function (e.g. physical, social, mental health) have been developed that require only a few minutes each to complete. Thus, clinicians can quickly obtain a profile of their patient's function across several dimensions.

Several instruments have been developed and are gaining increased usage. Two examples are the Functional Status Questionnaire (Jette, 1986) and the Medical Outcomes Study (MOS) Short-form (Stewart, 1988). The Functional Status Questionnaire (FSQ) is a brief, self-administered questionnaire consisting of 34 core items that takes approximately 15 minutes to complete and provides a comprehensive assessment of physical, psychological, social, and role function in ambulatory patients (Jette, 1986). FSQ results are broken into six subscales measuring difficulty with basic activities of daily living, intermediate activities of daily living, mental health, work performance, social activity, and quality of interactions. Each of the FSQ subscales has an alpha coefficient ranging from 0.64 to 0.82. The FSQ has been demonstrated to have construct validity with health-related measures such as bed disability days, restricted activity days, satisfaction with health, and frequency of social contacts (Jette, 1986). The FSQ has also been demonstrated to have predictive validity for the development of negative outcomes such as death, nursing home placement, and the need for assistance 24 hours a day.

The MOS Short-form is a twenty-item self-administered questionnaire that takes 3-4 minutes to administer and represents six health concepts : physical functioning, role functioning, social functioning, mental health, health perceptions, and pain. In the initial validation study, reliability coefficients ranged from 0.81 to 0.88 and statistically significant correlations between each of the health measures were demonstrated.

DIRECT OBSERVATION METHODS
OF MEASURING PHYSICAL FUNCTION

Theoretically, direct observation of a patient completing a functional task confers several advantages over self-report or proxy report of that person's ability to complete the task. Direct observation provides an objective, quantifiable measure of performance ; thus, this method eliminates possible discrepancies between what the patient or proxy reports and what the patient can actually do. As a result direct observation may provide more accurate and reliable information than self-report or proxy report. Other theoretical advantages of performance measures include face validity for the task being performed, better reproducibility, and perhaps, better sensitivity to change (Guralnik, 1987). Accordingly, direct observation may be useful both as a clinical tool and as a means of confirming the validity of self-report and proxy-report assessments.

On the other hand, direct observation of physical functional status has several drawbacks. First, it must be conducted in the presence of a trained examiner, in contrast to many self-report scales that can be completed at home at the patient's convenience. Therefore, additional staff time and effort are necessary. Furthermore, depending upon the task being observed (e.g. gait), the examiner may need to be a professional clinician. Second, many of these assessments rely on props, some of which need to be constructed and readily available. Some require additional clinical space to administer and may interfere with other patient care activities. Direct observation may also fail to capture the typical performance of a patient in his or her home environment. Patients may be more motivated to perform in a clinical or research setting when being observed. For example, a patient who wants to please his or her doctor may try harder to complete a functional task in the office compared to performance in the home setting. Conversely, a patient may be more motivated to complete a task at home when it represents a functional necessity. For example, a patient who may refuse to climb stairs in the physician's office may be forced to complete this task every day if his apartment is located on the second floor. Finally, some measures of physical function may be dangerous. For example, climbing stairs places patients at risk for falling or exertional angina.

To date, few methods for direct observation of physical performance have been reported. Some have focused on specific physical dimensions such as mobility (Tinetti, 1986) and manual dexterity (Williams, 1987 ; Jebsen, 1969). The Performance Test of Activities of Daily Living (PADL) measures a variety of tasks that are required for ADLs and IADLs (Kuriansky, 1976) including simulated dressing (putting on and removing a jacket), making a phone call, and simulated eating (transferring beans from a bowl to a can). The PADL, however, has not been incorporated into clinical or research settings for several reasons. First, it has not been validated in a community-dwelling elderly population. Second, the scoring of performance is frequently complicated. Finally, some of its items have been perceived as duplicative (Kane, 1981), and the instrument omits several dimensions of physical performance such as stamina/endurance and upper body strength.

Williams and colleagues have developed a Timed Manual Performance Test that measures manual dexterity including opening and closing of a series of door fasteners mounted on a plywood panel and several other tests of hand function (Williams, 1987). Advantages of this test include its ability to be administered by lay personnel and the use of timed measurements which do not require subjective interpretation. The use of timed measures has a theoretical advantage in that they measure more subtle decline than categorical measures of whether a person can complete a functional task. A patient experiencing functional decline may still be able to open a latch key door albeit more slowly than when healthy. The Timed Manual Performance Test is scored by summing the times needed to complete all tasks ; subjects taking longer than 50 seconds are more likely to require additional formal services or a change to a more dependent living arrangements in the following 12 months. In the initial validation study Williams reported sensitivity and specificity of (63 % and 67 %, respectively) to predict nonuse of services (Williams), but a subsequent study by Scholer et al. noted the test to be less sensitive (40 %) and more specific (74 %) in predicting the need for services (Scholer, 1990). The Timed Manual Performance test measures only upper extremity performance and requires the construction of props.

Tinetti et al. have reported a gait and balance scale that is performance-based and scored according to standardized rules with a maximum score of twenty-eight for the two scales combined (Tinetti, 1986). Subjects who had a total mobility score of less than 19 were 5.7 times as likely to have recurrent falls during the first three months of intermediate care facility residence as those who scored 19 or higher. The test assesses only lower body function and requires a professional assessor.

In an attempt to provide a performance-based measure that assesses both upper and lower body function that can be conducted by a lay observer and requires few simple props, we developed and conducted validation study on the Physical Performance Test (PPT) (Reuben, 1990 b). The PPT is an objective performance based measure of physical function that can be completed within 10 minutes requiring one examiner and a few easily obtainable props. Of the 9 items, two were from Jebsen (Jebsen, 1969) and Williams (Williams, 1987) (writing a sentence and simulated eating), one was from Tinetti (turning 360 degrees) (Tinetti, 1986), one was from the Performance Test of Activities of Daily Living (drinking from a cup and putting on and removing a jacket) (Kuriansky, 1976), one was from the Cooperating Clinics Committee of the American Rheumatism Association (50 foot walk test) (American Rheumatological Association, 1965) and three were new items (lifting a book and putting it on a shelf, picking up a penny from the floor, and climbing stairs). These were selected on the basis of their individual performance relative to the performance of the entire instruments and to represent the many aspects of physical functioning, e.g. upper extremity manual dexterity, mobility, endurance. Items were scored by measuring the time required to perform the task, by using previously described scoring rules, or by counting (e.g., number of stair flights).

One item (climbing stairs) was recorded as both the time required to climb one flight of stairs and number of flights of stairs climbed. A shortened (seven-item) version of the PPT that does not include the stair items was also created for three reasons : not all facilities have a staircase available, climbing stairs may be considered dangerous for some patients, and the number of stairs that constitutes a flight may vary.

The final nine-item and seven-item Physical Performance Tests and protocoles for administration and scoring are provided in Tables 4 and 5. The entire test takes 5 to 10 minutes. For each item, a five point scale (0-4) was created ranging from 4 being most capable or fastest to 0 being « unable to do ». Thus, scores on the nine-item scale could range from 0 to 36 and scores on the seven-item scale could range from 0 to 28.

Dimensions assessed by the PPT include : upper fine motor function, upper coarse motor function, balance, mobility, coordination, and endurance. Specific ADL activities that are simulated include eating, transferring, and dressing. In addition, the test measures physical capabilities that are necessary for other IADL activities that are difficult to measure in the office setting. For example, upper extremity strength is necessary to perform laundering ; climbing stairs is often essential to use public transportation.

The 9 items can be categorized by degree of difficulty, realizing that some variability is to be expected depending upon patients' physical or emotional handicaps. Items of perceived minimal difficulty are writing a sentence, simulated eating, and turning 360 degrees. Items of moderate difficulty are lifting a book (the Physician's Desk Reference), putting on and removing a jacket, picking up a penny from the floor, and walking 50 feet. The most difficult item is climbing stairs. By including items that extend across a broad range of difficulty ; the test provides measures of physical function for a diverse group of elderly patients, ranging from those who are dependent in ADLs to those who are fully independent in IADLs but may demonstrate impairment on an item such as stair climbing.

The Physical Performance Test has been evaluated in a validation study using 183 subjects (median age 79 years) in five populations ranging from residents of senior citizen housing to residents of board-and-care facilities. The PPT was reliable (Cronbach's alpha = 0.87 and 0.79, inter-rater reliability = 0.99 and 0.93 for the two scales, respectively) and demonstrated concurrent validity with self-reported measures of physical function. PPT scores for both scales were highly correlated (.50 to .80) with modified Rosow-Breslau, Instrumental and basic Activities of Daily Living scales and Tinetti gait score. PPT scores were more moderately correlated with self-reported health status, cognitive status, and mental health (.24 to .47), and negatively with age (− .24 and − .18). Thus, the PPT also demonstrated construct validity. Its value in predicting functional decline, use of services and change in level of care, and mortality remain to be determined.

CONCLUSION

Since the recognition of the importance of functional status in geriatrics, a variety of instruments have been developed and validated to measure function at all levels. The appropriate choice of an instrument depends upon the purpose of the information being obtained and the population being assessed. For clinical management of many older patients, formal instruments may not be necessary. Other patients who may have functional impairment in dimensions other than physical function may be identified with standardized multi-dimensional questionnaires. These standardized questionnaire instruments are also valuable in research settings but the most precise information about physical functioning may be obtained by using performance-based measures.

TABLE 4 :

PHYSICAL PERFORMANCE TEST SCORING SHEET

PHYSICAL PERFORMANCE TEST		
Time	Scoring	Score
1. Write a sentence _____ sec (whales live in the blue ocean)	10 sec = 4 10.5 – 15 sec = 3 15.5 – 20 sec = 2 20 sec = 1 unable = 0	_____
2. Simulated eating _____ sec*	10 sec = 4 10.5 – 15 sec = 3 15.5 – 20 sec = 2 20 sec = 1 unable = 0	_____
3. Lift a book and put it on a shelf	2 sec = 4 2.5 – 4 sec = 3 4.5 – 6 sec = 2 6 sec = 1 unable = 0	_____
4. Put on and remove a _____ sec jacket	10 sec = 4 10.5 – 15 sec = 3 15.5 – 20 sec = 2 20 sec = 1 unable = 0	_____
5. Pick up penny from floor _____ sec	2 sec = 4 2.5 – 4 sec = 3 4.5 – 6 sec = 2 6 sec = 1 unable = 0	_____
6. Turn 360 degrees	discontinuous steps 0 continuous steps 2 unsteady (grabs, staggers) 0 steady 2	_____
7. 50 foot walk test _____ sec	15 sec = 4 2 sec = 4 15.5 – 20 sec = 3 20.5 – 25 sec = 2 25 sec = 1 unable = 0	_____
8. Climb one flight _____ sec of stairs	5 sec = 4 5.5 – 10 sec = 3 10.5 – 15 sec = 2 15 sec = 1 unable = 0	_____
9. Climb stairs down _____	Number of flights of stairs up and (maximum 4)	
TOTAL SCORE (maximum 36 for 9-item, 28 for 7-item) _____ 9-item		7-item _____

* For timed measurements, round to nearest 0.5 seconds.

TABLE 5

PHYSICAL PERFORMANCE TEST PROTOCOL

Administer the Physical Performance Test as outlined below.
Subjects are given up to two chances to complete each item.
Assistive devices are permitted for tasks 6-8.

1. Ask the subject, when given the command « go », to write the sentence « whales live in the blue ocean ». Time from the word « go » until the pen is lifted from the page at the end of the sentence. All words must be included and legible. Period need not be included for task to be considered completed.

2. Five kidney beans are placed in a bowl, 5 inches from the edge of the desk in front of the patient. An empty coffee can is placed at the patient's non-dominant side. A teaspoon is placed in the patient's dominant hand. Ask the subject, on the command « go », to pick up the beans, one at a time, and place each in the coffee can. Time from the command « go » until the last bean is heard hitting the bottom of the can.

3. Place a Physician's Desk Reference or other heavy book on a table in front of the patient. Ask the patient, when given the command « go », to place the book on a shelf above shoulder level. Time from the command « go » to the time the book is resting on the shelf.

4. If the subject has a jacket or cardigan sweater, ask him or her to remove it. If not, give the subject a lab coat. Ask the subject, on the command « go », to put the coat on completely such that it is straight on his or her shoulders and then remove the garment completely. Time from the command « go » until the garment has been completely removed.

5. Place a penny approximately one foot from the patient's foot on the dominant side. Ask the patient, on the command « go » to pick up the penny from the floor and stand up. Time from the command « go » until the subject is standing erect with penny in hand.

6. With subject in corridor on in open room, ask the subject to turn 360 degrees. Evaluate on scale on PPT instrument.

7. Bring subject to start of 50 foot walk test course (25 feet out and 25 feet back) and ask the subject, on the command « go » to walk to 25 foot mark and back. Time from the command « go » until the starting line is crossed.

8. Bring subject to foot of stairs (9 to 12 steps) and ask subject, on the command « go », to begin climbing stairs until he or she feels tired and wishes to stop. Before beginning this task, alert the subject to possibility of developing chest pain or shortness of breath and inform the subject to tell you if any of these symptoms occur. Escort the subject up the stair. Time from the command « go » until the subject's first foot reaches the top of the flight of stairs. Record the number of flights climbed (up and down is one flight).

REFERENCES

Cooperating Clinics Committee of the American Rheumatism Association : A seven day variability study of 499 patients with peripheral rheumatoid arthritis. *Arthritis Rheum.*, 1965, 8, 302-334.
FILLENBAUM G.C. : Multidimensional Functional Assessment of Older Adults : The Duke Older American resources and services Procedures. Hillsdale, NJ, Lawrence Erlbaum Associates. 1988.
FITTI J.E., KOVAR M.G. : The supplement on aging to the 1984 NHIS. Vital Health Stat [1] no. 21. NCHS. Washington, DC, US Government Printing Office, 1988.
GURALNIK J.M., BRANCH L.G., CUMMINGS S.R., CURB J.D. : Physical Performance Measures in Aging Research. *J. of Gerontol. : Medical Sciences*, 1989, 44 (5), M141-46.

JEBSEN R.H., TAYLOR N., TRIESCHMANN R.B. et al. : An Objective and Standardized Test of Hand Function. *Arch. Phys. Med. Rehabil.*, June 1969, 311-319.

JETTE A.M., DAVIES A.R., CLEARY P.D. et al. : The functional status questionnaire : reliability and validity when used in primary care. *J. Gen. Intern. Med.*, 1986, 143-49.

KANE R.A., KANE R.L. : Assessing the Elderly. *D. C. Heath and Co.*, Lexington, Mass., 1981.

KARNOFSKY D.A., ABELMANN W.H., CARVER L.F., BURCHENAL J.H. : The nitrogen mustards in the palliative treatment of cancer. *Cancer*, 1948, (4), 634-656.

KATZ S., DOWNS T.D., CASH H.R., GROTZ R.C. : Progress in development of the index of ADL. *The Gerontologist*, 1970, 10 (1), 20-30.

KURIANSKY J., GURLAND B. : The Performance Test of Activities of Daily Living. *Int'l. J. Aging and Human Development*, 1976, 7 (4), 343-352.

LAWTON M.P., BRODY E.M. : Assessment of older people : self-maintaining and instrument activities of daily living. *The Gerontologist*, 1969, 9, 179-86.

MACKENZIE C.R., CHARLSON M.E., DIGIOIA D., KELLY K. : Can the Sickness Impact Profile Measure Change ? An Example of Scale Assessment. *J. Chron. Dis.*, 1986, 39, (6), 429-438.

NELSON E.B., CONGER B., DOUGLASS R. et al. : Functional Assessment of Elderly subjects in Four Service Settings. *J.A.M.A.*, 1983, 249, 3331-38.

NELSON E.C., WASSON J.H., KIRK J.W. : Assessment of function in routine clinical practice : description of the COOP Chart method and preliminary findings. *J. Chron. Dis.*, 1987, 40 (S 1), 55 S.

PROCTOR C.H. : Reliability of Guttman scale score, in American Statistical Association Proceedings of the Social Statistics Section, 1971, p. 348.

REUBEN D.B., SOLOMON D.H. : Assessment in geriatrics : of caveats and names. *Journal of the American Geriatrics Society*, 1989, 37, 570-572.

REUBEN D.B., MOR V., LALIBERTE L., HIRIS J. : A Hierarchical Exercise Scale to Measure Function at the Advanced Activities of Daily Living (AADL) Level. *Journal of the American Geriatrics Society*, 1990, 38, 855-861.

REUBEN D.B., SIU A.L. : An objective measure of physical function of elderly persons : The physical performance test. *Journal of the American Geriatrics Society* (in press, to be published in October 1990 issue).

ROSOW I., BRESLAU N. : A Guttman Health Scale for the Aged. *J. of Gerontology*, 1966, 21, 556-559.

RUBENSTEIN L., SCHAIRER C., WIELAND G.D. et al. : Systematic Biases in Functional Status Assessement of Elderly Adults : Effects of Different Data Sources. *J. of Gerontology*, 1984, 39, 689-91.

SCHOLER S.G., POTTER J.F., BURKE W.J. : Does the Williams manual test predict service use among subjects undergoing geriatric assessment ? *Journal of the American Geriatrics Society*, 1990, 38, 767-772.

SIU A.L., REUBEN D.B., HAYS R.D. : Hierarchical measures of physical function in ambulatory geriatrics. *Journal of the American Geriatrics Society, in Press.*

SPECTOR W.D., KATZ S., PURPHY J.B. et al. : The Hierarchical Relationship Between Activities of Daily Living and Instrumental Activities of Daily Living. *J. Chron. Dis.*, 1987, 40, 481-489.

STEWART A.L., HAYS R.D., WARE J.E. : The MOS Short-form General health survey : Eliability and Validity in a Patient population. *Medical Care*, 1988, 26 (7), 724-35.

TINETTI M.E. : Performance-Oriented Assessment of Mobility Problems in Elderly Patients. *J. Amer. Ger. Soc.*, 1986, 34, 119-126.

WILLIAMS M.E., HADLER N., EARP J.A. : Manual Ability as a Mark of Dependency in Geriatric Women. *J. Chron. Dis.*, 1987, 40, 481-489.

THE DEVELOPMENT AND USE OF THE IOWA SELF ASSESSMENT INVENTORY (ISAI)

Woodrow W. MORRIS[1], Kathleen C. BUCKWALTER[2], T. Anne CLEARY[3], Jerry S. GILMER[4], Patricia H. ANDREWS[5]

Summary. – *The Iowa Self Assessment Inventory (ISAI) is presented as a reliable, valid method of assessing the resources, statuses, and abilities of older persons. The purposes and some of the uses are discussed, along with the usual psychometric principles appropriate to a sound assessment tool. Attention is also paid to the need for additional data on cross-cultural populations. Scoring the instrument and profiling the results are presented. A copy of the ISAI is included.* (Facts and Research in Gerontology 1992)

Key-words : *assessment, multidimensional functional, self-assessment, elderly, cultural diversity.*

INTRODUCTION

In working with and for older persons there is a fundamental need to know systematically about their resources, statuses, and abilities in order to plan and develop sound programs which will respond to their service needs. This applies both to individuals and to groups of older persons. One way to accomplish this is through multidimensional functional assessment. The purpose of this paper is to introduce one

(1) Professor and Associate Dean Emeritus, College of Medicine, The University of Iowa.
(2) Professor, College of Nursing, The University of Iowa.
(3) Professor, Educational Measurement and Statistics, and Associate Vice-President, Academic Affairs, The University of Iowa.
(4) Assistant Research Scientist, Office of Consultation and Research in Medical Education, The University of Iowa.
(5) Program Associate, Iowa Geriatric Education Center, Department of Internal Medicine, The University of Iowa Hospitals and Clinics.

Address correspondence to Dr. W.W. Morris at the Aging Studies Program, 415 Jefferson Building, The University of Iowa City, Iowa, Iowa 52242.

such assessment tool, the Iowa Self Assessment Inventory (ISAI), to those potential users who are concerned with the provision of services to individual older persons or with gaining a better understanding of groups of elderly persons through survey research methods based on this kind of assessment.

The Iowa Self Assessment Inventory (ISAI) is a brief self-report instrument designed to help in the measurement of the resources, needs, statuses, and abilities of older people. (See Appendix A for a copy of the ISAI). In all cases the areas assessed are those deemed meaningful to older people.

The ISAI is a reliable and valid instrument (1, 2, 3) for the assessment of Economic Resources, Emotional Balance, Physical Health, Trusting Others, Mobility, Cognitive Status, and Social Support, the seven variables comprising the inventory. It is easy to administer and score, and is best used by trained individuals. Although administration time varies with each individual, the average older person completes the inventory in about 15 minutes. Manual scoring can be accomplished in another 4 or 5 minutes.

The ISAI focuses on the conscious self-perceptions of older persons, rather than on external measurement of the variable. Because of the self-report nature of the ISAI, it is designed to be used primarily with literate, relatively independent, well-elderly persons who can provide a written response. A high score on a particular scale suggests a positive perception, and a low score a negative perception of the construct being assessed.

Individual or group administration is feasible. The introductory section of the ISAI entitled "Background Information" solicits demographic information such as the respondent's gender, age, living arrangements, and level of education completed. This background section is followed by directions for completing the 56-item inventory. The respondent is asked to indicate the degree to which each statement is true about him or her on a 4-point scale with 1 = "true", 2 = "more often true than not", 3 = "more often false than not, and 4 = "false." The respondent indicates his/her rating by encircling the appropriate corresponding numbers. A description of the seven scales follows.

THE ECONOMIC RESOURCES SCALE (ER)

High scores on this scale are obtained by those who perceive their income and assets as adequate and, therefore, have no need for outside financial help, and do not participate in programs designed to supplement one's income. Those who perceive their economic status to be inadequate or impaired would obtain low scores on this scale.

THE EMOTIONAL BALANCE SCALE (EB) [ANXIETY/DEPRESSION]

Those with high scores on this scale are relatively worry-free, more or less calm, sleep well, and enjoy tranquil lives. Low scores indicate the opposite states, especially the presence of anxiety/depression.

THE PHYSICAL HEALTH STATUS SCALE (PH)

High scores on this scale are obtained by the individual who professes excellent health, seldom sees a doctor, and takes few prescribed medications. Those with low scores indicate that they have physical illnesses or disabilities, have more health problems than others, and whose ability to carry on daily activities has declined over recent years.

THE TRUSTING OTHERS SCALE (TO) [ALIENATION]

Individuals scoring high on this scale are those who believe that they have good, trustworthy friends, are friendly toward others, and generally amiable and affable in their interpersonal relationships. Low scores indicate that they question the motives of others, and believe others are against them ; that they are alienated from others.

THE MOBILITY SCALE (MO)

High scores on this scale are obtained by those who are mobile enough to carry on the usual activities of daily living and are able to get out to visit friends and relatives and participate in other social activities. Low scores represent their lack of such mobility.

THE COGNITIVE STATUS SCALE (CS)

Those who score high on this scale perceive themselves as intellectually intact, possessing good memory, orientation, and a continued ability to learn. Individuals with low scores tend to have trouble remembering things, forget appointments, and suffer a short attention span.

THE SOCIAL SUPPORT SCALE (SS)

High scores on this scale are obtained from respondents who believe they live in a comfortable social environment, peopled with friends and relatives with whom they enjoy close relationships. Low scores indicate that they perceive a less supportive social environment.

Items representing these seven scales are arranged in the inventory booklet in cyclic fashion as shown in Table 1 which is also used as a scoring form.

Ratings which are favorable, positive, or healthy are assigned a score of 4, while those of an opposite nature are scored 1, with intermediate scores of 2 and 3. Again, ratings of the items in the inventory reflect the respondents' perceptions of their status with respect to the several areas being measured by the scales.

Interpretation of the ISAI is based on a review of individual item ratings, scores on the seven scales compared with available large group data, and the integration of inventory data with information from other sources. For example, clinical examinations and interviews or other types of face-to-face assessments in addition to the ISAI scores are important components to consider in the interpretation of resource needs and status of an elderly person.

TABLE 1

SCORING KEY AND MANUAL SCORING FORM

SCALES	ITEMS								SCORES
Economic Resources	1R*	8R	15R	22S	29R	36S	43R	50S	_____
Emotional Balance	2S	9S	16S	23S	30S	37S	44S	51S	_____
Physical Health	3R	10S	17R	24R	31S	38R	45S	52R	_____
Trusting Others	4S	11S	18S	25S	32S	39S	46S	53S	_____
Mobility	5S	12R	19R	26S	33S	40R	47R	54R	_____
Cognitive Status	6S	13S	20S	27S	34S	41S	48R	55S	_____
Social Support	7S	14S	21R	28S	35S	42R	49S	56S	_____

''R'' means reverse scoring (i.e., a response choice of 1 is worth 4 points, a 2 is worth 3 points, etc.
''S'' means same scoring — no reversal.

PURPOSES AND USES

The ISAI measures an individual's resources, statuses, and abilities which have an influence on his/her adaptation to living in the later years. There are many situations in which assessment of the functioning of older persons is of value. It should be possible for agencies concerned with needs assessment, holistic health assessment, case management, evaluation of functioning over time, and admission to various types of living arrangements for the elderly to make more meaningful decisions with functional assessment data such as that provided by the ISAI in hand. In addition, self assessment can be a useful, economical tool in large-scale community surveys to determine the service needs of elderly citizens for planning service programs, new housing units, or simply to understand better the demographics of the elderly segment of the population.

Community Applications. — Multidimensional functional assessment is essential to good case management. It is a valuable tool for making informed decisions regarding older adults who may require special living arrangements, such as retirement homes, housing for low-income elderly and handicapped persons, congregate living arrangements for frail elderly individuals, and residential care facilities.

Long-term care providers need systematic and broad-based information about the functional levels of applicants to their facilities. They need to know that targeted behaviors can be measured accurately and how function changes over time. Thus, the functional assessment of applicants and residents can provide useful information regarding the extent to which the individual's functional level fits the level of care and pattern of services offered. If assessment is routinely conducted over time (perhaps once a year), changes in any of the seven areas assessed by the ISAI may be monitored, interventions or remedial strategies instituted, and their effects measured.

Studies conducted by the Comptroller General of the United States (4) are models of community survey uses of multidimensional functional assessment. The studies were valuable because they furnished information on differences between rural and urban elderly, differences found in various regions of the country and relative conditions with respect to health, security, loneliness, outlook on life, extent of impairment, need for services, unmet needs, and the predominant sources of help for older persons.

Large-scale surveys using self-assessment might be carried out at a fraction of the cost of those conducted by interviewers. An example of such a self-assessment survey may be seen in an Iowa City, Iowa mail survey designed to poll the interest of the elderly population of Johnson County in congregate living facilities. While this survey antedated the development of the ISAI, the principles of self-report were fundamental to the study. Time and cost constraints precluded conducting interviews with 284 respondents.

Although the original intent of the survey was a needs assessment for congregate housing, much more information was obtained. Upon the completion of the survey it was clear that the city knew more about its senior citizens and their needs than simply their interest in congregate living arrangements. Thus, self-assessment surveys can maximize information gathered while minimizing costs of such surveys.

Clinical Applications. – Multidimensional functional assessment could be a useful addition to the usual intake procedures in a wide variety of health care settings, including medical and dental outpatient clinics, hospitals, adult day health care programs, and community and home health care service agencies.

The geriatric patient needs to be seen and treated as a whole person rather than a conglomerate of presenting symptoms. Such a person will surely benefit if her/his conditions are seen in context of functional abilities assessed by the ISAI. Physicians, dentists, nurses, pharmacists, and other health care professional personnel need to be cognizant of the impact functional status in the seven identified areas has on the person's physical health and vice versa. Furthermore, the seven factors assessed by the ISAI are of value in selecting alternative sources of health care, such as whether care should be provided at home, elsewhere in the community, or in a long-term care facility.

PRINCIPLES OF USE

Targeted Population. – The ISAI is intended for use with elderly adults, age 60 and over. Because the instrument uses a self-report format, it is not recommended for persons unable to read nor for those cognitively unable to make a valid response.

The instrument has been validated with white, midwestern older Americans, but not yet with elderly individuals of differing cultural or ethnic backgrounds, although cross-cultural studies are underway at present. The ISAI has been translated into French and Spanish, and translations into Dutch and Italian are in process. Results obtained, therefore, from such culturally diverse respondents may not be directly comparable to the large-group data available at this time. This is not to say that important information cannot be obtained regarding the functional status of these respondents using the ISAI. Interpretation should simply be made with care, taking into consideration what is known of the respondent being assessed.

User Qualifications. – In general, those wishing to administer and interpret the ISAI should have an understanding of the functions and abilities measured by the instrument. The user should be mindful of the limitations of test interpretations. Users should understand that results obtained from the ISAI are always to be used in conjunction with other assessments of function in order to create a menaingful, functional profile for each respondent. Proper use of the instrument also assumes that the individual user will confer with ISAI consultants when necessary.

Ethical Issues. – As with any assessment procedure, this instrument should be administered only to consenting individuals.

Limitations. – Because the ISAI is a self-report measure, it may well be susceptible to conscious or unconscious distortions. For this reason, the ISAI should never be used as the sole method of assessing resources, statuses, and abilities where such information is to be used to influence important decisions about a respondent. The inventory is designed to supplement skilled judgments, not to replace them.

SCORING AND PROFILING THE ISAI

Scoring the ISAI. – The ratings of the items are scored according to the key provided in Table 1 which shows the cyclic arrangement of the items by scales. The form presented in Table 1 may be used to score the ISAI manually. There is space in this form to write the appropriate score for each item ; these may be totalled and written at the end of the row for each scale as the scale score. These raw scores are converted to standard scores when the raw scores are entered into the Profile Form (Figure 1). Separate manual scoring and profile forms are available from The

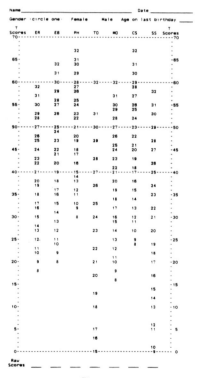

Figure 1

Iowa Self Assessment Inventory Profile Form.

Aging Studies Program, 415 Jefferson Building, The University of Iowa, Iowa City, Iowa 52242.

In Table 1, each item number is labelled with an "R" or an "S". Thus, for statement No. 1, labelled "R", "I have enough money to meet unexpected emergencies," a rating of "1", meaning "True" would be reversed giving it a value of 4. In the case of statement number 2 labelled "S", "I sometimes get tense as I think of the day's happenings," a rating of "1", meaning "True", would be given the same value (i.e., 1). Ratings of 2 or 3 are treated in the same manner.

In summary, transfer the ratings from the booklet to the scoring form, being sure to reverse all "R" ratings. Total the scores for each scale and write the total in the "SCORE" column. Finally, write the scale scores in the spaces provided at the bottom of the "Profile Form".

Profiling the Scores. – The means and standard deviations of the raw scores of the several scales vary significantly. To make scale scores comparable, they are converted to standard scores (T-scores) the distributions of which have a mean of 50 and a standard deviation of 10. Conversion of raw scores to T-scores and the creation of a profile is made easy by using the form depicted in Figure 1.

On the profile form, write the raw scores at the bottom of each column. Then look for that raw score in its column and circle or otherwise mark it. These points when connected will result in the "profile". Average scores are those falling within the range 40-60 (i.e., one standard deviation above and below the mean of 50). The meaning of the score ranges in the profile is suggested in the definitions of the scales and in numerical form.

THE IOWA SELF ASSESSMENT INVENTORY

BACKGROUND INFORMATION

Name _____ Date _____

Male ____ Female ____ Age on last birthday ____

How far did you go in school (Check one)

1. _____ Grade school or less
2. _____ Some high school
3. _____ High school graduate
4. _____ Business or trade school
5. _____ Some college
6. _____ College graduate
7. _____ Graduate/professional school

What is your race ? (Check one)

1. _____ White
2. _____ Hispanic
3. _____ Asian
4. _____ Black/African-American
5. _____ Native American-Indian
6. _____ Other, please specificy

Who lives in your houselbokl with you ? (Check one)

1. _____ No one - I live alone
2. _____ My spouse lives with me
3. _____ 1 live with another relative
4. _____ Other, please describe

DIRECTIONS

The statements on the following pages are about things that can affect our lives in one way or another. We ask you to describe your own situation using these statements. In this way we hope to understand some of your problems and needs.

1 - True
2 - More often true than not
3 - More often false than not
4 - False

Please read each statement carefully and then encircle the number corresponding to the answer that best applies to you. Wo realize that somo of the statements may not apply dhoclly to you all tho timo, but by to do the best you can. Do not worry about giving exacly the right answor ; your answor may simply mean the statement is true or false to some degree.

Please try to make an answer to evory statement.

1 - True
2 - More often true than not
3 - More often false than not
4 - False

1. I have enough money to meet unexpected emergencies.......................... 1 2 3 4
2. I sometimes get tense as I think of the day's happenings...................... 1 2 3 4
3. I have no physical disabilities or illnesses at this time........................ 1 2 3 4
4. People secretly say had things about me. 1 2 3 4
5. I need a cane, crutches, walker, or wheelchair to get around............ 1 2 3 4
6. I have trouble remembering things that happened recently.................... 1 2 3 4
7. There is no ove I can turn to in times of stress.............................. 1 2 3 4
8. I have enough money to boy those little extras.............................. 1 2 3 4
9. I frequently find myself worrying......... 1 2 3 4

10. I take 3 or more medicines each day..... 1 2 3 4
11. Friends are disloyal to me behind my back.................................. 1 2 3 4
12. I do my own shopping without help...... 1 2 3 4
13. I forgel where I put things.............. 1 2 3 4
14. There is no one I can depend on for aid if I poally nood it..................... 1 2 3 4
15. I have enough money to moot my regular dally expanses........................ 1 2 3 4
16. I tose sleep ovnt worry................. 1 2 3 4
17. My overall hoalth is excellent........... 1 2 3 4
18. I believe I am being plottod against...... 1 2 3 4
19. I de my own laundry................... 1 2 3 4
20. I have trouble remembering the names of people I know...................... 1 2 3 4
21. Thore is someone I can talk to about Important decisions................... 1 2 3 4
22. I need financial help.................. 1 2 3 4
23. I am bothered by thoughts I can't get out of my head......................... 1 2 3 4
24. My health is better than it was 5 years ago.................................. 1 2 3 4
25. Someone has it in for me.............. 1 2 3 4
26. Getting amound town is a problem for me 1 2 3 4
27. I lose my train of thought in the middle of a conversation.................... 1 2 3 4
28. There is no one I feel comfortable talking about problems with.................. 1 2 3 4
29. My finances at the present time are excellent................................. 1 2 3 4
30. I am a very nervous person............ 1 2 3 4
31. My ability te cary on my daily activities is worse than it was 5 years ego....... 1 2 3 4
32. I am sure I am being talked about....... 1 2 3 4
33. I am not able to prepare my own meals... 1 2 3 4
34. Leaming new things is harder for me than it used to be....................... 1 2 3 4
35. No one shares my concerns............ 1 2 3 4
36. My monthly expenses are so high I cannot always pay my bills............ 1 2 3 4
37. I get upsel over things................. 1 2 3 4
38. I have fewer health problems than most older people 1 know................. 1 2 3 4
39. Someone is controlling my thoughts...... 1 2 3 4
40. I walk without help.................... 1 2 3 4
41. I forget appointments................. 1 2 3 4
42. I know people I can depend on to help me if I really need it.................. 1 2 3 4
43. Have some savings and/or investments... 1 2 3 4
44. Worry over past mistakes.............. 1 2 3 4
45. During the past year I have been so sick I was unable to carry on my usual activities 1 2 3 4
46. Strangers look at me critically.......... 1 2 3 4
47. Can visit a friend or relative who fives out of own for ovenight or longer.......... 1 2 3 4
48. My mind is just as sharp as ever........ 1 2 3 4
49. It something went wrong no one would some to my assistance................ 1 2 3 4
50. Use food stamps..................... 1 2 3 4
51. Have more ups and downs than most people 1 2 3 4
52. During the past year I have been to a doctor lewer than 4 times.............. 1 2 3 4
53. See things when others do not.......... 1 2 3 4
54. Visit friends in their homes............. 1 2 3 4
55. Forget to take medicine when I am supposed to........................ 1 2 3 4
56. Do not have close relationships with other people.............................. 1 2 3 4

IOWA QUESTIONNAIRE

© 1985 par Woodrow W. Morris et Kathleen C. Buckwalter

Traduit en Français par Dr. Bruno Vellas, M.D., Ph. D., Centre de Médecine Gériatrique, C.H.U. Purpan ; Faculté de Médecine, Université de Toulouse, avec l'aimable collaboration de Kathy L. Heilenman, Associate Professor, Coordinator of French Language, Michel S. Laronde, Assistant Professor Départment de Français et Italien, et Anne Besco, candidat au maîtrise d'Anglais, départment d'Anglais, de l'Université d'Iowa.

INFORMATION GÉNÉRALE

Nom _____ Date _____

Homme _____ Femme _____ Age (dernier anniv.) _____
Scolarité (Cochez seulement une réponse)
1. _____ Ecole primaire
2. _____ Etudes secondaires
3. _____ Baccalauréat
4. _____ Ecole professionnelle ou école de commerce
5. _____ Etudes universitaires
6. _____ Diplôme universitaire (ou équivalent)
7. _____ Grandes écoles

Quelle est votre race ? (Cochez une réponse)

1. _____ Blanche
2. _____ Asiatique
3. _____ Noir
4. _____ Autre (précisez S.V.P.)

Indiquez quel est votre mode de vie en cochant seulement une réponse.
1. _____ J'habite seul(e)
2. _____ J'habite avec mon époux/épouse
3. _____ J'habite avec un(e) autre membre de la famille (spécifiez) _____
4. _____ J'habite avec une autre personne (spécifiez, S.V.P.)

INSTRUCTIONS

Les affirmations suivantes sont relatives à des événements qui peuvent affecter votre vie dans un sens ou dans un autre. Nous vous demandons de décrire votre propre situation en vous aidant de ces affirmations. De cette façon, nous espérons comprendre quelques-uns des problèmes et besoins des personnes âgées vivant à domicile. Il est demandé de répondre aux affirmations de la façon suivante :
1 – Vrai
2 – Plutôt vrai
3 – Plutôt faux
4 – Faux
Il est recommandé de lire chaque affirmation attentivement et ensuite d'entourer le chiffre correspondant à la réponse qui s'applique le mieux à votre cas. Nous savons que certaines questions ne peuvent pas s'appliquer directement à vous à chaque occasion, mais essayez de répondre tout de même. Il n'y a pas lieu de s'inquiéter de donner exactement la bonne réponse, votre réponse devant simplement dire si l'affirmation est vraie ou fausse dans une certaine mesure.

Répondez à chaque affirmation, s'il vous plaît.
1 – Vrai
2 – Plutôt vrai
3 – Plutôt faux
4 – Faux

1. J'ai assez d'argent pour faire face à une urgence inattendue.................... 1 2 3 4
2. Je deviens parfois tendu en pensant aux événements de la journée.............. 1 2 3 4
3. Je n'ai pas d'incapacité physique ou de maladies, en ce moment................ 1 2 3 4
4. Les gens disent du mal de moi en cachette 1 2 3 4
5. J'ai besoin d'une canne, béquilles, déambulateur ou chaise roulante pour marcher 1 2 3 4
6. J'ai des difficultés à me rappeler des souvenirs récents........................ 1 2 3 4
7. Je n'ai personne vers qui me tourner dans les moments difficiles............... 1 2 3 4
8. J'ai assez d'argent pour acheter des choses superflues......................... 1 2 3 4
9. Je me sens souvent préoccupé(e)....... 1 2 3 4
10. Je prends trois médicaments ou plus par jour 1 2 3 4
11. Mes amis me font des infidélités derrière mon dos........................... 1 2 3 4
12. Je fais mes courses sans aide......... 1 2 3 4
13. J'oublie où je pose les choses.......... 1 2 3 4
14. Je n'ai personne sur qui compter quand j'en ai réellement besoin............... 1 2 3 4
15. J'ai assez d'argent pour subvenir à mes dépenses quotidiennes................ 1 2 3 4
16. Je perds le sommeil car je suis trop préoccupé(e)....................... 1 2 3 4
17. Mon état de santé est excellent....... 1 2 3 4
18. Je crois que l'on conspire contre moi.... 1 2 3 4
19. Je fais ma propre lessive............... 1 2 3 4
20. J'ai des problèmes pour me souvenir des noms des gens que je connais......... 1 2 3 4
21. Il y a quelqu'un à qui je peux parler pour des décisions importantes............. 1 2 3 4
22. J'ai besoin d'une aide financière........ 1 2 3 4
23. Je suis tracassé(e) par des pensées que je ne peux pas m'enlever de la tête.. 1 2 3 4
24. Ma santé est meilleure maintenant qu'elle n'était il y a 5 ans................... 1 2 3 4
25. Quelqu'un a une « dent » contre moi..... 1 2 3 4
26. Circuler en ville est un problème pour moi 1 2 3 4
27. Je perds le fil de mes idées au milieu d'une conversation........................ 1 2 3 4
28. Il n'y a personne avec qui je me sente à l'aise pour parler de mes problèmes..... 1 2 3 4
29. Mes finances en ce moment même sont excellentes......................... 1 2 3 4
30. Je suis une personne très nerveuse...... 1 2 3 4
31. Mon aptitude à continuer mes activités journalières est pire qu'elle n'était il y a 5 ans 1 2 3 4
32. Je suis sûr(e) que l'on parle de moi..... 1 2 3 4
33. Je ne suis pas capable de préparer mes repas............................. 1 2 3 4
34. Apprendre des choses nouvelles est plus dur pour moi maintenant, qu'autrefois.... 1 2 3 4
35. Personne ne partage mes préoccupations 1 2 3 4
36. Mes dépenses mensuelles sont si élevées que je ne peux pas payer mes factures.. 1 2 3 4
37. Je m'inquiète pour tout................ 1 2 3 4
38. J'ai moins de problème de santé que la plupart des personnes âgées que je connais 1 2 3 4
39. Quelqu'un contrôle mes pensées........ 1 2 3 4
40. Je marche sans aide................. 1 2 3 4
41. J'oublie mes rendez-vous.............. 1 2 3 4
42. Je connais des gens sur qui je peux compter si j'en ai besoin.............. 1 2 3 4

43. J'ai quelques économies ou investissements   1 2 3 4
44. Je me préoccupe des erreurs passées...   1 2 3 4
45. Durant l'année dernière, j'ai été si malade que je n'ai pas pu continuer mes activités habituelles 1 2 3 4
46. Les personnes que je ne connais pas me regardent de façon critique 1 2 3 4
47. Je peux aller vois des amis qui vivent en dehors de la ville pour un ou plusieurs jours   1 2 3 4
48. Mon esprit est aussi vif qu'avant 1 2 3 4
49. Si quelque chose m'arrivait, personne ne viendrait à mon secours 1 2 3 4

50. J'utilise des tickets repas 1 2 3 4
51. J'ai plus de hauts et de bas que la plupart des gens 1 2 3 4
52. Durant l'année dernière je suis allé(e) chez le docteur moins de 4 fois 1 2 3 4
53. Je vois des choses que les autres ne voient pas 1 2 3 4
54. Je vais voir mes amis chez eux 1 2 3 4
55. J'oublie de prendre mes médicaments quand je devrais 1 2 3 4
56. Je n'ai pas de relations étroites avec d'autres gens 1 2 3 4

REFERENCES

1. MORRIS (W.W.), BUCKWALTER (K.C.), CLEARY (T.A.), GILMER (J.S.), HATZ (D.L.) and STUDER (M.) : Refinement of the Iowa Self-Assessment Inventory. *The Gerontologist,* 30, 2, 243-248, 1990.
2. MORRIS (W.W.), BUCKWALTER (K.C.), CLEARY (T.A.), GILMER (J.S.), HATZ (D.L.) and STUDER (M.) : Issues related to the validation of the Iowa Self-Assessment Inventory. *Journal of Educational and Psychological Measurement,* 49, 853-861, 1989.
3. GILMER (J.S.), CLEARY (T.A.) LU (D.F.), MORRIS (W.W.), BUCKWALTER (K.C.), ANDREWS (P.), BOUTELLE (S.L.) and HATZ (D.L.) : The factor structure of the Iowa Self-Assessment Inventory. *Journal of Educational and Psychological Measurement,* 51, 365-375, 1991.
4. U.S. General Accounting Office : Comparison of the well-being of older people in three rural and urban locations. Publication No. 80-41. Washington, D.C.

PAQUID : AN INTERDISCIPLINARY EPIDEMIOLOGIC STUDY OF CEREBRAL AND FUNCTIONAL AGING (1)

Pascale BARBERGER-GATEAU (*), **Jean-François DARTIGUES** (*),
Daniel COMMENGES (*), **Michèle GAGNON** (*),
Luc LETENNEUR (*), **Christine CANET** (**),
Jean-Louis MIQUEL (**), **Chakib NEJJARI** (*),
Jean-François TESSIER (*), **Claudine BERR** (***),
Marie-José DEALBERTO (***), **Arnaud DECAMPS** (****),
Annick ALPEROVITCH (***), **Roger SALAMON** (*)

INTRODUCTION

Although about 95 % of French elderly individuals aged 65 and over are community dwellers, few longitudinal studies have focused on this important part of the aged population. In France, cross-sectional studies of the elderly population, representative of 3 regions, provided prevalence estimates of handicap (1) ; subsequent follow-up of the subjects allowed identification of risk factors of mortality and dependence, measured by loss of mobility (2). In Midi-Pyrénées, a cohort of 645 persons aged 65 and over living in rural areas followed-up for at least 4 years showed that disability, subjective health and social involvement were independent predictors of mortality ; loss of autonomy was related to age, somatic pathologies but also low socio-

Address correspondence to : Pascale Barberger-Gateau, INSERM U. 330, Université de Bordeaux II, 146, rue Léo-Saignat, 33076 Bordeaux Cedex (France).

(*) INSERM U. 330, Université de Bordeaux II, 146, rue Léo-Saignat, 33076 Bordeaux Cedex (France).
(**) Laboratoire de Santé Publique Dentaire, Université de Bordeaux II, 146, rue Léo-Saignat, 33076 Bordeaux Cedex (France).
(***) INSERM U. 169, 16 bis, avenue Paul-Vaillant-Couturier, 94807 Villejuif Cedex (France).
(****) Centre de Gériatrie, CHR de Bordeaux, 33210 Lormont (France).

(1) **Acknowledgements :** The PAQUID research program is funded by the Fondation de France, Sandoz laboratories, AXA Insurance Company, the French Ministery of Research and Technology, the National Medical Insurance Companies CNAMTS and MSA, the Brain Institute, the Regional Council of Aquitaine, the General Councils of Gironde and Dordogne, the Regional Direction of Sanitary and Social Affairs of Aquitaine, the Inter-Firms Pension Aid Fund, CAPIMMEC and the National Institute of Medical Research (INSERM).

economic level and feeling of uselessness (3). However physical ability is not the only component of loss of autonomy in the aged : deterioration in cognitive functioning, and especially senile dementia of the Alzheimer type (SDAT), plays an important role in the burden of dependence (4) and is one of the major factors of institutionalization (5). However, the respective part played by physical or mental impairment, psychological distress such as depression, and social support, in the disability process and the resulting handicap is not yet known, and it requires longitudinal studies (6) ; these studies must focus simultaneously on the physical, psychological and social components of aging. This approach has been used in the PAQUID (« Personnes Agées QUID ») project. PAQUID is an epidemiologic cohort study of aging, with two main goals :

1) To study normal and pathological brain aging, by repeated psychometric measures of cognitive functioning and depression, and to identify prevalent and incident cases of Alzheimer's disease (AD). Follow-up will provide information on risk factors of cognitive decline, and perhaps identify early stages of senile dementia, where a preventive action could be feasible.

2) To describe the disability process after the age of 65, and identify its main risk factors and consequences, measured by institutionalization and mortality. Of particular interest is the relationship between the physical, cognitive, depressive and social components of dependence.

The objective of the present paper is to describe briefly the PAQUID project, and the specific sub-projects that have been developed using the subjects of the cohort. Such a research is a very long, ambitious and costly enterprise. It is therefore opened to other fields of research such as genetics, biochemistry, odontology, pneumology, ... leading to a multidisciplinary research team.

GENERAL METHODOLOGY OF THE PAQUID COHORT

The target population of PAQUID is the community population aged 65 and over, living in two departments of France : Gironde and Dordogne. A three-step sampling procedure stratified upon age, sex and size of urban units, led to 5 557 subjects, living in 75 different parishes of the departments ; 68.9 % agreed to participate in Gironde and 65.5 % in Dordogne, leading to a final sample of 3 777 individuals.

The management of the cohort is operated by INSERM U. 330 in Bordeaux. A one-hour home interview was carried by trained psychologists. Variables registered at baseline include socio-demographic factors, living conditions and habits, social network and support, social involvement, life satisfaction ; health status was assessed by hearing and visual impairment, dependence in Activities of Daily Living (ADL [7]) and Instrumental Activities of Daily Living (IADL [8]), subjective health, mobility, Rosow and Breslau scale (9), main symptomatologies and medications. Depressive symptomatology was assessed by the CES-D scale (10). A battery of psychometric tests was then administered, and included Folstein et al's Mini-Mental State Examination (MMSE [11]), to assess general cognitive functioning, followed by specific explorations of visual memory (Benton's Visual Retention Test [12]), verbal memory (Wechsler's Paired-Associates [13]), verbal fluency (Isaac's Set Test [14]), visuo-spatial attention (Zazzo [15]) and simple logical reasoning (Wechsler's Digit Symbol [16]).

Details about the methodology can be found elsewhere (17, 18, 19).

DSM-III criteria were applied, to screen for potentially demented patients. Patients who met the DSM III criteria for dementing syndromes were then seen by a neurologist who filled in the NINCDS-ADRDA criteria to precise the etiology of the deterioration (probable or possible Alzheimer's disease). All the subjects of the cohort are then followed-up for at least five years.

The 2 792 subjects living in Gironde underwent a baseline interview between January 1988 and March 1989. The first year follow-up was then carried on, using the same procedure, adding some variables such as life events in the past year, for 66 % of the subjects. For the remainder of the cohort, basic information, death and its cause, change of address, and institutionalization were obtained by a phone interview to the subject or to a proxy. The second year follow-up is now going on with a mailed questionnaire : variables of interest are institutionalization, hospitalization in the past year, main pathologies, mobility, ADL and IADL. The baseline interview has been completed in 1990 for the subjects of Dordogne.

MAJOR RESULTS

Detailed information about the first data of the study can be found in (18, 19, 20). The main results are :
– The strong inverse relationship between educational level, and the prevalence of dementia, after adjustment for age and sex : it decreases from 11.6 % in uneducated people, to 0.9 % in those who received at least 5 years of formal education (19).
– The major role played by depression and cognitive functioning in dependence, whichever the functional assessment scale used to measure dependence (18) ; in both women and men, 50 % of the subjects who are dependent on at least one of the IADL score less than 24 on the MMSE against 13.4 % only in the subjects who are completely independent.

A relationship between aluminium in drinking water and the prevalence of Alzheimer's disease was also found (21), but further analyses are still needed. Aluminium concentrations and other components are currently measured in water supplies of each parish. Complementary information about drinking and nutritional habits will be included in the next follow-up.

All these results are limited by the fact that we are dealing only with a community sample : confounding factors, related to institutionalization, could explain or weaken some of these relationships. Moreover, prevalence data in the community are influenced by the incidence of the disease under study (dementia or loss of autonomy), but also by the mean duration of the disease in that population, which in itself is related to death or institutionalization. For those reasons, we are now carrying the same project named PAVIN, on a representative sample of institutionalized elderly in Gironde.

THE PAVIN PROJECT IN INSTITUTIONALIZED ELDERLY

PAVIN (Personnes Agées Vivant en Institutions) is not really a sub-project of PAQUID, as it deals with different subjects, but can be viewed as a complementary study. A sample of 40 institutions was randomly selected in Gironde, after stratification according to the type of housing : retirement house with or without medical care, nursing home, psychiatric hospital, care family. In each institution patients are randomly drawn among the residents, to lead to 360 individuals. These subjects will undergo the same investigation as the PAQUID subjects, and will be followed-up. Data collection has started in June 1990.

Outcome of institutionalization will be assessed in terms of mortality, discharge to home and hospitalization. This study is coordinated with the International Collaborative Effort on Nursing Home Outcome, managed by Dr. J. van Nostrand at the National Center for Health Statistics (22). Alltogether, PAQUID and PAVIN will provide a comprehensive view of the elderly population of Gironde, and will give prevalence estimates by age and sex, of disability and dementia, whichever the place of residence. Moreover, levels of dependence in each type of institution will be known, allowing for international comparisons.

STUDY OF GENETIC FACTORS IN SDAT

Among the different hypotheses about the possible causes of SDAT that have been proposed, the genetic hypothesis has received considerable attention. The study of pedigrees of families with early onset AD (23) showed that the pattern of distribution of the disease was in agreement with a monogenic autosomal dominant inheritance. Linkage studies (24) performed on these families suggested a relationship between familial AD and a locus on chromosome 21. However, these results were not replicated by other studies (25). Discordant results were also found in case-control studies when the frequency of dementia was compared between first degree relatives of cases and controls (26, 27). The use of different methodologies and the presence of biases may explain in part the diversity of these findings.

Major selection biases observed in case-control studies will be avoided in a population based prospective study like PAQUID because the selection of the families will be done independently of the SDAT status of the subject.

The hypothesis of a genetic contribution to SDAT will be studied by asking subjects or a proxy whether their parents or siblings exhibited dementia signs (e.g., memory problems, aphasia, agnosia, disorientation and behavior disorders). The age of parents and siblings will be collected as well as the parent's age at the time of the subject's birth. Because the main feature of SDAT is its late-onset, data analyses have to be performed with censored data. Several methods were developed in order to take into account the problems of censorship.

To assess the role of genetic factors, the familial association has to be initially demonstrated. Two tests were developed for this purpose. The first test is based on the evaluation of the bivariate survival function of a parent-child pair, which allows for the computation of a coefficient of association (28). The second test is based on a logistic regression model that allows to test for familial factors while adjusting on other variables. Other statistical methods were also developed to examine the type of transmission of SDAT. A model of transmission based on the monogenic dominant hypothesis was designed. This model was characterized by the fact that censorship was taken into account for both parents and children.

SPECIFIC SUBPROJECTS OF PAQUID

Aside from the data collection designed to fulfill the main objectives of PAQUID, several specific projects have been developed with other research teams. These projects require an additional data collection, which may be performed for part or for the total cohort.

Bank of sera

Given the difficulty of obtaining definite diagnosis criteria for Alzheimer's disease, other than by autopsy or brain biopsy, a great interest is placed on the research of specific peripheric markers of the disease. These markers would be of particular interest for the early detection, when some therapeutic drugs could be tested, and help to understand the disease process. Unfortunately, no specific marker could be identified, until now, despite intensive research : the main field of investigation concerned peripheric markers of the cholinergic system, measured by the activity of choline acetyltransferase, but also less specific markers of immunologic or neuroendocrine disorders like the thyroid metabolism (29, 30).

For these reasons, we set up a blood collection among the PAQUID subjects who agreed to participate, with two objectives :
1) The immediate measure of two different aspects of metabolism related to aging and cognitive functions : thyroid disorders and free radicals production. Hypothyroidism is often responsible for cognitive deterioration in the aged, but high TSH levels have also been found to be associated with Alzheimer's disease, independently of a thyroid disorder (30). Free radicals are involved in general human aging, but could play a major role in cerebral aging (31). The enzymatic systems can be assessed by measuring Cu/Zn superoxide dismutase (SOD-1) and glutathion peroxidase (GSH-Px) activity in the red cells ; selenium is involved as a cofactor in the activity of the latter, and can be measured in serum or red cells.
2) The constitution of a sera bank of a few frozen blood samples for each individual. Follow-up of the subjects will allow the identification of clinically diagnosed Alzheimer's disease cases, which will then be compared to controls for different parameters of their serum, allowing perhaps for the identification of peripheric markers present in the serum prior to the clinical onset of the disease. The choice of the parameters to be measured will depend on the progress in knowledge about the disease process at that time.

Among the 2 792 PAQUID subjects of Gironde, 35 % agreed to give a blood sample. For each subject, 10 tubes of serum of 1.5 ml are frozen at − 180° C. TSH measure is actually conducted by radioimmunologic assay. For the study of free radical metabolism (in collaboration with INSERM U. 169 and CNRS URA 227 in Paris) additional blood samples with immediate separation of red cells and plasma are currently collected in 400 subjects. The preliminary results in 276 individuals show that a high level of TSH (> 4.5 ug/ml) was found in 8 % of the subjects, and a low level (< 0.4 ug/ml) in 4.3 %. Further investigation and follow-up is required to study the correlations of the measure with the clinical or psychometric characteristics of the subjects.

Study of Parkinson's disease

Parkinson's disease is one of the most frequent neurologic pathologies in the aged, but its prevalence in the community, its environmental risk factors and its consequences on cognitive functioning are not yet well known (32). The possible role of some agricultural toxics, like MPTP, has been raised (33). Dementia has often been found associated with Parkinson's disease and raises the question of its association with Alzheimer's disease, and perhaps of some common physiopathological mechanisms or risk factors (34). The study design of PAQUID allowed us to set up a complementary investigation of possible cases of Parkinson's disease and paired controls, which aims to give prevalence and incidence estimates of the disease, study its correlations with some environmental factors, and with cognitive deterioration.

Possible cases of Parkinson's disease among the PAQUID subjects are screened through two kinds of questions : complaining of symptoms of stiffness, slowness or resting tremor ; and anti-Parkinsonian medication intake. All these patients are then investigated by a neurologist, to eliminate false positive cases ; false negative cases are supposed to be very scarse with that screening procedure, and probably detected during the next follow-up of the cohort. Each case is paired with two not demented age and sex matched controls. Cognitive functioning is assessed in both cases and controls by a battery of psychometric tests, including among others the MMSE. A self-administered questionnaire includes several questions about past exposure to potential risk factors such as place of residence, well-water drinking, smoking, infectious diseases, professional exposure, agricultural toxics, nutritional habits.

The case-control study is completed by follow-up of the individuals, to identify the clinical evolutive patterns of Parkinson's disease and their health care use in the community. Among the 2 792 PAQUID subjects of Gironde, 74 (2.6 %) were taking anti-Parkinsonian drugs at the baseline interview ; phone interview to the general practitioners in charge of the patients revealed that 42 subjects took the drugs for other reasons than Parkinson's disease (mainly vascular diseases).

The remaining 32 cases would lead to a prevalence estimate of the disease of 1.14 % in the community, excluding institutionalized elderly. On the other hand, 6 % of the cohort answered « yes » to the question about resting tremor, and 10.3 % complained of slowness or stiffness in usual activity ; 2.8 % gave a positive answer to both questions. Further investigation and follow-up of the subjects will probably determine an additional percentage of undiagnosed Parkinson cases among them.

Sleep apnea and dementia

Sleep Apnea Syndrome (SAS) can be defined by the existence of at least 5 pauses of 10 seconds or more in respiration, per hour of sleep (35). The frequency of the syndrome although not well known, increases with age and has been found higher in demented patients (36), raising the question of its correlations as a contributory cause or consequence of the disease. For that reason, a complementary study of sleep patterns of the PAQUID subjects was undertaken, in collaboration with INSERM U. 169.

To detect potential cases of SAS, several items were used in a questionnaire, attached to the second year postal follow-up, exploring sleep apneas detected by the spouse, snoring and diurnal sleeping, which are frequently associated with SAS. Validation of the questionnaire by polysomnographic recording in 60 « cases » and controls will provide information on discriminative value of the questions. Selected items will give an estimate of the prevalence of SAS in community dwellers aged 65 and over, and allow-cross-sectional correlations with cognitive functioning. Subsequent follow-up will identify if the incidence of dementia or other disorders is increased in SAS patients.

Study of asthmatic patients : Paquidasm

The aim of this project is to describe the asthmatic patients among the PAQUID population. Indeed clinical characteristics, risk factors and disability related to asthma are insufficiently known in the elderly (37). In a preliminary approach, the survey concerns patients receiving a treatment for asthma. Among the whole population (n = 2 792) 88 people have been identified as receiving anti-asthmatic drugs. To assess the diagnosis of asthma, a phone interview to the general practitioner in charge of the patient was done. We used a very simple questionnaire to confirm the asthma diagnosis, to specify the importance of the disease, the number of consultations, and the possible association with another chest disease.

Asthma diagnosis has been confirmed in 50 patients : 46 % of them had another respiratory disease associated. Asthmatic patients differ from other PAQUID subjects for sex, residential area, socio-professional category, subjective health and importance of their disability. A complementary study is being undertaken to assess these differences by comparing asthmatic patients with non asthmatic paired controls. In a further step of the project we intend to focus our attention not only on treated patients but also on other asthmatic patients. Later this survey will be extended to the other geographical area of the PAQUID project and to institutionalized elderly.

Paquident : a dental project

Adequate nutritional intake is a factor of healthy aging and is probably protective against many degenerative disorders. Nutritional intake has even been suspected of playing a role against aging diseases such as cognitive decline (38, 39). However, it is often limited by dental impairments, or inadequate prostheses. For that reason, a team of dentists set up the Paquident study, which aims at describing the dental characteristics of the patients and assess the consequences of their diet. The initial group consisted in subjects living in the Gironde region, having accepted the one year follow-up of PAQUID, and a home visit for Paquident.

A questionnaire revealed hygiene habits (toothbrush, dental floss...), dental care (number of dental visits per year...) and enabled the evaluation of the use of dentures. A clinical examination described the dental state of the subject, accounting for caries, paradontopathies and general dental state. This dental information, in association with the medical information from PAQUID, enabled us to attain the objectives of this study, to be carried on over three years. Within the field of etiologic research, the second objective of this study will be to do a follow-up testing of the hypothesis of a relationship between dental defects, malnutrition and cerebral deterioration. The eventual results will be compared to similar types of studies (40) in order to validate, to begin with, the collected information.

CONCLUSION

The PAQUID project led to the constitution of a cohort of 3 800 individuals aged 65 and over, representative of two departments of the South-West of France. The survey protocol, the organization of the patients' interviews and follow-up, and data processing are managed by a team of epidemiologists, neurologists, statisticians and gerontologists, with the cooperation of the regional and departmental directions of social and sanitary affairs. Far beyond the initial objectives of PAQUID, the study design allowed introduction of new research projects, requiring only a minimum of additional information, either on a part or for the total of subjects of the cohort, or on characteristics of the area of residence, like water supply. Retrospective case-control studies are also possible, owing to the prevalent or incident cases of disease in the cohort, like SDAT or Parkinson's disease ; they are not biased by a recruitment limited to hospitalized or consulting patients. Inclusion of new data at each step of the follow-up is possible. One limit of such a study is the consent of the subjects : even if agreement is rather easily obtained for baseline interview and yearly follow-up, addition of home or phone interviews, at increasing rate, exhausts the elderly. For that reason, specific sub-projects must be limited and carefully discussed before implementation. Many research axes may however be investigated, using the data already collected and without requiring any additional information, like pharmacoepidemiology. On that condition, PAQUID is a project opened to researchers from the various fields of aging.

REFERENCES

1. COLVEZ A., ROBINE J., VARNOUX N. : Epidémiologie de l'incapacité des personnes âgées et facteurs associés. *Gérontol. Soc.*, 1984, 50-65.
2. COLVEZ A., ROBINE J., JOUAN-FLAHAUT C. : Risque et facteur de risque d'incapacité aux âges élevés. *Rev. Epidém. et Santé Publ.*, 1987, 35, 257-269.
3. GRAND A., GROSCLAUDE P., BOCQUET H., POUS J., ALBAREDE J.-L. : Predictive value of life events, psychosocial factors and self-rated health on disability in an elderly rural french population. *Soc. Sci. Med.*, 1988, 27, 1337-1342.
4. HAY J., ERNST R. : The economic cost of Alzheimer's disease. *Am. J. Public Health*, 1987, 77, 1169-75.
5. BARBERGER-GATEAU P., GROLIER L., MAURICE S., BORDE C., SALAMON R., GALLEY P. : L'hospitalisation en court-séjour des personnes âgées : premier pas vers l'entrée en institution ? *Rev. Epidém. et Santé Publ.*, 1990. In press.
6. EVANS J. : Prevention of age-associated loss of autonomy : epidemiological approaches. *J. Chron. Dis.*, 1984, 37, 353-363.
7. KATZ S., DOWNS T.D., CASH H.R., GROTZ R.C. : Progress in development of the index of ADL. *Gerontologist*, 1970, 10, 20-30.
8. LAWTON M.P., BRODY E.M. : Assessment of older people : self-maintaining and instrumental activities of daily living. *Gerontologist*, 1969, 9, 179-186.
9. ROSOW I., BRESLAU N. : A Guttman health scale for the aged. *J. Gerontol.*, 1966, 21, 556-559.
10. RADLOFF L.S. : The CES-D scale : a self-report depression scale for research in the general population. *Appl. Psychol. Meas.*, 1977, 1, 385-401.
11. FOLSTEIN M.F., FOLSTEIN S.E., MCHUGH P.R. : Mini-Mental-State : a practical method for grading the cognitive state of patients for the clinician. *J. Psychiatr. Res.*, 1975, 12, 189-198.
12. BENTON A. : Manuel pour l'application du test de rétension visuelle. Applications cliniques et expérimentales. *Centre de Psychologie Appliquée*, Paris, 1965.
13. WECHSLER D. : A standardized memory scale for clinical use. *J. Psychol.*, 1945, 19, 87-95.
14. ISAACS B., AKHTAR A. : The Set Test : a rapid test of mental function in old people. *Age Aging*, 1972, 1, 222-6.
15. ZAZZO R. : Test des deux barrages. Actualités pédagogiques et psychologiques. *Delachaux et Nestlé*, vol. 7, Neufchatel, 1964.
16. WECHSLER D. : Wechsler Adult Intelligence Scale Manual. In : *Psychological Corporation, eds*, New York, 1981.
17. DARTIGUES J., BARBERGER-GATEAU P., GAGNON M., ALPEROVITCH A., COMMENGES D., DECAMPS A., SALAMON R. : PAQUID : étude épidémiologique du vieillissement normal et pathologique. *Rev. Gériat.*, 1991. In press.
18. BARBERGER-GATEAU P., CHASLERIE A., DARTIGUES J., COMMENGES D., GAGNON M., SALAMON R. : Health measures correlates in a French elderly community population : the Paquid study. *Gerontological Society of America*, Boston (USA), 1990.
19. GAGNON M., LETENNEUR L., DARTIGUES J., COMMENGES D., ORGOGOZO J., BARBERGER-GATEAU P., ALPEROVITCH A., DECAMPS A., SALAMON R. : The validity of the Mini-Mental State Examination (MMS) as a screening instrument for cognitive impairment and dementia in French elderly community residents. *Neuroepidemiology*, 1990, 9, 143-150.
20. BARBERGER-GATEAU P., DARTIGUES J., CHASLERIE A., GAGNON M., SALAMON R., ALPEROVITCH A. : Conditions de vie et état de santé d'une population âgée au domicile ; premiers résultats du projet Paquid. *Rev. Gériatr.*, 1991. In press.
21. MICHEL P., COMMENGES D., DARTIGUES J., GAGNON M. : Study of the relationship between Alzheimer's disease and aluminium in drinking water. 2nd International Conference on Alzheimer's disease. Toronto (Canada), 1990 (abstr. n° 47). *Neurobiol. Aging*, 1990, 11, 264.
22. HING E., SEKSCENSKI E., STRAHAN G. : (National Center for Health Statistics). The National Nursing Home Survey, 1985, Summary for the United States. *Vital Health Statistics*, series 13, 1989, 97. *Public Health Service*, Washington.
23. POWELL D., FOLSTEIN M. : Pedigree study of familial Alzheimer's disease. *J. Neurogenet.*, 1984, 1, 189-97.
24. ST GEORGE-HYSLOP P., TANZI R., POLINSKY R. : The genetic defect causing familial Alzheimer's disease maps on chromosome 21. *Science*, 1987, 235, 885-9.
25. SCHELLENBERG G., BIRD T., WIJSMAN E. : Absence of linkage of chromosome 21 q21 markers to familial Alzheimer's disease. *Science*, 1988, 241, 1507-10.
26. HESTON L., MASTRI A., ANDERSON E., WHITE J. : Dementia of the Alzheimer type. *Arch. Gen. Psychiatry*, 1981, 38, 1085-90.
27. CHANDRA V., BELL P., LAZAROFF A., SCHOENBERG B. : Case control study of late onset « probable Alzheimer's disease ». *Neurology*, 1987, 37, 1295-1300.
28. COMMENGES D., LETENNEUR L. : Coefficient d'association pour données censurées : application à la maladie d'Alzheimer. *21es Journées de Statistiques*, Rennes (France), 22-26 mai 1989.

29. TOLEDANO J. : Recent views on possible early biochemical detection of SDAT. In : A. Bes, J. Cahn and R. Cahn, Eds. *Senile dementia : early detection*, Libbey, London, 1986, pp. 211-215.
30. CHRISTIE J.E., WHALLEY L.S., BENNIE J., DICK H., BLACKBURN I.M., BLACKWORD D.H.R., FINCK G. : Characteristics plasma hormone changes. *Br. J. Psychiatry*, 1987, 150, 674-681.
31. HARMAN D. : Free radical theory of aging : the « free-radical » diseases. *Age*, 1984, 7, 111-31.
32. BARBEAU A., ROY M., CLOUTIER T., PLASSE L., PARIS S. : Environmental and genetic factors on the etiology of Parkinson's disease. *Adv. Neurol.*, 1986, 45, 299-300.
33. RAJPUT A., VITTI R., STERN W. : Early onset Parkinson's disease in Saskatchewan. Environmental considerations for etiology. *Can. J. Neurol. Sci.*, 1986, 13, 312-316.
34. BOLLER F., MIZUTANI T., ROESSMANN V., GAMBETTI P. : Parkinson's disease, dementia and Alzheimer's disease : clinico pathological correlations. *Ann. Neurol.*, 1979, 7, 329-335.
35. KRIEGER J. : Les syndromes d'apnées du sommeil chez l'adulte. *Bull. Eur. Physiopathol. Resp.*, 1986, 22, 147-189.
36. ERKINJUNTTI T., PARTINEN M., SULKAVA R., TELAVIKI T., SALMI T., TILVIS R. :Sleep apnea in multi-infarct dementia and Alzheimer's disease. *Sleep*, 1987, 10, 419-425.
37. Public Health Service : Prevalence of selected chronic respiratory conditions USA 1979. *Vital and Health Statistics Series*, Atlanta, 1973, 84.
38. ABALAN F. : Alzheimer's disease and malnutrition : a new etiological hypothesis. *Med. Hypoth.*, 1984, 15, 385-93.
39. LA FOURNIERE F. (DE), PIETTE F., LEROUX P. : Syndromes démentiels d'origine métabolique. L'exemple des dysthyroïdies et des carences en vitamines B12. *Alzheimer Actualités*, 1990, 45, 5-7.
40. KANDELMAN D., LEPAGE Y. : Demographic, social and cultural factors influencing the elderly to seek dental treatment. *Int. Dent. J.*, 1982, 32, 360-368.

FOR WHOM IS RETIREMENT STRESSFUL ? FINDINGS FROM THE NORMATIVE AGING STUDY

Raymond BOSSE' [1, 2], **Michael R. LEVENSON** [3, 4],
Avron SPIRO III [1, 4], **Carolyn M. ALDWIN** [3],
Daniel K. MROCZEK [1, 5]

Summary. – A minority of male retirees have reported finding retirement stressful. This study addressed the task of characterizing that minority. Two types of retirement stress were distinguished : **transition stress,** the stressfulness of the retirement event itself among those who experienced it within one year of the survey, and **state stress,** the daily retirement hassles experienced by all retirees within the past three months. Social, situational, and personality variables were examined as predictors of both retirement transition and state stress. The study sample were 407 male participants in the Normative Aging Study who responded to mailed surveys in 1985 or 1988. The social variables most strongly associated with retirement transition and state stress were the experience of more stressful life events in the past year and more daily hassles. These were more important than (perhaps mediators of) variables assessing the circumstances surrounding retirement (e.g., the reason for retirement). Different personality descriptors from MMPI-2 clinical and validity scales were associated with retirement transition vs. state stress. Overall, men who reported the retirement transition to be stressful were less defensive, more introverted, and more depressed. On the other hand, state stress retirees had higher scores on the psychopathic deviate, psychasthenia, and mania, and lower scores on the lie and schizophrenia scales. Personality and social variables were found to be independent associates of retirement stress, demonstrating the importance of both person and environmental contributions to the perception of stress. (Facts and Research in Gerontology 1992)

Key-words : retirement, stress, aging, personality.

1. Normative Aging Study, Department of Veterans Affairs Medical Center, 200 Springs Road, Building 70, Bedford, MA 01730, USA.
2. Hellenic College, Brookline, MA.
3. Human Development & Family Studies, University of California, Davis, CA.
4. School of Public Health, Boston University, Boston, MA.
5. Psychology Department, Boston University, Boston, MA.

Support for this research was provided by the Medical Research Service of the Department of Veterans Affairs and by a grant from the National Institute on Aging (AG02287).

INTRODUCTION

Researchers at the Normative Aging Study have studied the health consequences of retirement for over ten years. Initial research, focusing on various measures of physical health, found few, if any, significant effects of retirement. While retirees in general report poorer health, this cannot be linked to retirement **per se.** For example, there were no significant differences in self-rated health changes between retirees and workers after controlling for retirement prompted by poor health (1). This finding held even when the population was stratified by white and blue-collar occupation (2). The frequency of somatic complaints increased slightly both in men who retired and those who continued working over a 3-5 year interval (3). Increases in health complaints were not associated with mandatory retirement and were not affected by former blue-collar vs. white-collar status, financial situation, or current participation in part-time work (2, 3). However, retirees as a group did have slightly greater mean increases in blood pressure and in cholesterol level, although this was within the normal range and did not translate into a greater incidence of hypertension among retirees relative to workers (4).

Having failed to demonstrate deleterious physical health consequences of retirement, we next considered mental health symptoms, assessed with the SCL-90-R (5), a widely used measure. Interestingly, retirees reported more psychological symptoms than workers, particularly on the subscales assessing depression, somatization, phobic anxiety, and obsessive-compulsive behavior. Differences in these subscales remained significant, even controlling for the retirees' worse physical health status, and did not appear to vary by length of retirement. Men who retired off-time, either early (before age 62) or late (after age 65), reported the highest number of symptoms, while late workers (those employed after the age of 65) reported the fewest symptoms (6). From this cross-sectional study, it was not clear whether retirement caused higher levels of psychological symptoms, or whether workers in poorer mental health were more likely to retire. Having collected the second wave of data in 1988, we followed up our cross-sectional findings with a longitudinal analysis (7). Specifically, we were interested in causal directionality – was retirement causing an increase in symptoms, or were those in poorer mental health retiring earlier ? In our analyses, we defined three groups, based on employment status in 1985 and in 1988. Continuing workers were employed at both surveys, recent retirees were employed in 1985 and retired in 1988, and long-term retirees were retired at both surveys.

We found that it was not the transition from work to retirement status which prompted the higher symptom level of the retirees, because there were no changes in mental health symptoms for any of the groups from T1 to T2, irrespective of change in work or retirement status. Nor was it the workers with more mental health symptoms who were more prone to retire, because the 187 men who were working in 1985 and retired in 1988 did not differ in mental health symptoms from those working at both surveys. Rather, it was the long-term retirees, those who were retired at both surveys, who reported more symptoms than either the workers or the recent retirees. We also found that those who retired early or for reasons of physical health reported more mental health symptoms at both occasions.

Although these findings might be interpreted as a cohort effect, such that retirement is associated with more distress in older cohorts than younger ones, we suggested an explanation which contrasts retirement as a **state** with retirement as a **transition.** This interpretation proposes that the recent retirees (less than 3 years) are in **transition** from work to retirement. They did not find retirement stressful, there may even be a bit of euphoria as frequently suggested in the literature, followed by disenchantment after being in the **state** of retirement for an extended period (8, 9). The disenchantment promotes some distress which is manifested in increased mental health symptoms. We will be better able to answer this question when the collection of our third wave of data is completed by the end of 1991. With these data, we will be able to examine changes in the mental health symptoms of the men who have passed from short-term or transitional retirement to the long-term state of retirement.

In the meantime, having found greater mental health symptoms among long-term retirees, we were prompted to investigate the stressfulness of retirement. Using the Elders Life Stress Inventory (ELSI) (10) which asks about stressful life events experienced in the past year, we found that the respondent's own retirement and spouse's retirement ranked 30th and 31st respectively on the 31 − item ELSI. This coincided with the report of Matthews and her associates (11) that retirement ranked 28th among 34 stressful life events which respondents had experienced at some point in their lifetime. (See also Neugarten [12]).

It is important to note that although retirement tended to be ranked as less stressful than other life events by most respondents and declared not to be stressful for a great majority of retirees, it nevertheless was stressful for a sizeable minority. Bosse' et al. (13) found 30.4 % of the men who retired in the past year (N = 200) reported retirement to be « somewhat », « very » or « extremely » stressful compared to 69.6 % who found retirement « not at all » or « a little » stressful. Comparable percentages were found for longer-term retirees with 68.9 % reporting no retirement-related problems during the previous three months, while 31.1 % reported a variety of problems such as boredom or finances.

Though these findings suggest that retirement may not be generally stressful, they leave unanswered more specific questions regarding retirement stress. The evidence now indicates that the research questions should no longer be general questions such as « Is retirement stressful ? » or « How stressful is retirement ? », but more specific questions such as « For whom is retirement stressful ? », and « What are the predictors of retirement stress ? » In other words, « What are the circumstances of the retirement event or the personal characteristics of the retirees for whom retirement is stressful and in what specific ways is retirement stressful for these retirees ? » Thus, one can examine both the social and personality predictors of retirement stress, in both its transitional and state aspects.

Based on our earlier work, we have made a conceptual distinction between retirement as a transition and retirement as a state. That distinction was originally based in part on the phases of retirement adaptation frequently alluded to in the retirement literature (e.g., 8, 9). In our earlier work, the distinction was operationalized based on the three-year interval between our surveys. That is, short-term retirees were those retired less than three years, while long-term retirees were those retired three years or more.

In the present context, we are concerned with identifying men who experience stress as a result of retirement. In our view, there are two sorts of stress that might be associated with retirement, the one experienced by men who have recently retired (i.e., retirement transition stress), and the other experienced by those men who have been retired for some time (i.e., retirement state stress).

Although we planned to organize the following review according to our transition-state distinction, this was not possible because most studies do not make this distinction. Length of retirement often is treated as a continuous variable, and included in analyses for purposes of statistical control. Thus, our review is organized by domains that have been identified in previous studies as being of relevance to retirement stress in general. Where possible, we will make distinctions between transition and state stress.

Predictors of Retirement Stress

Research has begun to provide partial answers to the question of who finds retirement stressful. For instance, women who were dissatisfied with retirement (presumably experiencing stress) were reported to have less **education** and **income,** fewer **social contacts** and poorer physical and mental **health** than the satisfied retirees (14). Men who found retirement stressful were those whose retirement was unexpected or **involuntary,** who were of **lower socioeconomic status** (15), who had experienced **more stressful events** in their lifetime (15, 16), and who reported less **social support** (16). Among NAS men who made the « transition » to retirement during the past year, poor health and finances were predictors of retirement stress (13).

Prior work stress. Wheaton (17) reported an inverse relationship between prior work stress and mental health in retirement for men but not for women. Specifically, he found that men who retired from low stress jobs reported an increase in mental health symptoms after retirement, while retirement had a cathartic effect for men who retired from high stress jobs and who subsequently reported a decrease in mental health symptoms. Jt should be noted, however, that Wheaton's research relates principally to work rather than to retirement stress.

Circumstances of the retirement event. The circumstances of retirement may play an important part in determining the stressfulness of that event. For example, early retirement, defined as retirement prior to age 62 – that is, before eligibility for pension benefits – may lead to more retirement stress than « on time » retirement. Men who retired early were found to report significantly lower income, less happiness and life satisfaction, or were more likely to have retired for health reasons compared to men who retired at or after age 65 (18). More generally, men who have relatively little control over the timing of the retirement event may find retirement commensurately more stressful.

Personality and retirement stress. It has been speculated for a long time that personality is related to retirement adjustment. Five types of male retirees were proposed by Reichard, Livson, and Peterson : the mature, the rocking-chair, the armored, the angry and the self-haters (19). This was among the first suggestions that personality was related to retirement adjustment, a view which has been expressed periodically since then but never explored systematically.

At the NAS, we examined whether neuroticism and extraversion, as assessed by the EPI-Q in 1975 (20), could predict problems in retirement state or retirement transition stress in 1985. However, in this earlier study (13), these personality traits did not predict either measure of retirement stress.

Present Study. Although the preceding studies (13, 15, 18) shed important new light on the question of retirement stress they are all limited in the number and combination of retirement stress predictors available to the investigators.

The present study has the advantage of utilizing the well-documented population of an on-going longitudinal study that spans nearly 30 years. Data are available on the key predictors of retirement stress suggested thus far in the retirement literature. The major focus of our prior research on retirement stress (13) was primarily to specify the extent to which retirement was considered stressful, and only secondarily to specify predictors of such stress. Since that initial publication, a new wave of retirement data is available on the NAS population, as is a more powerful measure of personality, the MMPI-2 (21). It was our expectation that the introduction of a wider selection of personality variables than we were able to utilize previously would reveal relations between personality traits and retirement stress.

In the present study, we sought to advance knowledge of specific retirement stresses and their personality and social predictors. We expanded the range of personality and social variables which may be associated with retirement transition or state stress in a larger sample of retirees than was previously available to us. The distinction between retirement transition and retirement state stress also allowed us to take into account the difference between retirement as a transition, on the one hand, and as an ongoing state, on the other.

Specifically, we expected men who were forced to retire because of health or business failures, for example, to find retirement transition or state more stressful than men who retired as planned.

In accordance with the findings of Matthews and Brown (15), we hypothesized that the experience of more stressful events in the year prior to retirement would be associated with greater retirement transition stress. An important determinant of retirement stress was expected to be the degree of control over the decision to retire. Men who were forced to retire because of age, health, business failures, or similar causes were hypothesized to find retirement more stressful than men who retired as planned.

Among the social variables that we considered is a measure of social class, indexed by blue-collar versus white-collar employment. Retirees from white-collar occupations may be more likely to find retirement stressful compared to blue-collar workers because of the greater autonomy, responsibility, and supervision of others experienced by people in these occupations. Former blue-collar workers, on the contrary, are hypothesized to find retirement less stressful because of the more arduous nature of these jobs, their taking rather than giving orders, or the greater job-related risks or stresses among some occupations. However, lower socioeconomic status in retirement among blue collar workers may obscure any such effect.

In addition to social variables, we also examined in greater depth the contribution of personality variables. The MMPI-2 (21) affords a more differentiated set of potential personality correlates of retirement stress than did the EPI-Q. In addition to the standard clinical scales, we were interested to know whether a measure of defensiveness can serve to alert investigators to a stress report minimization strategy by respondents. The MMPI K (subtle defensiveness) scale seems a promising candidate for such a measure (22). In general, we were interested to determine whether personality and social variables were independent predictors of perceived stress in retirement, both in terms of the transition from work to retirement, and in terms of retirement as a state.

MATERIAL AND METHODS

Sample

The male retirees who were the respondents in this study are participants in the Normative Aging Study (NAS) panel of the Department of Veterans Affairs in Boston, Massachusetts. Begun in 1963, the NAS is an interdisciplinary, longitudinal study of 2,280 men. Its primary objective is the investigation of biomedical and psychosocial aspects of aging. Since NAS participants were originally selected for good health and geographic stability, distributions of educational attainment, occupational level, and occupational stability are fairly similar across age cohorts. Although evenly split between white and blue collar occupations, the participants tend to be of higher social class levels than the general population from which they were drawn. The men generally have had a stable work career and many were in occupations or working for firms where employment stability was the norm. The volunteer nature of the Study, as well as its selection criteria, reduce the representativeness of the sample and thereby restrict the generalizability of its findings. On the other hand, the low attrition rate among NAS participants (less than 1 % annually) conserves the sample over time and aids the accurate description of within-individual change.

The NAS participants ranged in age from 21 to 81 at time of entry and currently range in age from 45 to 89. (More detailed descriptions of the NAS and of research findings prior to 1984 have been published [23-25]).

In the summer of 1985 the Social Survey was mailed to the 1,890 then currently active members of the NAS. Again in 1988, it was mailed to the 1,813 then active participants. After each mailing, a reminder letter was sent 3 weeks later. If the respondent still had not responded after an additional 3 weeks, another copy of the questionnaire was mailed. In 1985, 1,565 questionnaires were returned, and 1,484 in 1988, for response rates of 82.8 % and 81.9 % respectively.

The present study focused exclusively on the 407 NAS men who indicated on either the 1985 or 1988 survey that they had retired within 3 years of the survey data. This 3 year cutoff was used to coincide with the interval between the two surveys, so that a man would be included only once. Men who had retired, but returned to part-time work, were included. In 1985, 185 men had retired within the past 3 years, while 221 had retired within 3 years of the 1988 survey.

MEASURES

Independent variables

Year. To control for possible period effects due to the three-year difference between surveys, all analyses initially included a dummy variable for the 1988 survey.

Age. There was a wide range of ages (46-83). Forty-six year old retirees could have retired as young as 43, while 83 year old retirees would have had to work at least until age 80 since respondents were limited to those who had retired no more than three years prior to the study. The mean age of retired men in the 1985 survey was 63.4, while it was 63.1 for retired men in the 1988 survey (t [282] = .60, ns).

Occupation. For this study, the sample was divided into white-collar and blue-collar occupations. White-collar occupations included professional, technical, managerial, public officials and proprietors. Blue-collar occupations included clerical, craftsmen or trades, operatives and service workers. Respectively, 44 % and 38 % of the respondents in 1985 and 1988 were white collar workers. A dummy variable indicating a white-collar occupation was used in the analyses.

Reasons for retirement. Each respondent was asked to provide the principal and second most important reasons for their retirement. Their responses were grouped into seven categories : 1) health, 2) constraints on employment (e.g., loss of job or of business), 3) problems with aspects of job (e.g., dissatisfaction with pay or promotion, boredom), 4) disaffection with work role (e.g., tired of routine, worked long enough), 5) familial pressure to retire, 6) preference for leisure or new lifestyle, and 7) general readiness. These seven categories were then collapsed into three : retirement for reasons of health (1 above), for negative reasons (2-5 above), and positive reasons (6 and 7 above). Two dichotomous dummy variables were created, one indicating that the primary reason for retirement was health-related, and the other indicating that the primary reason for retirement was negative.

In addition, each respondent was also asked whether their retirement was mandatory or compulsory, and whether it was planned. Both of these variables were dichotomous.

Life events. Stressful life events were assessed by the Elders Life Stress Inventory (ELSI) (10), a 31-item list. Respondents indicated whether or not they had experienced each event during the past year, and also rated the stressfulness of those events they had experienced on a scale from 1 to 5 (« Not at all stressful » to « Extremely stressful »).

To reexamine the Matthews and Brown (15) finding that men who experienced more stressful life events also found retirement stressful, we generated a measure of life events by summing the number of events experienced by each man in the past year, excluding the event of retirement itself. The maximum score on this scale was 30 ; for men who completed at least 75 % (23) of the items, scores were prorated. Earlier work (10) has demonstrated that the simple count of events is highly correlated with the stress ratings on the ELSI.

Hassles. The survey also assessed daily stressors or « hassles » experienced in five life domains : health, marital (which could include marital problems and/or the wife's own difficulties), social relations, household finances, and work or retirement. The respondents indicated whether they had experienced a problem in any of these areas during the previous three months, and indicated how much they were troubled by that problem on a scale from 1 (« Not troubled at all ») to 7 (« The most troubled I've ever been »). (For additional information, see [26]). Ratings for four of the problem domains (health, marital, social relations, and household finances) were summed and divided by the number of valid items. The resulting measure thus provided an indicator of the stressfulness of hassles during the past several months.

Social support. Two types of social support were assessed (27). **Qualitative support** consisted of three items : 1) the number of confidants (0-5), whether or not the respondent in a time of crisis could rely on, 2) family and, 3) friends (both scored on a scale from 1-5). **Quantitative support** consisted of two types of questions : extensiveness of social networks and frequency of contact with network members. Social network questions included five items : marital status ; number of people in the household ; number of children ; number of relatives within an hour's drive ; and number of close friends. Marital status was recoded to single, currently married, previously married. The other four variables were reduced to a three-point score (0, 1, 2+). The frequency component included three items : frequency of seeing children, friends, and other relatives (0 = never, 1 = less than once a week, 2 = at least once a week).

Personality. In June 1986, the **MMPI-2** was mailed to the 1,882 then active NAS volunteers as part of the MMPI Restandardization project (21). Of the 1,882 potential respondents, 1, 550 returned questionnaires for an 82.4 % response rate. From the MMPI-2, we used three validity scales (L, K, F) and the 10 standard clinical scales : Hypochondriasis (Hs), Depression (D), Hysteria (Hy), Psychopathic Deviate (Pd), Masculinity-Femininity (Mf), Paranoia (Pa), Psychasthenia (Pt), Schizophrenia (Sc), Hypomania (Ma), Social Introversion (Si). A more detailed comparison of the NAS sample to the MMPI-2 normative sample is provided by Butcher et al. (28).

Dependent Variables

Two measures of retirement stress served as dependent variables, one assessing the stress associated with the transition to retirement within the past year, and the other assessing the extent of problems within the past three months associated with being retired.

Retirement **transition stress** was defined using the stressfulness rating (on a 1-5 scale) from the ELSI. Recall that only men who reported having retired within the past year were asked to indicate the stress associated with the event ; thus their stress rating was interpreted as indicating the stress associated with the transition to retirement. Men who did not experience the transition to retirement within the past year were defined as missing on the measure of transition stress.

Retirement **state stress** was defined using the item on hassles with retirement. In particular, we used the rating provided by men who reported a hassle with retirement during the past three months. Men who did not report a hassle with retirement in the past three months were given a score of 0.

For the 180 men with valid data on both measures of retirement stress, the correlation of transition stress with state stress was 0.49.

Analyses

The purpose of the analyses was to identify both the independent and the combined contributions of social and personality factors to the perception of retirement stress, considering both the transition to retirement and the state of retirement as outcomes. Since we had no *a priori* hypotheses about which of the factors should be most relevant, we used stepwise regression to identify them.

We began by considering the domains of social and personality variables separately, to identify the "best" predictors of the retirement stress measures. Then, once the best within-domain predictors were identified, we combined them and again used stepwise regression to identify the best predictors from the combined domains. In all of these analyses, we used the backward elimination method, in which all predictors are included initially. In successive steps, predictors which do not meet a preset significance level are eliminated from the model. Since this was an exploratory study, conducted with a relatively small sample size, we decided to use a liberal significance level. That is, a variable had to meet the .10 significance level to remain in the analysis.

RESULTS

Table 1 presents descriptive statistics for the social variables. The left-hand panel of the table presents means and standard deviations of the independent variables for men with valid data on the measure of retirement transition stress ($N = 188$). In addition, the correlation of each independent variable with transition stress is shown. In the right-hand panel of the table, corresponding values are shown for those men with valid data on the measure of retirement state stress ($N = 390$).

White-collar occupational status was modestly related to state stress but not to transition stress, as was survey year 1988. Among reasons for retirement, only an unplanned retirement was related to transition stress. Both number of negative life events and hassles ratings were strongly related to transition stress and to state stress. Neither quantitative nor qualitative social support was related to either type of stress, although the relationship between qualitative support and transition stress approached significance.

Table 2 shows the relationships of transition stress and state stress to 13 MMPI scales, including the 10 standard clinical scales and three other scales which assess evasive responding (L, F, and K). Both L and K were negatively related to state stress. Among the clinical scales, five (D, Pd, Pt, Sc, Ma) were positively related to transition stress. Pd and Pa were strongly positively related to state stress while there was a somewhat more modest relationship for Ma, Pt, Mf, and Hs.

TABLE 1

DESCRIPTIVE STATISTICS FOR SOCIAL VARIABLES,
BY TYPE OF RETIREMENT STRESS

	Transition (N = 188)			State (N = 390)		
	Mean	SD	r	Mean	SD	r
Control variables						
Year 1988 (%)	.56	.50	− .06	.56	.50	− .12*
Age	61.85	4.58	− .03	63.24	5.06	− .10
White collar (%)	.43	.50	.08	.41	.49	.11*
Reasons for Retirement (%)						
Health	.13	.34	.11	.14	.35	.09
Negative reasons	.26	.44	− .03	.30	.46	− .07
Mandatory retirement	.07	.25	.07	.11	.32	.00
Unplanned retirement	.63	.48	.16*	.65	.48	.10
Stress						
Life events	3.04	2.36	.29***	2.54	2.13	.32**
Hassles	2.21	1.76	.39***	1.98	1.66	.41**
Social Support						
Qualitative	9.70	2.80	− .13	9.93	2.75	− .08
Quantitative	11.93	2.20	− .01	11.85	2.12	− .05
Retirement Stress						
Transition stress	1.68	0.99		1.68	1.00	
State stress	1.11	1.97		1.11	1.97	

* p ≤ .05
** p ≤ .01
*** p ≤ .001

TABLE 2

DESCRIPTION STATISTICS FOR MMPI-2 PERSONALITY VARIABLES
BY TYPE OF RETIREMENT STRESS

	Transition (N = 161)			State (N = 339)		
	Mean	SD	r	Mean	SD	r
L	4.59	2.16	− .09	4.81	2.43	− .17***
F	3.60	2.33	.11	3.54	2.37	.07
K	16.66	4.47	− .15	17.16	4.55	− .13*
Hs	5.29	4.10	.14	5.11	3.91	.13*
D	19.47	5.54	.20*	19.20	5.09	.10
Hy	21.45	4.73	.13	21.51	4.63	.06
Pd	14.78	4.13	.23**	14.52	4.17	.22***
Mf	23.07	4.14	.03	22.67	4.28	.12*
Pa	8.93	2.78	.15	8.78	2.83	.05
Pt	9.28	6.96	.18*	8.44	6.74	.18***
Sc	8.09	6.54	.16*	7.69	5.98	.14*
Ma	14.80	3.73	.16*	14.43	3.64	.16**
Si	26.51	9.17	− .02	25.60	8.70	.04

* p ≤ .05
** p ≤ .01
*** p ≤ .001

Results of the stepwise regression analyses examining the relationship between social variables and the retirement stress measures are presented in Table 3, and show that social variables were significantly related to both transition stress, F (2, 148) = 11.93, p < .001, and state stress, F (3, 306) = 31.46, p < .001. Of the 11 variables initially entered in the model predicting transition stress, only the two general stress measures (life events and hassles) were significantly related (beta = .22 and .24, respectively). These two variables were also significantly related to state stress (beta = .20 and .36, respectively). For both outcomes, men who reported higher levels of life stress and hassles also reported higher levels of stress in both the transition to and the state of retirement. In addition, negative reasons for retirement was significantly negatively related to state stress (beta = −.09). In other words, men who retired because of business failure, loss of position, dissatisfaction with job or work role, or because of familial pressure, experienced less state stress in retirement. Together, the social variables accounted for a significant 14 % of the variance in retirement transition stress, and 24 % of the variance in retirement state stress.

TABLE 3

SUMMARY OF BACKWARD STEPWISE REGRESSION OF
SOCIAL VARIABLES ON RETIREMENT STRESS

	Transition (N = 151)				State (N = 310)			
	b	se	t	B	b	se	t	B
Life events	.088	.033	2.68**	.218	.182	.49	3.76***	.203
Hassles	.136	.047	2.90**	.236	.445	.066	6.76***	.364
Negative reasons for retirement					− .385	.217	− 1.78+	− .089
Intercept	1.084	.139	7.80***		− .125	.182	− 0.70	
R^2	.139				.236			
	F (2, 148) = 11.93 p < .001				F (3, 306) = 31.46 p < .001			

```
+   p ≤ .10
*   p ≤ .05
**  p ≤ .01
*** p ≤ .001
```

Similarly, stepwise regression of personality variables on the two retirement stress outcomes revealed that several traits significantly predicted both transition stress F (3, 157) = 5.75, p < .001, and state stress F (6, 332) = 6.18, p < .001 (see Table 4). Of the fourteen variables entered (survey year and 13 personality), only three were associated with transition stress. K and Si were negatively related (beta = − .19 and − . 30, respectively), while D was positively related to transition stress (beta = . 33). Thus, individuals who were defensive or introverted were less likely to report problems with the transition to retirement, while those who were depressed were more likely to report this transition as stressful. These personality variables accounted for 10 % of the variance in retirement transition stress.

Interestingly, a completely different set of personality traits was related to retirement state stress. L and Sc were negatively related (beta = − .11 and − .24, respectively), while Pd, Pt, and Ma were positively related to state stress (beta = .18, .22, and .12, respectively). In other words, individuals high on the Lie and Schizophrenia scales reported less stress with retirement, while those higher on the Psychopathic Deviate, Psychasthenia, and Mania scales were more likely to report problems in retirement. In addition, the dummy variable for survey year was significant, indicating that the men who retired within three years of 1988 reported lower levels of state stress. Personality explained 11 % of the variance in retirement state stress.

In sum, social and personality variables were related to both retirement transition and state stress. However, social variables, in particular other stressful life events and hassles, accounted for approximately twice as much variance in the outcomes as did the personality variables, when each domain was considered separately.

The final analysis combined the significant variables from the previous analyses to determine which personality and social variables were most closely associated with retirement stress (see Table 5). Again we used stepwise regression with backward elimination.

For transition stress, the independent variables included initially in the model were life events, hassles, K, D, and Si. In the final model, both life events and hassles were strongly associated with transition stress (beta = .15 and .27, respectively). However, of the three personality variables initially included, only D and Si were still significantly related to transition stress (beta = .23 and −.17, respectively) ; K was no longer associated. The final model accounted for 19 % of the variance, F (4, 152) = 9.03, < .001. This clearly indicates that both social and personality variables are independent predictors of perceptions of the stressfulness of the retirement transition.

TABLE 4

SUMMARY OF BACKWARD STEPWISE REGRESSION OF
PERSONALITY VARIABLES ON RETIREMENT STRESS

	Transition (N = 161)				State (N = 339)			
	b	se	t	B	b	se	t	B
K	− .043	.019	− 2.29*	− .193				
D	.060	.017	3.47***	.330				
Si	− .033	.011	− 2.93**	− .299				
Year					− .469	.200	− 2.34*	− .124
L					− .083	.045	− 1.86+	− .107
Pd					.082	.029	− 2.80**	.181
Pt					.062	.027	2.33*	.224
Sc					− .076	.033	− 2.31*	− .241
Ma					.064	.028	2.27*	.124
Int	2.115	.510	4.15***		.116	.691	0.17	
R2	.099				.100			
	F (3, 157) = 5.75 p < .001				F (6, 332) = 6.18 p < .001			

+ p ≤ .10
* p ≤ .05
** p ≤ .01
*** p ≤ .001

For retirement state stress, the independent variables included in the initial model were life events, hassles, negative reasons for retirement, survey year, L, Pd, Pt, Sc, and Ma. In the final model, two of the three social variables were significantly associated with state stress. Hassles and life events remained significant (beta = .38 and .13, respectively), while negative reasons for retirement was not. Of the six personality variables included, only one, Ma, remained significant (beta = .10). Together, these variables accounted for 22 % of the variance in retirement transition stress, **F** (3, 302) = 29.27, **p** < .001.

TABLE 5

SUMMARY OF BACKWARD STEPWISE REGRESSION OF
SOCIAL AND PERSONALITY VARIABLES ON RETIREMENT STRESS

	Transition (N = 157)				State (N = 306)			
	b	se	t	B	b	se	t	B
Life events	.062	.033	1.90+	.148	.117	.048	2.45*	.134
Hassles	.152	.047	3.22**	.266	.446	.063	7.06***	.382
D	.043	.018	2.38*	.232				
Si	− .019	.010	− 1.83+	− .170				
Ma					.055	.027	1.99*	.103
Intercept	.829	.293	2.83**		− .879	.405	− 2.17	
R²	.192				.225			
	F (4, 152) = 9.03 p < .001				F (3, 302) = 29.27 p < .001			

```
+   p ≤ .10
*   p ≤ .05
**  p ≤ .01
*** p ≤ .001
```

DISCUSSION

This study attempted to answer the question, « why do some men find retirement stressful ? » To this end, we identified the personality characteristics and social circumstances of retirees which are associated with the reporting of the stress associated with both the transition to retirement as well as with retirement as a stage of life. Men who retired within the past year (of the two surveys) were asked if they found retirement stressful, defined here as **retirement transition stress.** In addition, all of the respondents were also asked to indicate the extent to which they experienced daily hassles in five domains during the past three months. Hassles specifically associated with retirement were defined as indicators of **retirement state stress.** This question was answered by all retirees regardless of retirement duration. This differentiation between transition and state stress represents a refinement of the description of the retirement process.

Bivariate analyses indicated that both social and personality variables were associated with the two types of retirement stress. Among the variables assessing circumstances of retirement, having an unplanned retirement was associated with transition stress, while having had a white collar occupation was positively associated with state stress. However, the social variables which were most strongly associated with both transition and state stress were the number of negative life events and the stressfulness of daily hassles (other than retirement). These results not only support comparable findings by Matthews and Brown (15), but we expanded the field of stressors to include daily hassles as well as stressful life events.

Although others have found that retirement stress is greater among retirees who report less social support (16), we did not replicate this finding. However, our social support measure was considerably more refined in that it distinguished quantitative from qualitative support. Further, the NAS men were selected in part on the basis of their having extensive social ties to the area, so we may not have had enough respondents who qualified as social isolates to replicate earlier findings.

Bivariate analyses of personality variables revealed several associations with transition and state stress which were primarily positive, that is, associated with higher stress levels. Four of the MMPI-2 clinical scales (paranoia, psychasthenia, schizophrenia, mania) were related both to transition and state stress.

Additionally, the hysteria and masculinity-femininity scales were positively associated with state stress, while the depression scale was associated with transition stress. Two of three validity scales were negatively associated with retirement stress : the lie and defensiveness scales were associated with decreased reporting of state stress.

However, multiple regression analysis revealed a much different picture. Different personality variables were related to the two types of retirement stress, supporting the notion that transition and state stress are different aspects of the retirement process. Men who reported transition stress were less defensive, more extroverted, and more depressed. Retirement state stress was less likely to be reported by retirees who were high on the lie and schizophrenia scales, but more likely to be reported by those high on the psychopathic deviate, psychasthenia, and hypomania scales.

The relationships of the MMPI-2 scales to retirement stress must be interpreted with both caution and a measure of sophistication about the MMPI-2. Elevations on the MMPI-2 scales in a community residing, normal population cannot be interpreted to mean that such effects are due to clinical levels of the psychopathologies from which the scales derived their names. The names of the scales are somewhat misleading in this context, and require some interpretation. For example, a negative association between retirement stress and scores on the « Lie » scale does not mean that individuals who lie find retirement less stressful. Rather, higher scores on the Lie scale are taken to indicate that these individuals are especially likely to present a positive image of themselves to others. Such individuals may be more likely to underreport stress levels. Similarly, hypomania can be thought of as reflecting general energy levels, and there is a strong extraversion component in the psychopathic deviate scale (29). Thus, it is not unreasonable to suppose that individuals who are high in energy and enjoy social interaction are more likely to find retirement stressful.

Our last task was to examine whether the social and personality variables were independent or overlapping correlates of retirement stress. Combining both the significant social and personality variables into a single regression analysis revealed that there was some overlap or redundancy between these variables in that fewer remained significant. Nonetheless, both life events and hassles remained strong associates of both transition and state stress. Controlling for general stress due to both events and hassles, only three personality variables remained significant in the two models : Depression remained positively associated with transition stress, while introversion was negatively associated with it. Hypomania was the only personality variable to be associated (positively) with state stress.

While these findings could be interpreted as showing that social variables (e.g., stress levels) are more predictive of retirement stress than are personality variables, it should be remembered that the stress variables can be considered as proximal and the personality as distal with respect to retirement. That is, the stress variables were assessed at the same time as the retirement variables, and are the same types of variables, while the personality variables were assessed in a different survey and are different types of variables. Thus, we prefer the interpretation that both social and personality variables relate to the perception of the stressfulness of retirement.

A number of caveats need to be mentioned. First, although our findings make intuitive sense, it is not possible from these results to ascertain causal directionality. That is, we cannot determine whether other types of stresses make retirement stressful or whether certain individuals are simply more likely to report stress in general. However, the fact that the stress variables remained in the models even when personality variables were entered makes the latter interpretation less likely.

Second, stepwise regression was the procedure used in this study. We recognize the shortcoming of allowing the procedure to select the order in which variables entered the equation rather than doing so on an *a priori* basis. However, the use of this procedure was warranted in this instance. The research was exploratory due to insufficient literature on personality and retirement stress to guide the development of particular hypotheses. Further, stepwise regression allowed us only to test direct (as opposed to indirect) effects. It may be that much of personality's contribution to retirement stress is indirectly mediated by the perception of stress, and that this is why so many of the personality variables were no longer significant in the final equations. A statistical modeling procedure such as path analysis may be a more appropriate technique to use in the future. We will soon be able to accomplish this by including the third wave of data which we collected in the past few months.

Finally, our sample cannot be considered strictly random, which limits generalization of results. The men were selected for health and geographic stability, and constitute a relatively homogeneous sample. An offshoot of geographic stability is occupational stability, which may mitigate the impact of retirement, as compared to men who experienced more frequent job changes. However, it should be noted that the NAS men's mental health is similar to that of other community surveys (30), and the percentage who found retirement stressful is similar to that reported by others (11, 13).

In summary, in the course of this century, retirement has passed from a rare experience associated with superannuation into a normative life event (12). Thus, it is not surprising that the majority of men do not find it stressful. Nonetheless, a significant minority do find retirement problematic, and we need to understand further what personality or social circumstances contribute to this. This should allow for better anticipatory socialization into retirement, so that even fewer individuals will face retirement stress in the future.

REFERENCES

1. EKERDT (D.J.), BOSSE' (R.) : Change in self-reported health with retirement. *Int. J. Aging Hum. Develop.*, 15, 213-223, 1982.
2. EKERDT (D.J.), BADEN (L.,), BOSSE' (R.), DIBBS (E.) : The effect of retirement on physical health. *Amer. J. Pub. Health.*, 73, 7, 779-783, 1983.
3. EKERDT (D.J.), BOSSE' (R.), GOLDIE (C.L.) : The effect of retirement on somatic complaints. *J. Psychosomatic Res.*, 27, 1, 61-67, 1983.
4. EKERDT (D.J.), SPARROW (D.), GLYNN (R.), BOSSE' (R.) : Change in blood pressure and total cholesterol with retirement. *Amer. J. Epid.*, 120 (1), 64-71, 1984.
5. DEROGATIS (L.R.) : SCL-90-R Revised Manual. *John Hopkins University School of Medicine*, Baltimore, MD, 1983.
6. BOSSE' (R.), ALDWIN (C.M.), LEVENSON (M.R.), EKERDT (D.J.) : Mental health differences among retirees and workers. Findings from the Normative Aging Study. *Psych. Aging*, 2, 4, 383-389, 1987.
7. BOSSE' (R.), ALDWIN (C.M.), SPIRO (A.), LEVENSON (M.R.), WORKMAN-DANIELS (K.) : Psychological symptoms following retirement. Longitudinal findings from the Normative Aging Study. Presented at the Gerontological Society of America meeting, Minneapolis, November, 1989.
8. ATCHLEY (R.C.) : The Sociology of Retirement. *Halsted Press*, New York, 1976.
9. EKERDT (D.J.), BOSSE' (R.), LEVKOFF (S.) : An empirical test for phases of retirement : findings from the Normative Aging Study. *J. Gerontol.*, 40, 95-101, 1985.
10. ALDWIN (C.M.) : The Elders Life Stress Inventory (ELSI). Egocentric and nonegocentric stress. In M.A.P. Stephens, S.E. Hobfoll, J.H. Crowther, & D.L. Tennenbaum (Eds.), Stress and Coping in Late Life Families. *Hemisphere*, New York, 1990, pp. 49-69.

11. MATTHEWS (A.M.), BROWN (K.H.), DAVIS (C.K.), DENTON (M.A.) : A crisis assessment technique for the evaluation of life events : transition to retirement as an example. *Can. J. Aging,* 1, 28-39, 1982.
12. NEUGARTEN (B.L.) : Retirement in the life course. *Triangle,* 29, 2-3, 119-125, 1990.
13. BOSSE' (R.), ALDWIN (C.M.), LEVENSON (M.R.), WORKMAN-DANIELS (K.) : How stressful is retirement ? Findings from the Normative Aging Study. *J. Gerontol.,* 46, 9-14, 1991.
14. BLAU (Z.S.), OSER (G.T.), STEPHENS (R.C.) : Patterns of adaptation in retirement ; a comparative analysis. In Coping With Medical Issues : Aging, Kolker (A.), Ahmed (P.I.) [eds]. *Elsevier Biomedical,* New York, 1982, pp. 119-138.
15. MATTHEWS (A.M.), BROWN (K.H.) : Retirement as a critical life event. *Res. Aging,* 9, 548-571, 1987.
16. MATTILA (V.J.), JOUKAMAA (M.), SALOKANGAS (R.K.K.) : Retirement, ageing and adaptation (the Turva Project) Part II : design of the project and some preliminary finding. *Eur. J. Psychiat.,* 2, 46-58, 1988.
17. WHEATON (B.) : Life transitions, role histories and mental health. *Am. Sociol. Rev.,* 55, 209-223, 1990.
18. PALMORE (E.B.), FILLENBAUM (G.G.), GEORGE (L.K.) : Consequences of retirement. *J. Gerontol.,* 39, 109-116, 1984.
19. REICHARD (S.), LIVSON (F.), PETERSON (P.) : Aging and personality. A study of Eighty-Seven Older Men. *J. Wiley & Sons,* New York, 1962.
20. FLODERUS (B.) : Psycho-social factors in relation to coronary heart disease and associated risk factors. *Nordisk Hygienisk Tid Skrift Supplementum,* 6, Stockholm, 1974 (Special issue).
21. BUTCHER (J.N.), DAHLSTROM (W.G.), GRAHAM (J.R.), TELLEGEN (A.), KAEMER (B.) : Minnesota Multiphasic Personality Inventory (MMPI-2) : manual for administration and scoring. *University of Minnesota Press,* Minneapolis, 1989.
22. MEEHL (P.E.), HATHAWAY (S.R.) : The K factor as a suppressor variable in the MMPI. *J. Appl. Psychol.,* 30, 525-564, 1946.
23. BELL (B.), ROSE (C.L.), DAMON (A.) : The Normative Aging Study ; an interdisciplinary and longitudinal study of health and aging. *Aging Human Develop.,* 3, 5-17, 1972.
24. ROSE (C.L.), BOSSE' (R.), SZRETTER (W.) : The relationship of scientific objectives to population selection and attribution in longitudinal studies : the case of the Normative Aging Study. *Gerontol.,* 16, 508-516, 1976.
25. BOSSE' (R.), EKERDT (D.J.), SILBERT (J.E.) : The Veterans Administration Normative Aging Study. In Mednick (S.A.), Harway (M.), and Finello (K.M.) (Eds.), Handbook of Longitudinal Research, volume 2, Teenage and Adult Cohorts. *Prager,* New York, 1984, pp. 273-283.
26. ALDWIN (C.M.), LEVENSON (M.R.), SPIRO (A.) III, BOSSE' (R.) : Does emotionality predict stress ? Findings from the Normative Aging Study. *J. Personal. Soc. Psychol.,* 56, 618-624, 1989.
27. BOSSE' (R.), ALDWIN (C.M.), LEVENSON (M.R.), WORKMAN-DANIELS (K.), EKERDT (D.J.) : Differences in social support among retirees and workers : findings from the Normative Aging Study. *Psychol. Aging,* 5 (1), 41-47, 1990.
28. BUTCHER (J.N.), ALDWIN (C.M.), LEVENSON (M.R.), BEN PORATH (Y.), SPIRO (A.) III, BOSSE' (R.) : Personality and aging ; a study of the MMPI-2 in older men. *Psychol. Aging,* 6, 3, 361-370, 1991.
29. GRAHAM (J.R.) : MMPI-2 : assessing personality and psychopathology. *Oxford University Press,* New York, 1990.
30. ALDWIN (C.M.), SPIRO (A.) III, LEVENSON (M.R.), BOSSE' (R.) : Longitudinal findings from the Normative Aging Study. I. Does mental health change with age ? *Psychol. Aging,* 4, 3, 295-306, 1989.

VII

FACTS AND RESEARCH IN INTERNATIONAL GERONTOLOGY

GERONTOLOGICAL RESEARCH IN FINLAND

Eino HEIKKINEN (*)

INTRODUCTION

During the 1980s there has been a tremendous growth of gerontological research in Finland. The research effort has now been going on for several decades. The first scientific association was established in 1949. One of the most outstanding pioneers in the field of biogerontology was professor Eeva Jalavisto, who did extensive research into questions of biomedical gerontology in the late 1950s and early 1960s in Helsinki. Professor Ilmari Ruikka from Turku was a major influence in the field of geriatrics during the 1960s and 1970s, and professor Faina Jyrkilä, who did most of her work in Jyväskyla in the 1960s and 1970s, was particularly influential through her research in the field of social gerontology. The first chair of gerontology was established in 1975 under the Medical Faculty of the University of Tampere. Since then three chairs of geriatrics have ben established in the late 1980s in Turku, Helsinki and Kuopio, all under medical faculties.

The Academy of Finland has recently devoted considerable resources to the development of gerontological research in Finland. International cooperation has been expanding rapidly, and systematic efforts have also been made to develop researcher education. For information purposes a Finnish scientific journal was started in 1987, and an increasing number of researchers have also published in international journals.

RESEARCH INSTITUTIONS AND INTERESTS

In 1987 the Academy of Finland conducted a survey to evaluate the current status of gerontological research in Finland and to identify needs of development. According to its report there are ten or so universities and five research institutes in the country which produce significant gerontological research. In the field of biogerontology the most important research interests are the aging of connective tissue and

---

(*) Professor, Department of Health Sciences and Gerontology Research Centre, University of Jyväskylä, Finland.

the locomotor system (Heikkinen 1968, Suominen 1978, Kovanen 1989), biological and functional age (Jalavisto and Makkonen 1963 a, b, Heikkinen et al. 1974, 1984, Era 1987), and the efforts of aging on the nervous system (Hervonen et al. 1978, 1986). In the field of health sciences the main focus of research has been on epidemiological issues, functional ability, mental health problems, and on the connections between way of life, aging and health, particularly the relationship between physical activity and aging (Suominen et al. 1980, Heikkinen et al. 1989, Suominen et al. 1989, Pohjolainen et al. 1989). There have been a number of interview studies and clinical-epidemiological surveys with representative population samples (e.g. Ruikka et al. 1966, Heikkinen et al. 1983, Kivelä et al. 1988, Sulkava et al. 1985, Riekkinen et al. 1986, Takkunen et al. 1986, Jylhä et al. 1986, Enlund et al. 1986, Pahkala 1990).

In social gerontological research the main concerns have been the aging of the population and its social consequences (Martelin 1987, Valkonen and Nikander 1987), the position of elderly people in society, the living conditions of elderly people, community planning and living environment, social aging (Jyrkilä 1960, Pohjolainen 1988) and the psychic effects of aging (e.g. Ruth 1980, Ruth and Birren 1985, Aysto 1986).

The use of and need for services in the elderly has also been studied (e.g. Brommels 1984, Heikkinen 1989). There have been a number of surveys focusing on a selected town or municipality, and many of these have had their own development or experimental projects.

In recent years other disciplines have also been showing a growing research interest in the problems of aging : these include pedagogics (e.g. learning in old age), social history, folklore studies, linguistics, science studies, and theology.

The biggest, often multidisciplinary research teams currently work at the University of Jyväskylä, which in 1985 set up a multidisciplinary centre for gerontological research ; at the University of Tampere, which has the only chair of gerontology ; and at the universities of Helsinki, Turku and Kuopio, which have chairs of geriatrics and other disciplines related to geriatric research. Outside the university system, mention should be made of four research institutes : the Kuntokallio research and training centre and the research units at the Social Insurance Institution, the National Public Health Institute, and the Institute of Occupational Health. Currently gerontological research institutions engage around 100 researchers, although only an estimated 30 are full-time researchers.

SCIENCE POLICY PROGRAMS

In the early 1980s the Academy of Finland prepared a committee report on the development of gerontological research in Finland (Academy of Finland, National Medical Research Council 1982). The report specified certain areas that it thought should be given priority in the development effort, and it made various proposals for increasing research resources in the field (research grants, researcher education, university chairs of geriatrics and gerontology). In 1982 an association called The Society for Growth and Aging Research published its report on a research seminar which reviewed the state of gerontological research in the country. A Finnish bibliography consisting mainly of work in social gerontology came out in 1987, with a total of 16,411 references.

The same year also saw the publication of two research development programmes : The Role of Research in the Promotion of Good Aging (Publications of the Academy of Finland 3/1987 ; Helsinki 1987 ; in Finnish) and Better Welfare of the Aged (Ministry of Social Affairs and Health, Helsinki 1987, in Finnish).

These development programmes have set off several extensive research projects and programmes for researcher education. All of the country's major research units and teams are involved in these efforts. Financing is provided jointly by the Academy of Finland, The Ministry of Social Affairs and Health, universities, and gerontological research institutions.

Policy-making efforts have also been carried out under the auspices of the Nordic Council of Ministers. The Nordic Research Policy Council has given significant support to the planning and implementation of joint Nordic projects in gerontological research. Currently the responsibility for coordination of planning lies with the Gerontology Research Centre at the University of Jyväskylä. The Department of Health Sciences at Jyväskylä has been appointed by the W.H.O. as the national collaboration center in the field of socio-medical research in old age.

RESEARCH FUNDING

There are no estimates available on the current funding situation in Finnish gerontological research. Most of the funding is channelled from the state budget to universities and research institutes. A significant source of financing for a number of research projects is represented by grants. The total amount of research grants for 1990 is estimated at around FIM 4 million.

PUBLICATIONS

Research results of old-age studies are published in domestic and international journals. Up until quite recently comparatively few Finnish scholars have published in international scientific journals, but the situation has now been changing. In Finland, there are a number of fora for publication (Gerontology, journals in other disciplines, series published by university departments, the publications of the Ministry of Social Affairs and Health, etc.).

INTERNATIONAL SCIENTIFIC COOPERATION

Finnish research institutes have so far been engaged in relatively few international projects. However, the universities of Jyväskylä and Tampere have been involved in the comparative international research programme on old age sponsored by the W.H.O., and recently the Gerontology Research Centre at Jyväskylä (Functional Capacity of the Aged) and Kuntokallio (Way of Life of the Aged) have joined major Nordic research projects.

During the 1980s Finnish researchers have also been attending international scientific meetings to an increasing extent. The number of Finnish scholars on the editorial boards of international journals remains quite limited.

NATIONAL COOPERATION

There are two scientific associations in Finland which are active in the field of gerontology : Societas Gerontologica Fennica (est. 1949) and Society for Growth and Aging Research (est. 1980). Together, these associations have a membership of around 400.

A significant intermediate state in the development of scientific cooperation was represented by the Gerontology Cooperation Group, which worked for a number of years under the Academy of Finland in the early 1980s and involved some 20 (mostly young) researchers from different universities.

RESEARCHER EDUCATION

The number of doctoral dissertations published in the field of gerontology has been comparatively small (18 dissertations in 1980-1987). Currently over 30 persons from different universities and research institutes are involved in a researcher training programme sponsored by the Academy of Finland. There is very little researcher education abroad. In 1981 and 1984 the University of Jyväskylä organized Nordic postgraduate courses in gerontology and in 1987 a Nordic symposium in gerontology in collaboration with Kuntokallio. Other significant events from the point of view of researcher education have included the 1980 symposium on research of aging and care of the elderly (organized by the Jahnsson foundation), and the symposium on research of aging and public health in 1986 (organized by the Academy of Finland).

REFERENCES (only papers published in English are included)

BROMMELS (M.) : Future Hospital Care rort the Elderly. Implications of Change in Treatment Practice. In : Sjunde nordislea kongress i gerontologi (Eds Dehlin O., Steen B.), Technicattor Information AB, 1985, pp. 327-328.

ENLUND (H.), SAARINEN (H.), NISSINEN (A.), KIVELÄ (S.L.), TURAKKA (H.) : Self-Medication among the Elderly Finnish Men. In : 8th Scandinavian Congress of Gerontology, pp. 281-283, Tampere, 1986.

ERA (P.) : Sensory, Psychomotor, and Motor Functions in Men of Different Ages. Scand. J. Soc. Med., Suppl., 39, 1987.

HEIKKINEN (E.) : Transformations of Rat Skin Collagen with Special Reference to Ageing Process. Acta Physiol. Scand., Suppl. 317, 1968.

HEIKKINEN (E.), ARAJÄRVI (R.L.), ERA (P.), JYLHÄ (M.), KINNUNEN (E.), MÄSSELI (E.), POHJOLAINEN (P.), RAHKILA (P.), SUOMINEN (H.), TURPEINEN (P.), VÄISÄNEN (M.), ÖSTERBACK (L.) : Functional capacity of men born in 1906-1910, 1926-30 and 1946-50. Scand. J. Soc. Med., Suppl. 33, 1984.

HEIKKINEN (E.), KARHU (I.), JOKELA (J.) : Physical Exercise and Related Factrs among Elderly People in Four European Localities. In : Physical activity, ageing and sports. Vol. 1 (Eds. Harris R., Harris S.). Center for the study of aging, Albany, New York, 1989, pp. 157-177.

HEIKKINEN (E.), KIISKINEN (A.), KAYHTY (B.), RIMPELA (M.), VUORI (L.) : Assessment of biological age. Gerontologia, 20, 33-43; 1974.

HEIKKINEN (E.), WATERS (W.E.), BRZEZINSKI (Z.J.) [eds] : The Elderly in Eleven Countries. A sociomedical survey, WHO regional office for Europe, (Public Health in Europe), Copenhagen, 1983.

HEIKKINEN (R.L.) : Primary Care Services for the Elderly in Six European Areas at the Beginning of the 1980s. In : Health, Lifestyles and Services for the Elderly. World Health Organization (Public Health in Europe 29), pp. 75-98, Copenhagen 1989.

HERVONEN (A.), KOISTINAHO (J.), ALHO (H.), HELEN (P.), SANTER (R.M.), RAPOPORT (S.L.) : Age related heterogeneity of lipopigments in human sympathetic ganglia. Mechanisms of Ageing and Development, 35, 17-29, 1986.

HERVONEN (A.), VAALASTI (A.), PARTANEN (M.), KANERVA (L.), HERVONEN (H.) : Effects of ageing on the histochemically demonstrable catecholamines and acetylcholinesterase of human sympathetic ganglia. J. Neurocytol., 7, 11-23, 1978.

JALAVISTO (E.), MAKKONEN (T.) : On the assessment of biological age. I. Factorial analysis of physiological measurement in old and young women. Annal. Acad. Scient. Fenn., Ser. A., V. Medica 100, Helsinki 1963a.

JALAVISTO (E.), MAKKONEN (T.) : On the assessment of biological age. II. Factorial study of ageing in post-menopausal women. Annal Acad. Scient. Fenn., Ser. A., V. Medica 101, Helsinki 1963 b.

JYLHÄ (M.), LESKINEN (E.), ALANEN (E.), LESKINEN (A.L.), HEIKKINEN (E.) : Self-Rated Health and associated factors among men of different ages. J. Gerontol., 41, 710-717, 1986.

JYRKILÄ (F.) : Society and adjustment to old age. A sociological study on the attitude of society and the adjustment of the aged. Transactions of the Westermarck Society, *Vol V. Munksgaard,* Turku 1960.

KIVELÄ (S.L.), PAHKALA (K.), LAIPPALA (P.) : Prevalence of depression in an elderly Finnish population. *Acta Psychiatr. Scand.,* 78, 401-413, 1988.

KOVANEN (V.) : Effects of ageing and physical training on rat skeletal muscle. *Acta Phys. Scand.,* 135, suppl. 477, 1989.

MARTELIN (T.) : Trends in elderly mortality in the nordic countries. *Comprehensive Gerontology,* C1, 49-58, 1987.

PAHKALA (K.) : Social and environmental factors and depression in old age. *Int. J. Geriatric Psychiatry,* 5, 1990.

POHJOLAINEN (P.) : Social participation and life-style in old age. In : The aged in rural environment. [Eds. ASP (E.), SALONEN (T.), AHSANULLAH (A.)]. Department of sociology and political research, Sociological studies, series A, no 12, Turku 1988.

POHJOLAINEN (P.), HEIKKINEN (E.) : Longitudinal study of the physical activity of retired people. In : Physical activity, ageing and sports, vol. 1 [Eds. HARRIS (R.), HARRIS (S.)]. Center for the study of aging, Albany, New York 1989, pp. 219-224.

RIEKKINEN (P.J.), REINIKAINEN (K.), HELKALA (E.L.), SOININEN (H.), SIRVIÖ (J.) : Somatostatin in normal aging, in Alzheimer's disease and Parkinson's disease. In : 8th Scandinavian Congress of Gerontology, Congress proceedings, pp. 105-108, Tampere, 1986.

RUIKKA (L.), SOURANDER (L.B.), KASANEN (A.) : The health of the aged in Turku. *Ann. Acad. Sci. Fenn,* Series A, Medica 120, Helsinki, 1966.

RUTH (J.E.) : Creativity as a cognitive construct. The effects of age, sex and testing practice. Dissertation. The graduate school, University of Southern California, Los Angeles, 1980.

RUTH (J.E.), BIRREN (J.E.) : Creativity in adulthood and old age. Relations Intelligence, sex and mode of testing. *Int. J. Behav. Dev.,* 8, 99-109, 1985.

SUOMINEN (H.) : Effects of physical training in middle-aged and elderly people with special regard to skeletal muscle connective tissue and functional aging. *Stud Sport Phys. Educ. Health,* Univ. Jyväskylä, 1978, 11, 1-40.

SUOMINEN (H.), HEIKKINEN (E.), PARKATTI (T.) et al. : Effects of « lifelong » physical training on functional aging in men. *Scand. J. Soc. Med.,* 14, 225-240, 1980.

SUOMINEN (H.), RAHKILA (P.), ERA (P.), JAAKKOLA (L.), HEIKKINEN (E.) : Functional capacity in middle-aged male endurance and power athletes. In : Physical activity, ageing and sports. Vol. 1. [Eds HARRIS (R.), HARRIS (S.)]. Center for the study of aging, Albany, New York, 1989, pp. 213-218.

SULKAVA (R.),. WIKSTRÖM (J.), AROMAA (A.), RAITASALO (R.), LEHTINEN (V.), LAHTELA (K.), PALO (J.) : Prevalence of severe dementia in Finland. *Neurology* (Cleveland), 35, 1025-1029, 1985.

TAKKUNEN (H.), REUNANEN (A.), AROMAA (A.) : Impact of risk factors on cardiovascular mortality in old age. 8th Scandinavian Congress of Gerontology. Congress proceedings, Tampere, 1986.

VALKONEN (T.), NIKANDER (T.) : Demographic changes in the aged population of four nordic countries. *Yearbook of population research in Finland XXV,* pp. 9-19, 1987.

ÄYSTÖ (S.) : Neuropsychological functioning in elderly people. In : 8th scandinavian congress of gerontology. Congress proceedings, pp. 121-124, Tampere, 1986.

FACTS AND RESEARCH ON GERONTOLOGY IN JAPAN IN 1992

Hajime ORIMO (*)

ACADEMIC SOCIETIES

Japan Gerontological Society

The Japan Gerontological Society was established in 1959 as a national association for the fostering of studies and cooperation in the field of gerontology in Japan. This establishment took place 10 years after the foundation of the International Association of Gerontology (IAG), in which the Society became a member in 1960.

The Japan Gerontological Society was originally inaugurated as an organization amalgamating the Japan Geriatrics Society and the Japan Socio-Gerontological Society. However with the Japan Society for Biomedical Gerontology joining in 1981, and the Japanese Society of Gerondontology joining in 1991, it is expected to undergo considerable maturing by playing a major role in uniting the four societies.

A major activity undertaken by the Society is to hold a biannual academic meeting with its member societies. The contents of the meeting include special lectures and symposia, and free papers. The themes of the past four symposia were :

- Reconsidering the Indicators of Aging.
- Aging and Mental Functions – Is Man Destined to be Demented ?
- Dementia in Old Age and Related Problems.
- Focusing on Long Life Society – Designing an Optimal Life Cycle in Preparation for Coming Long Life Society.

Japan Geriatrics Society

The Japan Geriatrics Society was also founded in 1959 as was the Japan Gerontological Society. As of April 1991, 5,850 members belong to the society.

The following are the major activities in which the Japan Geriatrics Society is involved.

- *Hosting Academic Meetings*

A national academic meeting is held once a year. Averaging the past three annual

---

(*) Professor and chairman, Department of Geriatrics, Faculty of Medicine, University of Tokyo, Tokyo. President of Japan Geriatrics Society.

meetings indicates that approximately 1,300 people participated in each meeting, and that 397 free papers were presented. The major themes of the past three symposia are as follows :

- Characteristics of Water-Electrometabolism in the Elderly
- Problems in Drug Therapy for the Elderly
- Physiological and Pathological Aging
- Current Issues in Medical Care for the Elderly
- Free Radicals and Geriatric Diseases
- Progress of Coronary Atherosclerosis and its control.

In 1990, regional symposia started to be held in the nine districts throughout the country, twice a year respectively in each.

- *Publication of an Academic Journal*

The Japanese Journal of Geriatrics is regularly published biannually, and one supplementary issue also appears to include the papers published for the aforementioned annual national meetings. The average annual publication in the past three years amounted to 47 articles totaling 850 pages. The main themes in the journal are summarized in table 1.

TABLE 1

PAPERS PUBLISHED IN JAPANESE JOURNAL
OF GERIATRIC (1988-1990)

		%
Cardiology	28	20.0
Hypertension	13	9.3
Arteriosclerosis	3	2.1
Neurology	16	11.4
Cerebrovascular diseases	7	5.0
Dementia	15	10.7
Respiratory diseases	10	7.1
Metabolic diseases	12	8.6
Endocrinology	4	2.9
Osteoporosis	4	2.9
Nephrology	1	0.7
Hematology, Immunology	8	5.7
Infectious diseases	2	1.4
Gastroenterology	8	5.7
Rehabilitation	4	2.9
Laboratory medicine	2	1.4
Geriatric care	2	1.4
Clinical pharmacology	1	0.7
TOTAL	140	100.0

Note : Case reports are not included.

- *For Certifying Geriatric Physicians*

Enhanced knowledge and refine skills in geriatrics are becoming indispensable for all practicing clinicians with the rapid aging of the patient population. Program was established by the Society in 1988 to meet with such social demands. The purpose of the system is to offer a well-structured channel to train clinicians with the appropriate experience required to treat the elderly, and thereby to enhance the quality of medical care. The requirements for obtaining certification under this system are :

- must be a bearer of a current Japanese Medical Licence ;
- must have been a member of the Japan Gerontological Society for at least four consecutive years ;

– must have undergone more than three years of clinical training according to designated curriculums in facilities with consultant geriatric physicians accredited by the Society ;
– must pass the board examination of the Society.

The training curriculum includes topics such as geriatric medicine, surgery, ophthalmology and other subjects required to effectively treat the elderly. An applicant to this system is required to submit a summary of to medical records of more than 30 inpatients aged 65 and over with multipathology whom have been under the care of the applicant. The certification must be renewed every five years after the initial certification to ensure that the clinician is fully aware of recent studies and is employing the skills currently practiced. The first group of physicians are expected to receive certification under this system in 1992.

The Japan Socio-Gerontological Society.

This society was also founded in 1959 as was the Japan Gerontological Society. As of October 1990, it consisted of a total of 730 members.

The major activities of this Society are as follows.

• *Hosting Academic Meetings*

The Socio-Gerontological Society annually hosts a national meeting. According to the statistics of the past three meetings, the average number of participants per meeting was approximately 270 and the average number of presented free papers was 95. The major themes of the past five symposia were :

– Life-long Education in the 21st Century and Learning of the Elderly
– Establishing a Support Network for Old People Who Need to be Cared for
– Theme and Future Outlook of Social Gerontology toward the 21st Century
– Terminal Care for the Elderly
– Gerontological Approach for Staying Active in Later Life.

• *Publications of an Academic Journal.*

The Japanese Journal of Gerontology is published once annually. The average of the past five volumes amounts to 14 articles and 249 pages per volume. The content focus of the papers are listed in Table 2.

TABLE 2

PAPERS PUBLISHED IN JAPANESE JOURNAL
OF GERONTOLOGY (1986-1990)

		%
Family and generational relations	3	4.4
Roles in old age	2	2.9
Subjective well-being	10	14.7
Attitudes toward aging and the aged	5	7.4
Psychological aspects of the elderly	11	16.2
Care of the demented elderly	10	14.7
Health and physical functions	11	16.2
Care in the homes for the aged	3	4.4
Community services	5	7.4
Housing and environment	3	4.4
Demography	2	2.9
Educational services	1	1.5
Others	2	2.9
TOTAL	**68**	**100.0**

Japan Society for Biomedical Gerontology

Established in 1973, the name was changed to the Japan Society for Biomedical Gerontology, in 1981. The society also became a member of the Japan Gerontology Society in the same year. As of January 1990, it consisted of 514 members.

The major activities of this society are as follows.

- • *Hosting Academic Meetings*

A national convention is held every autumn and a symposium is held every spring.

The average number of participants the past three years was approximately 180 for the national convention and 150 for the symposium. An average of approximately 66 free papers were presented per national convention in the past three years. The major themes of the past five symposia were :

- – Strategies toward the Solution of Origin of Aging
- – Genetics of Aging
- – Experimental Animals in Aging Research 1989
- – Nutrition and Aging : Basic and Clinical Aspects
- – Aging of Proteins.

- • *Publication of an academic Journal*

Biomedical Gerontology, published biannually, documents the contents of the papers presented at the aforementioned academic meetings and symposia. The field of interest of the presentations from Volume 1 to 14 are given in Table 3.

TABLE 3

PAPERS PUBLISHED IN BIOMEDICAL GERONTOLOGY
(1977-1990)

		%
Cultured cells	112	16.6
Central and peripheral nervous system	80	11.9
Physiology (Acclimination)	9	1.3
Biology (C. elegans, Drosophila)	85	12.6
Immunology (T cells)	49	7.3
Nutrition	44	6.5
DNA/Gene	66	9.8
Biochemistry (Metabolism, Enzymes)	34	5.0
Pathology	32	4.8
Behavior and learning	8	1.2
Lipofusion and amyloids	17	2.5
Osteoporosis	8	1.2
Peroxide	9	1.3
Animal model for gerontological research	49	7.3
Hormone	25	3.7
Dementia	7	1.0
Others	39	5.8
TOTAL	673	100.0

RESEARCH ORGANIZATIONS AND PROMOTION OF RESEARCH

Promotion of Aging Research

In 1989, the national government announced its « Ten-Year Strategies for the Promotion of Health and Social Services for Senior Citizens » to formulate the strategies for expanding the health and welfare services essential during the last decade of this century. As one of the strategies, the Ten-Year Program for Promotion of Aging and Health Research will be executed as follows.

- *Establishing a National Research Center for Aging and Health (tentative name)*

Preparatory operations are being undertaken toward the opening of the center in the late 1990's.

According to the « Plan for the National Research Center for Aging and Health » reported in November 1990, the research fields which this center will explore include biomedicine, geriatrics, rehabilitation, nursing, basic care, technological development of health care devices, social sciences, and oriental & Chinese medicine. As of May 1991, however, the actual substance of its activities, including the research fields, have not been clarified yet. What has so far been decided are only the center's location in Ohbu City in Aichi Prefecture and the designation of the National Chubu Hospital there as its annex clinical facility.

There are three reasons for choosing this site : 1) there is a need for research associated with clinical medicine, 2) an existing national medical facility must be utilized efficiently and effectively, and 3) the prefecture's plan to construct long-term care facilities in the locate.

- *Establishment of a Private Foundation for Aging Research*

A private foundation to support aging research was established in December 1990. This foundation will serve to : 1) award research grants, 2) facilitate international cooperation and exchange, 3) train researchers, and 4) supply information.

- *National Grant Program for Project Oriented Aging and Health Research*

Since fiscal 1990, the national government has been awarding grants for research projects on aging undertaken by research of universities, research institutes, national hospitals and national sanatoriums. Research subjects range from biomedicine to social sciences as outlined in the « Plan for the National Research Center for Aging and Health ». A total of 900 million yen was granted to 62 research organizations in fiscal 1990.

As the plan for the research center become more tangible, expectation grows for achieving the coordination and systematization of the aferementioned three programs essential for promoting aging research.

Tokyo Metropolitan Institute of Gerontology

The Tokyo Metropolitan Institute of Gerontology (TMIG) was founded in 1972 by the Tokyo Metropolitan Government and it is the only academic research institute as of 1991, that specializes in and comprehensively conducts research on aging, geriatric diseases, and aging problems in Japan. The Institute went from a public to a private foundation in 1981, but most of its funding is maintained through subsidies from the Tokyo Metropolitan Government. It boasts a total of 177 full-time research staffs, with a total budget of approximately 3 billion yen allotted for fiscal 1991. One of the characteristics of the Institute is that the research is undertaken through close contact with a geriatric hospital and residential and nursing homes on the premises.

The Institute is organized into 33 departments ranging from biomedicine to socio-behavioral sciences. The emphasis is placed not only on the ordinary research undertaken by each department, but on the project-oriented research jointly conducted among multiple departments. The major themes of the projects being undertaken in fiscal 1991 are :

- Comprehensive Research of Age-associated Dementia
- Longitudinal and Interdisciplinary Study on Aging
- Environmental Factors and Aging
- Aging and Immuno-modulating System
- Quality of Life of Elderly People.

Collaborative research and academic exchange are actively undertaken with the National Institute on Aging, U.S.A. ; Institute of Gerontology, Academy of Science, U.S.S.R. ; and Beijing Geriatric Institute, Capital Institute of Medicine, People's Republic of China. TMIG is also designated by W.H.O. as a Collaborating Center for Health of the Elderly.

Other Research Organizations

Aging research is also being conducted in universities, hospitals and research institutes other than TMIG.

There are departments of geriatrics in thirteen university medical schools, where clinical research in geriatrics is exclusively undertaken through close contact with university hospitals. However, these medical school amount to only 15 % of the total of 85 medical schools in Japan. A number of departments of internal medicine in hospitals and clinics as well as medical schools also participate in, though only partly, clinical research in geriatrics. In addition, a focus is placed on subjects by the specialized medical centers established by prefecture governments such as the Tokyo Metropolitan Geriatric Center, the Center for Adult Diseases in Osaka, and the Research Institute for Brain and Blood Vessels in Akita.

Research in social gerontology is partly conducted in variety of departments in universities, including those of sociology, social welfare research, domestic sciences, psychology, mental health, public health, social medicine, nursing research, and architecture. However, these departments mostly stress individual research instead of systematically organized studies on gerontology. Another point to be noted is that gerontological research in major areas of social sciences such as economics, law and political sciences are still extremely limited. As present, no university department expressly specializes in social gerontology.

Research in biomedical gerontology is undertaken in : 1) departments of biology, and zoology in schools of sciences in universities, 2) departments of pathology, physiology, and biochemistry in medical schools, 3) research institutes related to these departments, and 4) research centers specializing in biomedicine established by national and local governments. However, these research organizations are not only very limited in number, but do not specialize in biomedical gerontology.

Acknowledgements

This report could not have been prepared without the valuable help of the following individuals and organizations, to whom go my sincere thanks : Mitsuaki Yamamoto of the Ministry of Health and Welfare, Yasuyoshi Ouchi of the Japan Geriatrics Society, and Yoshiaki Fujita of Japan Society for Biomedical Gerontology.

GERIATRIC MEDICINE IN THE UNITED KINGDOM : POLICY, ORGANISATION AND ACADEMIC RESEARCH

Paul F. HIGGS (*), Peter H. MILLARD (**)

Summary. – The review is in three parts. In Part 1 the specialty of geriatric medicine began in the United Kingdom (UK) because government placed responsibility for the chronic sick on the Regional Hospital Boards. That decision was made because of evidence of the benefits to be gained from introducing rehabilitation into the long stay wards. Now that the population is ageing government policy is changing. A favoured economic policy is foremost in the mind of government but implementation of the chosen plan is wasting money as well as being detrimental to the Health of the Nation. The policy is quicker Rehabilitation and better Community Care, but the reality is more people in privately run residential and nursing homes. Thus at the end of the 20th, government turns away from the specialist skills of geriatrics and in so doing emulates the fate of gerocomy in France at the start of the 19th century. The review concludes with a proposal that decisions should be made on statistically valid models and not on feelings.

In contrast, Part 2 gives factual information about specialist societies in the United Kingdom, and Part 3 reviews the research thrust of some of the Academic departments.
(Facts and Research in Gerontology 1992)

Key-words : geriatric, education, United-Kingdom.

INTRODUCTION

Biologically humans age in the same way, for ageing is a universal, intrinsic,

(*) Eleanor Peel Lecturer.
(**) Eleanor Peel Professor.
Division of Geriatric Medicine, Department of Medicine, St. George's Hospital Medical School, Cranmer Terrace, Tooting, London. SW17 ORE. United Kingdom.
Correspondence to : Prof. Peter H. Millard.

progressive and eventually deleterious phenomenon and nothing escapes, but despite the biological similarities Nations choose to organise their Health and Social Services in different ways. The United Kingdom has a National Health Service, and within that service there is a hospital based specialty of geriatric medicine which in most districts provides an acute, rehabilitative and long stay service for elderly people in the catchment area. Doctors training to be specialists in geriatric medicine in the St. George's department have recently published a review article on recent advances in Medicine in the Elderly (1). So, rather than repeating that work, we have chosen to consider the political, organisational and academic research activities of the specialty.

GERIATRIC MEDICINE : PAST, PRESENT AND FUTURE

Pre-1948 : the poor law infirmaries

Prior to the establishment of the National Health Service (NHS) in 1948, a separate medical specialty relating to older patients did not exist. Emptying of hospital beds to make way for expected war casualties, and the desire to create a comprehensive and universal health care system, laid the basis for the United Kingdom's specific hospital based geriatric medical model of provision for elderly people.

Health care provision for frail and infirm older people used to be provided "poor law" infirmaries. These infirmaries were originally developed as an element of a punitive social welfare system where the destitute were looked after only if they were prepared to give up all their individual rights and enter the "workhouse".

Workhouses were specifically designed to deter the able-bodied poor from seeking money from the parish instead of finding work. However by the early part of the twentieth century the poor law was mainly concerned with the frail and chronically sick elderly person. This was partly due to improvements in social insurance for workers and partly due to the haphazard development and organisation of the private and voluntary hospitals which often refused to treat elderly patients.

To overcome these and other deficiencies the opportunity created by the flexibility of war was grasped and a welfare state was created. Within that overall legislation government placed responsibility for the chronic sick both young and old on the newly formed Regional Hospital Boards, thus long stay care within the hospitals is free and social care is paid for according to one's means.

Post-1948 : separation of the frail and the infirm

Responsibility for the aged was split, but no new facilities were provided. After the war the wards containing the chronically sick were given to the hospital service whilst the units for the frail older person were left with local government. This distinction underpins the creation of the specialty of Geriatric Medicine. The theoretical foundations of a specialty of geriatrics had been suggested by Dr Marjorie Warren : she had demonstrated that many chronically sick people could be successfully rehabilitated, and made the case for geriatrics because it would improve the care of the chronic sick and free scarce hospital beds for others to use (2).

Warren had considered that responsibility for the frail aged should also be placed on the hospital service, and that recommendation was supported by a British Medical Association Working Party (3), for it is impossible to artificially separate the frail aged from the infirm aged, but the government ignored that recommendation – probably because bombing had displaced the frail aged to seaside towns (4). Thus the United Kingdom government has taken a medical approach to the problems of infirmity in old age and a social approach to the problem of frailty.

Development of a specialty : the place of rehabilitation

The idea that the chronic sick could be rehabilitated was revolutionary, and implementation of a policy based on an attack on bed-rest has led to many clinical developments and the establishment of related therapeutic disciplines such as occupational therapy and physiotherapy. Old age is no longer seen as being inherently debilitating in itself and the work of the specialists in Geriatric Medicine and their teams has played a major role in changing the attitudes of a Nation to the place of sickness in old age.

The formation of the British Geriatrics Society contributed to this major change in emphasis. All District Health Authorities (DHA's) now have a geriatric medical service in their catchment area. Each of these services is underpinned by the notion of rehabilitation ; most also provide an acute admission service as well as rehabilitative services, day hospitals, outpatient clinics, and domiciliary visits to individual old people in the community.

Problems caused by split responsibility

It would not, however, be accurate to claim that the story of British Geriatric Medicine is one of easy development to a harmonious conclusion. Division of responsibility brought the specialty into existence ; now some Health Districts focus on the more acute aspects of care, whilst the frail elderly referred to Social Service departments for admission to residential homes (and even the long stay patients) are denied specialist rehabilitation and aftercare.

Problems are now arising within the local authority residential homes and it is estimated that at least a quarter of the residents are in need of nursing care. That problem, which is inherent within the structure of the system, has been aggravated in the last decade because of an unprecedented increase in the numbers of elderly people in private rest and nursing homes (see later).

Lack of training in the residential sector

Problems arise because the general practitioners and the nursing and care staff have no special training in the care of the aged. Organisations are making attempts to overcome the deficiencies in training, however, there is no national policy. Also guidelines have been written with regard to training needs (6) and minimal standards and an inspectorate and registration authority has been formed, but there are no statutory minimal training qualifications for general practitioners, officers in charge and care attendants in residential homes. The only requirement for a nursing home is that there must be a registered nurse on duty, but such registration does not imply that the nurse has had specific training in the care of the frail and infirm aged.

The Royal College of Physicians has attempted to overcome lack of medical knowledge by developing a Diploma in Geriatric Medicine for general practitioners ; the Royal Institute of Public Health and Hygiene has also developed a certificated course and examination for care staff in residential homes (7). Government has also developed a Care Consortium in order to develop guidelines on training, but no report is expected until 1993.

Standards vary in long term care

Standards vary within the hospital, residential home and private sectors from the excellent to the appalling. Within the Hospital Service there is a Health Advisory Service which visits in order to keep up standards, but there are no minimum standards with regard to the facilities necessary for long stay care, and the choice with regard to the facilities allocated is left to the individual Districts. Concentration on the acute aspects of care, especially the development of an acute geriatric medical admission service integrated with general medicine has lead to development of National Health Service Nursing Homes (8, 9). These experimental homes differ little in their philosophy from experiments in long stay care in the hospital service, such as the Bolingbroke Hospital project (10), but they do differ in so much as responsibility for the medical care in the experimental nursing homes is not that of the physicians in geriatric medicine.

National Scandals

In the last two years the wife of the owner of a residential home for manslaughter has been prosecuted for manslaughter because of gross pressure sores in a patient discharged for care from a hospital, and in the residential sector a care assistant has been prosecuted for unlawful restraint. The two prosecutions demonstrate that on the one hand the country does not want to see the elderly sick neglected, and on the other hand they also do not consider that they should be unnecessarily restrained. The problem is to strike the necessary balance between care and risk.

It is increasingly becoming apparent that the distinction between nursing and residential care of the infirm and the frail is difficult to make and irrelevant to practical considerations. The practical problem is how, within a cash limited budget, does one provide the best quality of cost effective care.

Reemergence of the Poor Law Infirmary

From 1948 onwards local government started to build Old People's Homes (OPH) under part 3 of the National Assistance Act of 1948. By the end of the 1970's these provided accommodation to over 100,000 people. Since then the number of places first stabilised and then went into slight decline. In contrast the 1980's were marked by the rapid expansion of the private sector which by 1986 had trebled in size to provide 92,000 places for older people. Thus private sector residential home provision now matches public sector provision. Specialists in Geriatric Medicine have no specific access to these patients and with the profile of residents of these facilities showing greater infirmity and given the lack of skilled medical attention and the total absence of rehabilitation, the conditions of the poor law infirmary have been recreated.

Growth of private nursing homes

Private nursing homes have also mushroomed and now that sector has over 100,000 places. In contrast geriatric medicine has 51,400 beds. The growth of the private sector shows marked geographic variation, which as far as services for the elderly are concerned (seemingly) is more connected to the availability of property to convert into a home than to the health needs of the population. The ageing of the population, when coupled with constraints on National Health Service Hospital expenditure and local government expenditure caused by national government, has fuelled the expansion in care. But, ironically, the growth of the private sector has been funded by government through their open ended commitment to fund places in residential and nursing homes through the social security budget.

Government overspending, organisational reform and care in the community

Government expenditure on Board and Lodging allowance has risen from 8 million pounds a decade ago to 1,200 million pounds now and it is still rising. This prompted the Griffiths report into community care which eventually resulted in the Community Care Act (11). Care in the community is seen as the only acceptable way forward for providing non-acute care. It is premised on the assumption that institutional (especially hospital based) forms of care are not suitable for any group of clients, particularly elderly ones. However one of the ways that this policy will be put into operation is by using nursing homes to provide care for the highly dependent, a seeming contradiction but one sanctioned by the act as a way of reducing medical involvement in social care.

In order to facilitate this in 1993 the government intends to give local government control of the social security budget overspend ; to that end the wording of the 1948 Act which placed responsibillility for the long term care of the aged sick on the hospitals has been amended. Thus policy is returning to the pre-1948 position of having local government in charge of services for elderly people.

Contradictions between philosophy and practice

The contradictions between philosophy and practice are likely to become more acute in the future for two reasons. First, the introduction of competition between units into the health service will replace responsibility for particular catchment areas as the driving device for Geriatric Medicine and replace it with defined contractual arrangements for particular health care services. Second, the Community Care policy outlined above gives the primary responsibility for the assessment and purchasing of care to local government. This means that Geriatric Medicine may soon only be responsible for the acute and short term rehabilitation of the aged. Thus the place of prolonged rehabilitation and continuing care within hospitals becomes problematic and it is likely that the pressures of economic competition inside the NHS will lead to its disappearance. Couple that with the tendency for academic departments of geriatric medicine to change the in name to Health Care of the Elderly and one will see the specialty disappearing as well.

Gerocomy : a precedent from history

In 1803 in France doctors suggested the creation of a specialty for the aged called « gerocomie », which literally means the science of tending the aged. These demands ceased in 1830, demands when ageing was included in theses (12). It would be short sighted, to say the least, if the same thing happened to geriatric medicine in the United Kingdom. The provision of private rest and nursing homes has imbalanced service provision, and discharge and rehabilitation policies have been negatively affected by this imbalance. It would indeed be a dramatic irony if the specialty that was created by government legislation was also abolished by it for no more cogent reason than a zeal to implement a politically favoured form of economic organisation.

The need to take health care out of politics

The population of the world is ageing, and old people are known to consume more health care resources. Faced with the cost of medical leadership governments are tempted to save costs by removing trained physicians. Yet in so doing they undermine the principles of responsibility that underpin community care, and as the United Kingdom government has so ably demonstrated they end up spending more money. If other countries are to avoid the same pitfalls then decisions have to be made after consideration of the implications of change in scientifically valid models. A step in that direction has been taken by the publication at the end of 1991 of a paper from our department (13).

Time of occupancy is the forgotten fourth dimension

Time is recognised by physicists to be an important fourth dimension, but in hospital planning time of bed occupancy is ignored. Yet the words acute, rehabilitation and long stay imply dimensions of time as well as facilities, thus understanding of the interactions between the dimensions of time in the three sectors is central to planning.

Acute patients stay for days or weeks, rehabilitation patients for weeks or months, and long stay patients stay for months and years. If the average stay in long stay is two years then what happens to 10 long stay patients a year involves 20 beds. Given that rehabilitation patients stay a month then their beds could be used for up to 240 patients in the same year.

Decision making using models

The discovery that the pattern of bed occupancy in a department of geriatric medicine was expressed by a declining double exponential equation opened the way for the development of scientifically valid models. Confirmation of the validity of that observation in thirteen departments led to the development by a Professor of mathematics of a flow rate model. Using that model speed of treatment in geriatric medicine was found to correlate with the local availability of nursing homes. Thus style of practice was shown to be of secondary importance. This work lead to the development of a theoretical model, the use of which should enable plans to be made based on scientifically valid models. Time alone will tell whether that claim is correct.

THE SPECIALIST SOCIETIES

The United Kingdom does not have a National Institute of Gerontology or Geriatrics. Instead it has a network of autonomous bodies which act as a forum for the different professions. During 1991 attempts to create a National Institute by one independent organisation lead to a meeting of all interested parties. That meeting concluded that ageing in Britain was best served by autonomous groups.

British Geriatrics Society (BGS)

Hon. Secretary : Dr Ian R. Hastie.
Address : 1 St Andrew's Place, Regent's Park, London NW1 4 LB.
Telephone : 071 935 0074.
Journal : Age and Ageing.

Founded in 1947 the British Geriatrics Society now has over 1,500 members. Membership is open only to medically qualified doctors. The aim of the society is to encourage and develop a more positive understanding of the medical aspects of ageing and the problems created by those diseases that commonly afflict older people. It is organised into Regional groups with a central council and a secretariat. The regional group organise their own local programmes and there are two National meetings each year : the Spring meeting is held in the Regions and the Autumn meeting in London. Membership is open to overseas doctors.

British Society for Research on Ageing (BSRA)

Hon. Secretary : Dr. Ioan Davies.
Address : Unit for Biological Ageing Research, Department of Geriatric Medicine, Withington Hospital, Nell Lane, Manchester M20 8 LR.
Journal : Lifespan and Age and Ageing.

The society is open to all scientists who are interested in the study of ageing. It has 200 members from the biological and clinical fields. It organises scientific meetings once or twice a year. Membership is by application.

British Society of Gerontology (BSG)

Hon. Secretary : Maria Evandrou.
Address : Room R414, S.T.I.C.E.R.D., London School of Economics, Houghton Street, London, WC2A 2AE.
Telephone : 071-405 7686 ext. : 3030.
Journal : Generations Ageing and Society.

Established in 1973 the BSG is open to all who have an interest in the social aspects of gerontology. It has over 800 members from the social sciences and in addition to researchers it includes among its members doctors, social workers, occupational and physiotherapists, nurses and psychologists. Its annual meeting, a forum for the discussion of research based papers, is held in September.

British Association for Service to the Elderly (BASE)

Director : Cynthia Wilde.
Address : 119 Hassell Street, Newcastle-under-Lyme, Staffordshire, ST5 1AX.
Telephone : 0782 66 1033.
Journal : Action Baseline.

Formed in 1968, BASE provides opportunities for those who care for the elderly, either professionally or in a private capacity, to meet together informally, in order to

exchange and promote ideas and ways of providing better care services for elderly people. It organises local branch meetings, educational courses and a National Conference in November. Present membership is about 1,500 people.

Royal Society of Medicine (RSM) : Section of Geriatrics and Gerontology

Executive Director : Mr. R.N. Thompson.
Hon. Secretary of Section : Dr. Jacqueline Morris.
Address : 1 Wimpole Street, London. W1M8AE.
Telephone : 071 408 2119.

A newly formed section within the Royal Society of Medicine for doctors from all branches of medicine who are interested in the clinical, psychological, social and research aspects of ageing. Membership of the RSM is open to U.K. and overseas doctors and to senior scientists in allied clinical disciplines.

The Age Concern Institute of Gerontology

Director : Professor Anthea Tinker.
Address : King's College, University of London.
Telephone : 071-872 3035

Created in 1986 by joint agreement between Age Concern and King's College in the University of London, the Institute undertakes research, teaching and publishing. It organises conferences, seminars and public lectures. A part time MSc programme in Social Gerontology has been established.

Centre for Policy on Ageing (CPA)

Contact : Gillian Crosby, Assistant Director and Librarian.
Address : 25-31 Ironmonger Row, London EC1V 3QP.
Telephone : 071 263 1787

First established in 1947 as the National Corporation for the Care of Old People, this organisation redefined its role in 1980 and became the Centre for Policy on Ageing. The centre undertakes and usually publishes on its own behalf research on a wide variety of social, political and economic issues. The library offers a postal and telephone enquiry service.

Journal : co-sponsor of Ageing and Society.

The National Council on Ageing

The United Kingdom is characterised by a plethora of independent, sometimes government funded, voluntary organisations. Many relate to child health, some to cancer, others to specific diseases but there is also a host of others in the field of ageing. Over 100 of these come together in a loose confederation under the auspices of Age Concern, England. Information concerning this aspect of Age Concern's work can be obtained from

Director : Sally Greengross.

Address : 1268 London Road, London SW16 4EJ.

Telephone : 081 679 8000.

RESEARCH IN THE ACADEMIC DEPARTMENTS

This section was written after a postal survey of the Academic Departments. There are fifteen departments and ten replied. The survey shows the breadth and depth of interest in Research in the United Kingdom. All of the departments have clinical and teaching responsibilities as well. Responses have been broken down into subject matter rather than into departments. Much of the research has a service bias or is clinically orientated. Little of the research effort is being directed towards the study of ageing per se. The departments research activities represent the interests of the academic staff. There is no central direction.

Service Research

At the London Hospital Prof. Ebrahim's department has a quality of care programme funded for three years by the Royal College of Physicians. This work relates to standardised assessment, discharge summaries and long stay care. Work is also being undertaken into ethnic elders and the relocation of long stay patients. At Oxford Prof. Grimley Evans department, as part of a five centre national study on cognitive change and ageing, is studying reception of services by dementing people stress on carers. Carer stress is also being studied in Edinburgh by Prof. MacLennan's department and at the London Hospital Dr. Bennett is studying elder abuse.

The majority of the departments are undertaking research under the loose heading of audit. These studies are mainly associated with reviews of clinical practice. The problems of long term care are being studied at the London and at St. George's and the latter unit has a demonstration long stay project. Service orientated research is a strength of the St. George's department.

Rehabilitation Research

Research into muscle strength and aspects of locomotion are being undertaken by Prof. Young at the Royal Free and by Prof. Tallis at Manchester. The top priorities at the Royal Free are research into the practical, metabolic and immune consequences of age-related change in muscle, and Research into stroke illness. Rehabilitation Research is emerging as the major research interest in Prof. Tallis's department and at present they are concentrating on two problems : tactile neglect and muscle atrophy secondary to ageing and disease.

In Prof. Stout's Belfast department stroke illness is being studied with particular reference to prognostic indices and the metabolic response to acute stroke. Dr. Barer in Prof. Lye's department in Liverpool is developing a National Data Base on stroke illness. Stroke illness and its treatment is also being studied by Dr. Gray in Prof. Mac-Lennan's department in Edinburgh.

Epidemiological Research

An epidemiological perspective underpins the work of Prof. Grimley Evans in Oxford and Prof. Ebrahim at the London. In Oxford studies are ongoing into falls, cognition and the Guillain Barre syndrome. The latter study shows no age specific difference in the incidence of that disease. At the London the health status of ethnic elders, cardiovascular risk factors and hypertension in general practice are being studied. Prof. MacLennan in Edinburgh is using postal questionnaires to study giddiness in general practice.

Pharmacological

Pharmacological studies are ongoing in the majority of the departments. Specific focus is however given to these studies by Prof. Lye in Liverpool who is studying the pharmacodynamics of Ace inhibitors and enalapril and Prof. Cameron Swift at King's College in London ; Prof. Tallis in Manchester who focuses on drug interaction, better prescribing and the treatment of epilepsy. Self medication is being studied in Edinburgh and in Belfast drug utiisation in elderly patients is being evaluated. Prof. Livesley at Charing Cross, in London, is studying heart failure and work is ongoing with regard to cardiac function in Prof. Caird's unit in Glasgow.

Cognition/Dementia

Major centres for the study of cognition and dementia are in Prof. Wilcock's department in Bristol, in Prof. Arie's department in Manchester, in Prof. MacLennan's department in Edinburgh and in our department at St. George's. In Bristol attention is focused on Alzheimer's disease. In Nottingham the focus of attention is service delivery. In Edinburgh there is a MRC funded longitudinal study and at St. George's there is a clinico-neuropathological study. At Oxford Prof. Grimley Evans has a five centre study of cognition, Prof. Livesley at Charing Cross is studying assessment and writing skills, and Prof. Lye is involved in studies of the drug treatment of dementia.

Nutrition

In Edinburgh nutrition in long stay patients and in sheltered housing is being investigated. At Charing Cross immunological factors and nutrition are being studied, and at St. George's attempts are being made to alter the nutritional status of long stay patients by changing the diet.

Falls and Fractures

Few departments are directly studying the problem of falling. In Oxford fallers in middle and late life are being studied in order to determine related risk factors for intervention. Work is ongoing in Belfast on the prevention and treatment of osteoporosis with particular emphasis on the assessment of the benefit of increasing activity.

Infection

Immune responses to infection are being researched into in Belfast and at Charing Cross.

CONCLUSION

A considerable range of research studies are being undertaken in the Academic departments. This review has only skated over the surface of the work being done. Such activity augurs well for the future of the specialty in the United Kingdom. Whatever happens in the political scene research and scholarship will continue. Perhaps in future years there will be a Central Organisation which represents a National perspective concerning the Academic Educational and Research Activity in the United Kingdom. But until that occurs we have to rely on the enthusiasm of those who work in the field to let others know of their work : we thank my colleagues for their speedy response to our request and we hope that this overview will be of help to others.

REFERENCES

1. DIGGORY (P.), HOMER (A.), LIDDLE (J.), et al. Medicine in the elderly. *Postgrad. Med. J.,* 1991, 67, 423-445.
2. WARREN (M.W.) : Care of chronic sick. A case for treating chronic sick in blocks in a general hospital. *Br. Med. J.,* 1943, ii, 822-823.
3. British Medical Association, Report (1947) of the committee on the care of the elderly and infirm. *Br. Med. J.,* 1947, supp., 133-140.
4. THOMSON (D.) : Workhouse to nursing home. Residential care of elderly people in England since 1840. *Ageing and Society,* 1983, 3, 43-70.
5. MILLARD (P.H.) : A case for the development of departments of gerocomy in all district general hospitals : discussion paper. *J. Roy. Soc. Med.,* 1991 (in print).
6. Centre for Policy on Ageing, Home Life. A code of practice for residential care, CPA 1984.
7. GIBSON (S.), MOORE (W.) : The development and evaluation of a certificate course for care assistants in homes for elderly people. *Health and Hygiene,* 1991, 12, 115-120.
8. GRAHAM (J.) : Experimental nursing homes for elderly people in the National Health Service. *Age Ageing,* 1983, 12, 273-274.
9. BOND (S.), BOND (J.) : Outcomes of care within a multiple case study in the evaluation of the experimental NHS nursing homes. *Age Ageing,* 1990, 19, 11-18.
10. MILLARD (P.H.) : The Bolingbroke hospital long term care project. *In :* Denham (ed.) Long term care in hospital, *Croom Helm,* London, 1989.
11. HMSO : Caring for people. Community care in the next decade and beyond. *HMSO,* 1990.
12. STERNS (P.) : Old age in European Society. *Croom Helm,* London, 1977.
13. HARRISON (G.W.), MILLARD (P.H.) : Balancing acute and long term care : The mathematics of throughput in departments of geriatric medicine. *Meth. Inform. Med.,* 1991, 30, 221-228.

UNITED STATES DEPARTMENT OF VETERANS AFFAIRS HEALTH CARE FOR AGING VETERANS

Thomas T. YOSHIKAWA

Summary. – The United States Department of Veterans Affairs (VA) operates the largest health care system in the country. VA was established in 1930 and became formally affiliated with U.S. medical schools in 1946. With a rapidly growing aging veteran population, which will further expand over the next 30 years, VA has established a comprehensive health care delivery system that meets the needs of these individuals. These clinical services include, in addition to hospital and ambulatory care, a broad range of institutional and noninstitutional care programs as well as special geriatric activities. VA has also developed an extensive training and education program in geriatrics and long-term care for all disciplines, and has been recognized as a leader in geriatrics and gerontological research. (Facts and Research in Gerontology 1992)

Key-words : department of Veterans Affairs, veterans, health care delivery, aging, clinical services, training, education, research, nursing homes, geriatrics, long-term care.

The United States Department of Veterans Affairs (VA), previously called the Veterans Administration, achieved cabinet level status in 1989 through legislation. A Secretary for Veterans Affairs was appointed by the President. VA has three major responsibilities to eligible veterans : to provide socioeconomic assistance and support, health care, and burial services. Each of these responsibilities are managed, operated and administered by agencies or sub-departments within VA, i.e., Veterans Benefit Administration, Veterans Health Administration, and the National Cemetery Service.

VA through the Veterans Health Administration (VHA) operates the largest health care system in the U.S. Currently, VHA employs 195,000 persons which includes 6,600 full-time physicians (3,000 part-time physicians), and 59,000 nursing personnel. In

---

Communication and Reprint Requests to :
Thomas T. Yoshikawa, M.D., Office of Geriatrics and Extended Care (114), Department of Veterans Affairs, 810 Vermont Avenue, N.W., Washington, D.C. 20420.

VA, there are 172 medical centers, 340 outpatient clinics, and 126 hospital-based nursing home care units (NHCU). Annually, there are approximately 1,130,000 inpatients treated, 21,400,000 outpatient visits, and 27,000 VA NHCU admissions. The yearly operating budget for VHA alone is approximately $ 12 billion (1).

HISTORICAL PERSPECTIVE

Prior to 1930, veterans needs and benefits, i.e., insurance, medical care, compensation, and pensions were provided by a variety of legislation and various agencies and organizations (2). In 1930, the Veterans Administration was established through the consolidation of 47 Veterans' Bureau Hospitals, the Bureau of Pensions, and the National Home for Disabled Volunteer Soldiers. World War II brought on the need for expansion of benefits and medical care with the large numbers of returning veterans with illnesses and disabilities. On January 20, 1946, the Department of Medicine and Surgery (what is now called VHA) was created within the Veterans Administration with the passage of Public Law 79-293. Two weeks later, the Administrator for the Veterans Administration and the Chief Medical Director of the Department of Medicine and Surgery issued Policy Memorandum Number 2 which established affiliations and working agreements between VA hospitals and medical schools (3, 4). The Veterans Administration would operate the hospitals while the medical schools would recruit the physicians and establish the training and education programs. Today, 133 out of 172 VA medical centers are affiliated with 102 medical schools as dean's committee hospitals (5).

With the establishment of medical school affiliations, VA's Department of Medicine and Surgery's responsibility to veterans focused on three primary missions : medical care, training and education, and medical research. In 1982, Public Law 97-174 added a fourth mission of responsibility which was that the Department of Medicine and Surgery serve as the primary back-up to the Department of Defense during war or a national emergency for care of injured military personnel. In 1963, the President of the United States directed that 2,000 nursing home beds be created within VA through modification of existing facilities (2). Then in 1964, Public Law 88-450 authorized : (1) the establishment of 4,000 VA nursing home beds, (2) VA to contract the use of community nursing home beds at VA expense, and (3) per diem payments to State Veterans Homes providing nursing home care to veterans as well as matching grants to States for construction of State Home facilities. In 1972, Congress mandated that ambulatory care be made available. Since then, VA has evolved into a comprehensive health care delivery system as well as a major site for training and education of all health care disciplines and performance of high quality medical research.

DEMOGRAPHIC IMPERATIVE

The population served by VA is determined by military service. Health care provided by VA's Veterans Health Administration goes to only adults, and they are predominately men. It is, therefore, not surprising that there is a greater proportion of aging veterans relative to the total veteran population in comparison to the percentage of older adults in the general U.S. population. Whereas, the current percent of persons 65 years and older in the U.S. is approximately 12.5-13 %, the veterans who are 65 years and older comprise nearly 28 % of the entire veteran population (27 769 000) [6]. Table 1 summarizes the current composition of veterans by wars. It can be seen that the World War II and Korean Conflict veterans, whose median ages are 69.2

and 60.3 years, respectively, comprise one-half of the entire veteran population. Table 2 divides the veterans according to age groups at and above 55 years. Currently, 51 % of all veterans are 55 years and older, and 40 % are age 60 years and older (6).

TABLE 1

CURRENT VETERAN POPULATION.

Veteran Population	Totals (%)	Median Age (years)
Total	26,769,000 (100)*	55.4
World War I	72,000 (1)	90.5
World War II	8,643,000 (32)	69.2
Korean Conflict	4,770,000 (18)	60.3
Peace-time	6,412,000 (24)	45.6
Vietnam Era	8,303,000 (31)	43.9
Post-Vietnam Era	3,177,000 (12)	31.6

(*) Totals exceed 100 % and 26,769,000 because of veterans serving in more than one period of service.

TABLE 2

VETERAN POPULATION BY AGE

Age Group (years)	Totals	Percent
75 and older	1,645,000	6.1
70 and older	4,030,000	15.1
65 and older	7,469,000	27.9
60 and older	10,735,000	40.1
55 and older	13,638,000	50.9

Projections on the demographics of veterans over the next 40 years indicate that there will be a decline in the total number of veterans. However, there will be an increase in the number of aging veterans (i.e., 65 years and older) from the current figure of 7 469 000 over the next 30 years. By 2015, 46 % of the total veterans will be aging veterans. Equally important is that by 2005, over half of the aging veteran population will be comprised of veterans age 75 years and older — that segment of population which requires the greatest amount of health care and social support. Table 3 summarizes projected population data for veterans to the year 2030 (6).

TABLE 3

PROJECTED VETERAN POPULATION : 1990-2030.

Number of Veterans (millions)				
Year	Total	65 + (%)	75 + (%)	% 75 + veterans of total 65 + veterans
1990	26.9	7.3 (27)	1.6 (6)	22
1995	25.7	8.5 (33)	2.6 (10)	31
2000	24.1	8.9 (37)	3.8 (16)	43
2005	22.3	8.5 (38)	4.4 (20)	52
2010	20.5	8.2 (40)	4.4 (22)	54
2015	18.7	8.6 (46)	3.9 (21)	45
2020	17.1	7.8 (46)	3.7 (22)	62
2025	15.7	6.9 (44)	4.1 (26)	59
2030	14.6	6.0 (41)	3.7 (25)	62

CLINICAL PROGRAMS IN AGING

In response to the large increase in the number of older veterans, VA embarked on an aggressive but comprehensive and systematic approach to addressing the problem of care of the aging adult. VA developed a three-pronged plan involving clinical services, training and education, and research. The following information provides a brief description of the current clinical programs which are designed and established primarily for aging veterans.

Institutional long-term care

VA Nursing Homes. As mentioned earlier, VA's nursing home program was first established in 1963 through modification of existing facilities. The first new nursing home that was constructed using specific building criteria and standards was established in 1973 (2). Since then, VA has built numerous nursing homes, which now numbers to a total of 126. These homes are administered and operated by VA staff and are located on the grounds of a VA medical center. Comprehensive care is provided including medical, psychiatric, nursing, oral and dental, and rehabilitative services, as well as recreational therapy, family support services and patient and family education. Many of these VA nursing homes serve as important sites for training and education (7), which improves quality of care (8), and also are an important resource for clinical research (9, 10).

Community Nursing Homes. For veterans who require skilled and intermediate nursing care in order to make a transition from a hospital to the community, most VA medical centers can offer the services of a community nursing home through a contracted arrangement between VA and the community facility. VA pays a per diem, which is negotiated locally based on a predetermined formula and guidelines from VA's Office of Geriatrics and Extended Care. Veterans with nonservice-connected disabilities may remain in the community nursing home for up to six months ; service-connected veterans may stay for an indefinite period.

State Nursing Homes. Through a sharing agreement authorized by Congress, VA may provide up to 65 percent of the cost to construct a State nursing home or domiciliary. The state assumes the remaining cost for construction and is responsible for administering and operating the nursing home. VA pays a per diem to the state for the care of the veteran. The state is required to maintain a census of at least 75 percent veterans. A VA medical center of jurisdiction does an annual inspection of the State nursing home to assure quality of care and conformation to standards and criteria. Currently, there are 56 State nursing homes in 33 states.

VA Domiciliary. VA domiciliaries provide medical and rehabilitative care as well as other professional services for eligible veterans who are disabled by age, injury or disease and need care but who do not require hospitalization or nursing home services. Domiciled veterans are thus less functionally impaired than most nursing home residents. Currently, of the 34 VA domiciliaries, 26 also have an active program for homeless veterans.

State Domiciliaries. State domiciliaries are authorized to provide care for veterans under the same legislation and requirement for State nursing homes. The patient population and care provided are similar to those of the VA domiciliaries. There are 44 State domiciliaries in 32 states.

Non-institutional long-term care

Hospital-based Home Care. The first VA hospital-based home care (HBHC) program was established in 1970 (2). An interdisciplinary team from the hospital (physician, nurse, social worker, physical therapist, dietitian) visits the patient and caregiver at home. They provide necessary clinical care as well as training and supervision in nursing procedures, rehabilitation, and dietary instructions. Approximately 25 percent of HBHC programs also provide hospice care services in the home of the terminally ill veteran. Presently, 74 VA facilities have a HBHC program, with the entire program serving 16,100 patients and making 300,000 home visits annually.

Adult Day Health Care. For veterans who are still able to remain at home but require some clinical care, health maintenance, and therapeutic activities in a congregate setting, VA has established an adult day health care (ADHC) program. The ADHC program has obviated the continued and full time institutionalization of many veterans. This service is relatively new to VA, and only 15 medical centers have an ADHC program with an additional 24 facilities contracting the service with the community.

Community Residential Care. The community residential care (CRC) program offers residential care, in privately operated facilities. Veterans qualifying for CRC are those who are unable to resume independent living because of health conditions but who do not require hospitalization or nursing home care. VA inspects and screens the homes to meet specific standards, but the veteran pays for the cost of the CRC service.

Respite Care. Although respite care occurs in an institutional setting, its purpose is to facilitate and assist non-institutional forms of long-term care such as HBHC or ADHC. Veterans who reside primarily at home with clinical disabilities are eligible for intermittent respite care in a VA hospital or nursing home setting for up to 30 days a year. Respite care provides relief for the caregiver.

Geriatric care

Geriatric Evaluation and Management Program. The geriatric evaluation and management (GEM) program (also called geriatric evaluation unit or GEU) provides an interdisciplinary approach to comprehensive diagnosis, treatment, rehabilitation and discharge planning for elderly patients who are typically frail with complex medical and psychosocial problems. GEM programs are established in inpatient units or outpatient clinics or both. Presently, 93 VA facilities have a GEM program and another 35 VA medical centers will establish such a program in 1991. The clinical value and cost effectiveness of VA GEM programs have been studied and reported in the literature (11, 12).

Alzheimer's and Related Dementia Programs. Presently, 56 VA medical centers have established special programs for care of veterans with Alzheimer's disease or other dementias. These programs include 31 inpatient dementia units, 22 ambulatory dementia programs (e.g., day care center, hospital-based home care), and 25 outpatient assessment clinics.

Hospice Care. Hospice care is provided in VA as a special inpatient bed unit or by a hospice consultation team. Other patients are referred to community hospice care programs through Medicare.

EDUCATION AND TRAINING PROGRAMS IN AGING

VA began addressing the need to develop geriatric education and training programs in the mid-1970's. A number of specialized programs were established including fellowships in geriatrics for physicians and dentists, geriatric resident positions, training for clinical nurse specialists and allied health trainees, interdisciplinary team training programs in geriatrics, and training and education through VA's geriatric research, education and clinical centers (GRECCs). VA's geriatric physician fellowship program constitutes the largest single training pool for geriatric medicine in the U.S., accounting for 40 percent of physicians trained in geriatric medicine over the past 10 years. VA was one of the first as well as the largest trainer of geriatric dentists through its fellowship program. Recently, a geriatric psychiatry fellowship training program was initiated at eight VA medical centers throughout the country.

Through VA's seven regional medical education centers, and two continuing education centers – centers established to plan, organize, administer, implement, and evaluate training and education programs for VA staff – numerous national, regional and local conferences, seminars, workshops and symposia on topics and issues of aging have been made available to VA staff as well as trainees and non-VA professionals.

RESEARCH PROGRAMS IN AGING

VA's research budget is approximately $ 210 million annually. A significant portion of this budget goes toward funding aging research and research having some relevance to aging. In 1975, VA established centers of excellence in geriatrics called geriatric research, education and clinical centers (GRECCs). The mission of the GRECCs is to improve the health care and treatment of elderly veterans through research, training and education, and development of clinical models of care. There are presently 15 GRECCs throughout VA, each with special research foci (e.g., nutrition, diabetes mellitus, dementia, immunology, osteoporosis). Research activities include basic biological, clinical applied, and health services and care delivery investigations. Many of the leaders in aging research, as well as geriatric education and training, are staff of the GRECCs.

FUTURE DIRECTIONS

Despite its accomplishments in health care delivery, training and education, and research in geriatrics and long-term care, VA's strategic plan includes expansion of existing programs and services and establishment of new programs in aging. Before the year 2000, VA plans to have a GEM program, HBHC, and hospice care at every VA facility. Unused hospital beds will be converted to nursing home beds over the next five to six years. State nursing homes will continue to increase in number as well the number of community nursing home beds through VA contracts. The number of GRECCs will expand to nearly 20 by 2000 A.D. Training and education will focus increasingly on long-term care and psychiatric and behavioral disorders of the elderly person. A greater emphasis will be placed on funding research focused on aging-related issues that are especially unique to older veterans.

CONCLUSION

The Department of Veterans Affairs has played a leadership role in the development of health care for aging persons in the U.S. Through its numerous clinical services, VA provides a comprehensive continuum of care for the older veteran which includes acute hospital, ambulatory and long-term care. VA has led the nation in training physicians for a career in Geriatrics as well as paving the way for geriatric education and training in other disciplines. Aging research by VA investigators has been of the highest quality and has led to improved care of elderly persons and to a better understanding of the aging process.

Finally, VA remains poised to meet its yet greatest challenge in caring for older veterans over the next 30 years.

REFERENCES

1. Office of Strategic Planning, Veterans Health Administration. Department of Veterans Affairs, Washington, D.C., 1991.
2. MATHER (J.H.), ABEL (R.W.) : Medical care of veterans. A Brief history. *J. Am. Geriatr. Soc.*, 1986, 34, 757-760.
3. WORTHEN (D.M.) : The partnership between the VA and U.S. medical schools. *VA Practitioner,* June 1984, 53-58.
4. GRONVALL (J.A.) : The VA's affiliation with academic medicine : an emergency post-war strategy becomes permanent partnership. *Acad. Med.*, 1989, 64, 61-6.
5. HOLLINGSWORTH (W.J.), BONDY (P.K.) : The role of Department of Veterans Affairs hospitals in the health care system. *N. Engl. J. Med.*, 1990, 332, 1851-1857.
6. Demographic Division, Office of Planning and Management Analysis, Department of Veterans Affairs, Washington, D.C., 1991.
7. RUBENSTEIN (L.Z.), WIELAND (D.), PEARLMAN (R.A.) et al. : Growth of the teaching nursing home. The Veterans Administration experience. *J. Am. Geriatr. Soc.*, 1990, 30, 73-78.
8. WIELAND (D.), RUBENSTEIN (L.Z.), OUSLANDER (J.G.) et al. : Organizing an academic nursing home. Impacts on institutionalized elderly. *JAMA*, 1986, 255, 2622-2627.
9. FINNEGAN (T.P.), AUSTIN (T.W.), CAPE (R.D.T.) : A 12-month fever surveillance study in a veteran's long-staying institution. *J. Am. Geriatr. Soc.*, 1985, 33, 590-594.
10. RUDMAN (D.), HONTANOSAS, COHEN (Z.) et al. : Clinical correlates of bacteremia in a Veterans Administration extended care facility. *J. Am. Geriatr. Soc.*, 1980, 36, 726-732.
11. RUBENSTEIN (L.Z.), JOSEPHSON (K.R.), WIELAND (G.D.) et al. : Effectiveness of a geriatric evaluation unit. A randomized clinical trial. *N. Engl. J. Med.*, 1984, 311, 1664-1670.
12. RUBENSTEIN (L.Z.), WIELAND (D.), ENGLISH (P.) et al. : The Sepulveda VA geriatric evaluation unit : data on four-year outcomes and predictors of improved patient outcomes. *J. Am. Geriatr. Soc.*, 1984, 32, 503-512.

W.H.O. PROGRAM
FOR RESEARCH ON AGING

Stefania MAGGI (*), Jorge LITVAK (**)

INTRODUCTION

The W.H.O. Research Program on Aging was established in 1987, with the objectives of implementing a collaboration with the world scientific community to generate, collect and disseminate knowledge gained through research on aging.

The aims of the program include :

a. to advance understanding on the economic, social, cultural and humanitarian implications of the aging of world populations ;

b. to stimulate action-oriented policies and programs that will guarantee security for older adults and opportunities for them to participate in and benefit from the implementation of the programs ;

c. to encourage the development of appropriate education, training and research ;

d. to foster an international exchange of skills and knowledge in the field of aging.

The research focus is on the following scientific priorities : determinants of healthy aging, age-associated dementias, osteoporosis, and age-associated immune changes. The first three projects are already in progress.

ORGANIZATIONAL MODEL

The Program for Research on Aging has adopted an operational structure, as shown in figure 1.

The Secretariat of the Program for Research on Aging, with the collaboration of study groups, has the responsibility to prepare all research protocols and proposing the Coordinating Center and the participating countries for each project to the Stering

(*) Research Coordinator. Research Program on Aging. Program on Health of the Elderly. World Health Organization. National Institute on Aging, National Institute of Health, Bethesda, Maryland, 20892. Telephone : (301) 496-4692.

(**) Chief, Research Program on Aging. Program on Health of the Elderly. World Health Organization. National Institute on Aging, National Institute of Health, Bethesda, Maryland, 20892. Telephone : (301) 496-4692.

Organizational Model

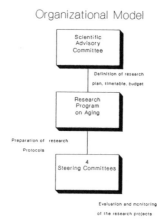

Figure 1 : Organization Model

Committees. The office of the secretariat is based at the National Institute on Aging, in Bethesda, M.D., U.S.A. For each research priority there is a Steering Committee with responsibilities for evaluating the research plans and monitoring the research project. It is composed by six to eight international experts on each field. The scientific plan, the timetable and the proposed budget approved by the Steering Committee are reviewed by the Scientific Advisory Committee, composed by 10 to 12 international experts.

For each of the priorities areas there is a Coordinating Center, responsible for the activities shown in figure 2.

Coordinating Center
Responsabilities

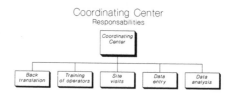

Figure 2 : Coordinating Center

The back translation is important to ensure comparability of the questionnaire and other instruments from one language to another. Any questions that are not the same as the original English version are identified, modified and the process of translation and back translation repeated until similarity to the original version is achieved.

The comparability of methods among all centers will be achieved by a common training of the field operators, annual site visits for updating, retraining, solving problems, and assessing progress in each center.

Other quality control procedures, in addition to the training sessions and visits to the centers, will include repeated administration of questionnaires and examinations in a sample of study subjects by personnel from the coordinating center.

Data entry and analysis will also be performed by the coordinating center.

PARTICIPATING COUNTRIES

The selection of the participating countries in each of the projects is based on the following criteria :

a) anticipated heterogeneity of rates across countries ;

b) sufficient stability of the population, to enable data collection and generalization of the findings ;

c) availability of reliable demographic data ;

d) ability to carry out epidemiological studies, in terms of existence of academic and institutional infrastructures, such as local research centers and health services.

RESEARCH PRIORITIES

A. Determinants of Healthy Aging

The Determinants of Healthy Aging project is envisioned as a cross-national longitudinal study, designed to identify factors affecting the full realization of physical, mental, emotional, social, and economic well-being of individuals as they age. The longitudinal aspect will provide essential measurements of changes over time, which in turn will provide policy-planners with information necessary to evaluate and develop programs which will assist the elderly in maintaining their autonomy. The baseline cross-sectional studies of samples of the elderly in participating countries will provide data to compare the prevalence of well-being in different cultures. Standardized, objective and concurrent measurements of function will provide the basis to determine whether reported differences in the prevalence of healthy, autonomous aging individuals in different cultures are due to differences in coping styles, support systems, or measurement and classification.

Study design

This project will include :

1. An extensive interview which will provide information on demographic characteristics, past medical history, self-reported health, social, and economic factors, physical function, cognitive ability, activities of daily living, depression, life events, social health and integration, health related behavior, housing, occupation and locus of control.

2. A physical examination which will include physical performance based testing and laboratory determinations.

The information will be used to describe associations of demographic, economic, biomedical, psychosocial, and cultural factors with the physical (1-6), mental (7-9), and social functional states (10-14) of individuals. Longitudinal follow-up of the participants will provide data to characterize how these factors influence transitions between functional states of well-being.

The research protocol has been sent out for critiques to a selected panel of international experts. Those critiques are being incorporated into a final draft protocol that will be submitted for approval to the Steering Committee of the project in January 1991.

B. Osteoporosis

The Osteoporosis project is a cross-national study, with cross-sectional, case-control and longitudinal components. It is designed to ascertain the incidence of hip fracture in participating countries, to identify risk factors for hip fracture and for the decrease of bone mass in postmenopausal women and to determine the age of peak bone mass and the distribution of bone mass in different populations by race, age and sex.

The cross-national exploration of differences in incidence of hip fracture and in risk and protective factors could help in developing etiological hypotheses and in planning specific preventive and therapeutic interventions.

Six to ten countries will be involved in this study. Candidate countries are : Brazil, Chile, China, Iceland, Japan, Hungary, and countries in Africa and in South-East Asia to be identified. The Coordinating Center will be located at the Columbia University, New York, under the direction of Dr. Jennifer Kelsey.

Study design

Five components are envisioned for this project :

1. The cross-national annual incidence of fracture of the hip in the population over 50 years of age will be estimated from hospital discharge data and from other sources of health information specific in each country (e.g. bone setters in Africa).

2. A population survey will be undertaken in order to validate the data available from these sources, with the goal of providing comparable incidence rates from one country to another, corrected for under-reporting.

3. A case-control study will be used to compare cross-culturally risk factors for fracture of the hip, such as family history (15-17), dietary habits (18-27), physical activity (28-34), medications use (35, 36), sensory impairments (37, 38), smoking habit (39-41), etc.

4. A study on peak bone mass, using Dual Photon X-ray (DPX), will assess the age of peak bone mass in each country, the factors affecting the peak bone mass and the bone mass distribution in each age group after the peak bone mass.

5. A longitudinal study is planned in two age-groups :

• group at the age of peak bone mass. The bone mass loss will be measured at 4 years follow up in individuals chosen by a probability sampling method, stratified by gender ;

• group of women in peri-menopause and early post-menopause (50-59 years old). Individuals identified during the population survey will be followed for 5 years in order to study the association between the occurrence of hip fracture and bone loss, calcium intake, physical activity and gender.

The research protocol was approved by the Steering Committee in september 1990.

C. Age-associated Dementias

This is a cross-national population-based survey of dementias in the elderly, with the purpose of comparing age- and sex-specific prevalence and incidence rates of dementias across countries. Rates can be compared across samples only if the information is collected using standardized methods. Therefore the first aim of the study is the development of reliable and valid instruments for the screening and clinical diagnosis of dementia which can be applied on a cross-national basis. Harmonization of instruments across cultures and standardization of the clinical diagnosis of dementias is the major goal of the study.

The participating countries are Canada, Chile, Malta, Nigeria, Spain, and USA.

The coordinating center is the SMID Center (Studio Multicentrico Italiano sulla Demenza) in Florence, Italy, directed by Dr. Luigi Amaducci.

Study design

A study sample of about 5,000 subjects 65 years old and over in each country will be assessed to ascertain prevalent cases ; two years later, the same sample will be reassessed and incident cases will be identified. Search for risk factors will be also performed and risk ratios will be estimated.

Cases will be diagnosed by means of a multi-phase procedure : a screening phase and an extensive clinical assessment for dementia syndrome and for different dementing disorders.

In the first phase, specifically trained lay-interviewers will administer the screening test (the IMC [42] or the MMSE [43]) and a structured interview on putative risk factors (i.g. age, sex, race, education, parental age at subject's birth, smoking, alcohol, hypertension, diabetes). Those subjects, identified as potential cases by the initial test, will enter the second phase to be conducted by the clinical investigator with the involvement of a surrogate respondent. The CAMDEX neuropsychological examination [44] will be administered. During the same session, the surrogate informant will be asked about the history of the present difficulty using the CAMDEX structured interview [44], the Activity of Daily Living scale and the Pfeffer functional questionnaire [45].

At the end of this session, the Clinical Investigator will exclude those subjects not presenting a cognitive impairment, on the basis of the results of both the functional and the neuropsychological assessment, with particular emphasis on the CAMCOG score. Subjects with confirmed mental impairment will be extensively studied to determine the final diagnosis. The clinical investigator will be requested to draw conclusions about the disease responsible for dementia. To diagnose dementia, both ICD 10 [46] and DSM III R [47] criteria for dementia must be satisfied and they will be made on the basis of the clinical, laboratory and neuroimaging findings.

To estimate the incidence rates of dementia and the relative risk values, all the non-cases will be reassessed two years later by means of the same multi-phase procedure. Where it is possible and acceptable, autopsy examination of cases and non cases will be an important research tool of the study. The relationship between cognition and post-mortem findings will assure the accuracy and the predictability of the entire procedure and of each instrument.

Moreover, several centers in developed countries have tissue banks, and they may be involved in the biological aspects on the research on dementia (examn of chromosome 21, skin fibroblast, brain tissue).

The Steering Committee approved the project on January 1990. At the present the participating centers are working on the standardization of the clinical diagnosis of dementias and on the harmonization of the instruments to be used in the pilot study.

CONCLUSION

The rapid aging of the population in developed and developing countries raises a considerable challenge to researchers and policy makers. Research on aging is needed at different levels, from basic research on the aging process of cells and organs to the study of the health, social and functional status of the elderly populations. Of particular relevance are the cross-national studies in representative samples of elderly individuals. One of the major effort of the WHO Program on Aging is to develop standard population survey instruments that measure the levels of physical and mental function and the degree of socioeconomic dependence of aged individuals in different cultural and environmental settings. Such instruments would allow for the establishment of data bases useful for understanding of the aging process and for the implementation of social and health services.

BIBLIOGRAPHIE

1. BELLOC (N.) : Relationship of health practices and mortality. *Prev. Med.*, 2, 67, 1973.
2. BELLOC (N.), BRESLOW (L.) : Relationship of physical health status and health practices. *Prev. Med.*, 1, 409, 1972.
3. BENFANTE (R.), REED (D.), BRODY (J.) : Biological and social predictors of health in an aging cohort. *J. Chron. Dis.*, 38 (5), 385, 1985.
4. BRANCH (L.G.), JETTE (A.M.) : Personal health practices and mortality among the elderly. *Am. J. Pub. Health*, 74 (10) : 1126, 1984.
5. BRESLOW (L.), ENSTROM (J.E.) : Persistence of health habits and their relationship to mortality. *Prev. Med.*, 9, 469, 1980.
6. BROWN (J.H.), KAZIS (L.E.), SPITZ (P.W.) et al. : The dimensions of health outcomes ; a cross-validated examination of health status measurement. *Am. J. Public. Health*, 74, 2, 159, 1984.
7. EVANS (J.G.) : Prevention of age-associated loss of autonomy : epidemiological approaches. *J. Chron. Dis.*, 37, 5, 353, 1984.
8. KOENIG (H.G.) : Research on religion and mental health in later life : a review and commentary. *J. Geriatr. Psychiatry*, 23, 1, 1990.
9. WELLS (K.B.), STEWART (A.), HAYS (R.D.) et al. : The functioning and well-being of depressed patients. *JAMA*, 262, 7, 914, 1989.
10. HOUSE (J.S.) and KAHN (R.L.) : Measures and concepts of social support in social support and health. New York, *Academic Press*, p. 83, 1985.
11. LUBBEN (J.E.) : Assessing social networks among elderly populations. *Fam. Community Health*, 11, 3, 42, 1988.
12. MAYFIELD (D.), McLEOD (G.), HALL (P.) : The CAGE questionnaire : validation of a new alcoholism screening instrument. *Am. J. Psychiatry*, 131, 1121, 1974.
13. ORTH-GOMER (K.) and UNDEN (A.L.) : The measurement of social support in population surveys. *Soc. Sci. Med.*, 24, 1, 83, 1987.
14. ROBERTS (N.), BENNETT (S.), SMITH (R.) : Psychological factors associated with disability in arthritis. *J. Psychosomatic Research*, 30, 2, 223, 1986.
15. EVANS (R.A.), MAREL (G.M.), LANCASTER (E.K.) et al. : Bone mass is low in relatives of osteoporotic patients. *Ann. Int. Med.*, 109, 870, 1988.
16. SEEMAN (E.), HOPPER (J.L.), BACH (L.A.) : Reduced bone mass in daughters of women with osteoporosis. *The New Engl. J. Med.*, 320, 9, 554, 1989.
17. MOLLER (M.), HORSMAN (A.), HARVALD (B.) et al. : Metacarpal morphometry in monozygotic and dizygotic elderly twins. *Calcif. Tiss. Res.*, 25, 197, 1978.
18. MATKOVIC (V.), KOSTIAL (K.), SIMONOVIC (I.) et al. : Bone status and fracture rates in two regions of Yugoslavia. *Am. J. Cl. Nutr.*, 32, 540, 1979.
19. HOLBROOK (T.L.), BARRETT-CONNOR (E.), WINGARD (D.L.) : Dietary calcium and risk of hip fracture : 14-year prospective population study. *The Lancet*, nov. 5, 1046, 1988.
20. RIGGS (B.L.), WAHNER (H.W.), MELTON (L.J.) et al. : Dietary calcium intake and rates or bone loss in women. *J. Clin. Invest.*, 80, 979, 1987.
21. ELLIS (F.L.), HOLESH (S.), ELLIS (J.W.) : Incidence of osteoporosis in vegetarians and omnivores. *Am. J. Clin. Nutr.*, 25, 555, 1972.
22. HEGSTED (D.M.) : Calcium and osteoporosis. *J. Nutr.*, 116, 2316, 1986.
23. HAFFNER (S.M.), STERN (M.P.), HAZUDA (H.P.) et al. : The role of behavioral variables and fat patterning in explaining ethnic differences in serum lipids and lipoproteins. *Am. J. Epidemiol.*, 123, 830, 1986.
24. HEGSTED (D.M.), LINKSWILER (H.M.) : Long term effects of level of protein intake on calcium metabolism in young adult women. *J. Nutr.*, 111, 244, 1981.
25. LUTZ (J.) : Calcium balance and acid-base status of women as affected by increased protein intake and by sodium bicarbonate ingestion. *Am. J. Clin. Nutr.*, 39, 281, 1984.
26. HEANEY (R.P.), RECKER (R.R.) : Effects of nitrogen, phosphorus, and caffeine on calcium balance in women. *J. Lab. Clin. Med.*, 99, 46, 1982.
27. SPENCER (H.), RUBIO (J.), RUBIO (E.) et al. : Chronic alcoholism. *The Am. J. Med.*, 80, 393, 1986.
28. DALSKY (G.P.), STOCKE (K.S.), EHSANI (A.A.) et al. : Weight-bearing exercice training and lumbar bone mineral content in postmenopausal women. *Ann. Int. Med.*, 108, 824, 1988.
29. SMITH (E.L.), REDDAN (W.), SMITH (P.E.) : Physical activity and calcium metabolism for bone mineral increase in aged women. *Med. Sci. Spt.*, 16, 60, 1981.
30. BORTZ (W.M.) : Effect of exercise on aging-effect of aging on exercise. *J. Am. Ger. Soc.*, 28, 2, 49, 1980.
31. MAZESS (R.B.), WHEDON (G.D.) : Immobilization and bone. *Calcif. Tissue Int.*, 35, 265, 1983.
32. DONALDSON (C.L.), HULLEY (S.B.), VOGEL (J.M.) et al. : Effect of prolonged bed rest on bone mineral. *Metabolism*, 19, 1071, 1970.
33. SCHAPIRA (D.) : Physical exercise in the prevention and treatment of osteoporosis : a review. *J. Royal Soc. Med.*, 81, 461, 1988.

34. ALOIA (J.F.) : Exercice and skeletal health. *J. Am. Ger. Soc.*, 29, 3, 104, 1981.

35. HAHN (T.J.) : Corticosteroid-induced osteopenia. *Arch. Intern. Med.*, 138, 882, 1978.

36. WASNICH (R.D.), BENFANTE (R.J.), YANO (K.) et al. : Thiazide effect on the mineral content of bone. *New. Engl. J. Med.*, 309, 344, 1983.

37. BLAKE (A.J.), MORGAN (K.), BENDALL (M.J.) : Falls by elderly people at home : prevalence and associated factors. *Age and Ageing*, 17, 365, 1988.

38. FELSON (D.T.), ANDERSON (J.), HANNAN (M.T.) et al. : Impaired vision and hip fracture. The Framingham Study. *J. Am. Geriatric Society*, 37, 495, 1989.

39. DANIELL (H.W.) : Osteoporosis of the Slender Smoker. *Arch. Intern. Med.*, 136, 298, 1976.

40. MacMAHON (B.), TRICHOPOULOS (D.), COLE (P.) et al. : Cigarette smoking and urinary estrogen. *The New Engl. J. Med.*, 307, 17, 1062, 1982.

41. DANIELL (H.W.) : Osteoporosis of the slender smoker : vertebral compression fractures and loss of metacarpal cortex in relation to postmenopausal cigarette smoking and lack of obesity. *Arch. Intern. Med.*, 136, 298, 1967.

42. BLESSED (G.), TOMLISON (B.E.), ROTH (M.) : The association between quantitative measures of dementia and of senile change in the cerebral gray matter of elderly subjects. *Br. J. Psychiat.*, 114, 797, 1968.

43. FOLSTEIN (M.F.), FOLSTEIN (S.E.), McHUGH (P.R.) : « Mini-mental state ». A practical method for grading the cognitive state of patients for the clinician. *J. Psychiatr., Res.*, 12, 189, 1975.

44. ROTH (M.), TYM (E.), MOUNTJOY (C.Q.), HUPPERT (F.A.), HENDRIE (H.), VERMA (S.), GODDARD (R.) : CAMDEX. A standardized instrument for the diagnosis of mental disorders in the elderly with special reference to the early detection of dementia. *Br. J. Psychiat.*, 149, 698, 1985.

45. PFEFFER (R.I.), KUROSAKI (T.T.), HARRAH (C.H.), CHANCE (J.M.), FILOS (S.) : Measurement of functional activities in older adults in the community. *Gerontol.*, 37, 323, 1982.

46. World Health Organisation. ICD-10, draft of chapter V, categories F00-F99. Mental, behavioural and developmental disorders, diagnostic criteria for research. Draft for fields trials, January 1989.

47. American Psychiatric Association. Diagnostic and statistical manual of mental disorders. Third edition-revised. *American Psychiatric Association*, Washington, DC, 1987.

RECOMMENDATIONS TO AUTHORS

• *Manuscripts proposed to Facts and Research in Gerontology must be submitted in accordance with the standards established by the International Committee of Editors of Medical Journals, Annals of International Medicine, 1982, 96, part 1 : 766-771, summarized below.*

• *The text should be submitted in the following format : title page, abstract and key words, text, acknowledgements, references, tables, illustrations and captions. It should be typed with double spacing, on one side only, on paper measuring 21 × 29,7 cm, leaving a left hand margin of 4 cm.*

• *The title page include : 1) the title of the article ; 2) the autors' forenames and surnames ; 3) the names of departments and institutions to which the authors belong ; 4) the main author's name and address ; 5) the funding sources (donation, award, grant, etc.).*

• *The second page should include the abstract and the key words.*

• *The third page includes a very short title (less than 40 characters) as a header for each edited page, and the main author's name.*

• *The text will be divided into : introduction, material and methods, results and discussion. Each part must begin on a new page.*

• *References in the text should be cited by numbers in square brackets, placed in line with the text and numbered in order of appearance. They should be listed in numerical order at the end of the paper in the form prescribed in the Uniform Requirements.*

• *Table : Each table should be on a separate page ; it should have a title and can be followed by an explanation. Each table should be cited in the text and should be numbered according to the order of appearance.*

• *Illustration for diagrams, original artwork : Black ink on white paper is preferred, but glossy prints will usually be acceptable. All illustrations should bear author's name and the number of the illustration on the reverse side, also an indication in soft pencil if only part of the illustration is required. Captions should be typed on separate sheets. It is the responsibility of the author(s) to ensure that any requirements of copyright and courtesy are fulfilled in reproducing illustrations and appropriate acknowledgements included with the captions.*

• *Copyright : Authors of accepted manuscripts must transfer copyright to Facts and Research in Gerontology, which holds copyrights to all articles, comments, reviews, and notes published in Facts and Research in Gerontology.*

• *Submission of manuscripts : Contributions and correspondence should be sent to :*

– Bruno VELLAS, Centre de Gériatrie, C.H.U. Purpan-Casselardit – 31300 Toulouse (France) or Clinical Nutrition Research Center ; (Aging Process Study) Department of Pathology, School of Medicine, U.N.M., Surge Building, Room 236. 2701 Frontier Place NE, Albuquerque, NM 87131 USA.

• *Two copies must be submitted. Submission of an article is taken to imply that its content has not previously been published and is not being considered for publication elsewhere. • Manuscripts are sent to two reviewers for recommendation and comment. Reviewers' comments are provided to authors by the Editor-in-Chief.*

CET OUVRAGE A ÉTÉ IMPRIMÉ SUR LES
PRESSES DES IMPRIMERIES FOURNIÉ
A FONSEGRIVES
31130 TOULOUSE/BALMA

DÉPÔT LÉGAL N° 2773 - AVRIL 1992

ISBN 0-8261-8170-8